FROM THE HEART
OF OUR PEOPLE

FROM THE HEART
OF OUR PEOPLE

Latino/a Explorations in Catholic Systematic Theology

Edited by
**Orlando O. Espín
and Miguel H. Díaz**

ORBIS BOOKS

Maryknoll, New York 10545

The Catholic Foreign Mission Society of America (Maryknoll) recruits and trains people for overseas missionary service. Through Orbis Books, Maryknoll aims to foster the international dialogue that is essential to mission. The books published, however, reflect the opinions of their authors and are not meant to represent the official position of the society. To obtain more information about Maryknoll and Orbis Books, please visit our website at www.maryknoll.org.

Manufactured in the United States of America
Copy editing and typesetting by Joan Weber Laflamme.

Library of Congress Cataloging-in-Publication Data

From the heart of our people   :   Latino/a explorations in Catholic
   systematic theology   /   edited by Orlando O. Espín and Miguel H. Díaz
         p.   cm.
   Includes bibliographical references and index.
   ISBN 1-57075-131-5 (pbk.)
   1. Hispanic American theology.   2. Catholic Church—Doctrines.
I. Espín, Orlando.   II. Díaz, Miguel H.
BT83.575.F76   1999
230'.2'08968—dc21   99-28082
                                                                              CIP

Para Ricardo, compañero y amigo.
Para Ramón, Jacqueline y mis nietos.

O.O.E.

Para Marian, compañera, amiga y esposa:
"la danza nupcial es nuestra comunión en la vida de Dios."
Para mis hijos Joshua, Ana y Emmanuel.

M.H.D.

Contents

Introduction

The present volume is not *about* or just *for* U.S Latinos/as. It is a collection of original essays that *explore* issues in Catholic systematic theology from the perspective of Latino/a[1] faith and culture. Furthermore, this book is an example of doing theology from that perspective.

Latino/a theology is not a monolithic discipline. Consequently, these essays do not represent the only way of doing Catholic systematics from the Latino/a experience. They are the result of a year-long process of discussion, mutual critique, and reflection by twelve theologians engaged in what has come to be known as *teología de conjunto.*[2] Therefore, the essays in this volume cannot be separated from the dialogical context within which they emerged. This way of doing theology is a departure from the usual style of European and European-American theological scholarship. The chapters in this book certainly represent the insights, research, and work of their individual authors; but as it will become clear to the reader, all the texts are engaged in mutual conversation. This volume, therefore, should be read as a whole.

At the 1995 annual meeting of the Academy of Catholic Hispanic Theologians of the United States (ACHTUS) in New York, Professor Miguel H. Díaz raised the question: "What would Catholic systematics look like if it were done *latinamente*?" The challenge was picked up by a number of theologians attending the ACHTUS meeting and by the editor-in-chief of Orbis Books.

In 1996 Professor Orlando O. Espín, on behalf of the Center for the Study of Latino/a Catholicism (of the University of San Diego), requested the necessary funding from the Lilly Endowment, which generously agreed to support a year-long symposium. Nine Latino/a Catholic systematicians were invited to participate in the process. A Latino biblical scholar, a Protestant Latino theologian and church historian, and a Latin American systematician joined the group in order to provide their expertise and distinct perspectives. Díaz's original question was posed to the group as the sole agenda. Two week-long meetings in San Diego, in January and July of 1997, separated and followed by frequent consultations among the participants, provided the context for the free-flowing and enriching conversations which gave birth to the essays in the present volume.

The conversations soon led the participants to realize that the task of "re-inventing" Catholic systematics from the Latino/a perspective would imply several more years of serious dialogue, further work on foundational and methodological issues, and deeper rethinking of specific systematic concerns. Therefore, the reader should be aware that this is but one of several forthcoming volumes.[3]

The twelve theologians also knew that doing Catholic systematics from a Latino/a perspective could not be accomplished if they were to follow the conventional (European) disciplinary divisions within systematic theology. Furthermore, given many of the available definitions of "systematic theology,"[4] serious questions were raised by the participants on the nature, definition, and purpose of "systematic theology" within the Latino/a context. Most Catholic definitions stress that a theological project is "systematic" because it has a foundational "principle of coherence" that explains and harmonizes structures, and relates the parts of Christian revelation and doctrine. We agreed. But, then, what is the principle of coherence of an authentically Latino/a systematic theology? The dialogical process that led to the present volume answered this question by retrieving and establishing *the faith and daily experience of the Latino/a people* as that principle of coherence.

The year-long process, earlier research, and frequent conversations taught the participants that the sources of Latino/a theology are broader than the conventionally accepted study of the written texts of scripture, the magisterium, and theologians. The daily reality and the living faith of the people are equally indispensable sources for theology. The participants further realized that popular Catholicism plays a crucial role as a symbolic expression of that Latino/a reality and faith. The awareness of the sources of Latino/a systematic theology, as well as the latter's "principle of coherence," in turn led to the choice of the unique thematic scheme of the present volume. The theologians involved in this project, therefore, decided to *explore some issues* in systematics "from the heart of our people," while honestly recognizing that the present volume is only a moment in the longer and still incomplete process of re-doing Catholic systematics from the Latino/a perspective.

The reader should also know that the participants' prior individual and collective publications will contribute to a better understanding of many of the issues raised in this book. The authors decided, however, not to repeat here what had already been published elsewhere by them—hoping instead that the enclosed selective bibliography, as well as the bibliographical indications in the articles' endnotes, would lead the reader to explore the broader spectrum of available texts on and from within Latino/a theology.

As the reader will discover, the defining role of culture and the critique of cultural oppression and of universalizing claims are themes that underlie most Latino/a theology. The preferential option for culture, if we may be allowed the expression, characterizes Latino/a theology. This option does not exclude other socioeconomic, racial, and historical dimensions but in fact presupposes them, since culture cannot exist without them. Similarly, and for the same reason, issues of gender are necessarily connected to this option.   To preferentially opt for Latino/a culture does not imply an idealization of that culture. Culture is an imperfect human creation, as capable of communicating and of distorting reality as any other human construct. Furthermore, the option for one culture does not indicate disregard for other cultures. It implies, however, a commitment of solidarity with, of "walking with," a specific human community. Indeed, a fundamental Christian doctrine already exemplifies the option for the particular—the Incarnation historically occurred among a people who were defined by a specific sociocultural reality, and yet this concreteness has never been understood to signify divine disregard for other peoples.

The importance of doing Catholic systematics *latinamente* has become an urgent task given the demographic presence of Latinos/as in the U.S. church. Nearly half of all U.S. Catholics are Latinos/as. And yet the theological academy continues to speak the cultural language of Central Europe. U.S. Catholic theology (and theological education) is at a turning point—either it speaks from the reality and faith of the Catholic community *as it exists in the country*, or it will become increasingly irrelevant to the U.S. church. This irrelevance can be quickly attained by insisting on models, methods, and themes that do not reflect the reality and faith of the Catholic people in this country. The alternative is not the addition of the occasional course on Latino/a theology, nor the superficial (and ultimately dismissive) inclusion of references to or footnotes on Latino/a authors in order to support ideas or arguments irrelevant to Latinos/as. What is needed is a profound conversion that occurs only when theologians are willing to listen to and be critiqued by the People of God. And this in turn can only be achieved when theologians seek to understand not mainly the faith of the elites, but the faith of the entire People of God *as this people exists*.[5]

The present volume and the process from which it came represent a different manner of doing theology. Building on the body of literature already available from Latino/a, Latin American, African American, feminist, and other cultural theologians, this collection of essays does not pretend to be exhaustive or definitive. Rather, as its subtitle indicates, it is only an exploration into systematic theology. It is our hope that these texts will trigger further reflection among Latinos/as, and among others in the theological disciplines.

As this book was in process, a collective volume of Latino/a Protestant theology appeared.[6] It too is the result of a process similar to the one in which we were engaged. Both theological projects seem to point in the same direction (i.e., the urgent need to do Christian systematics from the Latino/a faith and cultural perspectives). Each of the collective volumes also demonstrates both the denominational separations that persist as well as the shared richness that exists within Latino/a Christian theology. Our Protestant colleagues have acknowledged Latino/a Catholic contributions to their thought, just as we have always recognized theirs. Indeed, throughout our year-long project we counted on the participation and contributions of Professor Justo González, the respected United Methodist theologian and church historian.[7]

Latino/a Protestant and Catholic theologians can and will influence the overall ecumenical dialogue between and among our several churches. The intra-Latino/a ecumenical theological conversations are a fact already, in a spirit of mutual respect and learning. Much remains to be done and discussed, but we have begun to walk together toward the same goal. We pray and work for the day when Protestants and Catholics can come together and truly create a Christian systematics, an ecumenical *teología de conjunto*, acceptable to all, because it springs from our people's shared Christian faith and daily life. Until then, we Catholics acknowledge and build on the growing contributions, understanding, and support of our Protestant colleagues, just as they graciously acknowledge and build on ours.

We want to thank the twelve participants in the year-long symposium and Robert Ellsberg of Orbis Books. We are also grateful to the Lilly Endowment for its generous funding of the project; and to our colleagues at the University of Dayton and the University of San Diego, especially the latter's Center for the Study of Latino/a Catholicism, for their support and encouragement. Finally, we are gratefully indebted to our graduate assistants Janet Stanton, Veronica J. Murphy, and Elizabeth Remhof, who proved indispensable during the San Diego meetings and later throughout the editing process.

> — Orlando O. Espín
> University of San Diego
> — Miguel H. Díaz
> St. Vincent de Paul Regional Seminary

Notes

[1] In the present volume we have respected the way each author has chosen to name our people. Some have used "Hispanic," others "Latino," and still others "Latino/a," or a combination of these. Given intra-Latino/a discussions on the terms, we have provided useful descriptions and/or definitions (of these and other frequent terms) in the Glossary at the end of this volume.

[2] See Glossary.

[3] María Pilar Aquino's important essay in the present volume critically and systematically addresses questions related to foundations, method, loci, and

themes as these appear in the enclosed articles and in the broader discipline of Latino/a Catholic systematic theology. Prof. Aquino, who participated in the year-long process, wrote her text only after the other authors had finished theirs, and as the necessary introductory study to this collection. Discussions with Aquino, Goizueta, and García-Rivera led the co-editors to propose that the next volume in this collection be on the philosophical and epistemological foundations of Latino/a (Catholic) theology.

[4] See, for example: W. Kasper, *Theology and Church* (New York: Crossroad, 1989), 1-16; K. Rahner, "Theology," in *Encyclopedia of Theology: The Concise Sacramentum Mundi*, ed. Karl Rahner (New York: Crossroad, 1986), 1690-91; R. McBrien, *Catholicism*, new edition (San Francisco: Harper, 1994), 51-52; J. J. Mueller, "Theology" and "Theology, Systematic," in *The Modern Catholic Encyclopedia*, ed. M. Glazier and M. Hellwig (Collegeville, Minn.: Liturgical Press, 1994), 861 and 865 respectively; F. Schüssler Fiorenza, "Foundations of Theology," in *Handbook of Catholic Theology*, ed. W. Beinert and F. Schüssler Fiorenza (New York: Crossroad, 1995), 258-59, 261; W. Beinert, "Dogmatic Theology," in ibid., 190; I. Ellacuría and J. Sobrino, "Presentación," in *Mysterium Liberationis: Conceptos fundamentales de la teología de la liberación*, ed. I. Ellacuría and J. Sobrino (Madrid: Trotta, 1990), 10-11; C. Vagaggini, "Teología," in *Nuevo diccionario de teología*, ed. G. Barbaglio and S. Dianich (Madrid: Cristiandad, 1982), II:1688-1806.

[5] Interestingly, a similar intuition was proposed by the late Karl Rahner in "The Relation between Theology and Popular Religion," in *Theological Investigations, XXII* (New York: Crossroad, 1991), 140-47.

[6] J. D. Rodríguez and L. I. Martell-Otero, eds., *Teología en conjunto: A Collaborative Hispanic Protestant Theology* (Louisville: Westminster/John Knox, 1997).

[7] His essay in the present volume brings up very serious issues, from the Protestant perspective, that no Latino/a Catholic theologian can disregard any longer.

Theological Method in U.S. Latino/a Theology

Toward an Intercultural Theology for the Third Millennium

❦

MARÍA PILAR AQUINO

University of San Diego

The unity of the one and universal communion seems to be dawning in the local churches with the beginning of the Third Millennium.
—VIRGIL ELIZONDO, 1984

My contribution to the present volume deals with basic questions of theological epistemology, as these refer to the elaboration of a U.S. Latino/a systematic theology.[1] This chapter offers and discusses a number of perspectives that will allow the reader to better understand the identity, internal methodological structure, and purpose of our theology.

Open to critical dialogue and further development—as must be the case with every reflection that deals with human reality—I want to focus here on the epistemological and hermeneutic principles that underlie U.S. Latino/a theological activity, and which allow this activity to articulate the faith of our Christian communities in a reflective, methodic, and comprehensive manner.

Creating a complete system that would coherently explain and articulate the faith, beliefs, symbols, and formulations of the Christian communities throughout the world is an impossible dream for any contemporary theologian. The age of the *summae theologicae* is gone. The elaboration of systematic theology is increasingly a communitarian work that engages in critical dialogue and collective reflection. Two examples of this contemporary, collective approach to theology are the Academy of Catholic Hispanic Theologians of the United States (ACHTUS), and the several projects sponsored by the Center for the Study of Latino/a Catholicism at the University of San Diego. ACHTUS, for instance, understands its mission as seeking "to accompany the Hispanic communities of the United States, helping them discern critically the movement of the Spirit in their historical journey; thematize the faith experience of the people within their historical, socioeconomic, political and cultural contexts; encourage interdisciplinary scholarly collaboration . . . "[2] This chapter seeks to be consequent with that vision. Indeed, the very publication of the present volume is an example of theology done within that shared perspective.

In the first part of my essay I discuss a number of elements that will allow us to contextualize the work of U.S. Latino/a theology within its specific reality. These elements will raise for us a number of topics that will be treated later in the chapter. Consequently, the discussions of the first part must not be understood as sufficient in themselves but rather as integrally connected to the later thematic reflections, because both parts of this chapter respond to and are made possible by the reality within which our theologizing occurs.

In the second part of the essay I discuss the epistemological foundations, fundamental principles, and sources and loci which characterize U.S. Latino/a theology. The central proposition that runs throughout this chapter is that U.S. Latino/a theology is, from its very beginning, *an intercultural enterprise* that has no other route to theological knowledge but interculturality itself. Our theology elaborates its thematic reflection through an intercultural theological method, thereby offering the wider theological academy a workable and appropriate model. The social and religious relevance of theology in the third millennium will greatly depend on its ability to incorporate as methodological axis the *interculturality* that characterizes our contemporary world.

LATINO/A SYSTEMATIC THEOLOGY: PROBLEMS AND POSSIBILITIES

In this first part I want to discuss the problems, limits, and possibilities that U.S. Latino/a theology faces in its attempts to articulate methodologically the lived, reflected, and celebrated faith of our communities. I am thinking here of different elements or aspects which can be understood as components of the historical and cultural milieux within which we do theology.[3] These elements bear significant implications for the self-understanding, and for the theoretical and methodological development of our theology, just as they also point to the latter's ethico-political characteristics, concerns, challenges, and options. Not claiming to be exhaustive, I propose to reflect here on seven of these problems and possibilities.

The Weight of Western Theological Tradition

There are many definitions and understandings of systematic theology, with varying degrees of conceptual sophistication.[4] Together with the great tradition of Catholic theology, I understand systematic theology as an attempt to coherently and in an orderly fashion examine and explain the lived and reflected faith of the Christian community. The task of systematic theology is not the mere repetition of dogmas or of old formulas but is rather an effort at making understandable the central contents of the faith in accord with Tradition and the present-day experiences of the community. Even if today we must recognize the limits of all systematic theologies, the preceding understanding of its task implies a number of difficulties for a possible formulation and construction of U.S. Latino/a systematics.

Arguably, the greater difficulty comes from the current definitions of what *is* systematic theology. Today, at the doorstep of the third millennium, it is not enough simply to admit the intrinsically historical character of all theological knowledge. It is no longer enough to acknowledge that this historical character prevents us from employing metaphysical or conceptualist approaches to the task of theologizing. The historicity of all theological knowledge makes us recognize that dominant understandings of what *is* systematic theology—understandings which have been held as normative and universal—are no more than the condensation of Western theological traditions which have predominated in Europe and among European-American theologians.[5] Today we must also recognize that, although this contemporary theology is undergoing important transformations in method and contents, these changes are still occurring within the horizon of dominant Western culture. Furthermore, even those theologies which adopt critical-constructive methods, and which may allow us to identify the theoretical limitations of modern and liberation theologies, still construct themselves through the incorporation of perspectives *unilaterally* created within the Western academy.[6] In this sense, Western definitions of revelation, faith, and theology continue to be considered as rules of truth which should be assimilated or "inculturated" by other (i.e., non-European or European-American) communities of faith. This is why we should acknowledge that dominant understandings of what systematic theology is or should be remain profoundly *monocultural*. We must also recognize that the way the hegemonic theological academy constructs knowledge remains deeply embedded in the *patriarchal ideology* which has been so pervasive throughout the history of Christian theology. Consequently, Western understandings and definitions of what systematic theology is, or should be, are increasingly insufficient for a theological method—like U.S. Latino/a theology—that chooses to deal with the true historicity of faith.

The Need to Historicize the Fact of Theological Diversity

It is no longer enough simply to recognize, as an inevitable and established fact, the diversity of voices, faces, and knowledge which construct and articulate their own visions of God, of salvation, of the world, and of themselves. Every theological expression communicates the understanding it has of the Christian vision within the historic-cultural realities within which the faith is reflected upon and lived. Consequently, every theological expression bears the tensions embedded in the historicity of knowledge, thereby sharing historicity with all other theological expressions.

Every theological expression, as Fernando Segovia rightly points out, "is a voice in search of freedom, independence, and autonomy . . . a voice that wishes to lay claim to its own reality and experience, give expression to its own view of God and the world, and chart its own future."[7] These voices come from everywhere—from the poor, from oppressed women, from marginalized races and cultures, from the countryside and the city. What we must now recognize is that these voices reject the dominant intellectual traditions underlying the contemporary theological academy. In fact, these dominant traditions sprang from economic, cultural, and intellectual centers of power, and have demonstrated their inability to eliminate the great divisions that affect today's world—especially the North-South geopolitical divisions, the sexual divisions between men and women, and numerous other racial, ethnic, and religious divisions.

The new voices that embody today's theological diversity demand that the dominant intellectual traditions acknowledge their own historicity, their own epistemological assumptions, and examine their contribution to the creation and preservation of this increasingly divided world.[8] Historicity—a characteristic equally shared by all theological expressions— allows us to suggest that it is now time to examine rigorously the impact our theologies have on our societies and cultures; that we have the possibility of exchanging that which underlies our understanding of Christian life by recognizing the provisional and open nature of all theological affirmations; and that we can move beyond the monopoly exercised by dominant understandings without falling into either reductive relativism or the rhetoric of abstract unity. The fact of theological diversity, characterized by historicity, challenges the worldwide theological community to revise the very foundations on which contemporary theology rests.

"Parcels of Reason" and Intercultural Theological Dialogue

This third element is closely linked to the preceding one, although here I will underline the problem of communication among different rationalities. The emergence of many new theological expressions has generated new questions concerning the articulation of reason and rationality in contemporary theology.[9] For many theologians who are bringing forth new theological expressions, these questions have to do with their increased awareness that the current understandings of reason and rationality not only continue to bear a heavy monocultural and androcentric weight, but also that such notions have been used against them because of their refusal to work according to the univocal and unilateral rules that the dominant academy has given to these notions.

Leonardo Boff points out that "it is true that the pluralism of rational forms freed us from old hierarchies and totalitarian domination schemes, which used just one type of reason. But it gave way to another problem: how do the different rational forms relate between themselves?"[10] Roberto Goizueta raises the question: "Is theological pluralism possible?"[11] The possible answers must come not from prefabricated theories about knowledge in the abstract, or from nonexistent metaphysical realms. The answers to these questions must come from the historicity of the subjects of reason who know within their concrete reality. That is why I use the expression "parcels of reason," because each subject assumes his or her human existence as such, from it constructs a personal mode of arriving at knowledge, and creates *conceptual frameworks for grounding visions of the world with valid claims to universality*. This is the context within which we should raise the possibility of communication among historical subjects who share the human condition, and the task of theologizing from within it.

The contributions of Raúl Fornet-Betancourt to intercultural philosophy seem very pertinent to theology.[12] Instead of viewing the diversity of subjects who incarnate diverse rationalities as a problem without solution, Fornet-Betancourt proposes a first stage in which subjects and rationalities enter an *intercultural dialogue*:

> We see, in the multiplicity of voices through which reason may express itself, the fundamental motive that should bindingly summon us to dialogue, in that those voices are not ordered *a priori* by a metaphysical unity . . . they are historical voices, contingent expressions that articulate themselves as such from within the irreducible background of different life worlds. They are thus loaded with context and culture . . . That is why they are also voices of reason, manifestations of intellectual autonomy or autochthony. They affirm their right to "see" things from within their context and culture . . . That load of contextuality and cultural historicity . . . becomes a first challenge or

problem for intercultural dialogue, since it indicates that in that dialogue rationalities will confront each other . . . carrying in themselves
their own and specific historical load which in turn separates them;
but which, on the other hand, represents precisely that which each
(rationality) must transmit to the other. Therefore, far from seeing in
that historical-cultural load—in that dimension of lived and projected
history present in every form of rationality—an impediment to dialogue, we must assume it as the true possibility for non-dominant
communication.[13]

With this in mind, I suggest that today we need to move beyond the
mere recognition of the existence of "parcels of reason." We must move to
explore an intercultural theological dialogue in a consistent and systematic manner. For this dialogue to become a reality we must leave behind
the notion that some rationalities are like darkened mirrors, bad copies,
transplants, or partial "inculturations" of other rationalities held to be "superior." The proposed dialogue is not a confrontation between theological positions, nor is it "about" specific topics or controversial theories; it is
rather a theological dialogue "with" and "from" the limitations and possibilities opened by the historicity proper to each engaged rationality. This
intercultural dialogue is done by "doing" it, by entering the process of
interdiscursive communication as a condition for the possibility of creating new theological models that would do justice to the universal character of all parcels of reason.

The Critique of Dominant Intellectual Traditions

This element has to do with the critique of the present situation that
characterizes the dominant academy in the United States. Roberto Goizueta
rightly points out that a theology that seeks to systematize the faith as
reflected upon and lived by our people today has the duty of critiquing
and superseding the two intellectual traditions prevalent in the dominant
theological academy: *modern liberal individualism* and *postmodern
deconstructionism*.[14] Both traditions operate with notions of reason and of
the human person which are unacceptable to theologies linked to the faith
of marginalized groups and are impediments to any possibility of theological pluralism.

The first of these two traditions, founded on theoretical reason, leads to
reducing reality, truth, and knowledge to cold, quantifiable formulas:

The reduction of truth and knowledge to that which can be known
with certainty and objectivity has a further corollary: that alone is
true, and counts as knowledge, which can be universalized . . . thus
. . . the particularity and uniqueness of each human life is sacrificed

to the abstract, universal concept or number . . . Consequently, the judgments reached by theoretical reason have often been astonishingly unreasonable: the desire to create a completely rational world has resulted in a world torn apart by conflict, violence, distrust, fear and anxiety.[15]

The second of these traditions, instead of advancing or supporting a theology that communally reflects on what may have primacy in the Christian vision of the world, in fact erects walls that prevent all possibility of interdiscursive communication. Furthermore, this second tradition represents a radical break in the conditions that would permit any possible basic consensus on the fundamental truths that ground human dignity, justice, or the integrity of the world. Goizueta further indicates that

> for the postmodernist, "truth" and "knowledge" are always radically particular, radically contextual, radically relative, radically ambiguous, and always in flux. Differences are fundamental; similarities and unity are illusory. Indeed, everything is difference, or otherness. This includes the self, or the subject, who is also radically heterogeneous, an artificial pastiche of radically disparate and ever fluctuating relations, identities, and experiences. The self as such (as some coherent and relatively stable entity which unifies all these differences) does not exist; what we call the "self" is simply "social location" . . . Postmodern culture reacts to the modern sacralization of universal, theoretical truth by rejecting the possibility of truth altogether.[16]

The impact of these two traditions on the reality within which the U.S. theological academy exists has been dramatic. Furthermore, these traditions have strengthened the prevalent cultural context, which is distinguished by its insensitivity toward suffering peoples, its radical individualism, its personality cults, its absolute relativization of values, its immediatist pragmatism, and its reduction of nondominant rationalities to their particular racial or cultural territories. These two traditions have also strengthened the ideology assumed as evident by the majority of the country's population. This ideology accepts excessive social fragmentation and agrees with the ethical values of modern capitalism. As theologian and economist Franz Hinkelammert has shown, conservative Protestantism lent its cultural ethos and its theoretical paradigm to modern capitalism and to today's dominant ideology in the United States.[17] In fact, with rare exceptions U.S. theologians have shown great resistance against seriously incorporating into their work a critical analysis of the political-economic theories that accompany contemporary patriarchal capitalism.

In today's situation it is no longer enough to recognize that theology finds itself in a context marked by the confrontation of rationalities, each of these establishing its own validity rules. What we now need is to acknowledge that theology exists in a context in which rationalities confront each other from *unequal* positions of power within the same reality. We need to recognize that, in this confrontation, the dominant intellectual traditions were established by the elites of the Western academy, and these continue to judge as irrational the critical-liberating rationality of marginalized groups. For the dominant academy, the intellectual discourse coming from these groups lacks theoretical rigor, it has not yet reached the necessary maturity to establish the parameters of a theological epistemology that could claim to be valid and true for the whole Christian community, and, consequently, the intellectual discourse of marginalized groups is seen as applicable only to the "contextual," "ethnic," or "particular" groups themselves. In this way feminist, Latino/a, African-American, and Native rationalities are relegated to a position of structural disadvantage in the intellectual world.

Theologians must recognize that the critique of dominant intellectual traditions includes a further critique of all theories and theologies that ultimately serve to perpetuate the anthropological reductionism that supports sexism, racism, homophobia, implicit or explicit colonialism, and a world fragmented in radically autonomous "monoculturalities." It is important to understand that if we do not recognize this, and if we do not judge it to be an opportunity for devising a new theological discourse, the present situation will continue to lead us down the path to dialogical breakdown, to a crisis of ethico-religious references, to the demise of collective projects founded on justice, to the destruction of hope, and finally to the acceptance of death. The result could only reflect a social reality ruled by the dominant principle of "divide and conquer."

It is no longer enough to speak of theological pluralism, because present social and intellectual reality have closed most doors.[18] The only road still open for us is the creation of new ways of thinking founded not on abstract theories but on the real life of our faith communities. According to Fornet-Betancourt, "the task would then be to start reformulating our means of knowledge from within the dispute of the several voices of reason and/or cultures, within a context of open communication; and not to start rebuilding theories which are monoculturally established."[19] This suggested route offers us better intellectual alternatives for dealing with the situation that currently characterizes the dominant U.S. academy, as well as dealing with the social interests and needs of our own communities. Consequently, Latino/a theology does not adopt reductive notions of reality, of the human person, of truth, or of knowledge, which are still evident in the dominant theological academy. On the contrary, our theology searches for notions and meanings from within the world of the victims of injustice, from within their humanizing reason, from within their creative intellectual traditions, and from within their liberating praxis.

The Redefinition and Broadening of Terms in Theological Discourse

Contemporary critical theologies, notably the various liberation theologies, exhibit great flexibility in their use of terms, concepts, and notions that, in most cases, have their roots in the conceptual constructions of the Western European academy. This intellectual "mobility" allows them to apply terms without greater precision, while at the same time abandoning many of the rigid conceptual rules of the several Western theoretical disciplines. Most of the time this flexibility applies to terms that name specific operations of knowledge within philosophy, logic, and theories of knowledge in general. The implied variety attends to not only the terms but also to the order and sense given in the development of discourse or argumentation, as in the case of such concepts as *principle, proposition, premise, assumption, presupposition, criterion, element, imperative,* and others. These terms are often applied without further explanation or justification. Furthermore, we can find in liberation theologies a number of discourses that propose to speak about the same reality or on the same subject employing these terms, and yet each of these discourses may use the same terms with different meanings, or perhaps employ different terms for the same meanings, or even apply them differently and for different purposes. Let me offer a few examples of what I mean.

A given liberation theology may state that its starting point is "the lived experience, the consciousness of oppression and of liberation, and the struggle for life," but this same affirmation(s) may then be variedly referred to (by the theology's several authors) as "methodological principle,"[20] "pre-condition" of the theological task,[21] "a common perspective . . . a challenge and an imperative,"[22] "'first stage' in the methodological process,"[23] or simply the locus where we may discover a "theological method."[24] Although these terms individually have their own meaning and function, they are indistinctively employed in the articulation of theological discourse to refer (without further explanation) to the same methodological element—in this case, the starting point of a given theology. Even the English translations of some works by Latin American liberation theologians have adopted this terminological "mobility": what Jon Sobrino calls *el presupuesto fundamental*, in Spanish,[25] is translated as "the basic premise"[26]; what Raúl Vidales calls *primer momento fontal* [27] is simply eliminated in the translation and another phrase put in its place, thereby changing the meaning and power of the Spanish original.[28]

Another example refers to concepts or notions central to the Christian vision of liberation. The use, explanation, or application of these concepts or notions allows for terminological and epistemological diversity. Such is the case with *option for the poor*, which has been theologically referred to as an "epistemological category,"[29] a "global horizon, explanatory principle, practical and epistemic locus, theological and ecclesiological locus,"[30] the "content of God's revelation,"[31] that which has "radicality, primacy, and ultimacy,"[32] and as an "ecclesiological characteristic,"[33] a "theological insight,"[34] an "antecedent option,"[35] the "core of liberation theology,"[36] and the "starting point of theology."[37]

The point I want to make by mentioning these few examples is that contemporary liberation theologies have adopted an attitude of great freedom vis-à-vis the intellectual traditions of the dominant Western academy. Liberation theologies have not rejected the Western academy's contributions; rather, they *have dialogued* with them, and they have *changed the uses and meanings* of inherited terms *from within* liberation theologies' *own historicity*, language, and theological goals. This flexibility could be interpreted as an arbitrary transgression of the methodological coherence of hegemonic theories. In fact, it should be seen as a relocation—a conceptual redefinition of terms whose meanings are found in the structural whole of each theological tradition. I am thereby suggesting that this flexibility is revealing an important conceptual movement: the transition from monocultural hegemonic theories to critical theories, which in the very process of their constitution consciously adopt an intercultural character, and which, in that movement, enrich, correct, and broaden the prevalent ways of knowledge. Furthermore, as Fornet-Betancourt points out, this movement fosters "the broadening of our hermeneutical, methodological and epistemological resources, thereby introducing us into a dialogic process with other life and thought traditions."[38] That is why we can no longer claim that liberation theologies (especially those from the Third World[39]) are just incomplete or "babbling" versions of Western hegemonic theories simply because the former employ conceptual elements from the latter.

The Influence of Latin American Liberation Theology on U.S. Latino/a Theology

Latino/a theology in the United States has always been aware of its intimate relationship with its sister, Latin American liberation theology. U.S. Latino/a theologians have clearly acknowledged this relationship: "As its grateful heirs and dialogue partners, U.S. Hispanic theologians have appropriated many of the key insights of liberation theology, especially its methodological insights . . . The dialogue and friendship between Latin American and U.S. Hispanic theologians are stronger and more fruitful than ever."[40] The theological visions of Latino/a theologians "reveal a clear option for the optic and methodology of liberation theology."[41] "The link between Latin American and U.S. Latino theology is strong . . . Latino theologians in the United States soon recognized their need for a theology concerned with changing the lives of the exploited."[42] "[Latin American] liberation theology, especially its praxis-oriented methodology, was embraced by a new generation of U.S. Hispanic thinkers with enthusiasm and hope."[43] "Theology from the perspective of Latina women recognizes itself . . . within the arena or common inspiration of both *feminist liberation theology* and *Latin American liberation theology*."[44] As I will discuss later, Latin American influence appears mostly on U.S. Latino/a theology's method,[45] hermeneutic,[46] and overall intention.[47]

However, U.S. Latino/a theology very early understood that the best way to incorporate seriously the contributions of Latin American liberation theology was to develop a theology that would sink its roots in, respond to, and accompany the faith experience of the Latino/a communities *in the United States*.

Latino/a theology also exposed some of the lacunae of Latin American theology, not as conceptual insufficiencies but as significant limitations of a theological project that wants to be rooted in the faith of the people. In my view, there are four main critiques that U.S. Latino/a theology brings to Latin American theology. The first one underlines the unilateral and reductive character of the social analysis carried out by Latin American theology, especially when it seems to exclusively emphasize the economic-political dimension of reality, dismissing its cultural, aesthetic, and racial dimensions. The second critique has been amply discussed by Orlando Espín, who underlines that liberation theology "has tended to downplay popular religion's role in the Church"[48] and has disdained popular Catholicism in theological epistemology, in spite of its being the omnipresent expression of the faith of the people throughout the continent.[49] The third critique exposes the androcentric and sexist character of that theology, which ignores violence against women, dismisses critical feminist theories and theologies, and condones the patriarchal foundations of Latin America's societies, churches, and cultures. The fourth critique addresses the scorn (often more implicit than explicit) with which a number of Latin American theologians view U.S. Latino/a theology. Woefully ignoring Latino/a theology's basic perspectives, some Latin Americans judge Latino/a theology to agree with neocapitalism's hegemonic ideology. These Latin Americans often assume that Latino/a theology "sold out" to "the system," that it ignores what real poverty is, has reneged of its Latin American cultural identity, and "fools around" with the extreme rationalism typical of the dominant theological academy in the United States.

Anyone aware of U.S. Latino/a theology, and of its social, cultural, and religious reality, might be surprised at such simplistic and erroneous analyses. Paradoxically, this same group that so severely misunderstands and misjudges U.S. Latino/a theology seems oblivious to the institutional benefits it seeks and receives from universities and foundations of the First World in general and from U.S. Latino/a theologians in particular. It is indeed interesting to note the fact that when U.S. universities and theological centers want to discuss third-world theologies, they seek out the "outside" (in this case, Latin American) dialogue partners while dismissing or ignoring the theologies and theologians of the Third World "within" their own borders.

Dismissing without a hearing the whole of U.S. Latino/a theological contributions, this Latin American group assumes that *because* Latinos/as *geographically* reside in the United States they *must* also share in the wealth and hegemony.[50] Evidently, these gross misunderstandings and unfounded judgments reflect a provincial and reductive attitude untenable in today's "global village."

On the other hand, just as there are limitations in Latin American theologies, there are also clear examples of very serious attempts at dialogue and elaborating replies to these and other critiques. For example, Juan Luis Segundo noted the scant self-criticism of Latin American theologies and the need for their engaging other contemporary theological and epistemological critical theories.[51] João Batista Libânio has responded to criticism coming from conservative and neoconservative theologies.[52] Diego Irarrázaval acknowledges the impact of popular religion on theology,[53] as well as the theological contributions of native peoples, blacks, and women.[54] Gustavo Gutiérrez has recognized the contribution of feminist theology and is increasingly interested in U.S. Latino/a theological contributions.[55] Latin American women theologians have themselves critically articulated feminist theology in the continent, thereby exposing the sexism and patriarchal ideology of much of liberation theology.[56]

U.S. Latino/a theology's criticism of Latin American theology is intended solely as a call to dialogue. It is an invitation for it to adopt a more comprehensive critical and analytic perspective, to assume a more realistic vision of concrete reality, to move beyond its onesidedness and its conceptual reductionism, and to help create a space where all Christian voices will be welcome. This invitation stands as a call to dialogue with our sisters and brothers of the Latin American theological community as all of us struggle in faith and hope.

The Temptations to Which U.S. Latino/a Theology Is Exposed

Although there are arguably more temptations than we may be aware of, for our purposes here I will indicate only three. The first one is the temptation to construct theology according to the vocabulary and methodological canons of the dominant Western academy. In his work on the conditions and criteria for *intercultural theological dialogue*, Virgilio Elizondo points out that third-world theologians, "in their effort to successfully create a new theological reflection faithful to their particular cultures, may frequently feel constrained by their own and constant dependence on the theological and philosophical works"[57] that predominate in first-world churches and theologies. We must recognize that this temptation is still here for us, even after U.S. Latino/a theology's claim of autonomy—as expected of any theology conscious of its historicity. To confront this temptation we must further explore the Christian vision to which our communities witness through their daily resistance and struggle for liberation, as well as through their practical, spiritual, and intellectual resources. Because our theology is born out of multiple and complex expressions of faith, we can (a) accompany the Latino/a communities' journey with conceptual lucidity, (b) authentically dialogue with other theologies, (c) critically appropriate and creatively reformulate the best contributions of the Western academy, and (d) establish norms of academic excellence, of theoretical quality, and of political effectiveness in accord with the identity and goals of our theologizing.[58]

The second temptation is linked to the first. In opposition to dominant theology, U.S. Latino/a theology, from its very beginning, refused to be imprisoned in the university world. Our theology has always recognized its necessary and intimate connection to the religious and cultural reality of marginalized U.S. Latino/a communities. From the very beginning, our theology also recognized that these communities are traditionally excluded from the academic world and its production of knowledge. "We stand against a-historical, rationalist and conceptualist epistemologies,"[59] which only reinforce this exclusion from the hegemonic academy. This recognition, however, carries with it the temptation to think that our theology should merely or mainly address catechetical or "pastoral" concerns, and/or that Latino/a theology's academic language is "too sophisticated" for "the people," and/or that the popular religion which so permeates the daily lives of our people does not require "theoretical elucubrations." To fall into this pluriform temptation would imply the denial of the epistemological statute of popular religion, and it would tear apart our communities' power to define knowledge. This temptation would invalidate and reject the intellectual rigor required by the study of popular religion. In fact, the construction of a theoretically solid theology implies the rejection of dominant ideology in culture, society, and church—the very dominant ideology that still regards Latino/a communities as "not good enough" and as only deserving and capable of mediocre theologies. As Roberto Goizueta points out, "If the best, most sophisticated scholarship is not placed in the service of our communities, then it will continue to be used against them."[60] That is why we must continue exploring new ways to deal creatively with the existing tensions between the university and pastoral action, between the classroom and the parish, between the academy and the *barrio*. In the U.S. context we cannot afford the luxury of establishing false dichotomies or claims of autonomies between or among these contexts.

The third temptation derives from dominant society's ideological and cultural context. Latino/a theology does not accept any monocultural version of reality, and it rejects those ideologies which fragment persons and cultures. Nevertheless, our theology finds itself immersed in a social context that moves toward the economic and cultural homogenization of the world. This movement seeks to impose, on a global scale, the model of society promoted by neocapitalism (in its U.S. form) and a vision of the world founded on the dynamics of the marketplace. By imposing the dominant, exclusive vision of culture and society, this movement deepens the marginalization of those peoples and cultures without equal power to communicate to the world their alternative vision of reconciliation through justice, of human dignity, and of earth's oneness. It is in this context that U.S. Latino/a theology must deal with the temptation which claims that, in order to oppose the homogenizing avalanche of dominant ideology, Latino/a theology should entrench itself exclusively within Latino/a cultures. In other words, our theology may be tempted to articulate its religious vision of the world by appealing only to our own communities' spiritual or wisdom resources. This route, however, would inevitably lead to the imprisonment of Latino/a theology "within its own house." In order to confront this temptation we must underline our theology's understanding of the tension between the "universal" and the "particular."

Latino/a theology rejects the pretensions to abstract universality on which U.S. dominant ideology and society operate. At the same time, our theology believes that it cannot give up its liberating religious vision. It cannot give up the spiritual strength found in the historical experience of peoples and theologies that have created counter-hegemonic visions— against dominant homogenization, against the fragmentation of peoples, and against the assimilation of their distinct cultural world. U.S. Latino/a theology recognizes its fundamental connection with the worldwide movement of peoples and theologies which—from within their own realities, from within their own articulation of the believing word, and from within their own particularity—seek to strengthen a vision of worldwide solidarity as today's only possible alternative to the neocapitalist hegemonic avalanche. Only here, within the interrelatedness and interdependence of the several efforts to save our common home, can we question the tension between the universal and the particular. Only here can we utter and understand the expression so dear to Latino/a communities: *mi casa es su casa* (my home is your home). In "my" particular home "your" struggles for justice also find a home, because they are my struggles too, because the struggle is universal. In this sense, Raúl Fornet-Betancourt points out,

The question now is not how to integrate the particular in the movement of the universal. Rather, the question is how to graft the diversity of the world in the particular. We should thereby break the dia-

lectic circle of conflict between the "universal" and the "particular,"
and leave behind, as a false question, the difficulty of recognizing
the "particular" without prior justification vis-à-vis the "universal."
We would then see that we only have universals. The trunk proper
to each culture is a concrete universal. There are no "particularities"
and no "universality," only historical universalities. And it will all
depend then on whether these universalities empower themselves,
or not, for the solidarious encounter among themselves.[61]

In this same sense, U.S. Latino/a theology understands that, by articulating its theological word, it is denouncing the message of death contained in the dominant ideologies. It is also giving up any participation in
the neocapitalist hegemonic movement which produces and reproduces
so much dehumanization and violence. As articulation of the believing
word of women and men who live and work in the midst of this world's
powers, U.S. Latino/a theology understands its vocation as the cultural
and spiritual empowering of our people in order to infuse a vision of justice and hope in our "common home." Latino/a theology's universal dimension is grounded in this vision.

EPISTEMOLOGICAL FOUNDATIONS
OF U.S. LATINO/A SYSTEMATIC THEOLOGY

In order to understand the foundations and principles of knowledge in
U.S. Latino/a Catholic systematic theology, it is important to remember
that we are speaking of a discipline that bears the weight of older, pre-
established, unilateral definitions. That is why it seems prudent to raise
the question of the prior conditions necessary to a theological method that
would allow a knowledge of the faith lived in and by U.S. Latino/a communities. The very act of raising the question is an acknowledgment that
Latinos/as in the United States do not form a monolithic or homogeneous
block but a *dynamic historical reality* formed by diverse communities, traditions, and cultures. The internal differences within this reality range from
rituals and beliefs proper to each community, to the several ways in which
U.S. governments and society have accepted and dealt with particular
Latino/a communities and cultures. Religious practices and social acceptance play an important role in determining the U.S. Latino/a theological
agenda, given that not all communities have received the same degree of
acceptance, opportunities, or resources to empower some of their members' incorporation into theology. Nevertheless, the common dynamic historical reality Latinos/as share may be described as follows: (a) it was
born out of a double conquest—first European, and then European-American; (b) it is articulated religiously and culturally by popular Catholicism;

(c) it is marked by a history of struggles for socioeconomic, political, and intellectual emancipation as well as by struggles for self-determination, for liberation, and for human dignity; d) it is immersed in an adverse social context which is also diverse and conflictive; (e) it bears ethical and religious values that defend the dignity of the human person in community, although it also reproduces patriarchal modes in human relations; and (f) it demonstrates an extraordinary wealth of resistance, joy, and hope.[62] Consequently, from within this dynamic historical reality I am writing on a theology that, because it is "U.S. Latino/a," seeks to articulate itself in a new way: within the perspective of intercultural thought.

What prior conditions would make possible this new way of systematizing Christian faith from within this concrete historical reality? A consideration of these conditions is important because they affect the method this theology adopts in order to arrive at knowledge of the faith. Following the directions suggested by Raúl Fornet-Betancourt, I will indicate five of these prior conditions.[63]

1. *To free our own word.* This is the first and arguably the most important condition for the construction of a U.S. Latino/a systematic theology. Its importance arises from the fact that, as a colonized people, we must find our own voice in the midst of a theological ambience already weighed down by "rigorous" discourses which would lead us to silence. The liberation of our own word implies that we not abandon our criticism of colonializing theories and dominant theologies, that we continue the work of theological and cultural decolonization, that we strengthen the development of a liberating hermeneutic, and that we give up those ways of thinking which diminish our dignity or distort our intellectual capacity.

2. *Solidarity.* This is the intercommunicative platform on which we must establish relations with other voices. This platform is not "ready made"; rather, it is a process which allows us to interweave several discourses from a perspective of mutual recognition and respect. Solidarity forbids the reduction or instrumentalization of other theological voices, while it empowers the debate among differences without ever closing off communication. In this process we learn to recognize the profiles of situated universals and their interrelational character.

3. *The "whole" as culturally plural truths.* This prior condition lets us understand that the "whole" of truth occurs in the very process of exchange among culturally plural "truths." As explained by Fernando Segovia, we give up the idea that a single theology or a single culture "represents the sole and superior embodiment of the Christian tradition."[64] That is why we must move beyond the notion that the "whole" implies "the truth," or that "the truth" exists in an abstract "whole." In this sense, we must understand truth not as a condition or situation but as a process. No theology and no culture can give us the truth but only the possibility of seeking it. The process of interdiscursive communication, in equality of

conditions, is the means of turning into a whole the diverse voices that actively participate on the way to truth.

4. *Respectivity*[65] *of reality*. In his explanation of the unity of all historical reality, Ignacio Ellacuría pointed out that "the whole of intramundane reality constitutes a single, complex and differentiated physical unity, in such a way that unity does not cancel differences nor differences cancel unity."[66] To understand respectivity as a prior condition in the construction of a U.S. Latino/a systematic theology implies that we choose to know, not by imprisoning reality in a closed conceptual system, but by affirming that reality as a foundational "opening" that is "respective" to other modes of reality. Because respectivity forbids a totalitarian conception of reality, it allows us to affirm plural versions of reality without fragmenting or isolating them. Respectivity also moves us beyond intellectual or historical relativism, opening formal spaces for a reflection on reality's substantial inner connection.

5. *Radical broadening of the sources*. In the context of U.S. Latino/a theology, this prior condition assumes that we take seriously into account the historical and cultural experience of our people as bearer and transmitter of divine revelation. This experience is especially clear in the constellation of practices and thoughts mediated by religion, with its rituals, symbols, and language, and also in the daily relations among genders and races, as well as in the myriad musical, literary, scientific, philosophical, and political forms that gather the "utopic soul" of the people. The broadening of the sources implies that we bear in mind all that constitutes and expresses the people's interests and experience, precisely because it affects theological knowledge. It is part of theology's hermeneutic role to interpret that experience as it may empower or obstruct justice, freedom, compassion, solidarity, and human dignity according to God's saving intent.

Having reflected on these prior conditions, and in view of the next section of this essay, I want to indicate briefly what I understand by *theological epistemology* and by *theological method*. First, I understand that theological epistemology has as its object the discernment and exposition of the cognitive moment of theological activity. As such, it shows the categories and principles that theoretically ground a concrete mode of theological thinking, as well as the operations that intervene in the intelligence of the faith. As an academic discipline, theological epistemology certainly has its proper autonomy, but as a human and Christian activity it constitutes a moment in human knowing, subject to unavoidable historical conditionings as well as being inevitably "respective" to the reality within which it finds itself.[67] In this way, theological epistemology necessarily involves interpretive horizons and directions as it brings about the knowledge of the faith. In this sense, a theology that seeks to articulate the liberating hopes of oppressed groups requires a hermeneutic that is critical, popular, feminist, and intercultural, as well as a method that is congruent with that theology's aims.

Second, and to specify the theological method, we must begin by stating how U.S. Latino/a theology conceives of what is specific to theologizing. Latino/a theology understands the specificity proper to theologizing as intelligence of the faith, understanding this intelligence as critical reflection on the praxis of the faith. As such, therefore, it refuses to view theology as a merely theoretical, speculative activity, affirming instead that the intelligence of the faith is an activity centered primarily on the apprehension of lived reality in order to confront and deal with it. Together with the Ecumenical Association of Third World Theologians (EATWOT), U.S. Latino/a theology understands that "our methodologies are not principles to be applied to reality; they are a guide to clarify our commitment and praxis. Our aim is not new doctrines, but new relationships and lifestyles. Method implies a direction, and liberation is the direction."[68]

Theological method is referred to the horizon that embraces the whole of theological activity, as it also embraces the global direction of thought within which that activity occurs and the critical road which that activity travels in the very dynamic of traveling it. This is why method cannot be viewed as separate from theological contents, or as free from an ethical, political option. In order to determine which is U.S. Latino/a theology's option and which principles intervene in its method, it is first necessary to look into the explicit self-understanding that U.S. Latino/a theology has of itself.

In the Tradition of Culturally Plural Christianity

U.S. Latino/a theology, as all Christian theologies, knows that its ultimate foundation lies on divine revelation. It understands that revelation is its foundational principle and the primary hermeneutic rule of theological knowledge, its universality residing therein.[69] Revelation "discovers" for humanity God's saving intentions. Orlando Espín rightly points out that the *Christian* experience of God is due to revelation: "Divine revelation allows us to glimpse the being of the one God as lovingly relational . . . and it is this relational God that Christians also and consequently encounter in the human experience of grace."[70] However, U.S. Latino/a theology—as any liberation theology would—underlines that revelation always occurs and is apprehended within the historicity of the believing community.

From the perspective of critical feminist theology, Elizabeth Schüssler Fiorenza indicates that "the [Second Vatican] council takes seriously the principle of incarnation when it asserts that divine revelation is only given in human, cultural, and societally conditioned language."[71] According to

Espín, both revelation and the experience of grace are necessarily mediated by human cultures in the way the latter are experienced in and through daily life. That is why "there is no acultural Christianity, just as there is no acultural option for God, love, and salvation."[72] Accordingly, if the aim of revelation is to incorporate the human person and the world into the process of divine salvation, this salvation acquires its historical form in liberation. As we learned from Ignacio Ellacuría, "liberation is a concept that represents the very essence of the revealed message, God's saving gift" to women and men of all times.[73] That is why we understand our participation in God's saving work as a struggle for liberation from sin and injustice—a struggle whose ultimate origin can be no other but revelation. This participation is made possible by the power of divine grace, since through grace we accept and respond in faith to the mystery of God in our lives— a mystery that urges us to eliminate the oppression and darkness that weigh heavily on women, men, and indeed on all of creation.[74]

Consequently, U.S. Latino/a theology "discovers" and apprehends revelation and salvation from within the historical, religious, cultural, and bodily context of Latino/a communities. The particularity of this historical context, as would be the case with any other faith community, is what makes possible our people's participation in God's universal saving plan. It is from within this context that we can reach knowledge of the faith, as well as grasp the implications of revelation and salvation for our communities' concrete lives. In this respect, Alejandro García-Rivera (herein) can suggest, through the comparison of a European and a Latino/a Christmas devotion, that Latino/a metaphysics is best conceived of as cosmology; as such, it constitutes a "whole" of aesthetic values founded on God's love for the particular. The several available articulations of the contents of revelation are necessarily contextual, given the historical character of revelation and of human knowledge. These articulations clearly demonstrate the plural character of Christianity. That is why we can also speak of the reality of revelation as a culturally plural reality. U.S. Latino/a theology sees the need to move beyond the monocultural and patriarchal perspectives found in many of the available articulations of revelation, which we too inherited from Western Christian tradition. We should readily recognize that Latino/a theology must still develop a more consistent and explicit systematic reflection on revelation and salvation.

U.S. Latino/a Theology's Self-understanding—Its Intercultural Cradle

U.S. Latino/a theology may not renounce its intercultural cradle. This is a theology born within a reality where a number of religious traditions and several theological formulations converge. European, Latin American, European American, Afro-Latin and African American, Native American, and feminist traditions and elaborations have been welcome and critically embraced. And yet, U.S. Latino/a theology acquired its own personality because its cradle lies within the concrete and complex reality of the Latino/a communities of the United States, which in turn constitute an intercultural community. This community is the fastest growing segment of the U.S. population as well as of the Catholic church in the United States. As Jeanette Rodríguez points out, "The most recent census estimates a Latino/a population of 29.3 million, with a projected increase to 40.1 million by the year 2009. We come from many different lands of origin, representing no less than twenty-one Latin American countries."[75] Allan F. Deck says that "fully one-third of today's U.S. Roman Catholics are Hispanic and, if the trends persist . . . Hispanics will constitute the majority of Roman Catholics sometime in the first decade of the next millennium."[76] Sociologist Gilbert Cadena also asserts that "by the year 2010 Latinos will constitute over one-half of the (U.S. Catholic) church."[77] Given its demographic composition, the Catholic church in the United States has begun to have a predominantly Latino/a face, and this reality requires a rethinking of ecclesiology that can inspire and organize *all of the church's life* in the United States. The chapter by Gary Riebe-Estrella in the present volume explores the characteristics and challenges of an ecclesiology elaborated not so much around "topics" that might interest Latino/a culture but through the methodological perspectives of U.S. Latino/a theology.

The starting point of Latino/a theology's reflection is faith as lived by our communities; from this cradle our theology establishes its connection with the larger society and with the worldwide Christian church. In one of the classics on liberation theology—the collective book *Irruption of the Third World: Challenge to Theology*—Virgilio Elizondo writes that "we feel that this type of theological reflection is not only more honest but even more universal . . . We are convinced that the more universal one tries to be, the less one has to offer to others. Conversely, the more particular a thought is, the more its universal implications become evident."[78]

U.S. Latino/a theological reflection, then, starts from the lived faith of the community, which welcomes God's presence in its midst; celebrates it in its popular rituals, ceremonies, and prayers; and witnesses to it through the community's words and deeds. This reflection unveils and reveals— to our community and to the world—the encounter between the mystery of God and the mystery of human experience. In this way, if theology speaks of the deeper meaning of our being and our doing under the light of revelation, then theology needs, demands, and implies an anthropology. In fact, the strength of any theological project greatly depends on the theological anthropology it subscribes to. Similarly, the relevance of and reception given any theology depends on the theological anthropology it proposes. There can be no theology without a corresponding anthropological foundation. This explains the importance of theological anthropology for U.S. Latino/a theology. Two articles in the present volume approach two major components of this anthropology, both of them within an organic-relational anthropological model. Through his interpretation of the *fiesta* in U.S. Latino/a cultures, Roberto Goizueta points to the implications the notion of aesthetic praxis has for a theological anthropology. Miguel Díaz explores Latino/a popular narrative as source for a theological anthropology.

Within this very brief discussion of Latino/a theology's self-understanding, I want to quickly highlight five Latino/a perceptions of our own theology in order to indicate the latter's identity, how we understand our theological task, and what we see as our theology's contribution to the broader theological community. (1) Virgilio Elizondo points out that spirituality is a constitutive element of U.S. Latino/a theology because "[this theology] is a joint enterprise of the believing community, which is seeking the meaning of faith and the direction of its journey of hope lived in the context of charity."[79] (2) In an earlier text I have indicated the formal specificity that defines Latino/a theology as a discipline founded on faith:

> "Theo-logy" is the proper language through which we seek to permanently, critically and systematically understand the faith which the community lives, celebrates and proclaims. Insofar as it is a reflective effort (*logos*) about God (*theos*) and about the experience of God, it is carried out from within the richness of the believing experience. In fact, more than a *science of the intellect*, theology is the vocabulary of *affectus*—of love aimed at the full manifestation of God's activity in human history. Theological reflection starts with the experience of faith, while it is also a fruit of the latter. Theological reflection is a permanent dynamism which again fertilizes and interweaves the same experience of faith that is informed by the *living word of God* in past and present history . . . The act of theologizing neither precedes nor follows the experience of faith—between the former and the latter there remains a fecund and creative tension.[80]

(3) In yet another text I indicated that U.S. Latino/a theological activity, as a discourse rooted in our *mestizo/a* condition, "presents itself as a critical reflection on the lived experience which our people have of God in their daily struggles against suffering, oppression and violence. The *object* of Latino/a theology is God, but a God discovered within the native worldview of the Latino/a communities."[81] (4) Roberto Goizueta underlines the distinctive emphasis of U.S. Latino/a discourse: "As critical reflection on praxis, the theology being developed by U.S. Hispanics is informed by the methodology of Latin American liberation theology," but due to the fact that this praxis is necessarily historically situated, "the concrete historicity of U.S. Hispanic communities will furnish new insights into the very meaning of historicity, or praxis itself . . . by emphasizing

the popular religious character of historical praxis."[82] (5) Arturo Bañuelas points to the communitarian and committed character of our theology: "U.S. Hispanic theologies are the result of a process called *pastoral de conjunto*"; but because this process involves active participation in and the analysis of reality, it "assures that Hispanic theologizing is grounded in human experience, especially the experience of oppression," just as it also requires a new kind of theologian—committed, and with a conscience—"since their common project, their *teología de conjunto*, is the liberation of Hispanics as part of God's salvific plan for a new humanity."[83]

Based on these understandings, I want to return to two earlier points. It is only now, within the context of reality as assumed by Latino/a theology and theologians, that we can situate those two earlier points. First, with respect to the influence of Latin American theology on U.S. Latino/a theology: it is evident that U.S. Latino/a theology also declares its self-understanding as critical reflection on the praxis of faith under the light of revelation; it is equally committed to the option for the poor and marginalized as fundamental principle; and it seeks to actualize salvation—within personal and social processes of liberation—as participation in God's salvific act. Second, with respect to the theological method U.S. Latino/a theology shares with other third-world theologies: I already indicated that method implies a direction and is not free from an ethical, political option; consequently, the horizon and aim of Latino/a theology is the achievement of integral humanization, of liberation, of a better quality of life for all, and of social justice—especially for those whose suffering is caused by any form of injustice or violence.[84] This theological method allows Latino/a theology to give better account of God's mystery in the religious complexity of U.S. Latino/a communities.

I now want to reflect on the fundamental hermeneutic-epistemological principles of U.S. Latino/a systematic theology's method, aware that we are and have always been within culturally plural Christianity.

Fundamental Hermeneutic-Epistemological Principles

I want to underline here the three foundational principles from which U. S. Latino/a systematic theology starts. I speak here of fundamental principles because these are the propositions admitted as starting points by this theology, constituting the bases which its practitioners share in the process of constructing the knowledge of faith. These propositions—as fundamental principles—establish the formal nucleus of U.S. Latino/a systematic theology; since they intervene in the process of theologizing, they radically determine the internal structure of the theological method as well as the very identity of this theology. That is why, methodologically, none of these principles can be understood separately from the others; rather, each acquires its cognitive consistency and its intellective magnitude in relation to the others. Together, these principles govern faith's *epistemic locus* by granting theology its methodological coherence; because they are rooted in the *sociocultural locus* of Latino/a communities, these principles also determine the selection and interpretation of theological contents.

First principle: The faith of the people. The centrality of the "faith of the people"[85] lies in the conscious option, made by U.S. Latino/a theology, to take *this* faith and not another as the starting point for theological reflection as organizing principle of our theologizing. It could be argued that, as understandings of the faith, all theologies presuppose and imply faith. But what Latino/a theology emphasizes is that the faith of the people is the faith lived and expressed primarily and fundamentally within the concrete reality of popular Catholicism. In this sense, any theology can say that its starting point is the experience of faith, but most theologies do not take seriously—as fundamental principle of theological knowledge!—the faith of the people lived within popular Catholicism.[86]

In order to justify *this* faith's priority in Latino/a theology, it is important to first reflect on the subject of this faith—the ones who bear and share this faith. In this sense, Roberto Goizueta points out that the bearers of this faith are "men and women of Latino/a descent, who are victims of a marginalization based not only on culture but on language, social class, gender or race."[87] We are speaking of concrete persons, of men and women who identify their history "with the history of violence and suffering made visible in Jesus' grimace of pain on the cross . . . The blood and the wounds are the visible memories of his and our suffering. To erase them is to erase those memories and, with them, our very identity as persons, without which there can be no liberation that arises out of our own history as subjects."[88] Orlando Espín confirms that "Latinos/as have no doubt about the reality of suffering . . . It is true that some in our communities are not poor, but they are clearly the exceptions . . . Poverty and marginalization still shape the more frequent context of Latino/a life in the United States. And this context is diversely experienced as and through suffering."[89] U.S. Latino/a theology, consequently, has chosen to give high priority to the faith of these people who seek to be liberated from suffering; it also chooses to take very seriously the pervasive reality of suffering among our people, trying to accompany the people in their confrontations with that suffering. In this sense, the cry of the suffering people is the "pre-comprehension" for Latino/a theology. To choose to see and listen to *this reality* is prior to any other option. To seriously take into account the faith of the poor and suffering means that one recognizes that in this people the self-manifestation of God takes place, and that this people is at the same time the privileged *hermeneutic locus and the horizon* for apprehending and interpreting the whole of revelation.

It is undeniable, as Virgilio Elizondo rightly points out, when discussing intercultural theological dialogue, that "poverty and suffering, because they are universal, are above the Church, doctrine and theology, and may yet become the foundation for an authentic dialogue aimed at a common Christian struggle."[90] Consequently, U.S. Latino/a theology does not opt for a theological concept per se, which may operate as an organizing or systematizing principle of its reflection—as *hope, suffering, reign of God, discipleship* could be. Rather, Latino/a theology opts for a reality that brings together the object and the subject of theology. All theological concepts find their proper locus in the faith of the people, even though we still face the task of continued exploration of this faith's fabric. This fundamental reality, therefore, radically determines both the mediations of theological knowledge as well as the contents of the faith.

Second principle: The option for the poor and oppressed. This is the identifying mark of all theologies that belong to the wider family of liberation theology. In U.S. Latino/a theology, this option is "the most important *epistemological precondition for Christian faith*: to know God we must first opt for the poor . . . To turn a deaf ear to the cries of the poor is implicitly to identify God's voice with that of the status quo and, hence, its established power structures."[91] The option for the poor and oppressed has special relevance for Latino/a theology not only because of the situations I described in the first part of this article, but more fundamentally because this theology is born from and develops in the heart of a societal model rooted in the markets and ideologies of globalizing neocapitalism. Dominant intellectual traditions and contemporary theologizing also occur within that context. According to Franz Hinkelammert, the neocapitalist model of society—also called neoliberalism and globalization—is capitalism's new face,

> [The neocapitalist model] was introduced in the decade of the eighties under the guise of "structural adjustments," and for the globalization and homogenization of the world through the marketplace . . . Neoliberal economic theory doesn't speak about reality. It only speaks of markets, without the least reference to the concrete realities within which the markets operate . . . The market is the *societas perfecta* that achieves its perfection through its own globalization . . . When today we search for alternatives, we do so within a market economy which has transformed the marketplace into the sole and complete criterion for social decisions.[92]

Neocapitalism comes dressed in the neoliberal ideology that presents economic efficiency and market competitiveness as supreme and exclusive "reasonable" criteria for society's life, although these criteria cover up the real consequences of the global market in the real lives of real people. The neoliberal ideology is deaf to the cries of the ever-growing segments of the world's population denied access to means of living. This ideology is blind to the serious ecologic destruction produced by the global marketplace. This ideology presents global capitalism as the practical fulfillment of all utopias, and as the final achievement of human aspirations. It refuses, however, to take responsibility for the new and very serious human holocausts the markets have produced. While global neocapitalism announces a heaven on earth, its neoliberal ideology hides the hells that markets produce on earth, often calling on the name of God to justify neocapitalism's founding theoretical paradigm. In its utopian pretension, the neoliberal vision of the "totalized society" through "global markets" embodies a mystique of collective suicide—a rationalized spirituality of the irrational—which denies the status of rational to any alternative vision of justice, of human dignity, or of the earth's wholeness which might seek to subvert neoliberalism's own irrationality.[93] In reference to this, the chapter by Jeanette Rodríguez in the present volume emphasizes the need to revisit our native religious traditions in order to search for new theological answers to the challenges posed by the current social model.

We are at the doorstep of the third millennium. Instead of rejoicing at the progress made in the quality of life of all peoples, we must witness everywhere in the world the widening and deepening of poverty and exclusion. In a 1998 pastoral letter, Brazilian bishop Pedro Casaldáliga amply describes the effects and global consequences of contemporary neocapitalism. Casaldáliga also points out what the church and theology can do to confront the latter.

Some believe that it is time to change our paradigms. They are uncomfortable with martyrs in postmodern or postmilitant memory . . . Meanwhile, neoliberalism, the global market, the "geopolitics of chaos" . . . the "economic horror" . . . are still here, murdering the world . . . In this end of century and end of millennium, 15% of the world's population owns 79% of the wealth, while 85% of the population are left with the remaining 21%. Absolute poverty punishes more than one and a half billion people, who must live with less than a dollar per day. The number of the poor is being tripled . . . *Hunger* is today, more than ever before, the "silent bomb," and most deadly. Twenty-five of the world's children die of hunger every minute—thirteen million every year. Eighteen percent of humanity consumes 80% of all the available *energy*. In just two years there would not be a tree left on the planet if the rest of the world consumed the same amount of paper as the United States (which barely represents 6% of the world's population). The First World invests some 50 billion dollars per year in the *underdeveloped* world, but every year it

takes out more than 500 billion dollars from those same countries—
not counting the interest on the latter's debt . . . *Migration* is quickly
becoming an "itinerant nightmare," a kind of world war between
desperation and lockout . . . Speaking on the First World's resistance
to immigrants, Vivianne Forrester has rightly defined this "witch-
hunt of the foreigner" as really a "witch-hunt of the poor." It will
prove a useless hunt . . . *Discrimination against women* continues growing at an alarming rate at the end of this supposedly democratic century. That wall has not fallen . . . *Our governments are turning
"globalitarian;"* but the fact remains that just 200 transnational
megacorporations control a fourth of the planet's economic activity
. . . In the midst of this neoliberal night, [we can see] the new shine of
many stars of alternative creativity throughout the world. [These
stars] are the reply of life to a system of death which cannot be
humankind's destiny.[94]

Given this description, we must reaffirm that the option for the poor
and oppressed does not belong to a past theological paradigm; rather, it
remains a fundamental Christian imperative—a required norm for the
protection of our rationality. This option is a "scandal" for modern theoretical reason, and "madness" for postmodern theoretical reason, but it is
still strength and wisdom for Christian liberating reason. For U.S. Latino/a
theology, the option for the poor and oppressed demands a rigorous critique of neocapitalist political economy, of its corresponding neoliberal
"utopization" of the laws of the marketplace, of its pretended globalization of a culture of exclusion, of its patriarchal and racist roots, and of its
rampant ecological destruction.

Our theological reflection would become a rhetorical discourse about
marginalization, unable to explain the latter's systemic causes if we do
not contextualize our concrete reality within the above framework; if we
do not localize all religious, social, cultural, racial, and sexual
marginalization in that context; and if we fail to see the relationship between marginalization and the ecological crisis. As Hinkelammert has
pointed out, the option for the poor and oppressed lets us determine the
concrete and historical locus wherein God's revelation occurs, while at the
same time it obliges us to historicize our theological contents through a
critical and ongoing analysis of the hegemonic system understood as "totalization" of all personal and social life.[95] This kind of analysis enables us:
(1) to expose all the dimensions and potentialities of the "faith of the
people," as it is lived in Latino/a popular Catholicism; (2) to recognize
the specific profile of the *bearers* of the faith of the people as embodied,
racial, sexual, and interrelated beings; and (3) to establish more clearly
practical and conceptual networks with other Christian communities
throughout the world who are also engaged in confrontation with global-

izing neocapitalism. That is why the option for the poor constitutes today a privileged space for intercultural communication, and that is why it is more important today than ever before.

Third principle: Liberating praxis. Latino/a theology is internally articulated by the principle of liberating praxis. Under this light, U.S. Latino/a theological reflection understands itself as a praxis of accompaniment *with*, *within*, and *from* the Latino/a communities in the latter's struggle for a new reality free of violence, dehumanization, and exclusion.

The praxis of accompaniment is seen as a category that grounds theological activity. It is a criterion which determines methodological method, as well as a criterion with which to search and verify the truth of the faith. This praxis is also a principle of theological interpretation and a principle of articulation for the knowledge of faith. Lastly, the praxis of accompaniment is both imperative of liberating reason and privileged locus for the acquisition of a liberative mode of knowledge. Hence, this praxis has an epistemological privilege.

We understand human praxis—both personal and communitarian—to be constitutive of reality's historical process as a whole: complex and plural, rational and aesthetic, dynamic, concrete and transcendent, open and innovative, respective, structural and individual, transforming and constructive, ethical and political. That is why human praxis cannot be reduced to a single process or a single dimension of reality.[96] Praxis is not an "object" which may be taken or left behind; rather, it constitutes historical reality *within daily life*. It is in *lo cotidiano*[97] of existence where we live, understand, and give direction to human praxis. Roberto Goizueta points out that Latino/a popular Catholicism helps us comprehend human praxis more adequately: communitarily, aesthetically, ethically, politically, and rationally. Popular Catholicism helps us understand that "human action, or praxis is 1) sacramental; 2) essentially and intrinsically communal, or relational; 3) an end in itself; 4) empowering; and, therefore 5) liberating."[98] Therefore, U.S. Latino/a theology must be rooted in a notion of human praxis that harmonizes beauty with justice. More specifically, it shows the connection that exists between the aesthetic dimension and the ethical, political dimension of human action.

Sources and Loci of U.S. Latino/a Theology

In the Catholic theological perspective, the concept of *locus theologicus* refers to the sources of theological knowledge.

When explaining the theological teaching of Melchor Cano (1509-66) on the *loci theologici*, Evangelista Vilanova says that for Cano "theological loci are not fundamental or controversial doctrines; rather [they are] the *domicilia argumentorum*, that is, the *tituli fontium* from which theological argumentation must proceed."[99] Both Vilanova and Yves Congar regard

Cano as the creator of modern theological methodology because of his clarification, reformulation, and systematic organization of the concept of locus.[100] U.S. Latino/a theology holds that the privileged locus of theological reflection is the *popular religious experience* of the Latino/a community, because that experience is the context of revelation and of its consequent reception, interpretation, and transmission. Insofar as it is the context of revelation and of its interpretation, this locus is also *source* of theological knowledge—because it carries the contents of the faith, and offers both the material and the interpretive principles for a coherent formulation of theological discourse. In this sense, the sources of theological knowledge are not restricted to the written texts of the past, which may have documented certain contents of the faith—the apprehension and documentation of which may contain certain interpretive codes which correspond to a specific historical and social place.

Both U.S. Latino/a theology and Latin American liberation theology reject any abstract separation between sources and theological loci. Sixto García indicates that "the sources and foundations of Hispanic theology can never be divorced from the privileged locations . . . These locations qualify, shape, and condition the identity of the sources for such a theology."[101] Ignacio Ellacuría points out that, although "locus" and "source" may be methodologically distinguished, "the distinction is not strict and, much less, exclusive; because in some ways *locus* is *source* insofar as the former makes the latter give from within itself this or that, in such a way that thanks to locus and because of it specific contents may be actualized and made really present."[102]

With the above reflection in mind, I want to make a further conceptual distinction on our understanding of theological locus. U.S. Latino/a theology is elaborated from within popular religious faith, thereby acknowledging this experience as its formal *locus theologicus*. As the context which contains revelation and grounds theological knowledge, this locus functions as the *epistemic locus* of faith. The theological locus, however—and *because* it is situated within historical coordinates—implies the option for a specific *sociocultural location* within which the deliberate selection of theological material, its interpretation, and its presentation take place. The theological locus of U.S. Latino/a theology is clearly determined by the *sociocultural location* constituted by marginalized men and women who seek justice, solidarity, and human dignity. This conceptual distinction, however, does not indicate or accept that the epistemic locus be separated from the sociocultural location. Rather, both loci intervene in the same process of knowledge as components of the one theological method. The relationality between both loci is clearly explained in the chapter by Jean-Pierre Ruiz in the present volume. In this text Ruiz critically examines, interculturally, the place of the Bible in Latino/a communities.

The above reflections and observations allow me to contextualize the three sources and loci we are discussing in this section.

Latino/a Popular Catholicism

In U.S. Latino/a theology the centrality of popular Catholicism as source and locus of revelation and theology is simply undeniable.[103] There are three basic reasons which justify this centrality. First, popular Catholicism is the most distinguishing, most pervasive, and omnipresent reality in the religious life of *Catholic* Latino/a and Latin American communities throughout the continent. It is the privileged space wherein the people live and celebrate their faith, and it has special relevance in the lives of the women of marginalized races and groups. It is in the popular Catholic space that the Word of God happens as an event. Second, and as Orlando Espín asserts, "Latino/a popular Catholicism is a religion. More concretely, it is the religion of those treated as subaltern by both society and Church in the United States."[104] As such, this religion contains, offers, and transmits the theological contents and principles that ground a hermeneutic of the faith. Third, according to Virgilio Elizondo, "the popular expressions of the faith . . . are the ultimate foundation of the people's innermost being and the common expression of the collective soul of the people."[105] In this sense, Latino/a popular Catholicism guides the elaboration of a theological discourse which connects and illuminates the community's religious life to *lo cotidiano* of its existence.

The above three reasons—which justify the evident centrality of popular Catholicism in Latino/a theology—also justify the use of the adjective *popular*, which we attach to Latino/a Catholicism in order to more correctly name the people's religion. Furthermore, as Miguel Díaz clearly demonstrates in the introductory part of his chapter in this volume, popular religion has generated numerous narratives which are popular *because* they first came from socially marginalized persons and were later appropriated by equally marginalized communities.

Another reason to understand Latino/a popular Catholicism's centrality is the type of rationality that operates within it. Popular religion displays a thought structure based on participation, incarnation, and reciprocity. Because of this, it adopts a "logic of vital synthesis" within which knowledge is acquired through affective participation, and in which the criterion for determining "what is true" is that which sustains dignified living. Consequently, U.S. Latino/a theological epistemology has consciously opted for the *praxic* character of knowledge, so as to correspond to Latino/a popular Catholicism's rationality, which is communitarian, aesthetic, rational, critical, liberating, ethical, and political.[106]

The option for Latino/a popular Catholicism in theologizing has diverse functions and meanings. In *epistemological* terms, the multiform, differential, and consistent character of the material that actualizes the faith brings about a truly Catholic theology. In *hermeneutic* terms, Latino/a popular Catholicism embraces the faith of the people and thus constitutes the locus and central code for interpreting the tensions inherent in human life and caused by human action in the world; this includes "the meaning of life, personal and collective destiny, the origin and destiny of the universe and of history, and the end, origin and meaning of evil, of pain, of death, of the mysterious and the marvelous."[107] In *methodological* terms, the whole structure of the faith finds rationality, order, and coherence in popular Catholicism's contents, symbols, rituals, and languages. In *theological* terms, the contents of theology cannot be determined from pre-established discourses but only from the lived and reflected historical expression of the faith of the people; that is, Latino/a popular Catholicism offers us the material to discover and name the present and always challenging mystery of God, and on this foundation to redo and rewrite every other central topic in systematic theology. In *ethical-political* terms, because it articulates the whole of personal and communal relations, Latino/a popular Catholicism is the appropriate space within which to deconstruct dominant social relations and to build new ones free of violence and oppressive patriarchal power. In *soteriological* terms, Latino/a popular Catholicism is the religion within which people construct a complex and dynamic vision of the world, connect their religious experience to other ecclesial traditions of life and thought, resist the avalanche of dominant religions and ideologies, and confront historical reality's present contradictions and future possibilities. Popular Catholicism has salvific value because God dwells therein, among the scorned of the earth. The poor and oppressed are the body of Christ, and this body shows the world the meaning of sin and grace, of perdition and salvation.

The Reality of Mestizaje

There are a number of readily available books and articles that explain *mestizaje*[108] as central category, as fundamental epistemological-hermeneutic principle, and as *locus theologicus* of U.S. Latino/a theology.[109] Here I only want to highlight its particular relevance to a *theological method* which consciously opts for *inculturality as central methodological axis*.

U.S. Latino/a theologians are aware of the current debates on such issues as diversity, pluralism, and multiculturalism. They are also well aware of the ongoing discussions on the question of how to deal theologically with the excessive monocultural character of Western Christianity, and with cultural and theological diversity. We are familiar with the several European alternatives proposed as answers to this question. Perhaps the best-known alternative was initially offered by J. B. Metz. He advocated a culturally polycentric church which would parallel the cultural and theo-

logical polycentrism already evident in Christianity.[110] Echoing this proposal, Spanish theologian Juan José Tamayo also suggested that "to a cultural polycentrism, like the one which irrevocably characterizes today's
civilization, must correspond—also irrevocably—an ecclesial and theological polycentrism."[111] For his part, Roberto Goizueta suggests that U.S.
Latino/a theology must take part in the emergence of a polycentric church:
"What kind of theology is appropriate to a polycentric church? . . . A polycentric church demands a new theological subject, or, more properly, new
theological subjects."[112] These alternative proposals, although well inten-
tioned, are nevertheless insufficient. In fact, the very idea of theological
polycentrism is untenable and undesirable in the context of today's global
neocapitalism. Furthermore, polycentrism cannot even exist because it is
today impossible to think that theology's *inter*discursive dynamic could
take place within some sort of "self-centered" dynamic in every religious-
cultural system. In today's world, even if we were to admit the existence
of many epistemological "centers," these cannot dialogue under *equal* conditions. The fact is that any theological discourse that takes seriously into
account the plural fabric of reality and of knowledge must deal also with
the asymmetric character of social power relations at all levels. Theological discourse must critically confront the ethnocentric tendencies of all
cultures, including its own, as well as avoid romanticizing its notions of
family, community, and people. These notions, because they are founded
on and structured along patriarchal gender relations, often cover up violence against women and children. Theological discourse should explore
the possibilities opened by the intercultural sensitivity that today guides
many Christian communities throughout the world.

Raúl Fornet-Betancourt argues that "what is radical in this perspective is
not, therefore, that we have a polycentric Christianity today, but, rather, a
culturally plural Christianity . . . Intercultural dialogue radicalizes the program of a polycentric Christianity; more precisely, it supersedes it," because,
while it recognizes the irreducible value of the many theological discourses,
it leads to the recognition "that the question for 'Christian identity' can no
longer be posed but from the perspective of intercultural exchange."[113]

In this sense, I believe that *mestizaje* offers a more adequate and more
realistic theological answer to the questions emerging from our own historical reality. I mean here not only the biological *mestizaje*, which created
a new race, but especially the cultural and intellectual *mestizaje* that created a new *intercultural reality* and, consequently, an *intercultural theology*.
In the words of Virgilio Elizondo, "*mestizaje* is simply the mixture of human groups of different makeup determining the color and shape of their
eyes, skin pigmentation, and makeup of bone structure . . . Biologically
speaking, *mestizaje* appears to be quite easy and natural, but culturally it
is usually feared and threatening."[114] This definition admits the mixture

of blacks and whites too—a process commonly referred to as *mulataje.* Evidently, *mestizaje* is a historical fact that still opens up old wounds, just as it is also the opportunity to build an intercommunicative platform with other voices who speak from their own irreducible cultures. As Elizondo notes, *mestizaje* occurs in several ways, although it emerged as a massive reality only through conquest and colonization, "giving rise to a new people . . . and in them begins a new history."[115]

Precisely because *mestizaje* has been portrayed by dominant cultures as carrying a social value only worthy of exclusion, a *mestizo/a* theology will highlight the vital syntheses which "new peoples" have interculturally created in order to explain their own vision and their own identities. The *mestizo/a* biological condition does not automatically lead to intercultural consciousness. It is not a necessary requirement to arrive at truth. It is, however, the opportunity for recognizing the intercultural character of our origin, of our being, and of our identity. As such, the reality of *mestizaje* also implies a conscious option for intellectual, cultural, and theological *mestizaje.* Incorporated as fundamental principle of the intelligence of the faith and as methodological axis, this option constitutes the basis on which to articulate an intercultural vision of Christian identity. Along these same lines, Anne E. Patrick indicates that *mestizaje* is "an increasingly important category for ethical and theological reflection."[116]

As historical locus where different cultures and experiences converge, each carrying its history of suffering and struggle against the powers of death, *mestizaje* becomes a privileged space for a theology that navigates on the current of solidarity among peoples who seek to confront their suffering. This same current led Johann-Baptist Metz to make the transition between the *polycentric* to the *intercultural* discourse. According to Metz, "More universal and more interculturally communicative than the language of western rationality and of western science, is the language that articulates the memory of suffering . . . This memory of suffering is what makes a given culture sensitive and accessible to all other cultural worlds."[117]

Given its intercultural cradle, its *mestizo/a* condition, and its epistemological options, Latino/a theology can greatly contribute to that authentic theological dialogue which seeks to discern the exigencies of God's revelation in the present historical reality within which our communities live. The very future of Christianity is implicated in this search—a future that can only be intercultural. In the words of Jeanette Rodríguez: "The concept *mestizaje,* as developed by U.S. Latino/a theologians, is one that will prove useful to future generations as they learn to deal with, to engage and be creative about the realities of the future."[118] The title of one of Virgilio Elizondo's books has become an imperative for theology in the third millennium: *The Future Is Mestizo: Life Where Cultures Meet.*[119]

Lo cotidiano

We must first recognize that *lo cotidiano* (daily life) is a category of analysis developed by feminist critical theory. As cultural notion, it has always been present in Latino/a cultures as a way of designating the whole of the doing and thinking of our people in their daily and recurring routine. Although daily life has been a space controlled by dominant ideologies and religions, twentieth-century currents of liberation thought underestimated *lo cotidiano*'s critical weight, the analytic magnitude of daily living, and its counter-hegemonic political value.

The analytic pertinence of daily life was discovered by feminist critical theory and not by androcentric liberation theologies. This category emerged within the context of the feminist philosophies and sociologies developed in eastern Europe and Latin America, in the 1960s and 1970s, in order to confront ideological totalitarianism and monolithic meta-discourses current at the time. Their aim was the reinvention of the ethical and political foundations of true democracy in social life.[120]

As analytical category, *lo cotidiano* has been one of critical feminism's most important contributions, because it permitted the exposure of the hierarchical historical dynamics—especially patriarchal ones—that affect people in their *daily living*, in the day after day of human relations lived in the home, in social institutions, at work, in culture, and in religion. Daily life, in this sense, radically critiques today's social models, which dehumanize and polarize persons. At the same time, daily life articulates an alternative democratic and aesthetic view of the world, of history, and of life. Within this perspective, a new model of life rejects all social relations based on social, sexual, or racial hierarchies; it puts a stop to ecological destruction and understands social power as the power to create a new rational daily life. *Lo cotidiano* is understood as a *dynamis* that seeks to make hegemonic and universal the logic of human rights—including the rights to friendship, bread, employment, and beauty.

For feminist theory, daily life leads to a new perspective for the future of persons and of the world through the radical transformation of all of life's dimensions. Because it has to do with everything that affects *lo cotidiano* of existence, it brings to the fore those topics left unattended by androcentric theories—culture, aesthetics, beauty, affects, happiness, reproductive rights, sexuality, and the development of personality. In this sense, the notion of aesthetic praxis positively corrects the reductive and utilitarian emphasis which often characterized the modern understanding of historical praxis. Just as it also broadens our comprehension of human praxis as transformation toward true liberation. With daily life, feminism inaugurated a new way of conceptualizing what is meant by *life*—not as mere abstract living, but as a good life that can be continually supported by the whole of society. That is, a life where people may *everyday* enjoy a greater and better quality of life—a life *worth* living.[121]

The theological significance of daily life as source and locus of U.S. Latino/a theology is grounded in the fact that it is here where the real life of real people unfolds, and where God's revelation occurs.[122] We have no other place but *lo cotidiano* to welcome the living Word of God or to respond to it in faith. The faith of the people, as lived and expressed in popular Catholicism, happens within the dynamics of daily existence. The chapter by Orlando Espín in the present volume clearly establishes the epistemological and hermeneutic centrality of daily life for U.S. Latino/a theology. *Lo cotidiano* is presented there as the context within which occur all experiences of evil and hope, of grace and sin, of salvation and condemnation. Espín argues that it is here, in daily life, that we must religiously and culturally construct the categories for interpreting these experiences.

A theology that seeks to act as mediation of humanization and liberation must be engaged in the humanization and liberation of daily life, until every people, person, and living thing achieves a life worth living. The methodological importance of daily life is grounded on its being the privileged locus for an intercultural theology, since the cultures and religious experiences of our communities converge in it. Theologically, daily life has salvific value because the people themselves, in *lo cotidiano* of their existence, let us experience the salvific presence of God here and now in their daily struggles for humanization, for a better quality of life, and for greater social justice. At the same time, daily life urges us to join actively in the long march toward a new humanity and a future of fulfillment still latent in the heart of creation, until we reach God's definitive salvation.

CONCLUSION

For U.S. Latino/a theology, the current theological search for a comprehensive, ordered, and systematic articulation of the faith of the people involves a critical and deliberate option for *interculturality* as methodological axis. This option opens the way to face the challenges inherent in the processes of truth of the faith and of revelation. Within these processes, where culturally plural truths find their wholeness, we discover our task as contributing to the incorporation of the world and of human persons into the universal circle of divine salvation. As a theology which solidariously accompanies the faith of the people, the primary identity of Latino/a theology comes from its way of welcoming and *co*-responding to the mystery of God in our lives. Therefore, this theology's elaboration involves a journey, a direction, and a commitment. These three seek to speak these truths:

The Truth of Reality

We see the historical dynamics within which we currently live as moments of grace and as signs of the times, calling us to rethink the whole of the theological enterprise. Face to face with neocapitalist, systemic currents which see in themselves the model for the total satisfaction of human aspirations, U.S. Latino/a theology proclaims that the ways of God lead us to journey toward another reality shaped by other currents. The faith of the people, so hopeful in the midst of so much violence, believes that God's dwelling place cannot be in the global marketplace. The economic and sociocultural processes of neoliberal globalization increasingly demonstrate the similarities of situations lived across the world: the violence and impunity with which the "powerful" of the world perpetrate crimes and injustices (with concomitant increases in fear and poverty among the "weak") are well documented global facts.

On the other hand, there is also a growing similarity in the response of peoples and cultures who, grounded on a religious vision of justice and human dignity, fight for an alternative civilization, for greater humanization, and for the end of violence. Because Latino/a theology navigates on these currents, our theological word wants to speak the language of liberation and hope, as the truer word of our people. To further identify and illuminate this word, U.S. Latino/a theology now needs to take more into account the contributions of relational theological anthropology, of intercultural liberation philosophy, of critical theories of systemic analysis—including critical feminist and ecologic theories—and of other sciences compatible with Christianity's liberating identity.

Latino/a theology is elaborated within a context of communities that transcend geographic and intellectual borders. Nevertheless, this theology still sees the pertinence of Christianity's liberation traditions, within Catholicism and within our own cultures. As such, ours is a theology with global implications. It stands *against* the hegemony of systemic domination, while it is *in favor of* the hegemony of worldwide solidarity and of compassion toward suffering peoples.

The Truth of Theology

As all theological activity, ours is exposed to the traps of the reversed reality and seductive utopias created by the dominant intellectual traditions. Latino/a theology will be faithful to its nature, identity, and mission as knowledge of the faith as long as it maintains its connection to the tradition of culturally plural Christianity and its deliberate attention on the epistemologic-hermeneutic principles which ground it: the *faith of the people*, the *option for the poor and oppressed*, and *liberating praxis*. Faithfulness to these will offer Latino/a theology the possibility of speaking by recognizing truth through theological knowledge, even if it cannot guarantee it.

The Truth of God

Our theological task is carried out in the midst of a world that permanently threatens the faith of our community with the idolatrous message of profit and superficial happiness. To speak the truth of God in this world means that we must denounce the idol's evil and sin. It also implies that we must proclaim the God encountered in the religion of the people—in their celebrations, rituals, *fiestas*, prayers, and reconciliations. Popular Catholicism goes on revealing a God who defends, protects, corrects, and nourishes the very same social groups the world disdains. Latino/a theology must discover and proclaim this God who is preferentially revealed in the *faith of the people*, in the reality of *mestizaje*, and in the *daily life* of our communities.

I want to conclude by insisting that my reflections here ultimately speak of what theology is and has been in my life, and of how I understand the journey I share with my colleagues in the theological community. My becoming a theologian and my personal identification with U.S. Latino/a theology are, before everything else, a vocation whose ultimate justification is found in God alone. For a *mestiza* woman like myself, daughter of poor Mexican migrant workers, theology is not a given, nor can it be taken for granted. In my family and cultural contexts, there was no support or encouragement for women to become involved in the intellectual life. With my theological word I am attempting to reclaim, for myself and for women of similar background, a place in the world as builders of knowledge. I learned early enough that theology is not the concern of an individual or a mere academic "career," as I suspect it's often perceived in the United States. For me, theology is the process of faith lived with the Christian community with which I share joy and suffering, company and loneliness, and with which I often spend "days of mourning in hope." Theology, as aware and informed faith, guides the core options of my life and inspires the decisions I make in *lo cotidiano* of my existence. In a word, theology is not something I do, as if it were an object external to my life. Theology is a central axis of my identity as a Catholic woman, and it is the way I *co*-respond to the mystery of God in my life. Theology takes me down the great rivers of resistance and hope that irrigate *lo cotidiano* of the popular classes from which I come. It is the privileged way I have for finding strength, inspiration, and hope in my life.

Notes

¹ On the use of *Latino/a*, please see the Glossary in the present volume.

² Mission Statement, Academy of Catholic Hispanic Theologians of the United States, ACHTUS Constitution, art. I.

³ Professor Raúl Fornet-Betancourt's work on an intercultural philosophical model has proven very useful to me in this and in subsequent parts of the present article. I find his philosophical perspectives very important for U.S. Latino/a theology's future development. From among Fornet-Betancourt's many publications, see especially "El cristianismo: Perspectivas de futuro en el umbral del Tercer Milenio a partir de la experiencia de América Latina," *Pasos* 51 (1994), 1-8; and *Hacia una filosofía intercultural latinoamericana* (San José, Costa Rica: Departamento Ecuménico de Investigaciones, 1994).

⁴ See, for example, Karl Rahner, "Theology," in *Encyclopedia of Theology: The Concise Sacramentum Mundi*, ed. K. Rahner (New York: Crossroad, 1986), 1690-91; Richard P. McBrien, *Catholicism* (San Francisco: Harper, 1994, new edition), 51-52; J. J. Mueller, "Theology, Systematic," in *The Modern Catholic Encyclopedia*, ed. M. Glazier and M. Hellwig (Collegeville, Minn.: Liturgical Press, 1994), 865; Francis Schüssler Fiorenza, "Foundations of Theology," in *Handbook of Catholic Theology*, ed. W. Beinert and F. S. Fiorenza (New York: Crossroad, 1995), 258-59, 261; Wolfgang Beinert, "Dogmatic Theology," in Beinert and Fiorenza, *Handbook of Catholic Theology*, 190; Francis Schüssler Fiorenza, "Systematic Theology: Tasks and Methods," in *Systematic Theology: Roman Catholic Perspectives*, ed. F. S. Fiorenza and J. P. Galvin (Minneapolis, Minn.: Fortress Press, 1991), 1:3-87.

⁵ In order to see the reason for this affirmation, the reader needs only to review the publications cited in the preceding note, as well as the authors and sources they use when defining and explaining theology as a whole, its topics, and its several disciplines.

⁶ Cf. Francis Schüssler Fiorenza, "Systematic Theology," 35-85. See also the chapters included in T. W. Tilley, ed., *Postmodern Theologies: The Challenge of Religious Diversity* (Maryknoll, N.Y.: Orbis Books, 1996).

⁷ Fernando F. Segovia, "Two Places and No Place on Which to Stand," in *Mestizo Christianity: Theology from the Latino Perspective*, ed. A. Bañuelas (Maryknoll, N.Y.: Orbis Books, 1995), 35.

⁸ Cf. Roberto S. Goizueta, "El mestizaje hispano-americano y el método teológico," in *Revista Latinoamericana de Teología ReLAT* 168 (1993), www.uca.ni/koinonia/relat/168.htm, 4.

⁹ On the articulation of theological knowledge in Latin American liberation theology, see Jon Sobrino, *The True Church and the Poor* (Maryknoll, N.Y.: Orbis Books, 1991), 7-38.

¹⁰ Leonardo Boff, "Post-Modernity and the Misery of Liberating Reason," *Pasos Review* 1 (1995), 5.

¹¹ Roberto S. Goizueta, *Caminemos con Jesús: Toward a Hispanic/Latino Theology of Accompaniment* (Maryknoll, N.Y.: Orbis Books, 1995), 167.

¹² Cf. Fornet-Betancourt, *Hacia una filosofía intercultural*.

¹³ Fornet-Betancourt, *Hacia una filosofía intercultural*, 16.

¹⁴ For the definition and meaning of these terms, see "Rationality or Irrationality? Modernity, Postmodernity, and the U.S. Hispanic Theologian," in Goizueta, *Caminemos con Jesús*, chap. 6, 132-72; see also his contribution to the present volume, especially the section "The Self in Modernity and Postmodernity."

¹⁵ Goizueta, *Caminemos con Jesús*, 134-35.

¹⁶ Goizueta, *Caminemos con Jesús*, 137, 154. Leonardo Boff says that, for

postmodern theories, "none of the types of rationalization should assume the monopoly of reason. On the contrary, several types of rationalization should be valid, autonomous, and irreducible" (Boff, "Post-Modernity and the Misery of Liberating Reason," 2).

[17] Franz J. Hinkelammert, "Capitalismo y socialismo: La posibilidad de alternativas," *Pasos* 48 (1993), 10-15; idem, "El cautiverio de la utopía: Las utopías conservadoras del capitalismo actual, el neoliberalismo y la dialéctica de las alternativas," *Pasos* 50 (1993), 1-14.

[18] Goizueta, *Caminemos con Jesús*, 169.

[19] Fornet-Betancourt, *Hacia una filosofía intercultural*, 20.

[20] Ecumenical Association of Third World Theologians (EATWOT), "Final Statement of the Sixth EATWOT Conference," in *Doing Theology in a Divided World*, ed. V. Fabella and S. Torres (Maryknoll, N.Y.: Orbis Books, 1985), 188.

[21] "Final Statement of the 'Women against Violence' Dialogue," in *Women Resisting Violence: Spirituality for Life*, ed. M. J. Mananzan et al. (Maryknoll, N.Y.: Orbis Books, 1996), 183; see also Sixto J. García, "Sources and Loci of Hispanic Theology," in Bañuelas, *Mestizo Christianity*, 120.

[22] "Final Document of the Intercontinental Women's Conference, Oaxtepec, Mexico, December 1-6, 1986," in *With Passion and Compassion*, ed. V. Fabella and M. A. Oduyoye (Maryknoll, N.Y.: Orbis Books, 1988), 186, 188.

[23] Raúl Vidales, "Methodological Issues in Liberation Theology," in *Frontiers of Theology in Latin America*, ed. R. Gibellini (Maryknoll, N.Y.: Orbis Books, 1979), 43.

[24] Final Reflection, "Commonalities, Divergences, and Crossfertilization among Third World Theologies: A Document Based on the Seventh International Conference of the Ecumenical Association of Third World Theologians (Oaxtepec, Mexico, December 7-14, 1986)," in *Third World Theologies: Commonalities and Divergences*, ed. K. C. Abraham (Maryknoll, N.Y.: Orbis Books, 1990), 200.

[25] Jon Sobrino, "Centralidad del Reino de Dios en la teología de la liberación," in *Mysterium Liberationis: Conceptos fundamentales de la teología de la liberación*, ed. I. Ellacuría and J. Sobrino (Madrid: Editorial Trotta, 1990), 1:496 (English translation: *Mysterium Liberationis: Fundamental Concepts in Liberation Theology* [Maryknoll, N.Y.: Orbis Books, 1993]).

[26] Jon Sobrino, "Central Position of the Reign of God in Liberation Theology," in Ellacuría and Sobrino, *Mysterium Liberationis: Fundamental Concepts in Liberation Theology*, 374.

[27] Raúl Vidales, "Cuestiones en torno al método en la teología de la liberación," in *La nueva frontera de la teología en América Latina*, ed. R. Gibellini (Salamanca: Ediciones Sígueme, 1977), 50.

[28] Vidales, "Methodological Issues in Liberation Theology."

[29] Goizueta, *Caminemos con Jesús*, 173.

[30] Juan José Tamayo, *Presente y futuro de la teología de la liberación* (Madrid: San Pablo, 1994), 31-32.

[31] Jon Sobrino, "Opción por los pobres," in *Conceptos fundamentales del cristianismo*, ed. C. Floristán and J. J. Tamayo (Madrid: Editorial Trotta, 1993), 881-85.

[32] Jon Sobrino, *The Principle of Mercy: Taking the Crucified People from the Cross* (Maryknoll, N.Y.: Orbis Books, 1994), 25.

[33] Ignacio Ellacuría, *Conversión de la Iglesia al Reino de Dios* (Santander: Editorial Sal Terrae, 1984), 84.

[34] Andrés G. Guerrero, *A Chicano Theology* (Maryknoll, N.Y.: Orbis Books, 1987), 159.

[35] Leonardo Boff, *Faith on the Edge: Religion and Marginalized Existence* (Maryknoll, N.Y.: Orbis Books, 1991), 60.

[36] Leonardo Boff, *Cry of the Earth, Cry of the Poor* (Maryknoll, N.Y.: Orbis Books, 1997), 107.

[37] João B. Libânio and Alfonso Murad, *Introdução à teologia: Perfil, emfoques, tarefas* (São Paulo: Edições Loyola, 1996), 172-73.

[38] Fornet-Betancourt, *Hacia una filosofía intercultural*, 38.

[39] Within the Ecumenical Association of Third World Theologians (EATWOT), and in other scholarly contexts, it has become common practice to refer the expression *Third World* to the impoverished peoples and marginalized cultures of the geopolitical South (i.e., Latin America and the Caribbean, Asia, and Africa), as well as the impoverished peoples and marginalized cultures within the rich countries of the geopolitical North (i.e., the Third World within Europe, North America, and Japan). In this sense, the Third World exists within the First, as the First also exists within the Third. See "The Irruption of the Third World: Challenge to Theology: Final Statement of the Fifth EATWOT Conference, New Delhi, August 17-29, 1981," in *Irruption of the Third World: Challenge to Theology*, ed. V. Fabella and S. Torres (Maryknoll, N.Y.: Orbis Books, 1983), 191-206. In its most recent statement, EATWOT indicates that "the term 'Third World' remains the official identity of our Association. Its meaning primarily arises from the social, economic, political, religious and cultural forces which render our people expendable" ("Search for a New Just World Order: Challenges to Theology. Final Statement of the EATWOT Assembly at Tagaytay City, Philippines, December 10-17, 1996," *Voices of the Third World/EATWOT* 20:1 (1997), 24.

[40] Goizueta, *Caminemos con Jesús*, 174.

[41] Fernando F. Segovia, "Hispanic American Theology and the Bible: Effective Weapon and Faithful Ally," in *We Are a People! Initiatives in Hispanic American Theology*, ed. R. S. Goizueta (Minneapolis, Minn.: Fortress Press, 1992), 45.

[42] Gilbert R. Cadena, "The Social Location of Liberation Theology: From Latin America to the United States," in *Hispanic/Latino Theology: Challenge and Promise*, ed. F. Segovia and A. Isasi-Díaz (Minneapolis, Minn.: Fortress Press, 1996), 179.

[43] Allan Figueroa Deck, "Introduction," in *Frontiers of Hispanic Theology in the United States*, ed. A. F. Deck (Maryknoll, N.Y.: Orbis Books, 1992), xiv.

[44] María Pilar Aquino, "Perspectives on a Latina Feminist Liberation Theology," in Deck, *Frontiers of Hispanic Theology in the United States*, 25.

[45] For an approximation to the now classic method of Latin American liberation theology, see Ignacio Ellacuría, "Hacia una fundamentación del método teológico latinoamericano," in *ECA [Estudios Centroamericanos]* 322-23 (1975), 409-25; Clodovis Boff, "Epistemology and Method of Liberation Theology," in Ellacuría and Sobrino, *Mysterium Liberationis: Fundamental Concepts*, 57-84; Gustavo Gutiérrez, *A Theology of Liberation* (Maryknoll, N.Y.: Orbis Books, 1993), 3-12, 83-120; Tamayo, *Presente y futuro de la teología de la liberación*, 25-73; and the excellently edited collection *Gustavo Gutiérrez: Essential Writings*, ed. J. B. Nickoloff (Maryknoll, N.Y.: Orbis Books, 1996), 23-77.

[46] For an introduction to theological and biblical hermeneutics in the early stages of liberation theology, see Juan José Tamayo, *Para comprender la teología de la liberación* (Estella: Editorial Verbo Divino, 1989), 53-70, 98-114; Gilberto da Silva Gorgulho, "Biblical Hermeneutics," in Ellacuría and Sobrino, *Mysterium Liberationis: Fundamental Concepts*, 123-50; Carlos Bravo G., "Del Exodo at seguimiento de Jesús," in *Cambio social y pensamiento cristiano en América Latina*, ed. J. Comblin, J. I. González Faus, and J. Sobrino (Madrid: Editorial Trotta, 1993), 79-100; Nickoloff, *Gustavo Gutiérrez: Essential Writings*, 78-148; Carlos Mesters, *Defenseless Flower* (Maryknoll, N.Y.: Orbis Books, 1989).

[47] On Latin American theology's fundamental intentionality, centered on the

notion of *integral liberation*, see the two preceding notes. See also the text that, in my opinion, is the most representative and the most important one on the topic, although it is one of the least known: Ignacio Ellacuría, "Liberación," in Floristán and Tamayo, *Conceptos fundamentales del cristianismo*, 690-710. For a more recent understanding of the fundamental intentionality, based on the notion of Christian love as mercy, justice, and liberation, see Sobrino, *The Principle of Mercy*, 27-46; and also Jon Sobrino, "De una teología sólo de la liberación a una teología del martirio," in Comblin, González Faus, and Sobrino, *Cambio social y pensamiento cristiano en América Latina*, 101-21.

[48] Orlando O. Espín, *The Faith of the People: Theological Reflections on Popular Catholicism* (Maryknoll, N.Y.: Orbis Books, 1997), 64.

[49] Espín, *The Faith of the People*, 91.

[50] See note 39, supra.

[51] Juan Luis Segundo, "Críticas y autocríticas de la teología de la liberación," in Comblin, González Faus, and Sobrino, *Cambio social y pensamiento cristiano en América Latina*, 215, 217-36.

[52] João B. Libânio, "Panorama de la teología de América Latina en los últimos veinte años," in Comblin, González Faus, and Sobrino, *Cambio social y pensamiento cristiano en América Latina*, 72-78.

[53] Diego Irarrázaval, *Rito y pensar cristiano* (Lima: Centro de Estudios y Publicaciones, 1993); idem, *Tradición y porvenir andino* (Puno/Lima: Instituto de Estudios Aymaras/Asociación de Publicaciones Educativas, 1992).

[54] Diego Irarrázaval, "How Is Theology Done in Latin America?," *Voices from the Third World/EATWOT* 18:1 (1995), 59-78.

[55] Gutiérrez, *A Theology of Liberation*, xxxvi.

[56] María Pilar Aquino and Ana María Tepedino, eds., *Entre la indignación y la esperanza: Teología feminista latinoamericana* (Bogotá: Indo-American Press, 1998).

[57] Virgilio Elizondo, "Condiciones y criterios para un diálogo teológico intercultural," in *Concilium* 191 (1984), 45.

[58] On this, see Arturo J. Bañuelas, "U.S. Hispanic Theology: An Initial Assessment," in Bañuelas, *Mestizo Christianity*, 77; Roberto S. Goizueta, "Rediscovering Praxis: The Significance of U.S. Hispanic Experience for Theological Method," in Bañuelas, *Mestizo Christianity*, 85; García, "Sources and Loci of Hispanic Theology," 106; Ada M. Isasi-Díaz, *Mujerista Theology* (Maryknoll, N.Y.: Orbis Books, 1996), 79; María Pilar Aquino, "Directions and Foundations of Hispanic/Latino Theology: Toward a *Mestiza* Theology of Liberation," *Journal of Hispanic/Latino Theology* 1:1 (1993), 8.

[59] Goizueta, "El mestizaje hispano-americano," 4.

[60] Goizueta, *Caminemos con Jesús*, 9.

[61] Fornet-Betancourt, *Hacia una filosofía intercultural*, 34.

[62] Fornet-Betancourt, *Hacia una filosofía intercultural*, 39; Bañuelas, "U.S. Hispanic Theology: An Initial Assessment," 72; Segovia, "Two Places and No Place on Which to Stand," 35; Espín, *The Faith of the People*, 32, 63, 68-70.

[63] Fornet-Betancourt, *Hacia una filosofía intercultural*, 21-26, 47.

[64] Fernando Segovia, "Aliens in the Promised Land: The Manifest Destiny of U.S. Hispanic American Theology," in Segovia and Isasi-Díaz, *Hispanic/Latino Theology*, 16.

[65] *Respectivity* is a classic and fundamental concept in X. Zubiri's philosophy. Zubiri was one of the most important influences on Ignacio Ellacuría's thought, considering that Ellacuría was Zubiri's closest disciple and his best interpreter. According to Zubiri: "Since reality is an 'open' formality, it is not reality except 'respectively' to that to which it is open. This respectivity is not a relation, be-

cause every relation is the relation of a thing or form of reality to another thing or form of reality. Respectivity, on the contrary, is a constitutive moment of reality's formality itself and as itself" (Xavier Zubiri, *Inteligencia sentiente: Inteligencia y realidad*, 3d ed. [Madrid: Alianza Editorial, 1984], 120). See also X. Zubiri, *Estructura dinámica de la realidad* (Madrid: Alianza Editorial, 1989), 25, 215, 314, 318; idem, *Inteligencia y razón* (Madrid: Alianza Editorial, 1983), 285-86, 342, 349; idem, *Inteligencia y Logos* (Madrid: Alianza Editorial, 1982), 22-32.

[66] Ignacio Ellacuría, *Filosofía de la realidad histórica* (Madrid: Editorial Trotta, 1991), 30.

[67] Cornelius Ernst indicates that "the notion of a theological epistemology . . . is itself historically conditioned . . . The search for identity in the new nations of the post-colonial era, in a tension between traditional religions and new technology, is a preoccupation with the redefinition of meanings . . . [These] support the suggestion that the reformulation of theology taking place in our time demands a corresponding reformulation of theological epistemology" (C. Ernst, "Theological Methodology," in Rahner, *Encyclopedia of Theology*, 1677).

[68] EATWOT, Final Reflection, "Commonalities, Divergences, and Crossfertilization," 200.

[69] Wolfgang Beinert, "Revelation," in Beinert and Schüssler Fiorenza, *Handbook of Catholic Theology*, 602-3; Libânio and Murad, *Introdução à teologia*, 172, 245-46.

[70] Orlando Espín, in the third part of his essay in the present volume.

[71] Elizabeth Schüssler Fiorenza, *Discipleship of Equals. A Critical Feminist Ekklesialogy of Liberation* (New York: Crossroad, 1993), 101-2.

[72] Orlando Espín, in the first part of his essay in the present volume. See also Espín's important study on the overall role of culture in theology and church: "A 'Multicultural' Church?: Theological Reflections from 'Below,'" in *The Multicultural Church: A New Landscape in U.S. Theologies*, ed. W. Cenkner (New York: Paulist Press, 1995), 54-71.

[73] Ellacuría, "Liberación," 690; idem, *Conversión de la Iglesia*, 191-204.

[74] Second Vatican Council, *Dei Verbum*, nos. 2-5; Paul VI, *Evangelii Nuntiandi*, nos. 9, 29.

[75] Jeanette Rodríguez, "U.S. Hispanic Theology: Context and Challenge," *Journal of Hispanic/Latino Theology* 5:3 (1998), 6.

[76] Deck, "Introduction," xi.

[77] Cadena, "The Social Location of Liberation Theology," 176.

[78] Virgil Elizondo, "Toward an American-Hispanic Theology of Liberation in the U.S.A.," in Fabella and Torres, *Irruption of the Third World*, 54-55.

[79] Virgil Elizondo, "*Mestizaje* as a Locus of Theological Reflection," in Bañuelas, *Mestizo Christianity*, 9.

[80] María Pilar Aquino, *La teología, la Iglesia y la mujer en América Latina* (Bogotá: Indo-American Press, 1994), 10-11.

[81] Aquino, "Directions and Foundations of Hispanic/Latino Theology," 8.

[82] Goizueta, "Rediscovering Praxis," 90.

[83] Bañuelas, "U.S. Hispanic Theology: An Initial Assessment," 73. See Glossary for *teología de conjunto*.

[84] On this understanding of theological method, see Ellacuría, "Hacia una fundamentación," 419; Goizueta, *Caminemos con Jesús*, 206-7; Sobrino, *The True Church and the Poor*, 22-23; José Ramos Regidor, *Jesús y el despertar de los oprimidos* (Salamanca: Ediciones Sígueme, 1984), 97; and "Final Statement of the 'Women against Violence' Dialogue," 180.

[85] See Glossary.

[86] See Glossary.

[87] Goizueta, "El mestizaje hispano-americano," 1.

[88] Roberto Goizueta, "U.S. Hispanic Popular Catholicism as Theopoetics," in Segovia and Isasi-Díaz, *Hispanic/Latino Theology*, 275.

[89] Espín, *The Faith of the People*, 166-67.

[90] Elizondo, "Condiciones y criterios para un diálogo teológico intercultural," 48.

[91] Goizueta, *Caminemos con Jesús*, 177. See also the biblical, theological, and soteriological foundations for the option for the poor in Gustavo Gutiérrez, "Option for the Poor," in Ellacuría and Sobrino, *Mysterium Liberationis: Fundamental Concepts*, 235-50; Pablo Richard and Ignacio Ellacuría, "Pobreza/Pobres," in Floristán and Tamayo, *Conceptos fundamentales del cristianismo*, 1030-57.

[92] Franz Hinkelammert, *Cultura de esperanza y sociedad sin exclusión* (San José, Costa Rica: Departamento Ecuménico de Investigaciones, 1995), 15, 141, 143, 158.

[93] Hinkelammert, *Cultura de esperanza*, 19, 167-78, 303-7, 315-18.

[94] Bishop Pedro Casaldáliga, "El cuerno del jubileo," *Reflexión y Liberación* 10:37 (1998), 5-8.

[95] Hinkelammert, *Cultura de esperanza*, 358.

[96] For the notions of liberating praxis and accompaniment, see the works by Roberto Goizueta, which I use in the present article, especially *Caminemos con Jesús*, 86-102, and "El mestizaje hispano-americano," 1. See also María Pilar Aquino, *Our Cry for Life: Feminist Theology from Latin America* (Maryknoll, N.Y.: Orbis Books, 1993), 11-13; idem, "Directions and Foundations of Hispanic/Latino Theology," 8-9; idem, "Perspectives on a Latina Feminist Liberation Theology," 34-37; and Ellacuría, *Filosofía de la realidad histórica*, 470-72.

[97] See Glossary.

[98] Goizueta, *Caminemos con Jesús*, 103.

[99] Evangelista Vilanova, *Historia de la teología cristiana* 3 vols. (Barcelona: Editorial Herder, 1989), 2:612.

[100] Vilanova, *Historia de la teología cristiana*, 2:611; Yves Congar, *A History of Theology* (Garden City: Doubleday, 1968), 163-65.

[101] García, "Sources and Loci of Hispanic Theology," 106.

[102] Ellacuría, *Conversión de la Iglesia al Reino de Dios*, 168.

[103] It is worth noting that, following Virgilio Elizondo's suggestions in that direction, Orlando Espín and Sixto García were the first U.S. Latino/a theologians to propose and elaborate (starting in the early 1980s) a critical examination of popular Catholicism as source and locus for Latino/a systematic theology.

[104] Espín, *The Faith of the People*, 92, 162; see also Goizueta, *Caminemos con Jesús*, 21-23.

[105] Virgil Elizondo, "Popular Religions as Support of Identity—Based on the Mexican-American Experience in the United States," in *Spirituality of the Third World: A Cry for Life*, papers and reflections from the Ecumenical Association of Third World Theologians (EATWOT) 1992 Assembly, in Nairobi, Kenya, ed. K. C. Abraham and B. Mbuy-Beya (Maryknoll, N.Y.: Orbis Books, 1994), 56.

[106] On this type of rationality, see Goizueta, "Rediscovering Praxis," 94-97; idem, *Caminemos con Jesús*, 140-41; Cristián Parker, *Popular Religion and Modernization in Latin America* (Maryknoll, N.Y.: Orbis Books, 1996), 258-64; Manuel M. Marzal, "The Religion of the Andean Quechua in Southern Peru," in *The Indian Face of God in Latin America*, ed. M. Marzal et al. (Maryknoll, N.Y.: Orbis Books, 1996), 90; Xavier Albó, "The Aymara Religious Experience," in Marzal et al., *The Indian Face of God*, 141-44.

[107] Parker, *Popular Religion and Modernization in Latin America*, 377.

[108] See Glossary.

[109] The entire book *Mestizo Christianity*, edited by Arturo Bañuelas revolves around this theme. Therein, especially see Virgil Elizondo, "*Mestizaje* as a Locus of Theological Reflection," 7-27; Fernando Segovia, "Two Places and No Place on Which to Stand" 29-43; and Arturo Bañuelas, "U.S. Hispanic Theology: An Initial Assessment," 55-82. See also Aquino, "Directions and Foundations of Hispanic/Latino Theology," 5-21; Fernando Segovia, "In the World but Not of It," in Segovia and Isasi-Díaz *Hispanic/Latino Theology*, 195-217; Ada M. Isasi-Díaz, "Afterwords: Strangers No Longer," in Segovia and Isasi-Díaz, *Hispanic/Latino Theology*, 367-74; Allan F. Deck, "Latino Theology: The Year of the *Boom*," in *Journal of Hispanic/Latino Theology* 1:2 (1994), 51-63; Rodríguez, "U.S. Hispanic Theology: Context and Challenge," 6-15.

[110] Johann-Baptist Metz, "La teología en el ocaso de la modernidad," *Concilium* 191 (1984), 37-39; idem, "Standing at the End of the Eurocentric Era of Christianity: A Catholic View," in Fabella and Torres, *Doing Theology in a Divided World*, 85-90.

[111] Tamayo, *Presente y futuro*, 29.

[112] Roberto Goizueta, "United States Hispanic Theology and the Challenge of Pluralism," in Deck, *Frontiers of Hispanic Theology in the United States*, 15, 19.

[113] Fornet-Betancourt, "El cristianismo: Perspectivas de futuro," 7-8.

[114] Elizondo, "*Mestizaje* as a Locus of Theological Reflection," 9-10.

[115] Elizondo, "*Mestizaje* as a Locus of Theological Reflection," 10, 12.

[116] In M. P. Aquino and R. Goizueta, eds., *Theology: Expanding the Borders*, Annual Publication of the College Theology Society, vol. 43 (Mystic, Conn.: Twenty-Third Publications, 1998), 10.

[117] Johann-Baptist Metz, "Perspectivas de un cristianismo multicultural," in *Cristianismo y liberación: Homenaje a Casiano Floristán*, ed. J. J. Tamayo (Madrid: Editorial Trotta, 1996), 36.

[118] Rodríguez, "U.S. Hispanic Theology: Context and Challenge," 11.

[119] Originally published in French as *L'avenir est au métissage* (Paris: Nouvelles Editions Mame, 1987). In English, *The Future Is Mestizo: Life Where Cultures Meet* (Oak Park, Ill.: Meyer-Stone Books, 1988).

[120] Among the pioneering authors, see Agnes Heller, *Historia y vida cotidiana* (Mexico City: Editorial Grijalbo, 1972); idem, *Sociología de la vida cotidiana* (Barcelona: Editorial Península, 1977); idem, *La revolución de la vida cotidiana* (Barcelona: Editorial Península, 1982); Teresita de Barbieri, *Mujeres y vida cotidiana* (Mexico City: Fondo de Cultura Económica, 1984); Julieta Kirkwood, "El feminismo como negación del autoritarismo," in *Teoría feminista: Selección de textos*, ed. Ediciones Populares Feministas (Santo Domingo: Ediciones del CIPAF, 1984); Ana Sojo, *Mujer y política. Ensayo sobre feminismo y sujeto popular* (San José, Costa Rica: Departamento Ecuménico de Investigaciones, 1985).

[121] On these perspectives, see Alfonso Ibáñez, ed., *Agnes Heller: La satisfacción de las necesidades radicales* (San José, Costa Rica: Departamento Ecuménico de Investigaciones, 1991), 11-17, 55-59; and Oscar Jara, "Prólogo a la edición centroamericana: De la amistad, el pan y la belleza," in Ibáñez, *Agnes Heller*, i-iv.

[122] See my work on daily life in theological method in Aquino, "Perspectives on a Latina Feminist Liberation Theology," 33-34; idem, "Feminismo," in Floristán and Tamayo, *Conceptos fundamentales del cristianismo*, 519-20; idem, *Our Cry for Life*, 38-41, 109-21; idem, "Latin American Feminist Theology," *Journal of Feminist Studies in Religion* 14:1 (1998), 104. See also Ada M. Isasi-Díaz, *Mujerista Theology*, 66-73.

2

Theology's Contribution to Society

The Ministry of the Theologian

VIRGILIO P. ELIZONDO

Mexican American Cultural Center

In our Hispanic quest for life, liberty, and the pursuit of happiness in the United States, the Hispanic theologian has a very crucial contribution to make. Emerging out of the common struggles of our people, the theological word is an essential element of our quest. Without it, the efforts of others will remain incomplete. We are a deeply religious people. Religious expressions are interlaced throughout our language and culture; religious themes appear throughout our novels, songs, and art work; religious imagery is the most common and persistent element of our Hispanic language—whether English, Spanish, Náhuatl, *Cholo*, *Pocho*, Mayan, or otherwise. For us, religion is not just a Sunday observance but everyday life. Our God-imagery is the deepest element of our identity. Will our religion bind us to an enslaving past or liberate us? Is it a power unto survival or a fatalistic force condemning us to subservience and to domination by others?

Religion is a power, but how that power is used must be named and directed. That is the task and challenge of the religious thinker of the group. Others can help, but no one can do it for us. As long as we do not explore and articulate this element of our being, we will remain a spiritually colonized and oppressed people. As Hispanic culture is fundamentally Chris-

49

tian *Mestizo*, our theologians have an important role to play in envisioning and articulating the future of our people in this.

The 1960s were a time of great enthusiasm, critical movements, and world-changing events. In the secular world of the United States, the various minorities were claiming their rightful place in the dominant society of our country. We were claiming the most basic right to existence! Hispanics were claiming the right to inclusion in the various structures of society, to speak Spanish, to self-studies in the various fields of history, psychology, and the social sciences. We were tired of being told who we were and where we belonged—now we were going to speak for ourselves.

During this same period, the Catholic church was undergoing one of the most important moments of its life since Pentecost: Vatican Council II. Our church told us to use our own language, to incorporate our arts and music into the liturgy, to celebrate our heritage, to make the anxieties and hopes of our people those of the church, and to develop our own spiritualities and theologies based upon the Word of God in dialogue with the wisdom and philosophy of the local people. Traditions of long standing were to be respected and cherished. The church would never really take root and be at home until it developed its own local thinkers, liturgists, spiritualities, and theologies—this is the way of the Incarnation.[1]

Furthermore, in the process of building church the poor had a very privileged role, for it is through their cries for justice that the church is constantly purified and kept from becoming simply another institution of this world. In the faces of the broken and disinherited of the earth, the church sees the body and face of her own crucified Lord. In their cries it hears the clearest call to conversion, solidarity, and communion. Action on behalf of justice is a constitutive element of evangelization. The poor have an evangelical instinct to know when the gospel is being served or when it is being diluted or falsified. The poor are not to be at the margins of the church, but they are to take center stage![2] I would add to this the basis of my own doctoral thesis: If the poor and excluded are God's privileged children, then the God-expressions of the poor and excluded are privileged expressions of God and thus a fundamental source of theological reflection.[3]

Since the majority of U.S. Hispanics were poor and excluded from the structures of society and church, and of a different culture than the mainline United States, these two aspects of Vatican II would become fundamental in the future of our Hispanic apostolate, and indeed of our theological challenge.

The convergence of our *movimientos* throughout the United States with the movement of Vatican II brought about the urgent awareness that we needed a distinctively U.S. Hispanic spirituality and liturgy based upon a serious theological reflection on the faith of our people, especially as lived and expressed in the lives of our Hispanic poor. *It wasn't just Hispanic*

culture as such that was of ecclesial interest to us, but Hispanic culture as the
culture of the poor, marginated, excluded, and often exploited people. True theology could only emerge out of the heritage, tears, struggles, survival tac-
tics, and dreams of our people in dialogue with the foundations of our
faith. So we started, and it has been an exciting beginning.

In my studies of theology, I was always told that theology was faith
seeking understanding. Yet in all the theology which I studied, I never
seemed to be studying about the faith of *my* people, the faith which I had
received through the practices, devotions, and rituals of our Latino Catholic
tradition and of the church which I had experienced and loved since childhood. Theology seemed to be more of an intellectual exercise than a deepening of the faith. It was the same for other subjects I studies—I was studying about "them" but not about "us." There was no theology in existence
which explored the living faith of our *Mestizo* Latin American Christians.
This is changing rapidly.

Theologizing is a life process. It is the story of my life and quest in the
context of the life and quest of my people. For me, it was first the Mexican-
American people of the southwestern part of the United States, and now
the Hispanic people of the United States. In that sense it started not only
at my own birth, but at the birth of our people: the birth of Latin America.
Theologizing is very personal but not individualistic, because it is about
the common "us" that lives in me. U.S. Hispanic theology is the effort to
articulate the evolving Christian consciousness of our people as it is in
itself and as it relates to others in our society and our church.

In a way *our theology is a collective autobiography.* I dare to say this not
because I am so presumptuous as to think that I, or any of us who are
theologizing, am speaking for everyone but because what we try to study,
conceptualize, and verbalize, we have received not only from our own
families and neighborhood friends—our first and most fundamental
school—but also from the thousands of Hispanics whom we have been
privileged to work with and listen to during our entire lifetime. This has
been so especially during the last thirty years, since the foundation of
PADRES, LAS HERMANAS and MACC, the ENCUENTROS, the *Instituto*
de Liturgia Hispana, ACHTUS, and the many other efforts that are multiplying across the United States. During this time we have worked, ago-
nized, searched, laughed, cried, dreamed, joked, prayed, and celebrated
with literally millions of our own people from California to New England, Miami to Seattle, San Antonio to San Juan, New York to Anchor-
age, and all points in between—from the *ranchitos* to the cities, from universities to parish halls, from meetings with militants to working with
the U.S. military. Our U.S. Hispanic people are everywhere and are as
different as we might be. Indeed, we are a people, we are a nation! We
have a common soul! *Somos un pueblo en marcha!* (We are a people on the
move!)

We are not mere Latin Americans from Latin America, but neither are we "pure, red-blooded Americans," WASPs, or general, run-of-the-mill melting-pot Americans without a conscious sense of our heritage. We have a space in the world and a time in human history that is very definitely our own.

Our common story is our collective soul—our poets recite it, our story-tellers write novels about it, our songwriters sing it, our actors dramatize it, and our artists paint it. But for the scholars and thinkers, theologians and liturgists, politicians and business people, human scientists and so-cial workers, educators and administrators of mainstream United States we still remain an unidentified mystery. They see us as a problem to be solved. They want to help us by making us into their own image and like-ness so that we can say with them, "And God saw that it was good." But that would be a betrayal of God, who did make us, as we are, in God's own image and likeness.

What we feel in our hearts and sing passionately with our lips, we must conceptualize and verbalize theologically, so that we may understand with our minds what we experience spiritually in the depths of our being. As we "name" ourselves, we can begin to introduce ourselves properly not only to one another but to others in society and in the church—no longer apologetically or arrogantly, but simply as fellow human beings, as fel-low Christians. It is in the midst of the struggles for self-identity, libera-tion, and determination, especially the struggles of the poor among our people, that I place the urgent, critical, and creative task of the U.S. His-panic theologians.

Our theological work is the story of the universal human quest for life as lived and expressed by the Hispanic Christians of the United States—whether recent immigrants or long-time residents. Hence, precisely because it is so historically and culturally conditioned, it can be so universal—as any good story is universal! Our historical memory, our contemporary struggles, and our religious faith are the ultimate basis of our identity as a people. Our theologizing is a Christian interpretation of our struggle for life, survival, identity, human dignity, legitimacy, equality, liberty, hap-piness, and belonging. It is not abstract theory but living reality seeking understanding, expression, and direction.

Our theology seeks to be prophetic in that it denounces injustices. It is visionary in that it dares to dream of the new earth of an America without borders. It is imaginative and creative in that it dares to do theology in a new way and out of very different theological contexts. It is communitarian because it is done together with our people. It is practical in that it works with the grassroots in community organizing and other local projects. It is spiritual in that it seeks to articulate and promote the spiritual treasures of our evolving *Mestizo* heritage. It is evangelical in that it seeks to know and proclaim Jesus of Nazareth as he related to his own culture and heritage, as a model for our own relationship to our heritage and culture. But most of all, it is a rare combination of critical and romantic, passionate and engaged narrative, for it seeks not only to deepen our understanding of ourselves and our mission in the United States, but also to articulate exciting dreams—like the prophets of Israel—about a new future wherein no one will have to suffer what we have suffered in the past.

As Archbishop Patrick F. Flores has frequently said, "Just give us a chance and you will see how much we have to offer." It is a challenging and exciting time for U.S. Hispanic theologians, and we are just beginning.

Notes

[1] Vatican II, *Ad Gentes*, no. 22.

[2] Vatican II, *Lumen Gentium*, no. 8; World Synod of Bishops, *Synod on Justice* (1971); Second Conference of Latin American Bishops, *Medellín Conclusions* (1968); Paul VI, *Evangelii Nuntiandi* (1975); John Paul II, "Opening Speech at the Third Conference of Latin American Bishops," *Puebla Documents* (1979).

[3] Virgilio Elizondo, *Mestizaje: The Dialectic of Cultural Birth and the Gospel*, 2 vols. (San Antonio, Tex.: Mexican American Cultural Center, 1978). This is the English translation of the original French text, *Métissage, Violence Culturelle, Annonce de l'Évangile: La Dimension Interculturelle de l'Évangélisation*, presented at the Institut Catholique, Paris.

3

The Whole and the Love of Difference

Latino Metaphysics as Cosmology

ALEJANDRO GARCÍA-RIVERA

Jesuit School of Theology, Berkeley

It may surprise some that a theology that self-consciously proclaims to be based on the particular may attempt a "systematics." Systematics in the twentieth century, after all, followed the great German tradition of an elegant systematizing principle whose main effect is the totalization of reality and the subordination of particularity. Indeed, such systematic attempts destroy the very insight of Latino theology on the crucial role the "particular" plays in theology. Up to this point, however, Hispanic theology has been satisfied to claim the starting point of particular Hispanic practices with little reflection on its philosophical basis. Some Latino theologians may even argue that there is no need for such accounting. I disagree. Seductive as it may sound, faith may not escape the challenge of reason. Reason, understood in its broad sense as *intellectus* rather than *ratio*, makes faith "visible."[1] Indeed, reason is the flower of faith. Thus, the intended project of this chapter is to give an accounting of the crucial Latino insight on the essential role of the particular.

Such accounting follows a series of related questions. On what grounds can one claim the significance of the particular? Is not the particular a totalizing principle as well? Does it not swallow up, in reverse fashion, any generalities we, as Hispanic theologians, may observe or wish to claim? Is there an understanding of the particular that avoids this totalizing tendency? Such questions suggest that the notion of the particular in order to avoid becoming a totalizing principle requires a corresponding notion that grounds its understanding while preventing its imperious aspirations. Such a notion, I claim, is the *Whole*. By *Whole* I do not mean the generic Whole of the Scholastic tradition that relates to the particular as genus to species. Neither do I mean the German Romantic Whole that relates to the particular as immanent Spirit to particular manifestation. By Whole I mean an aesthetic Whole that grounds the particular even as the particular constitutes the Whole.

It may be obvious by now that such a Whole (a Whole that founds particularity) is unlike the metaphysics so despised and discredited in our day. Such a Whole emphasizes the reality of contingency in the midst of permanence, and a reality of relations forging real individuals (a reconceived realism) over a reality of independent individual identities with which only the mind can relate (nominalism and Kant).

The proposal for such a Whole will be developed by examining a quintessential Latino devotion: the *Nacimiento*, or Nativity scene. The *Nacimiento* suggests the Whole as *Cosmos*, a *uni*verse of aesthetic values grounded in the founding element of God's love for the particular. As such, a Hispanic accounting of the Whole turns out to be a metaphysics—but a metaphysics conceived as cosmology. Indeed, I would claim that the discrediting of traditional metaphysics has been due to the loss of a viable Christian cosmology, rather than the bankruptcy of a philosophical tradition.

The promise of such a reconceived metaphysics, then, would be manyfold. Not only would it ground Hispanic claims for the theological significance of the local Latino church but also revitalize a tradition once thought to be bankrupt. The *Nacimiento* of Hispanic devotion will also be compared here to Schleiermacher's wonderful little work on a German Nativity scene, *Die Weihnachtsfeier: Ein Gespräch.*[2] The comparison of the two *Nacimientos* will have two objectives. First, the comparison will demonstrate that the Christian Nativity scene presents a visual theodicy, or rather, an aesthetics of sign which signifies a theodicy.[3] And, second, that the Latino *Nacimiento* differs in a very special way from its European counterpart. The visual theodicy expressed in the *Nacimiento*, I will argue, emphasizes the cosmic over the Spirit. As such, the *Nacimiento* was shaped in great part by an indigenous theodicy which placed a greater emphasis on cosmic order rather than on human redemption.[4]

DIE WEIHNACHTSFEIER

A Strange Nativity: Schleiermacher's Die Weihnachtsfeier

The father of liberal Christianity, Friedrich Schleiermacher, wrote, in a fit of inspiration, a marvelous little work entitled *Die Weihnachtsfeier: Ein*

Gespräch (*Christmas Eve: A Dialogue*). Schleiermacher wished to present this work, written in the form of a Platonic dialogue, to his friends on Christmas 1805. A charming dialogue, whose setting is a comfortable nine-teenth-century home around Christmas time, this work also contains some of Schleiermacher's most profound theology. Indeed, *Die Weihnachtsfeier* articulates the most difficult topic a theologian must eventually confront: the relationship between human suffering and a loving God. Schleier-macher locates the heart of this relationship in the doctrine of the Incarna-tion, visually represented in the Protestant (and Roman Catholic) popular practice of the Nativity scene.[5] In doing so, Schleiermacher's *Die Weihnachtsfeier* becomes a dialogue on the Incarnation. As such, Schleiermacher's understanding of the Incarnation contains a surprising element.

Three main actors unfold Schleiermacher's theodicy in *Christmas Eve*: Sophie, the women, and the men.[6] One must resist the temptation to iden-tify in the different voices of the dialogue the voice of Schleiermacher him-self. Schleiermacher reveals his thought through all the characters.[7] Sophie, however, may be seen as expressing the author's deepest reflections. She is pure experience: unpretentious, innocent, and spontaneous. She starts the dialogue with music, singing each note "with reverence," anticipating and cherishing the notes with humble caring.[8] As such, she represents the spirit of Christmas itself. Sophie describes the Nativity scene:

> "Arranged informally about the table, and with tolerable skill, were representations of many of the important moments within the exter-nal history of Christianity, only a few episodes dividing them. In the same vicinity, one could see the baptism of Christ, Golgotha and the Mount of the Ascension, or the outpouring of the Spirit, the destruc-tion of the Temple, and Christians ranged in battle against the Saracens over the holy Sepulcher. In another grouping there was the pope marching in solemn procession to St. Peter's, the martyrdom of Hus, and Luther's burning of the papal bull; in another the bap-tism of the Saxons, missionaries in Greenland and Africa, a Herrnhuter Brethren churchyard, and the Halle Orphanage. The origi-nal desire had apparently wished to give special emphasis to the latter, as the most recent great accomplishment of religious zeal. The child had obviously taken pains to employ flame and water through-out the whole composition, making a fine pattern with the two con-flicting elements. Streams actually flowed, and fires flickered."[9]

The above description strikes one with its emphasis on the connected-ness of history.[10] Indeed, Sophie appears to be able to empathize with his-tory to such a degree that the present becomes meaningful through her childlike empathy. A view of history presents itself. The fires and streams become eloquent witnesses to Schleiermacher's view of history as spiritual. Something else, however, strikes us about the description of the Nativity scene:

"Now among all these highlighted objects one sought for a long time in vain for the birth scene itself, for she had wisely contrived to conceal the Christmas star. One had to follow after the angels and after the shepherds gathered around a campfire, then open a door in the wall of the structure . . . and there in an enclosure, which actually lay out-of-doors, one looked upon the holy family. All was dark in the lowly shed, save one beam of light streaming down from some hidden source upon the infant's head and casting a reflection on the bowed face of his mother. In contrast to the wild flames on the other side, this mild splendor seemed like a heavenly over against an earthly light."[11]

The infant Jesus is nowhere to be seen! Such invisibility ought not to be considered an oversight. Schleiermacher makes a deliberate point. The nature of that point will be the subject of the next few sections. For now, I only point to the strange character of Schleiermacher's Nativity scene. What kind of Incarnation is it that hides its flesh and blood? Yet Schleiermacher has been one of the most influential thinkers (if not the founder) of liberal Christianity. In the next few sections we will attempt to place Schleiermacher's strange statement on the Incarnation within a tradition of the visual representation of Jesus' birth, and within German thought. Having then located Schleiermacher's *Die Weihnachtsfeier* within its own local tradition of German thought, as well as within the wider ecclesial tradition of the Nativity scene, I will contrast *Christmas Eve* and *La Pastorela* in order to argue my case for a reconceived metaphysics in terms of cosmology.

Hodie Natus Est: *The Nativity Scene Tradition in the Wider Church*

Visual representations of Jesus' birth reveal a compact cosmology. Shepherds (human creatures), tending their sheep (animal creatures), hear angels (angelic creatures) singing in the heavens while the newborn Child lies in a manger filled with hay (vegetative creatures). Meanwhile, three Magi (cultural creatures) representing the three major geographic areas of the then known world—Europe, Asia, and Africa[12]—follow a star (cosmic creature). The Nativity scene deliberately and self-consciously brings together a Christian cosmic universe, the visible and the invisible, in a visual mosaic of the Incarnation. For this reason alone, the Nativity scene makes a powerful statement about the role of cosmology in Christian theology. Moreover, the Nativity scene comes to us as part of an ancient and well-loved tradition.

The Nativity scene, this visual representation of Jesus' birth, may be one of the oldest examples of popular Catholicism. Based, in part, on the scriptural infancy narratives (Lk 2:7-20; Mt 1:18—2:23), the history of the Nativity scene as popular Catholicism, the *praesepre* tradition, begins at a cave-like grotto alleged to be Jesus' actual birthplace. Origen, in the third century, alludes to the grotto as a center of pious devotion.[13] In fact, the empress Helena later built a basilica over the spot. Later writings assert that figures of the Holy Family were placed there as far back as 400 C.E. Indeed, it was and remains a site of pilgrimage. In 354 C.E., Pope Liberius established the Nativity as a special feast on December 25 to distinguish it from the Epiphany. Liberius dedicated a basilica, eventually known as Sancta Maria ad Praesepre, entirely for this new feast and did so by bringing relics of the "true" *praesepre* from Bethlehem. These relics were placed in a side chapel to which Pope Gregory III (731-41 C.E.) added figures of Mary and the Child.

At this point an interesting transformation takes place that reveals the genius of popular religion. The relics of wooden boards from Jesus' "actual" manger are displayed not in the usual manner of a reliquary, but put together in the form of a manger or *praesepre*. This manger-reliquary becomes, amazingly enough, the altar where the pope puts the consecrated host on Christmas Eve. Others imitate this liturgical (and popular) act, and soon other churches place the actual figure of the Child Jesus within the manger.[14] Perhaps the most dramatic development in this curious mix of popular Catholicism and high liturgy takes place in the Middle Ages through the influence of St. Francis of Assisi.

In the year 1223, Francis receives papal permission to erect in the church at Greccio a *praesepre* at which he places a live ox and donkey. The Nativity Mass itself is celebrated over the manger. The impact of this Nativity scene must have been great. A certain John of Greccio, for example, claims to have seen a Child sleeping in the manger and that the Child awoke at the sound of Francis's voice and embraced him. The hay from that manger was later credited for the miraculous cures of animals.[15]

Such powerful visual representations call for commentary. Indeed, the Nativity scene took on dramatic form in the Middle Ages. Such plays as the *Officium Pastorum* (shepherds' play) were extremely popular. Indeed, the visual representation of the Nativity and its enactment through ritual drama were made for each other. The *praesepre* tradition apparently presents a profound insight of faith that calls for articulation. It is theology expressed perhaps in its most profound way: an aesthetic narrative of immense popular appeal. Such aesthetic narratives find in visual representation insights with unfathomable capacity for reflection.

Schleiermacher's *Christmas Eve* obviously owes a great debt to the *praesepre* tradition. It too attempts to visually represent not only the scriptural infancy narratives but also elements borrowed from the contemporary culture. Like the Nativity scene of the *praesepre* tradition, Schleier-macher's *Die Weihnachtsfeier* takes the form of an aesthetic narrative. Less a shepherds' play than a Platonic dialogue, Schleiermacher's Nativity dialogue, nonetheless, becomes a profound theological commentary on the Incarnation. As such, it is also a cosmology of sorts. Indeed, the context of Schleiermacher's *Christmas Eve* may be seen as a response to a cosmological revolution.

Spirit and Time: Two Cosmological Revolutions

Friedrich Schleiermacher faced a crisis within his own society, at the height of the Enlightenment. The religious wars of the Reformation, the scientific revolution, and the discovery of the Americas were rapidly changing not only Europe's worldview but also its way of life.[16] The Reformation wars had brought home the issue of religious difference, while the peoples of the Americas had brought to sharp focus the issue of human difference. And perhaps most problematic to Schleiermacher, the scientific revolution had raised the issue of temporal difference. Indeed, science had given birth to a new cosmology.[17] Newton had mechanized the cosmos and left little room for spirit.[18] The result was not only a cosmological revolution but also a philosophical revolution.

Newton's mechanical universe, in a sense, solved the ancient philosophical problem of Being and Becoming by splitting their organic unity. The Becoming of a thing—that is, changes such as a seed growing into a tree—had in ancient or medieval thought been united through the "soul" or "nature" of the Being acting causally (materially, formally, efficiently, finally).[19] Though most scholars would place modernity's dichotomies at the feet of Descartes, I would emphasize the role played by Newton's new cosmology.

Newton's great achievement, in my opinion, was his notion of time. Using the new concept from calculus (the "infinitesimal") Newton transformed the philosophical notion of Becoming into the scientific notion of motion. By making time, or rather, temporal difference, infinitesimal, Being and Becoming undergo radical transformation. Infinitesimal time, after all, knows little of final causes. Infinitesimal time is, simply, a moment—an infinitely small moment—of time. As such, efficient cause jumps to the forefront of cosmic explanation.

Some Greeks saw Nature as organic, being endowed with a soul seeking a way to its proper place in a cosmic hierarchy—a *scala naturae*. Thus, Aristotle was able to explain the transformation of a tiny seed into a huge oak. So Nature's Becoming was less a deficiency of being and more a manifestation of soul. No wonder Aquinas saw in Aristotle's cosmology a splendid foundation for a grand *Summa* of theological reflection. The search for a proper place in a cosmic hierarchy assumes, nonetheless, a cosmos that is essentially complete. The cosmos, in this perspective, is essentially a place, or a set of spaces, within which a hierarchy can be discerned. Dynamism can exist in such cosmology but only as a function of the spaces. A cosmology of space supports the notion of final cause. Indeed, final cause lends itself well to a view of the cosmos as a well-ordered arrangement. Final cause then becomes the organic connection between the soul and its cosmic space.

Newton's transformation of the cosmos of spaces into a cosmos of infinitesimal temporal units makes final cause an incongruous element in the new cosmology. Infinitesimal time knows nothing of finality. It exists for the moment. Such cosmology brings a new notion of Becoming into the universe. Becoming is then unrelated to Being. Indeed, Becoming may be viewed as an end in itself. Thus, Newton's cosmology sets the stage for a new dynamism in the cosmos. Movement in Newton's cosmos is explained not through final cause but solely through efficient cause. Efficient cause strips the spirit's organic relationship to the natural. Nature is not so much the organic manifestation of spirit but the efficient motion of its parts. Nature becomes a watch, and God a marvelous Watchmaker.

Newton's transformation of Becoming into motion created the classical field of physics.[20] As such, Newton made time a "spirit-less" entity. If ancient time—the temporal of Becoming—had been a sign of the soul's final cause, then Newtonian time became a sign of simple efficient cause, that is, the machine. For philosophy and theology, the transformation was devastating. No longer could theology convincingly state along with Augustine:

Not with doubting, but with assured consciousness, do I love Thee, Lord. Thou hast stricken my heart with Thy word, and I loved Thee. Yea, also heaven and earth, and all that therein is; behold, on every side they bid me love Thee; nor cease to say so unto all, that they may be without excuse . . . And what is this? I asked the earth, and it answered me, "I am not He"; and whatsoever are in it confessed the same. I asked the sea and the deeps, and the living creeping things, and they answered, "We are not thy God, seek above us." I asked the moving air; and the whole air with his inhabitants answered, "Anaximenes was deceived. I am not God." I asked the heavens, sun, moon, stars, "Nor (say they) are we the God whom thou seekest." And I replied unto all the things which encompass the door of my flesh: "Ye have told me of my God, that ye are not He; tell me something of Him." And they cried out with a loud voice, "He made us." My questioning them, was my thoughts on them: and their form of beauty gave the answer. And I turned myself unto myself, and said to myself, "Who art thou?" And I answered, "A man." And behold, in me there present themselves to me soul, and body, one without, the other within. By which of these ought I to seek my God? I had sought Him in the body from earth to heaven, so far as I could send messengers, the beams of mine eyes. But the better is the inner, for to it as presiding and judging, all the bodily messengers reported the answers of heaven and earth, and all things therein, who said, "We are not God, but He made us." These things did my inner man know by the ministry of the outer: I the inner knew them; I, the mind, through the senses of my body. I asked the whole frame of the world about my God; and it answered me, "I am not He, but He made me."[21]

If, for theology, natural phenomena could no longer be seen as signs of God's greater reality, neither could philosophy argue for a greater reality beyond natural appearances, that is, a metaphysics. Appearances may be signs, but they are signs ultimately of the mind, a mind consisting of different "stuff" from Nature's "stuff," *res cogitans* versus *res naturans*.[22] Thus, natural appearances ultimately point to mental realities.[23] Such transformation effectively transforms Greek speculations on Nature as ontology into the modern preoccupation with reality as epistemology. If philosophy is to look for the roots of the contemporary demise of metaphysics, let it find them here. At stake, I am arguing, is the unspoken foundation for any metaphysics: cosmology.

Newton's mechanical cosmology, however, was but one of two cosmological revolutions. If Newton's cosmological revolution took the human spirit out of the universe, then the other cosmological revolution had made the human spirit the center of the universe. The crucial question to put to Newtonian cosmology may be given new phrasing: Where can the human spirit be found in a mechanical universe? The inspired answer of German thinkers of the time was a philosophy of history known as *historicism*. Historicism can be traced to Giambattista Vico's *New Science* (1725) and Johan Gottfried Herder's *Also a Philosophy of History* (1774). Vico felt

that the study of social reality requires methods fundamentally different from those of the natural sciences because society, unlike nature, cannot be reduced to the "insensible motion of bodies"; rather, it consists of the conscious acts and volitions of individuals which take place in the stream of time.[24]

Thus a new interest in the past gave way to a particular modern attitude toward history, that is,

the positive value of history understood as human progress in its immanent, worldly, and secular reality. What distinguished this new outlook from major Enlightenment patterns was its rejection of a mechanistic worldview; its belief that history, far from being a collection of abuses and superstitions, was itself the key to the understanding of man as a social and political being.[25]

George Iggers here describes a new cosmic hierarchy. This hierarchy, however, has to do with time rather than space. Progress defines a new temporal hierarchy. If the classical hierarchy of being describes a ladder from "down" to "up," then the new temporal hierarchy of becoming describes a ladder from "primitive" to "modern." Indeed, German genius replaced Newton's infinitesimal time with "modern" time. Modernity becomes (as Newton's infinitesimal time) a moment. But it is a very special moment. Coming at the end of the temporal chain of being, "modern" time defines a special type of finality: the end, or rather, the edge of progressive history. Moderns, for example, can always situate themselves in the present. Thus the present, in a sense, acts as the "final" cause of modernity. Modernity becomes fulfilled in the "present." Historicism brings back a new version of final cause into a revised cosmology of time. There is something unique, however, in the German conception of history.

What distinguished the German tradition of history, with which we are dealing, so radically from other expressions of historicism in the eighteenth and nineteenth centuries was its emphasis upon the uniqueness and irrationality of values transmitted by history.[26]

This German twist can (as usual) be traced back to Luther.

Ernst Troeltsch has pointed at the peculiar twist which Luther gave to the theory of natural law. In the place of a concept of a rational Law of Nature, Luther substituted an irrational Law of Nature. Luther argued in accordance with St. Paul's admonition that "there is no power but of God: the powers that be are ordained of God." Every state represented the will of God, and thus required the complete obedience of the Christian in all matters temporal. Reason therefore expressed itself not in abstract moral commandments, but in historical institutions. The positive authorities were the concrete manifestations of natural law. Luther's political and social ethics are thus conservative. His concept of society lacked any real concern with change.[27]

It was Herder, however, who radicalized the historicist principles into their German form.[28] Historicism was based on two concepts: individuality and meaning. The concept of individuality was a direct challenge to the concept of natural law. It assumes a lack of universal values. All is change, although nations possess a certain stability. They are alive and can grow. "Nations have the characteristic of persons: they have a spirit and they have a life span. They are not a collection of individuals, but are organisms."[29]

Historicism restored organicity to the universe. Unfortunately, such organicity belonged specifically to a very special creature. Historicism recognized the major weakness of Newtonian science, the methodical exclusion of spirit, and reworked a cosmology of time unique to spirit itself. As such, this cosmology of time—history—can only be perceived by empathy since reason cannot suffice. Herder expresses it thus:

> Since according to the ideas of the [Red Indian] Americans every river, every tree, every meadow has a spirit, should not the German rivers and mountains also have one? Let someone, therefore, defend the national spirit . . . and show by examples that Germany has since the earliest times had a fixed national spirit in all classes, still has it at the present time, and according to its organization will have it everlastingly.[30]

Two other trends of thought affecting German philosophy at the time were the concepts of *Humanitätsideal* and Idealism. *Humanitätsideal*

> agrees with the Enlightenment that there is a common humanity, a certain nobility and dignity present in seed form in all men . . . Still, if the Enlightenment stresses the common characteristics of man and his rationality, the *Humanitätsideal* stresses the diversity of man and the interrelating of all aspects of his personality, of rationality and irrationality, into a harmonious whole. Every individual is different, and the task incumbent upon each one is to develop his own unique personality to the fullest.[31]

The concept of *Humanitätsideal*, however, has another dimension to add to the concept of individuality:

> For Wilhelm von Humboldt the individual is not found in the empirical person we perceive, but in the higher idea he represents. The purpose of man's life is thus emphatically not "happiness," but rather the fulfillment of this idea.[32]

In this concept of Idealism there exists a link from a person as an expression of an idea to a collective group, such as a nation, also being the expression of an idea and thus possessing *individuality*. This progression

> . . . from the individuality of the person to that of the nation or state occurred in countless German thinkers of the early nineteenth cen-

tury—notably in Fichte, Schelling, Schleiermacher, and even, in a sense, Hegel. The state and society were no longer regarded as rational constructions, the result of contractual arrangements between individuals in the manner of the Enlightenment; they were "superpersonal" creative forces, which build from time to time, out of the material of particular individuals, a spiritual Whole and, on the basis of that Whole, proceed from time to time to create the particular political and social institutions which embody and incarnate its significance.[33]

The counterpart to Newtonian cosmology, the spiritual Whole, was not to be found in the natural but in human history. German scholarship had introduced an alternative to Newton's infinitesimal time: historical time. Newton's cosmology of motion now had a powerful challenger, the human cosmology of history. This cosmology was, in a sense, the exact opposite of Newton's cosmos. If the mechanical universe knew nothing *of* spirit, then the historical universe knew nothing *but* spirit. One of the contemporary legacies of such scholarship is the modern academy, split into what C. P. Snow has called the "two cultures."[34] Such a view has theological consequences. Schleiermacher's *Christmas Eve* exemplifies them.

Die Weihnachtsfeier: *Revisiting Schleiermacher's* Christmas Eve

We now return to *Die Weihnachtsfeier* to answer the question posed at the beginning of the chapter. Why the missing Child in the Nativity scene? Only as we approach the end of the dialogue does an answer present itself. Schleiermacher uses the men in *Christmas Eve* to raise philosophical questions.[35] The question of history emerges out of the men's discussion on the origins of the feelings related to and evoked by the Christmas festival.

It is the distinctive nature of this festival that through it we should become conscious of an innermost ground out of which a new, untrammeled life emerges, and of its inexhaustible power, that in its very first germ we should already discern its finest maturity, even its highest perfection . . . However unsatisfactory the historical traces of his life may be when one examines it critically . . . nevertheless the festival does not depend on this. It rests on the necessity of a Redeemer, and hence upon the experience of a heightened existence, which can be derived from no other beginning than him.[36]

The reason Christmas has so much meaning for us is the actual historical presence of Jesus. We know this by our empathy with the festival. This empathy, in turn, is an empathy with history. We sense Jesus' historical presence across the centuries. Time connects us to Jesus; it does not separate us. Jesus' presence becomes "present" in the Nativity scene. The Nativity scene, however, facilitates our empathy with Jesus' historical presence, not effects it. Thus, Jesus needs not be symbolized in the manger, for his historical presence becomes known to us through empathy and not through symbol.

The shift from symbol to empathy raises serious questions. Not everyone looks at a Nativity scene and "senses" Jesus' presence. A theory of symbol can easily explain this. Schleiermacher's new cosmology has a more difficult task. The question continually confronting Schleiermacher now comes to the forefront: Why are some individuals separated from the Christ-consciousness that history provides?

This, of course, is a question of theodicy. The question of evil now presents itself as a separation from a historical Christ-consciousness. Schleiermacher attempts a solution in Eduard's answer:

> "In himself what else is man than the very spirit of earth, or life's coming to know in its eternal being and in its ever-changing process of becoming? In such a state there is no corruption in man, no fall, and no need of redemption. But when the individual fastens upon other formations of his earthly environment and seeks his knowledge in them, for the processes of coming to know them dwell in him alone: this is only a state of becoming. Then he exists in a fallen and corrupt condition, in discord and confusion, and he can find his redemption only through man-in-himself."[37]

The new cosmology now begins to make its presence known. The very "spirit of the earth" is an "ever-changing process of becoming." As such, the answer supports a particular strand of theodicial tradition: Irenaeus's evolutionary history of human development.

Justo González has aptly demonstrated Irenaeus's intriguing and appealing account of evil and human suffering.[38] Adam and Eve did not so much willfully sin as stumble into sin, as inexperienced children may get into trouble for lack of maturity. God placed them out of the Garden in order to protect them rather than to punish them. Eventually, Adam, Eve, and their progeny will mature and learn how to live without getting into trouble. For Irenaeus, human suffering is due to human immaturity, which causes us to make bad judgments. Such a theodicy stands in sharp contrast to the theodicy of the Augustinian tradition. Augustine's theodicy sees the root of human suffering not in human immaturity but in human will. As such, human suffering need not have been, but tragically began due to an original act of the human will. As such, humanity has continued to "devolve" rather than evolve. Irenaean theodicy supports a cosmology of history or evolution; Augustine's does not. Indeed, John Hick saw Schleiermacher's thought as an Irenaean theodicy.[39]

The new cosmology of history allows Schleiermacher to answer the question of evil in terms of those who do not empathize with a historical Christ-consciousness. Only if sin is seen as discord and confusion can human tragedy be understood in evolutionary terms. Confusion keeps us from accessing the Christ-consciousness. Thus, Schleiermacher's Irenaean theodicy tends to "naturalize" the fact of evil.[40] It does so by making it an integral part of this new cosmology of becoming. If "man" is the very "spirit of earth," an "ever-changing process of becoming," then sin naturally enters such cosmology as part of the process of becoming. Such theodicy has consequences for an understanding of redemption. Schleiermacher continues Eduard's discussion:

> "He finds redemption, that is, in that the same union of eternal being and of the coming into being of the human spirit, such as it can be manifested on this planet, arises in each person and thus each contemplates and learns to love all becoming, including himself, only in eternal being. And insofar as he appears as a process of becoming he wills to be nothing other than a thought of eternal being; nor will he have his foundations in any other expression of eternal being than in that which is united with the ever-changing, ever-recurrent process of becoming. In fact, the union of being and becoming is found in humanity not incidentally but eternally; and this is because that union exists and comes into being as man-in-himself does."[41]

Thus redemption amounts less to radical transformation (a new becoming) than to clear empathy (with eternal being). Therefore, Schleiermacher answers the puzzling fact that even in an optimistic evolutionary cosmology, tragedy, and suffering exist.

The last sentence of the above quote could be seen as an answer to Newton's de-spiritualizing the universe. Newton may be correct in saying that the objects in the universe correspond to non-spiritual laws of motion, but in one particular object of the universe—the human being alone—"the union of being and becoming is found . . . not incidentally but eternally." Because of Jesus' incarnation, historical time possesses an eternal dimension that Newton's infinitesimal time does not. Historical time breaks through infinitesimal time's tyranny of the present to allow the past to be felt in the present. But what does Schleiermacher mean by "man-in-himself"? Is he proposing an extreme individualism? Letting Eduard continue, Schleiermacher asserts:

> "In the individual person, however, [this union] as it has reality in his own life, must come into being both as his own thinking and the thinking which arises within a common life and activity with other men; for it is in community that that knowledge which is proper to

our planet not only exists but develops. Only when a person sees humanity as a living community of individuals, cultivates humanity as a community, bears its spirit and consciousness in his life, and within that community both loses his isolated existence and finds it again in a new way—only then does that person have the higher life and peace of God within himself."[42]

The above makes clear that Schleiermacher did not have individualism in mind in his phrase "man-in-himself." The individual emerges from a communal whole. Schleiermacher boldly calls us to "cultivate humanity as a community" for only in community can the individual lose his or her "isolated existence" and "[find] it again in a new way." "Man-in-himself" refers to the greater reality of the communal Whole as exemplified in the individual. The individual is an exemplar of the Whole.

Schleiermacher's understanding of redemption now becomes clear. Redemption is found in the communal Whole that seeks clear empathy with the historical Christ-consciousness and keeps individual consciousness from discord and confusion. The communal Whole par excellence, for Schleiermacher, turns out to be the church.

John Hick found Schleiermacher's theodicy the most defensible and attractive to the alternative theodicy of the Augustinian tradition. Indeed, Schleiermacher's theodicy beckons us like a siren's call to join that community of redemption, the church, in order to expand our consciousness to include the historical presence of Christ.

Schleiermacher's system has much appeal to Hispanic/Latino theological themes. The emphasis on the community of redemption, the celebration of humanity as community, the recognition of individuality within community, the emphasis on history—all these could also be said to be themes of Latino theology.[43] Yet something appears to be not right. Schleiermacher's theodicy lacks something that the Augustinian tradition best exemplifies: a strong sense of the seriousness of suffering and the radical nature of sin. Hispanic/Latino theologians must ask whether suffering can truly be seen as a matter of discord and confusion. Has not our experience been more radical? Are 23 million deaths in the space of fifty years during the early colonial period in Mexico simply a matter of discord and confusion?[44] An answer may lie in comparing Schleiermacher's wonderful literary and theological work with another dialogue on the Incarnation, the Hispanic/Latino drama known as the *Pastorela*.

LA PASTORELA: A DIFFERENT "WHOLE"

The encounter with indigenous America gave the *praesepre* tradition a new popularity and career. The early missionaries, in order to teach catechism to the natives, used the strategy of what Robert Ricard has called the "edifying play."[45] Building on the strong indigenous tradition of ritual drama, the missionaries adopted aesthetic narrative as a means of teaching Christian doctrine. Thus, the *praesepre* became the *Nacimiento* of Latino popular Catholicism, under the influence of both indigenous traditions and missionary efforts. The *Nacimiento* became both a visual representation and an enacted drama to serve the purpose of evangelization. What made the *Nacimiento* uniquely American, however, was the mixture of Western and Amerindian[46] interpretation that took shape and is still taking shape today. Though many *Nacimientos* may appear to be identical with Western Nativity scenes, a semiotic analysis would demonstrate a distinctive representation.

An example of such *mestizaje* of Western and native elements may be seen in the corresponding ritual enactments associated with the *Nacimientos*. The medieval "shepherds' play," for example, was substantially indigenized by using local actors and performing the play in the native Náhuatl language. This early play became very popular and in time came to be known as the *Pastorela*. The above demonstrates the intricate relationship between the Nativity scene and ritual drama, in general, and the *Nacimiento* and the *Pastorela*, in particular. Each helps interpret the other. Hispanic devotion to the *Nacimiento* includes several dramas. Along with the *posadas*,[47] the *Pastorela* enacts and interprets the significance of the *Nacimiento* in Hispanic/Latino popular devotion. Though having its origins in medieval "shepherds' plays," the *Pastorela* became indigenized through the subsequent missionary efforts in the Americas. Thus, it is worthwhile to keep in mind the elements of the traditional medieval *Officium Pastorum* as these developed into the elements of the *Pastorela*.

The *Officium Pastorum* began with an angel appearing to the shepherds announcing, "natus est vobis hodie Salvator mundi in civitate David." The shepherds then go on singing "transeamus usque Bethlehem," when they are met by two angels asking the famous "quem queritis?" The *quem queritis* forms the conversation between the shepherds and the angels. This dialogue is modeled after the Easter trope, *Quem queritis*, which in turn is modeled after the scriptural dialogue between Mary and the angels on the day of the Resurrection.[48] The latter conversation, the *quem queritis in sepulchro?*, now becomes the shepherd's dialogue: *quem queritis in praesepre?* Thus are revealed the deep theological underpinnings of these plays—an understanding of redemption and suffering. After the dialogue, the angels show the shepherds the *praesepre* while the shepherds sing "Puer natus est" or "Natus est nobis hodie."

The *Pastorela*, as mentioned above, is modeled after the *Officium Pastorum* but with significant differences. Some historians place the beginnings of the *Pastorela* in 1527, when *la comedia de los reyes* was presented at the cathedral in Cuernavaca. None other than Fray Juan de Zumárraga (first archbishop of Mexico) ordered, in 1530, a "shepherds' play" to communicate the Christian tradition of Christmas to the natives. Andrés de Olmos, in response, composed in Náhuatl his famous *La Adoración de los Reyes Magos* to celebrate the Epiphany. Olmos, however, was surprised by the response of the Amerindians. He had struck a common chord with indigenous traditions. Soon, native celebrations of *La Adoración* took on decidedly non-Western overtones. Roman authorities interpreted such overtones as *limpiar el aire de los malos espíritus* (clearing the air of evil spirits), and the Inquisition condemned them around the beginning of the seventeenth century. Nevertheless, the Jesuits, arriving in the Americas in 1572, became major promoters of this indigenous celebration, which continued even after the Inquisition's ban.[49]

Since then, these native plays entered the domain of the popular, composed and recomposed again and again according to local sentiments and, at various times, including political and social critiques. The rough, rural language proper to shepherds characterizes such *pastorelas*. They lend themselves to much improvisation, and their authors typically remain anonymous. A striking characteristic is their biting humor. This comic element, however, underlines what is basically a commentary on evil, with Western and indigenous elements mixed in. Though Western missionaries came preaching a gospel of redemption, the Amerindians understood suffering in terms of cosmic order.

The *pastorelas* mix these elements through their basic storyline of humble shepherds who receive the news—brought to them by Gabriel the archangel—of the Child's birth in Bethlehem. On the way there, they are frustrated by the action of Luzbel (the devil) who, jealous of the Redeemer, is determined to play havoc on the shepherds. Michael, the archangel, intervenes and restores order to the chaos created by Luzbel for the shepherds. The *Pastorela* ends with a visual representation of the *Nacimiento*. If a comedy is a tragedy with a happy conclusion, then the *Pastorela* is a comedy of redemption, but a tragedy still, in terms of the cosmic havoc that is eventually "ordered." Although these elements vary in every local *Pastorela*, the basic structure remains the same. For that reason, I will here refer to (and throughout use the text of) the *Pastorela* enacted in my home parish in San Leandro, California.

San Leandro's local *Pastorela* begins with a narrator, much like the author of Luke's gospel, setting the redemptive significance of the events that are to take place. The first scene begins with a dramatic representation of the Annunciation. The *Pastorela* is thus far faithful to the scriptural narrative and follows the *Officium Pastorum*.

But an interesting addition is made to the otherwise traditional narrative of the Annunciation. When the narrator explains that Joseph and Mary must travel to Bethlehem for the census, the *Pastorela*'s directions call for a scene where Joseph and Mary walk toward Bethlehem accompanied by two angels. The presence of the angels accompanying Joseph and Mary to Bethlehem is also seen in another Hispanic/Latino popular devotion— the *posada*. In the *posada*, the *peregrinos* (Joseph and Mary) walk along with two angels to different homes in the community, where they ask for *posada* (lodging), "in the name of heaven." The *Pastorela* itself will have two arch- angels playing major roles throughout: Gabriel, who announces, and Michael, who battles evil. They represent two themes interwoven into the *Pastorela*—announcing good news and battling personalized evil. In other words, in the *Pastorela* we already see a divergence from Schleiermacher's *Weihnachtsfeier*—Christmas is not just about joy. It is about joy that occurs in the midst of struggle. Moreover, the struggle involves cosmic elements. Angelic creatures mix with human ones as the drama of the Incarnation begins.

The next scene presents Rebeca, Ismael, and Borrego[50] awakening at dawn. Already a mix of indigenous and Western notions of evil can be seen in the chorus the *pastores* sing before starting the new day's work:

"Gracias mil, Dios todopoderoso, que nos das la luz del día. Toma en cambio nuestras almas, toma en pago nuestras vidas. Al ir al trabajo rogamos, Señor, nos prestes tu ayuda en toda ocasión. Vivimos gustosos, teniéndote fe, queriendo en la muerte la gloria también. Gracias damos con el alma al Señor de la Creación, esperando dicha y calma de Quien la vida nos dió."

Although at first sight the chorus appears traditional, certain elements indicate that traditional forms of thought have been reinterpreted.

The first line begins with a eucharist, that is, a giving thanks. Thanks are given to God, the Creator, who brings the sun up every day (an indig- enous essential element). In exchange, God can have our lives. Here ap- parently appears a reference to the ancient practice of human sacrifice guaranteeing the sun's rising. Such reference, however, needs to be placed in the entire context of the chorus. The *pastores* expect *dicha y calma* (cos- mic order) from the Lord of Creation. Atoning sacrifice and cosmic order mix together in this passage to reveal a curious mix of indigenous and Western theodicies. The *Pastorela*, of course, does not include a scene of human sacrifice. Nonetheless, the subject of the *Pastorela* is the Child, who will become, in a sense, a human sacrifice.

The shepherds then begin a conversation, in a biting, insulting, but still comic way. This element of the *Pastorela* signals its dramatic form. The *Pastorela* is a comedy. As I mentioned earlier, a comedy may be defined as a tragedy with a happy ending. Throughout the *Pastorela*, the shepherds bring in comic elements that begin tragically but are then given a comical twist. More will be said about this later. For now it is enough to notice that this Christmas story is more about empathetic laughter than about empathetic joy.

The next scene, significantly lengthy, involves the encounter of the devil Luzbel with the archangel Michael. Michael comes to offer Luzbel pardon for his earlier defection. Luzbel declines and vows to beat Michael in battle. However, Michael quickly defeats him and the scene shows Luzbel writhing on the ground with rage. This scene points to the elements of battle or struggle found in any *Pastorela*. But the confrontation of Michael and Luzbel may not be interpreted as a Manichaean struggle between Good and Evil. This particular battle, after all, is hardly a struggle. Luzbel does not stand a chance. Nonetheless, there is encounter and confrontation. Evil may be, as Augustine proposed, a *privatio boni*, but in the *Pastorela* such privation of the goodness of God's Creation involves a confrontation with those elements that would deprive us of enjoying that goodness.

The *Pastorela* introduces the surprising presence of metaphysical evil into the theme of human suffering—surprising, at least, for those who claim that metaphysics has no place in theologies that take human experience or culture seriously. Surprising, as well, for those who claim that metaphysics is above human experience. In the *Pastorela* metaphysical elements mix with human experience. As such, metaphysics here relates to human experience not as "above" or "beyond" but as "with." By "with," I do not mean "side by side" but a "web." Metaphysics concerns the web of human experience.[51] Therefore, metaphysics is not identical to human experience but provides the connections, the *real* relations, with all nonhuman realities that together form the totality of human experience. This makes metaphysics a cosmology rather than an epistemology or an ontology.

The adventure of the *pastores* begins with an element typical of the medieval *Officium Pastorum*. An angel, in this case Gabriel the archangel, appears to the shepherds to announce the birth of the Messiah.

> "Pronto se aproxima de Dios el Hijo, causando asombro profundo. Ha de venir a este mundo como el profeta predijo. Vagad por las cercanías de Belén. Y en el portal, para librarnos del mal, debe nacer el Mesías. El os dará nuevas leyes, el signo de Redención. A prestarle adoración vendrán poetas y reyes. ¡Al llegar ese momento, que mi vos aquí propala, han de vestirse de gala la tierra y el firmamento. Cantarán mejor las aves, será el cielo más azul, y por sus celajes de tul correrán brisas suaves! . . . ¡Dejad los campos sin flores, bendecid las profecías, que va a nacer el Mesías! ¡Id a adorarle, pastores!"

Gabriel announces the traditional refrain from Luke's gospel but adds a distinctive American note: The birds shall sing sweeter, the sky shall become bluer, even the clouds shall ride on breezes softer than the present.

The cosmic order shall be transformed into even greater harmony. The message here is not the replacement of the cosmos but its more beautiful, or rather, more harmonious transformation. As such, this cosmology reveals not progress toward an eschatological end but instead an intensification of what already is. Such is consistent with the above notion of metaphysics. If metaphysics concerns more a cosmology than an epistemology or ontology, then Gabriel (a nonhuman creature) informs human experience not in the manner of "coming to know" (an epistemology) or revealing the "is-ness" of reality (an ontology); rather Gabriel announces a reality and a call to action. Gabriel connects the shepherds to what goes on in the larger cosmic web—the total cosmic web of reality—and in doing so becomes part of the shepherds' human experience.

The archangel's call to action is revealing. He tells the shepherds: "*Leave the fields without flowers . . . Go and revere him, shepherds!*" Gabriel calls not for repentance, as traditionally understood, but for repentance in cosmic terms. Collect all the flowers from the fields in order to offer them to the infant! This aesthetic reference further enriches our understanding of the metaphysical cosmology of the *Pastorela*. Gabriel reveals redemptive transformation of human experience in aesthetic terms. Repentance begins with a gathering of flowers. This reference to the garden reminds us of the Yahwist account of the Fall from the Garden. As such, the *Pastorela* has much affinity with the Augustinian tradition of theodicy.

The next scene strikes us with its humanity. Mary and Joseph are on their way to Bethlehem when Mary tells Joseph that she cannot go on any longer. She has grown extremely tired. Joseph encourages her to go on. They have a sacred prophecy to fulfill. Mary continues to complain of fatigue. Joseph relents and calls for a rest. After a while, Joseph begins to get ready to journey again. Mary tries to get up but cannot. She kneels and asks God for help in fulfilling her mission. Gabriel appears and says:

> "Dios ha escuchado tu ruego y hasta ti gozoso llego, para calmar tu agonía, lleno de amor y concordia te ha elegido el Santo Padre porque serás Reina y Madre, llena de misericordia. Y allí de Dios, a la diestra, cercano se halla el portal donde el Niño ha de nacer, para humillar el poder del espíritu del mal. He de servirte de guía, por la voluntad de Dios ¡Qué Dios te salve María!"

Gabriel reveals to Mary that he will be her guide, for the Child to be born is to humble the *power of the spirit of evil*. Perhaps it is here that the early colonial Inquisition saw indigenous syncretic elements, although the above, of course, does not interpret the Incarnation as the crushing of a pagan evil principle or spirit. Another interpretation offers itself if a cosmological metaphysics is presumed.

First, one must note Gabriel's offer to be a guide. Gabriel, a nonhuman creature, makes himself available to guide human experience to an unseen yet quite present reality. Gabriel, a metaphysical element, allows human action to be guided, to be shaped, according to invisible realities. Jesus' birth humbles the evil spirit *as a beautiful reality humbles a lesser vision*. Such *humillación* may be compared to a confrontation between reality and ideology rather than a confrontation between two realities. The confrontation is not lesser in effect than if it were the encounter between two antagonistic realities. Such interpretation reveals the indigenous concern for cosmic harmony and order. Redemption is, above all, a matter of beauty. Metaphysical guides such as Gabriel allow us to see such beauty above the lesser visions that confront and confound our lives.

The next scene is striking as the most different from the traditional "shepherds' play." Luzbel, frustrated and humiliated by Michael, hears one of the shepherds approach. In a scene full of indigenous imagery, Luzbel, like an *hechicero* (sorcerer), moves his arms in a circle and "attracts" the poor shepherd (against his will) to his side. The shepherd's first words on seeing Luzbel, "¡Ay qué cara! ¡Vaya tío!," reveal once again the aesthetic underpinnings of the *Pastorela*'s theodicy. One can sympathize with the missionary friars at such imagery. Being carried against one's will contradicts Christian notions of human liberty and its relationship to sin. The *hechicero*'s act could imply a non-Christian statement about free will ("the devil made me do it"). A cosmological perspective, however, reveals as well an element of breaking the natural order of things. Evil, as represented by Luzbel, has cosmic order and free will as antithetical references. The significance of this fact becomes clearer in the next line.

Luzbel now asks the poor shepherd: "¿Qué buscas?," the famous *quem queritis?* of the *Officium Pastorum*. Surprisingly, in this "shepherds' play," the *quem queritis* is asked not by an angel but by Luzbel himself! Whereas in the *Officium Pastorum*, the question is intended to help the shepherds reach the Christ Child, here the question is meant to confound the shepherds in their journey. The shepherd, as in the traditional play, responds that he is seeking the *Nacimiento*, the birthplace of the Christ Child. Luzbel, unlike the traditional play, informs him that the *espíritu del mal* does not want him to continue. The shepherd struggles to free himself from Luzbel and denies him. He will go on to find the *Nacimiento* even "aunque me cueste el pellejo." Luzbel, angered, now kicks the poor shepherd, leaving him with a "devilish tail."

This comical dimension has been brought about through two elements running continuously in the *Pastorela*: the encounter with forces that would break the harmonious beauty of the *campos* and the free will of the shepherds. These two components mix inseparably in the cosmic theodicy of the *Pastorela*. The cosmic elements, however, are prevented by the comical dimension from joining a dualistic struggle between the forces of order and the forces of chaos. Creation's goodness and the Creator's justice are safeguarded not by stressing the goodness of Creation over and against the free will of human creatures, but by allowing Creation a dynamic aesthetics, a drama with tragic occurrences that resolve themselves around the beautiful climax of the *Nacimiento*. Thus, Creation becomes more than some static painting hung on the walls of the universe for the Creator to admire; it is rather a dynamic comedy carried to the very heart of the Creator (as represented in the *Nacimiento*).

The comical element in the *Pastorela* continues as the other shepherds join the shepherd now "en-tailed." The following scene is as rich in humor as it is in tragedy. His companions pull and pull on the unfortunate shepherd's tail until, finally, it comes off. The scene reveals the shepherds as thoroughly confused and sidetracked from their journey. Ismael (one of the shepherds), reflecting the nature of their situation, prays with eyes looking toward the heavens, "¡Tú, Señor, que ves aquí tanta criatura apenada, muéstranos la senda ansiada!" (You, O Lord, who beholds here so many contrite creatures, show us the desired path). Once again revealing the aesthetic underpinnings, Ismael prays for sight. At this point, the archangel Gabriel appears and, like the angel in the *Officium Pastorum*, exclaims: "¡Pastores! ¡Mirad allí!" At this point, the *Nacimiento* appears in all its glory. Angels, oxen, mules, Joseph, Mary, and the star mix in a cosmic, total vision centering on the Child. The tragedy of the unfortunate encounter with the *espíritu del mal* and the chaos that sent them into confusion now become a comedy as the harmony of the scene puts the other elements of the *Pastorela* in perspective.

CONCLUSIONS: A TELLING COMEDY

The *Pastorela* differs in substance from Schleiermacher's *Christmas Eve* dialogue. The nature of that difference revolves around an understanding of evil, understood as a cosmology.

Schleiermacher founds his theodicy upon a unique cosmology—one of history, existing side by side with another Western cosmology, Newton's. As such, Schleiermacher's provides an alternative to Newton's. Humanity is the very "spirit of the earth," even as Newton's earth cannot allow for spirit. Schleiermacher's theodicy makes a critical separation of the human from the natural. His thought splits the cosmos between nature and history. History is the cosmos upon which the spirit may fly and manifest itself while nature stands by unaffected, playing a very small role in the drama of the Incarnation. The effect of this critical separation is subtle. It nonetheless reveals itself in the lack of a visual representation of the Christ Child in the Nativity scene. This self-conscious element in

Schleiermacher's *Die Weihnachtsfeier* reveals a christological oddity: Jesus' incarnation appears to have meaning only in history but not for the natural cosmos. Jesus' redemption offers itself as a historical consciousness affectively accessed through communal empathy. As such, Schleiermacher reveals a profound iconoclasm. There is no room for sacred symbol. It is the consequence of his cosmology. If symbol is making the invisible visible, then Newton's naturally visible cannot partake in Schleiermacher's historically invisible in order to allow the symbolic manifestation of the spiritual. Thus Schleiermacher's refusal to represent the Christ Child in the Nativity scene. The Christ Child is not to be seen but felt.

Schleiermacher, then, would have no use for the *quem queritis?* That which cannot be seen cannot give rise to a search. Schleiermacher's Nativity scene has no need of angelic sight, for there is no need to see the Child—there is need only to empathize with Jesus' historical consciousness. In other words, Schleiermacher has traded history for symbol. If symbol makes visible an invisible reality, Schleiermacher's history sees no need for visibility. Historical consciousness is always accessible through empathetic communal consciousness. The cosmological consequences for Christianity are profound.

There is little room for symbolic perception in Schleiermacher's cosmos. There is no need to struggle and make visible the invisible realities of the world. Instead, the invisible manifests itself in the visible realities of history. Indeed, the visible subordinates to the invisible. Thus, there is struggle in Schleiermacher's theodicy but no tragedy. There is perception, empathetic feeling, but no struggle to perceive, *quem queritis?* No wonder, then, that Schleiermacher's *Die Weihnachtsfeier* contains little humor. Although Schleiermacher's dialogue shows history progressing to a happy ending, without tragedy such happiness is humorless. Schleiermacher substitutes joy for humor. Schleiermacher's redemptive history can know joy but not humor.

The option for joy instead of humor, in a dramatic play, reveals the nature of its aesthetics. Joy lends itself well to conclusions. Indeed, dramatic joy is basically a happy ending. Thus, a drama whose consistent theme is joy will be nothing else than one long happy ending. Such is Schleiermacher's *Christmas Eve: A Dialogue.* Humor, on the other hand, is drama's eyes. Humor allows one to see beyond the dramatic structure itself. Yet more than simple sight, humor allows discovery of that which remains invisible to the actors and to the audience. Thus, only humor lends itself to the *quem queritis?* of the "shepherds' play."

Weihnachtsfeier's lack of humor reveals an interior sight that can only see that which is self-contained within a community's capacity to "see," that is, its capacity for empathy. Historical consciousness cannot be "discovered." It is already present in the communal consciousness. As such, Schleiermacher's theodicy calls for redemption in terms of becoming part of a community. Thus, Schleiermacher's theodicy will not allow a community to be in pilgrimage. The community of redemption has already reached its vision.

Therefore, there is no need to go above a community's interior sight. The community of redemption provides access to the Whole. This Whole is not, of course, the community, but rather the historical consciousness with which a community may or may not empathize. Schleiermacher's Whole does not allow a metaphysics, for there is no "meta," or mediation, involved in the communal empathy of historical consciousness. Empathy's vision is direct, not mediated. As such, there is no need for mediations or mediators. There is no need for angels, or stars, or devils, or oxen, or mules. There is no need for metaphysics, for "meta-sight," for seeing above and beyond the communal experience. Thus, the drama of redemption becomes strictly restricted in vision to that which only the dramatic structure directly intends. Such a drama, surprisingly, has no audience but only actors.

A drama of redemption that contains only actors and no audience is a curious thing. No catharsis is possible. This raises the serious question menacing Schleiermacher's proposed theodicy in *Weihnachtsfeier*. Can there be true empathy in a drama without an audience, without catharsis? And, without catharsis, can there be true human transformation, that is, redemption? These questions reveal the very nature of redemption when seen in aesthetic/dramatic perspective. Redemption and, therefore, theodicy, necessarily involve a highly visual element which involves the audience, capable of seeing the drama in order to participate in its experience. However, if there is no audience, then the drama becomes pure history, with few if any aesthetic elements.

The cosmological implications are surprising. Newton's mechanical cosmology has not been overcome by Schleiermacher but simply duplicated in a historical cosmology. Newton's relentless effective cause becomes effective spirit in Schleiermacher's human cosmology. Neither cosmology allows for a true aesthetic Whole—only a Whole which explains the effective motion of nature (Newton) or the effective motion of spirit (Schleiermacher). Newton's Whole becomes a watch, while Schleiermacher's is an empty Nativity scene. Neither allows catharsis. Though Newton's cosmos allows for an audience (the scientist), such may not, indeed cannot, find catharsis in Nature's effective motion. Schleiermacher's cosmos, on the other hand, does not allow for an audience.

The *Pastorela*, on the other hand, presents a quite different cosmos. Its comical element necessarily involves an audience. The audience, in this case, is the actors. Indeed, the whole play is about seeing an action even as the action takes place in the midst of such seeing. The shepherds "see" the play through the angels who bring them vision. Angels give vision to Jesus and Mary. A star guides the three kings. Vision thus allows those who are taking part in the play also to be its audience. This is possible not only because human creatures are the actors but because all the creatures of the cosmos participate as well. All the members of this cosmic community have their particular roles to play, yet none of them alone is the drama. Moreover, each member needs the others in order to play its particular role. The need is for vision—a vision that guides and discovers. Indeed, the need for vision makes the drama dynamic.

The need for vision also allows for the tragic element. The shepherds fumble in confusion until the archangel Gabriel shows them where to look. Yet the need for vision in the *Pastorela* emerges not simply out of the desire to see, but because vision is confounded by both natural and moral evil. Mary, exhausted in her pregnancy, cannot go on until an angel shows the way to the *Nacimiento*. Luzbel brings in the element of moral evil in a unique mix of indigenous and Western notions of moral action. He takes the traditional question of the *quem queritis?* and makes it the focus of moral action. In the context of a cosmic drama, Luzbel's question makes moral action not simply a choice between doing good or evil, but a call to a lesser vision and a halted journey.

Thus, Luzbel tries to scare the shepherd to settle for lesser sight and impede the search for the beautiful *Nacimiento*. The *Pastorela*'s drama involves the need for vision as well as the struggle to see. Need and struggle, visually enacted, become the axle and wheel of the *Pastorela*'s theodicial dynamics until they find their visual rest in the cosmic order and harmony of the *Nacimiento*. The need and struggle of the *Pastorela*, however, are cosmic. Nature participates in the drama in its visible (the star) and invisible (angels) forms. Moreover, these cosmic elements become mediators of sight. They allow for a "meta-vision" that in this context leads the actors to be audience as well. In other words, cosmic elements as mediators of sight allow audience participation in the drama of redemption.

The *Pastorela*'s *Nacimiento* has no empty manger. Joseph and Mary are present there with a very visible Child at the center. The *Nacimiento* becomes the Whole of this metaphysics, revealing our tragedies to be comedies. Humor is thus possible, for the vision of this metaphysics presents our suffering as more than tragedy and, more profoundly, as the comical elements that true vision shall see someday. This is no lightweight humor, nor does it make light of human suffering. Rather, it is a humor that sees deeply into the tragic nature of human suffering while it mediates its sting. It hopes in the alternative of despair. It is a humor that unveils the lesser visions and ideologies that confound our journey to the Whole. The Whole, then, becomes an essential element of Hispanic systematics. For only a system that allows for the audience's laughter can escape the easy optimism of human progress or the debilitating despair of human tragedy.

The question of the audience, therefore, becomes *the* question of Latino metaphysics. Can a particular cultural community become aware of its own significance? Can a particular cultural community be involved in true cultural transformation, that is, one that does not destroy the nature of the community's particularity while it addresses its needs and struggles? Can a particular cultural community mediate vision to other particular cultural communities? All of these questions pertain to metaphysics. These are also questions that only an audience can answer. The connection between audience and metaphysics may perhaps be Hispanic theology's most original contribution. It is a connection that can only be made assuming a particular type of Wholistic reality—an aesthetic Whole, a redemptive comedy involving the entire cosmos itself. As such, Latino metaphysics is a cosmology.

Yet a question remains. Where can one find such a Whole in the theological and philosophical tradition? Does a cosmological perspective take us too far afield from the received tradition? Duns Scotus gives us a clue. He argued for a new philosophical notion, the *forma individualis*, in the name of love. Love, Scotus reasoned, cannot relate to an abstract universal. Love relates only to unique individuals. Thus, the form of the abstract universal cannot account for love's necessity of a concrete individual. There must exist a "form" that grants uniqueness and particularity to creatures in order that we may love them. Scotus's philosophy of love provides an advantageous point for the Hispanic theologian. This philosophical clarity given to the relationship between love and the particular allows Latino theology an intersection with the classical tradition. Scotus's philosophy of love, however, still begs the question of the Whole. Where does love and the particular "fit" in the question of the Whole?

An answer may be formulated. David Burrell tells us that philosophy ought not be assumed to play a foundational role in theology. Rather, revelation is the starting point upon which philosophical analysis must build. But where in revelation ought a Latino metaphysics begin its systematic endeavor?

If the question of human suffering is the starting point of Latino theology, then the answer concerns the doctrine of Creation. The doctrine of Creation asserts a God who created the world and saw that it was good. If God created the world "good," then how can such a God allow evil to happen in the world? As such, the question is essentially an aesthetics: God *saw* the work of Creation and judged it *good*. Indeed, Christian answers to this question have invariably taken the form of an aesthetics. The goodness of a work of art, however, is but one dimension of an aesthetics. The other essential dimension is love. And this brings us back to Duns Scotus.

At the time of Scotus a furious debate raged over the absolute power of God. If God is omnipotent, then can God create other worlds besides this one? I do not want to discuss the impact of this debate. Others have done it admirably.[52] I would, however, point out that the question can be rephrased in a much more profitable way. Why did God create this world and not another one? Put this way, the question reveals the aesthetic dimensions of Creation. God created *this* world because God loves *this* world. Thus, the question ties God's love with the *this-ness* of Creation. And that *this-ness* is expressed in the marvelous diversity of creatures. God, apparently, loves difference. Yet such differences also form the *this-ness* which is the concrete but total work of art that revelation tells us is Creation. The Whole as work of art is no abstract universal but a concreteness to be seen and admired.

In other words, only as an aesthetic work do both the Whole and its particulars achieve concreteness. A work of art is particular in its wholeness even as it must be constituted by very concrete bits of particularities. But when such philosophical musings turn to the revelatory fact of Creation, one discovers a relationship between the Whole work of art and its particulars. The planets and the stars, the foxes and the rabbits, the rising of the sun and the setting of the moon, all achieve their cosmic order because God loved the world into being. Not a detached Watchmaker but a Passionate Lover of Beauty created the world. *It is not cold logic that orders the world and its particulars, but love that arranges its unique creatures into a beautiful and unique Whole.* At this point, then, the Hispanic theologian enters the *mestizaje* of philosophy and theology. Creation becomes a cosmology and metaphysics a vision for God's creatures. If love orders the world into a Whole, so that the world may be "seen" as God "sees" it, then theological reflection demands a metaphysics of love.

Such a metaphysics has consequences for theodicy. If love brought about the cosmic order of the world, then evil becomes not so much an antagonism but an incongruity in that order. Our suffering is real as the incongruous is real. Indeed, it is that very incongruity that alerts us to our suffering. For how else would we know that we suffer unless there were a loving order that provides reference to our chaos and confusion? Incongruity, however, has its reality only in reference to that loving order. Augustine's *privatio boni*, then, is given new conception with insight from indigenous America. It is not so much privation of good as incongruity with the cosmic order that best describes metaphysical evil. Metaphysical evil, in other words, is the lesser vision.

As such, a metaphysical cosmology grounds the basis of Christian hope. Hope becomes a matter of a greater vision in the midst of suffering, chaos, and confusion. Hope becomes the discernment of the cosmic order, which, in turn, means the discernment of love arranging the world. Hope becomes the love of difference so that the Whole may be discerned.

If the contemporary religious situation may be described as one of despair, then a Latino metaphysics gives intellectual substance to the Christian affirmation of hope. A Latino metaphysics can shed the light of reason on an affirmation which, after Auschwitz, Vietnam, and Bosnia, seems unwarranted and arbitrary. As such, Hispanic theology joins other theological traditions, together forming the overall rich Catholic tradition of "faith seeking understanding." A Latino metaphysics as cosmology gives witness to faith in the midst of struggle, to hope in the face of lesser visions, and, above all, to the love of difference.

Notes

[1] *Intellectus* is reason that includes the affections and is, I believe, the meaning understood in the wider tradition. *Ratio*, on the other hand, is a reduction of the meaning of the intellectual occasioned by the mechanization of both nature and thought that took place at the time of the Enlightenment. By making "visible," I mean the challenge of incarnating faith in the world of believers and nonbelievers alike (see Alex García-Rivera, *St. Martin de Porres: The "Little Stories" and the Semiotics of Culture* (Maryknoll, N.Y.: Orbis Books, 1995).

[2] Friedrich Schleiermacher, *Christmas Eve: Dialogue on the Incarnation*, trans. Terrence N. Tice (San Francisco: Edwin Mellen Press, 1990).

[3] The "visual theodicy" which comprises the Nativity scene may be discerned by analyzing the signs and symbols constituting the scene—signs and symbols that emerge out of the culture. In other words, I am claiming that the Nativity scene is a cultural "text" or, rather, a cultural "mosaic" on which a semiotic analysis is appropriate (see, e.g., García-Rivera, *St. Martin de Porres*, chap. 3).

[4] Please note that I am not claiming that the Latino *Nacimiento* does not express a theodicy that contains a belief in human redemption. Rather, the claim is that the indigenous emphasis on cosmic order is a unique element which has been added to our understanding of human suffering and redemption.

[5] Popular religion need not be solely identified as the practice of the poor. As argued by Robert Schreiter (*Constructing Local Theologies* [Maryknoll, N.Y.: Orbis Books, 1985]) and myself (*St. Martin de Porres*), popular religion cuts across classes. Moreover, Protestants as well as Roman Catholics practice popular religion. See, e.g., R. W. Scribner, *Popular Culture and Popular Movements in Reformation Germany* (London: Hambledon Press, 1987).

[6] The comparison between Schleiermacher's *Christmas Eve* and Latino popular Catholicism could have been made on the Hispanic sense of *fiesta*. The gathering of this German middle-class family for Christmas is, after all, a *fiesta* of sorts. Roberto Goizueta's description of *fiesta* as "life in the subjunctive" would, I believe, prove to be quite profitable if applied here.

[7] Richard R. Niebuhr, *Schleiermacher on Christ and Religion* (London: SCM Press, 1964), 41.

[8] Schleiermacher, *Christmas Eve*, 31.

[9] Ibid., 33.

[10] Another interesting point is his mention of missionaries. Schleiermacher's connection to the Moravians is well known. The Moravians are also known for their missionary work among the natives of North and Central America. In fact, the Moravians at the time had a mission to the natives in Bethlehem, Pennsylvania. This author spent six years in Allentown, a city next to Bethlehem, as pastor of a parish and got to know the Moravian community rather well. The Moravians were also known for their Nativity scenes and their love of the Christmas festival. In fact, there exists at the Moravian College in Bethlehem, Pennsylvania, a Nativity scene or creche very similar to the one described by Schleiermacher.

[11] Schleiermacher, *Christmas Eve*, 33.

¹² Such is Baudet's thesis. See Henri Baudet, *Paradise on Earth: Some Thoughts on European Images of Non-European Man* (Middletown, Conn.: Wesleyan University Press, 1988).

¹³ Origen, *Contra Celsum*, I, 51, in Migne *PG*, xi, 756.

¹⁴ Karl Young, *The Drama of the Medieval Church* (Oxford: Clarendon Press, 1933), chap. 17.

¹⁵ This account comes from Thomas of Celano in the thirteenth century, recounted in P. Sabatier, *Vie de S. François d'Assise* (Paris, 1894), 328-29. The actual deposition may be found in *Acta Sanctorum* (Paris and Rome, 1866), Oct., ii, 706.

¹⁶ J. Samuel Preus, *Explaining Religion: Criticism and Theory from Bodin to Freud* (New Haven, Conn.: Yale University Press, 1987).

¹⁷ A vast literature exists documenting the changes. A brief selection includes H. Butterfield, *The Origins of Modern Science 1300-1800*, rev. ed. (New York: Macmillan, 1960); Edwin Arthur Burtt, *The Metaphysical Foundations of Modern Physical Science* (Garden City, N.Y.: Doubleday, 1954 <1952>); John L. Casti, *Paradigms Lost: Images of Man in the Mirror of Science* (New York: William Morrow & Co., 1989); A. C. Crombie, *Science in the Middle Ages: 5th to 13th centuries*, vol. 1 (Cambridge: Harvard University Press, 1961); A. C. Crombie, *Science in the Later Middle Ages: 13th to 17th centuries*, vol. 2 (Cambridge: Harvard University Press, 1961); Stanley Jaki, *The Origin of Science and the Science of its Origin* (South Bend, Ind.: Regnery / Gateway, 1979); Stephen Toulmin, *The Discovery of Time* (New York: Harper & Row, 1966); Stephen Toulmin, *The Return to Cosmology: Postmodern Science and the Theology of Nature* (Berkeley and Los Angeles: University of California Press, 1982).

¹⁸ Such a statement might be a bit unkind to Newton. I believe that he would have been appalled by modern science's insistence on maintaining a "value-free" nature. Nonetheless, Newton's thought naturally led to a "value-less" nature, even if he himself did not see it at the time. See, for example, E. J. Dijksterhuis, *The Mechanization of the World Picture*, ed. C. T. Dikshoorn (Oxford: Oxford University Press, 1961). Also, for a more positive view of Newton's thought, see H. S. Thayer's "What Isaac Newton Started," in *Newton's Philosophy of Nature* (New York: Hafner Publishing Co., 1953).

¹⁹ See R. G. Collingwood, *The Idea of Nature* (Oxford: Oxford University Press, 1960 <1945>).

²⁰ The non-scientist ought to know that since the early twentieth century another revolution in cosmology has taken place through quantum mechanics. Newtonian mechanics is known in the physics world as classical mechanics. Though many theologians who write on the relationship between theology and science concentrate on the significance of quantum mechanics, classical mechanics is far from gone in contemporary physics. Both of Einstein's theories of special and general relativity are instances of classical mechanics. Indeed, the calculations of the trajectories that put an American on the moon was the product of Newtonian or classical mechanics. There exists a strong movement to unite quantum and Newtonian mechanics. See, for example, Stephen Hawking, *A Brief History of Time* (New York: Bantam Books, 1996 <1988>). Note that this movement centers on a renewed understanding of time.

²¹ St. Augustine, *The Confessions of Saint Augustine* (Oak Harbor, Wash.: Logos Research Systems, 1995), Book VI.

²² I am referring, of course, to Descartes' famous distinction and how it becomes expressed in Kantian philosophical psychology. I have argued that postmodernity made an extreme of modernity's understanding of signs. Postmodernity would have signs as simply pointing only to themselves—the ul-

timate effect of Newtonian cosmology (see Alex García-Rivera, "Creator of the Visible and the Invisible: Liberation Theology, Postmodernism, and the Spiritual," *Journal of Hispanic/Latino Theology* 3:4 [1996], 35-56).

[23] Skittish Kantian philosophers might vehemently argue with me. Naturally, I recognize Kant's inspired attempt to preserve the relationship between appearance and reality. Nonetheless, a cosmology of space and time, as categories of a quasi-mechanical organization of mind, still follows the Newtonian pattern of efficient cause.

[24] George G. Iggers, *The German Conception of History: The National Tradition of Historical Thought from Herder to the Present*, rev. ed. (Middletown, Conn.: Wesleyan University Press, 1983), 30.

[25] Ibid., 33.

[26] Ibid., 33.

[27] Ibid., 33-34. Troeltsch put it this way: "This might perhaps apply to the peculiarly irrational idea of Natural Law that enabled Lutheranism to accept the existing conditions of authority, regarding the Law of Nature as though these conditions of authority, together with sin and inequality, were all part of the unchanging Divine Order, to which the soul [which remains inwardly free] gives itself up to labor and to endure" (*Die Soziallehren der christlichen Kirchen und Gruppen*, in *Gesammelte Schriften* [Tübingen: Paul Siebeck Verlag, 1912], 1:596). The translation is mine.

[28] Herder is also known for his concern over the place of the Amerindians in world history. He provided a theoretical framework for studying them in *Outlines of a Philosophy of the History of Man* (1784). He was a good friend of Alexander Von Humboldt, the brilliant German anthropologist, whose *Vues des cordilleres* greatly increased European interest in the Aztec civilization. The details of their relationship to the Americas is discussed in Benjamin Keen, *The Aztec Image in Western Thought* (New Brunswick, N.J.: Rutgers University Press, 1971), chap. 10.

[29] Iggers, *The German Conception of History*, 35.

[30] Note here the reference to the indigenous American. Little scholarship has been done to document the influence of the European encounter with the Americas on German philosophical and theological thought. Rohan D. Butler, *The Roots of National Socialism* (New York: E. P. Dutton & Co., 1942), 26.

[31] Iggers, *The German Conception of History*, 38.

[32] Ibid., 39.

[33] Stevens Luke, "The Meanings of Individualism," *Journal of Historical Ideas* 32 (1971), 56.

[34] That is, the natural sciences and the humanities. I claim that both represent different cosmologies. See C. P. Snow, *The Two Cultures* (Cambridge: Cambridge University Press, 1969).

[35] The theme of the feminine and the masculine runs throughout *Christmas Eve*. For a detailed discussion of this aspect, see Marylin Chapin Massey, *Feminine Soul: The Fate of an Ideal* (Boston: Beacon Press, 1985); see also, Dawn de Vries's challenge to Massey's interpretation in "Schleiermacher's Christmas Eve Dialogue: Bourgeois Ideology or Feminist Theology?" *Journal of Religion* 69 (1989), 169-83.

[36] Schleiermacher, *Christmas Eve*, 80.

[37] Ibid., 82.

[38] See Justo L. González, *Christian Thought Revisited: Three Types Of Theology* (Nashville, Tenn.: Abingdon Press, 1989).

[39] John Hick, *Evil and the God of Love* (London: Macmillan, 1966), chap. 10.

[40] Dieter Schellong argues that Schleiermacher's theology reflects his privileged position in Prussian society. He charges that Schleiermacher's evolutionary view

of the world entails a "naturalization" of evil (*Bürgertum Und Christliche Religion: Anpassungsprobleme Der Theologie Seit Schleiermacher In Theologische Existenz Heute*, no. 187 [Munich: Kaiser Verlag, 1975], 21, 44-45).

[41] Schleiermacher, *Christmas Eve*, 82.

[42] Ibid., 83.

[43] Gary Riebe-Estrella struggles in this book with the Latino theme of *pueblo*. The struggle, in part, consists in avoiding a view of community such as Schleiermacher proposes here.

[44] See David Cook Noble, *Demographic Collapse: Indian Peru, 1520-1620* (Cambridge: Cambridge University Press, 1981).

[45] Robert Ricard, *The Spiritual Conquest of Mexico* (Berkeley and Los Angeles: University of California Press, 1966), chap. 12.

[46] See Glossary.

[47] A *posada* is a ritual procession that reenacts the journey of Mary and Joseph, from Nazareth to Bethlehem, seeking shelter and hospitality.

[48] Young, *The Drama of the Medieval Church*, 4-5.

[49] http://www.intermex.com.mx/navidad/pastorela.html (designed by Patricia Saavedra, last revised December 1996).

[50] *Borrego* means "lamb," and it is used here in a comic sense to describe the "Cantinflas" (a famous Mexican comedian) type of buffoonery displayed by this character.

[51] More and more Hispanic theologians are emphasizing the cosmic notion of a web of creatures. As Jeanette Rodríguez-Holguín points out in her essay, we are more than socioeconomic entities. We are, more fundamentally, creatures. See also my proposal for an anthropological understanding of the human person as a creature among other creatures in a web of cosmic community, that is, "*criaturas de Dios*," in *St. Martin de Porres*.

[52] See, for example, Amos Funkestein, *Theology and the Scientific Imagination: From the Middle Ages to the Seventeenth Century* (Princeton, N.J.: Princeton University Press, 1986).

4

Fiesta

Life in the Subjunctive

❦

ROBERTO S. GOIZUETA

Boston College

"María, the Church welcomes you, and joins your parents and friends
to celebrate with you your fifteenth birthday, your *quince años*. This
celebration should be a thanksgiving for having received life, and an
acceptance of the duties life brings with it, when you live it according to love and the commandments of God."[1]

Those words, enunciated by a priest, begin a typical *quinceañera* celebration in the Mexican-American community; after the music that accompanies the entrance procession ends, the congregation gives thanks to
God for the gift of life. Following the religious ceremony, the celebration
will continue as the *quinceañera*, family and friends repair to a dance hall
for the fiesta, where all will celebrate the occasion with wonderful food
and drink, and especially music and dance.

The writings of U.S. Latino/a theologians have repeatedly underscored
the central role of such rituals and celebrations in the life of U.S. Latino
communities. U.S. Hispanics are, in many respects, a people of the "fiesta," a fact often depicted in popular U.S. culture, film, literature, and
television. Indeed, one might go so far as to say that, in the United States,
Latinos and Latinas have come to be identified with the fiesta. While the
phenomena of specific Latino festivals have been examined in a number
of social scientific studies, the present chapter explores the significance of

the fiesta for, specifically, the elaboration of a Christian theological anthropology. That is, the essay will suggest that the fiesta, as a thanksgiving for having received life, reflects and expresses a profound sense of the
human in relationship to the Sacred.

Before analyzing the features of that theological anthropology, however,
we examine the anthropology underlying modern and postmodern con-
ceptions of the self, as well as the notion of the human person implicit in
Latin American liberation theology, which represents both a continuation
and a critique of modern notions of the self. Finally, we argue that an explicitly theological appreciation and interpretation of the fiesta, in light of the
foregoing anthropologies, can offer important insights into the Christian
understanding of the human person and the person's relationship to God.

THE SELF IN MODERNITY AND POSTMODERNITY

Among the salient characteristics of modernity is the emergence of the
human subject as active historical agent; modernity signals the birth of
the human person as, not merely the object of external historical agents,
whether natural or supernatural, but as the autonomous agent of his or
her own life. The ramifications of this axial shift in human self-understanding have been far-reaching. For instance, one of the consequences of
the modern "turn to the subject" has been the reconceptualization of the
character of human action in the world, a radical transformation of our
understanding of what constitutes human life.

As the sole agent of his or her activity in the world, the modern subject
does not so much live in history as *make* history. History is not merely a
stage upon which human beings play roles assigned to them by fate or
providence; it is, rather, the product of human activity, or *praxis*, in the
world. Like a sculptor in the presence of a block of marble, the modern
subject looks upon the world, and indeed, upon his or her own life, as raw
material to be chiseled and molded into a shape in accord with his or her
designs, a shape much more beautiful than the mere matter from which it
was sculpted. Our very language reflects this understanding of human
life as *made* rather than lived: the modern subject "makes" a living, "makes"
love, and strives to "make something" of himself or herself. Whether my
own life or the life of another, human life becomes, then, some*thing*, an
object to be acted upon. The modern subject thus becomes alienated from
his or her own life and the lives of others, as a subject divorced from the
object, since the separation of the subject from the object (that is, the entire
world "outside" the ego) is a necessary precondition for the subject to
control the object in order to manipulate it: I can only "work upon" that
which I can grasp, in other words, that which lies outside and separate
from me.[2]

This notion of human agency or praxis has been an essential precondition for many of the great advances of modernity, whether in the natural sciences, the social sciences, medicine, politics, technology, or industry. Modern advances have been made possible by our recognition that, far from being mere pawns in the hands of fate, human beings can control and transform their natural and social environments, as well as their own lives. The emergence of the modern subject as agent and maker of history was thus accompanied by a profound confidence in the possibility of historical progress; we have not only the ability and the right but, indeed, the responsibility to move history forward, to improve our own lot and the lot of humankind as a whole. Thus, the modern idea of progress is a corollary of the modern notion of the self as autonomous agent-subject.

As autonomous, the modern self was not only alienated from its own life, and other human lives, but from God as well. Perhaps the most powerful symbol of this shift was the French Revolution, especially the dethroning of Mary at Notre Dame Cathedral and her replacement by the Goddess of Reason. If the medieval person had perceived God as the foundation of human existence, the modern person would look to Reason as the source of life, the instrument by which a better future would be fashioned. It was not long before the Jacobin revolution began to show its seamier side, as the great hopes for a free and just society confronted the cruel reality of the guillotine. Yes, there has been progress, but too often at the point of a gun, either literally or figuratively. To know the underside of modernity is to have discovered that, in the words of the German Jewish philosopher Walter Benjamin, "every great work of civilization is at the same time a work of barbarism."[3] To know the underside of modernity is to have discovered that the twentieth century has witnessed more victims of human violence than all previous centuries combined.

Although *postmodernity* has been defined in numerous ways, one possible way of defining the notion is precisely as the West's increasing consciousness of the inherently ambiguous character of human history. The millions of victims have, in Gustavo Gutiérrez's words, "irrupted" into history, which can no longer be seen as an unambiguous history of progress.[4] As we enter the third millennium, the modern subject, who makes history, and the modern ideology of progress, the belief that human history is a process of uninterrupted improvement, are under attack as never before.

In all its varied guises, postmodernity represents the unmasking—or deconstruction—of the autonomous modern subject, not only the "rational" subject but also the "agent" subject. Insofar as modernity identified human action with doing, making, producing, or achieving, thereby divorcing the person from his or her environment (which was to be "worked upon" in order to "make" history), it has laid the foundation for the devastation of the natural and human environment. Thus, the Holocaust and the ecological crisis are not aberrations but direct consequences of the modern turn to the subject, especially the identification of the human person as a maker or producer.

The postmodern deconstruction of the subject has resulted, at least in its more radical poststructuralist form, in a concomitant deconstruction of the modern subject-object dichotomy. Poststructuralist views of human action, therefore, favor more indeterminate, fluid, and diffuse notions of the relationship between the "subject" and the environment, even eliminating the separation altogether. It should come as no surprise, then, that postmodernity has resulted in a recovery of the notion of human action as *play*. If the modern subject was a worker, *homo faber*, the postmodern "subject" is a player, *homo ludens*. In contrast to the modern subject's desire to control the environment in order to work upon it, human action-as-play dissolves the subject-object disjunction as the player loses himself or herself in the festive activity; creation becomes recreation. Postmodern play is thus the antithesis of modern work.[5]

In religion, this shift has resulted in a recovery of spirituality and mysticism, those human activities which had been depreciated and discarded by the modern subject because they were seen as useless and unproductive. From the burgeoning New Age spiritualities, to the fascination with angelology, to the renewed interest in medieval Christian mystics, to the growth of neoconservative forms of Christianity, women and men in contemporary Western societies are valuing and engaging in useless, unproductive, playful activities through which they experience a unity or harmony with their environment that they cannot experience while they are at work, acting, producing, making. The shift from the modern notion of the person as *homo faber* to the postmodern notion of the person as *homo ludens* finds its religious parallel in a shift from an identification of *religious* action with ethical behavior, "doing" good, to an identification of religious action with aesthetic or affective behavior, "feeling" at one with God, others, one's self, the environment, the cosmos, and so on. If doing good required commitment, engagement, struggle, self-sacrifice, and suffering, feeling at one with the cosmos calls for celebration, enjoyment, pleasure, recreation, "being" rather than "doing," and so forth.

LATIN AMERICAN LIBERATION THEOLOGY

In several ways, the liberation theology movement in Latin America has, in its own particular context, reflected the shift from the modern anthropology of *homo faber* to the postmodern *homo ludens*. The greater emphasis liberation theologians have increasingly given to women's experience, *lo cotidiano*, spirituality, and popular religion as *loci theologici* reflects, at a deeper, fundamental level, precisely such a shift in theological anthropology and, more specifically, in the understanding of human action, or praxis.[6] Conversely, the relatively little attention paid to popular religion in the initial stages of the liberation theology movement reflected—arguably, I think—a certain suspicion toward forms of human activity which did not explicitly contribute to the struggle for justice and which were, therefore, "useless" in the light of that struggle.[7]

In the area of theological anthropology, liberation theology was significant precisely in that it brought Catholic theological reflection into the modern world, criticizing static notions of the person and "human existence" which, in their inattentiveness to praxis, wittingly or unwittingly legitimated the status quo. The human person, insisted the Latin Americans, cannot be understood or known except through his or her historical praxis. Moreover, it is in and through historical praxis that we come to know the God who is revealed in history. The Christian faith demands not merely contemplation or prayer but action as well.

However, insofar as it adopted the specifically Marxian, modern notion of praxis, liberation theology assimilated Marx's instrumentalist anthropology, wherein the human person is viewed as *homo faber*; to be a human being is to be engaged in the transformation of society, to become an agent of change. Since popular religion and, much less, play or celebration do not involve direct action for change, these were, to some extent, ignored in early liberation theology literature (with some notable exceptions). At the very least, these forms of action were given comparatively little attention. As I have argued elsewhere, Marxists as well as liberation theologians tended to conflate the original Aristotelian distinction between praxis (human action that is its own end, with no external purpose) and poiesis (human action that seeks some external end, or product).[8]

In the wake of the failure of Marxist-inspired social movements in Eastern Europe and Latin America, and the growth of Protestant evangelical and Pentecostal groups in Latin America, some of these anthropological assumptions are being increasingly questioned. In the first case, a principal reason for the failure of Marxist revolutions has been precisely their instrumentalist approaches to human suffering and injustice. Since they assume the modern dichotomy between the subject-as-agent and the world-as-object, instrumentalist notions of historical praxis necessarily turn human beings and society into objects to be manipulated—in this case, in the cause of transformation and liberation.[9]

In the second case, liberation theology's initial inattentiveness to the fundamental character of human action as "useless" resulted in an inattentiveness to the importance of celebration, ritual, popular religion, and family life in the ongoing struggles of the poor. Protestant evangelical and Pentecostal groups have been able to fill that vacuum by, among other things, affirming and valuing the affective, celebratory dimensions of popular religion and addressing the forms of suffering (for example, domestic violence, alcoholism) which, though often the most immediate forms of oppression experienced by the poor in their everyday lives, had been too often ignored by liberation theologians influenced by the modern under- standing of human action as that which takes place in public, in the streets, in the marketplace, in the factory, as it is here that history is "made."

This phenomenon is noted by Phillip Berryman: "An anthropologist studying the differences between active Catholics and evangelicals in an Indian town in Guatemala told me he was finding little difference in be- liefs about God or Christ or other doctrinal points or even about politics. The sharpest cleavage was over liquor . . . For many men becoming evan- gelical is heavily identified with renouncing alcohol—and for their fami- lies it signifies the end of alcohol-related abuse."[10] In another study, "the Salesian priest and sociologist Luis Corral Prieto interviewed 270 Protes- tants who had formerly been Catholics . . . When asked what had changed in their lives, many said 'everything': They no longer smoked or drank, their marriage and family life was completely changed, and even their economic situation had changed for the better."[11]

By retrieving the central theological significance of popular religion, U.S. Latino/a theologians are also responding to this new reality, not by rejecting liberation theology, but by adopting, adapting, and helping to deepen the groundbreaking and radical insights of liberation theologians. Indeed, as liberation theologians themselves become more open to the "faith of the people," the process of theologizing out of the context of that faith will certainly become a process of mutual accompaniment. Without in any way deprecating the necessity of sociopolitical transformation, Latin American theologians like Gustavo Gutiérrez have themselves been in- creasingly insisting on the necessity of appreciating another essential di- mension of the faith as lived by the poor, namely, the gratuity of God's love.[12]

The challenge for those of us who have been inspired and influenced by liberation theology, then, is to appropriate the fundamental insights of that movement while, at the same time, drawing from our different expe- riences and historical contexts in order to engage Latin Americans in a dialogue that will foster the further development and deepening of those fundamental insights—in this case, insights concerning the nature of the human person and human action. In the light of our own historical con- text, U.S. Hispanic theologians have already developed a sustained, sys- tematic theological reflection on Latino popular Catholicism, elaborating many of its anthropological and theological implications.[13] In other writ- ings, for example, I have examined the notion of "aesthetic praxis"[14]; in the remainder of this chapter, I would like to make more concrete this notion—and its implications for theological anthropology—by exploring the meaning and significance of that activity which is central to the lives of all Latinos and Latinas, the fiesta.

THE FIESTA

My thesis in this section is that the fiesta, as a central element of Latino culture, reflects and expresses a theological anthropology fundamentally different from the modern notion of the autonomous subject-as-agent and that, as such, the fiesta is a principal form of cultural resistance. That is, the understanding of human life underlying and expressed through the fiesta is one in which the attitude of agency (doing, making) is grounded in an attitude of receptivity and response; more specifically, the former mediates the latter. In turn, it is precisely in his or her character as receiver and respondent that the human person is *capable* of celebrating. Thus, what lies at the heart of the Latino affinity for festive celebration is not necessarily a happier, warmer, or more easy-going *temperament*, but a fundamentally different *understanding* of the human and, specifically, of the nature of human activity in the world.

Viewing himself or herself fundamentally and primarily as one who receives and responds rather than as one who makes or produces, the U.S. Hispanic is free to celebrate life—all of life—as a gift of absolute value. In the context of the dominant U.S. culture, especially, such celebration has a prophetic and, indeed, a political character: to celebrate life as gift in the midst of a culture that views life as an object to be controlled is a prophetic act; to "waste" time celebrating in the midst of a culture where time is a priceless commodity ("time is money") is a subversive act.

At the same time, such celebration remains ambiguous to the extent that it becomes assimilated into or coopted by the dominant culture. So, for example, if the attitude of receptivity to life-as-gift is not mediated by a commitment to political liberation, such an attitude may readily serve simply to reinforce stereotypes of Latinos/as as lazy or passive. Or the celebration of life-as-play may assimilate the consumerist values of the dominant culture.

The fiesta, as I will be using the term, is *not* a "party." In the words of Cuban researchers Rafael Brea and José Millet, "The most general and accepted meaning [of the term] is a solemn religious or civil affair with which an important event is commemorated."[15] Thus, while merriment is often—or usually—an important element of the festivities, what defines the fiesta, properly speaking, is not the presence of merriment but the activities' character as commemoration, or celebration. This will be an important distinction if we are to avoid a certain romanticization of fiestas, or the more stereotypical understanding (in the dominant culture) of the fiesta as merely a party, an "escape" from daily drudgery, or a way to put our troubles behind us for a time. That may be the primary function and significance of partying in U.S. culture—and it is one element present in many fiestas—but it is not the primary function and significance of the fiesta in Latino culture. The fiesta is, at the same time, play *and* work.

The above definition also blurs the distinction between religious and civil celebrations; a fiesta may be either, or both. As Ronald Grimes observes in his landmark study of the fiestas of Santa Fe, New Mexico, "Denials of the validity of a church-state or religion-culture dualism are common among both Indians and Hispanos of New Mexico."[16] Indeed, while the varied cultural groups which compose the ancestry of Latinos and Latinas are each distinct in many important ways, the rejection of such dualism is a common trait of all. And the absence of such dualism is nowhere more evident than in the cultural phenomenon of the fiesta.

The fiesta represents a fundamental challenge to the very subject-object dichotomy that grounds the modern autonomous subject-as-agent. In addition to the absence of religious-cultural dualism, several other characteristics of fiestas reflect and express a challenge to modern anthropology. Among these features are the nature of the fiesta as: (1) an expression of *communitas*; (2) human action "in the subjunctive mood"; (3) the confluence of play and work; and, therefore, (4) a form of liturgical action. As a liturgical act, the fiesta reveals an understanding of the human person and human action which, though not necessarily expressly religious or spiritual, represents a *theological* anthropology in the truest sense—that is, an understanding of human life as *gift* and, consequently, of the human person as one who (in gratitude) *receives* and *responds* to that gift. At bottom what is celebrated is life as gift, and the fiesta is the liturgical act whereby the community receives and responds to the gift. As an act of reception and response for the gift of life, the fiesta—whether expressly civil or religious—is a fundamentally religious act.

This gift, however, is not abstract; its irreducible value derives from its Source. The value of life as a gift to be celebrated is grounded in the intrinsic connection between the gift and its Giver. The gift of life is made concrete in the Creator's love for us and in our active response to that love, a response made manifest not only in the act of celebration but also in that love of neighbor and commitment to justice which are the sociohistorical verification of our belief in life-as-gift. The only adequate celebration is one which affirms the irreducible value of *all* life and which, therefore, emerges within a commitment to social justice, a commitment to resist all forms of instrumentalization and objectification.

Consequently, Latino popular Catholicism commonly places the Cross at the center of its celebrations. Paradoxically, the Cross represents the concrete manifestation of the irreducible value of life; Jesus' gift of his life on the Cross reveals the value of all life as gift.[17] More specifically, Jesus' solidarity with and compassion for the outcasts of his society, that is, his active affirmation of the value of *their* lives, alone makes possible—and credible—the celebration of life as a gift. Unless we first affirm the absolute value of the outcast's life as itself a gift of God, we cannot, with integrity, affirm and celebrate the value of "life"; liberation is the concrete form which all authentic celebration must take.

In his analyses of non-Western public rituals, especially *Carnaval*, Victor Turner describes the liberating dimension of public celebrations precisely as rooted in their affirmation of solidarity with and among marginalized groups; such celebrations represent a transition "from systems of status roles to *communitas*, the I-thou relationship, and Buber's 'essential We' as against society regarded as 'It.'"[18] This notion is further specified by Brazilian anthropologist Maria Goldwasser in her study of *Carnaval*: "Communitas is the domain of equality, where all are placed without distinction on an identical level of social evaluation, but the equivalence which is established among them has a ritual character."[19] *Communitas* is neither static nor chaotic (whatever the surface appearances); it is a dynamic "shared flowing" which "denotes the holistic sensation when we act with total involvement, when action and awareness are one (one ceases to flow if one becomes aware that one is doing it)" and, therefore, "just as a river needs a bed and banks to flow, so do people need framing and structural rules to do their kind of flowing . . . It takes a great amount of order to produce a 'sweet disorder,' a great deal of structuring to create a sacred play-space and time for antistructure . . . This is not dead structure, but living form; Isadora Duncan, not classical ballet."[20] The dynamic, "flowing" character of *communitas* and its leveling function represent a reversal of "hard-won bourgeois values."[21]

In U.S. Latino fiestas, an essential "river bank" that structures the "flow" of *communitas* is precisely the U.S. Latino cultural identity. In his analysis of the fiestas of Santa Fe, for instance, Grimes notes that "ethnicity is emphasized repeatedly by the fact that most of the rhythms are mariachi . . . That the music is not 'mere' entertainment becomes obvious when participants are asked whether they would mind using the songs and rhythms of some other linguistic and ethnic tradition. 'The fiesta would no longer be the fiesta,' they say. The music is essential, not accidental, to what makes a fiesta."[22] In a study of the Puerto Rican community in Chicago, Felix Padilla makes a similar observation: "The leading social event was the celebration of *El Día de San Juan* (St. John's Day) . . . *El Día de San Juan* soon became the major social event for the Puerto Rican community . . . Overall this event signified the ethnic solidarity shared among the city's Puerto Rican population."[23] "Nowadays," observes Almudena Ortiz in her study of *quinceañeras*, "one of the main reasons behind having a *Quinceañera* is still one of ethnic identity."[24]

Thus, in the words of Turner and Buber quoted above, fiestas are a principal way through which the Latino community celebrates its life as an "essential 'We'" over against "society regarded as 'It.'" That this "We" (*nosotros*) is constituted and celebrated "*over against*" society as "It" (that is, the dominant culture) already suggests the subversive character of the fiesta in U.S. Latino communities. Whether by refusing to surrender traditional celebrations like the *quinceañera* or by "taking over" public thoroughfares and neighborhoods during the celebration of the Way of the Cross on Good Friday, the Latino community asserts its identity, visibility, and vitality in the face of a dominant culture that demands assimilation.

A further subversive aspect of the fiesta is suggested by its liminality. As a transition from hierarchy to equality ("We"), from "dead structure" to "sweet disorder," *communitas* is always a *liminal* event. As Victor Turner suggests,

> Most cultural performances belong to culture's "subjunctive" mood. "Subjunctive" is defined by Webster as "that mood of a verb used to express supposition, desire, hypothesis, possibility, etc. rather than to state an actual fact . . . " Ritual, carnival, festival, theatre, film, and similar performative genres clearly possess many of these attributes. The indicative mood of culture . . . controls the quotidian arenas of economic activity, much of law and politics, and a good deal of domestic life . . . It is perhaps significant that, as the *Concise Oxford Dictionary* puts it, "subjunctive = verbal mood, obsolescent in English."[25]

In other words, it is no coincidence that the subjunctive mood plays a much greater role in the Spanish than in the English language, and that "learning the subjunctive" is usually the most difficult obstacle confronting a native English-speaker trying to learn Spanish.

Given Turner's definition of liminality, then, one might argue that the fiesta (whether *cinco de mayo* or Marian festivals) is a public ritual wherein "the village greens or the squares of the city are not abandoned but rather ritually transformed. It is as though everything is switched into the subjunctive mood for a privileged period of time . . . Public liminality is governed by public subjunctivity."[26]

At the same time, this subjunctivity (as well as the spirit of *communitas*) always remains, to some extent, fragile insofar as "any liminal situation has a tendency to revert to its structured opposite, that is, the status system."[27] The public subjunctivity of the fiesta, or its ability to evoke future possibilities, is also fragile insofar as any subjunctive situation has a tendency to revert to indicativity; that is, to lose its ability to celebrate the present *as projected into* a possible future. The subversive character of liminality lies precisely in its "in-betweeness"; in the case of temporal liminality, in its lying in between the present and the future, thereby representing an implicit challenge to the status quo. When fiesta loses its character as a celebration of the present *as intrinsically linked to the remembered past and the hoped-for future*, it degenerates into a celebration of the present-as-status-quo, the present as disjoined from the past and future. Then, celebration merely legitimates the status quo, allowing us to "escape" it for a brief time. The structure of Latino fiestas, from the music to the narratives and dramatic reenactments that are so often an essential element of the celebrations, serves to link the present celebration to the past (often in the form of the "dangerous memory" of suffering) and the future (as the anticipated, full realization of *communitas*).

The always-ambiguous character of the fiesta is reflected in the role of the young *quinceañera*. In the *quinceañera* celebration, there is a reversal of roles, wherein the girl becomes the center of attention. The woman, who usually finds herself marginalized in the public life of the community, now takes center stage. Yet this ritualized "reversal" remains ambiguous precisely insofar as it does not lead to an ethical-political reversal. In the absence of this, women will continue to be idealized in the public fiesta at the same time that they are subordinated to the man in everyday life.[28]

The same ambiguity is evident at the economic level. The extraordinary amount of money so often expended by Latino families to celebrate *quinceañeras* in a "proper" fashion is sometimes justified as the necessary cost of maintaining this important tradition. At the same time, the felt need to spend those exorbitant sums too easily becomes assimilated into the consumerist values of the dominant U.S. culture.[29]

The structured character of the fiesta, as a precondition for the freedom and equality experienced and projected in the celebration, also prevents us from interpreting it as *mere play*; the fiesta reflects a confluence of play *and* work. When the fiesta is interpreted as mere play (for example, within a postmodern notion of play as unstructured and free-floating), it too easily becomes romanticized. Moreover, it is especially in its character as work, or *structured* play, that the fiesta is always in danger of reverting to "the status system." An aspect of all fiestas is the work necessary to structure the celebration, to prepare and set aside time and space. When this aspect of fiesta as work is ignored (in, for example, the romanticization of fiesta as party) the ways in which unjust social structures can become replicated in the structure of the fiesta will be obscured. So, for instance, patriarchal social structures can become replicated when women are expected to do the "work" of the fiesta without being allowed to participate fully in the "play." Precisely as *communitas* "in the subjunctive mood," the fiesta represents a prophetic challenge to the failure of its participants to fully realize that *communitas* in the present.

Inasmuch as the fiesta is a dramatic event in which *communitas* is *effected* in the present (even if incompletely) and *projected* "subjunctively" into the future, the entire celebration is itself "work"; conversely, the preparation and structuring of the fiesta are themselves integrated into the celebration as important aspects of the fiesta. (I have elsewhere observed, for example, how the Easter Triduum celebration is really one celebration encompassing three days, with the preparatory and clean-up work that takes place between the distinct celebrations of Holy Thursday, Good Friday, and Easter Sunday actually becoming itself solemnized and ritualized.[30]) Representing a unity of play and work, the fiesta challenges and subverts both an escapist (postmodern) understanding of play and a mechanistic (modern) understanding of work.

If the above interpretation of the fiesta as it functions in the U.S. Latino community is correct, then the fiesta can be understood as a *liturgy*, that is, a "work or action performed by a people in public, usually according to a prescribed ritual."[31] Theologically, this "work or action" is a communal act of *worship*, that is, an act of praise and thanksgiving which commemorates the saving love of God as this has been manifest in the remembered past, is experienced in the celebrated present, and is anticipated in the promised future. The liturgical act of worship is thus a *communal action* of *receptivity* (of the saving love of God) and *response* (praise and thanksgiving). What defines the act of worship—at its core—is that, in the celebration, a human community expresses its self-understanding as fundamentally recipient and respondent rather than as fundamentally doer and maker (though, as suggested above, doing and making are always a part of celebration). That is, in worship, human action manifests itself not simply as a doing, making, or achieving—not simply a mechanistic, physical movement of the environment-as-object, or simply a "going from here to there"—but as, above all, a receiving. Yet this act of reception in no way implies passivity (as it would be viewed in the eyes of the modern autonomous subject), since it necessarily entails an *active* response, that is, the liturgy itself. Moreover, the recipient and respondent is not fundamentally the "I" but the "We."

This understanding, however, begs a further question: If worship always involves an act of reception and response, what or whom are we receiving and to what or to whom are we responding? In explicitly Christian worship, the answer might be something like this: "We are receiving God's saving love and, in turn, offering a response of praise and thanksgiving." This, however, prompts a further question: In what does God's saving love consist? If we pursue this line of argumentation, we eventually arrive at the conclusion that the gift we have received from God is creation itself, life itself, as incarnated most completely (for the Christian) in God's own self-gift in the person of Jesus Christ.

What we are receiving and responding to is *the gift of life*, not in a sentimental sense, but in an ontological sense: we know that whatever "we" do, make, or achieve is ultimately gift; we know that whatever relationships we construct are grounded in the prior constitutive relationship with the One who has loved us first; we know that who we are is not dependent on what we do, make, or achieve; we know that life—all of life—is *gift* before it is an "object" that we work upon, mold, transform, or liberate. And, we know that unless we acknowledge and affirm all of the above, all that we do, make, achieve, or liberate will go for naught. That is, the historical struggle for justice—the construction of a world that truly images the God of life, the "Giver of life"—must be grounded in the prior, more fundamental attitude and act wherein we acknowledge our dependence on a God who *is* Life. If doing, making, and achieving imply an attitude of control, receiving and responding imply an attitude of trust. If, for the modern subject, receptivity implies weakness and passivity, for the Latino community receptivity is the most fundamental form of human praxis, through which one is freed and empowered to act, to think "subjunctively," to celebrate *communitas* in the very midst of its enemies, who seek its destruction. Praxis-as-doing is grounded in and made possible by praxis-as-receiving.

The fiesta represents precisely that attitude of trust in the ultimate goodness of life, both as a reality in the present and as an unrealized future that challenges and subverts the status quo. If religious worship does this explicitly, fiesta does it implicitly—sometimes explicitly as well. To celebrate life itself as good, even when we cannot control it, is to acknowledge life as gift, as being in the control of Someone else; it is to acknowledge and affirm a Giv*er*, even if only implicitly. Insofar as the fiesta celebrates the *ultimate* goodness of life (even in the midst of suffering and, indeed, as the "subjunctive" denial of the ultimacy of death), it celebrates life as a gratuitous gift *that cannot be destroyed* by a dominant culture that, objectifying life, would destroy it.

All of the characteristics of fiesta outlined above subvert a dominant culture constructed on the basis of the modern autonomous subject who "makes" history. The fiesta reflects a theological anthropology which, even when not explicitly religious, understands the human person as *constituted* by relationships, not only relationship to the human community which precedes and forms the person, but especially by relationship to the primordial, triune Community whose love *is* life. When we are open to that life, when we trust in the ultimate goodness of life even in the midst of struggle, when we refuse to lose hope, when we refuse to be reduced to mere objects or mere machines of production, we are then—and only then—freed to celebrate.

Notes

[1] Angela Erevia, *Quinceañera* (San Antonio, Tex.: Mexican American Cultural Center, 1980), 15.

[2] On the modern subject as defined by the act of "making," see Matthew Lamb, "Praxis," in *The New Dictionary of Theology*, ed. Joseph Komonchak, et al. (Wilmington, Del.: Michael Glazier, 1987), 784-87; idem, *Solidarity with Victims* (New York: Crossroad, 1982); Jürgen Habermas, *The Theory of Communicative Action* (Boston: Beacon Press, 1984); idem, *Theory and Practice* (London: Heinemann,

1974); Hans-Georg Gadamer, "Hermeneutics and Social Science," *Cultural Herme-neutics* 2 (1975), 307-16; Richard Bernstein, *Beyond Objectivism and Relativism: Sci-ence, Hermeneutics, and Praxis* (Philadelphia: University of Pennsylvania Press, 1985); idem, *Praxis and Action: Contemporary Philosophies of Human Activity* (Phila-delphia: University of Pennsylvania Press, 1971); Nicholas Lobkowicz, *Theory and Practice: History of a Concept from Aristotle to Marx* (Notre Dame, Ind.: University of Notre Dame Press, 1967); Joseph Dunne, *Back to the Rough Ground: 'Phronesis' and 'Techne' in Modern Philosophy and in Aristotle* (Notre Dame, Ind.: University of Notre Dame Press, 1993). See also Roberto S. Goizueta, *Caminemos con Jesús: To-ward a Hispanic/Latino Theology of Accompaniment* (Maryknoll, N.Y.: Orbis Books, 1995), esp., 77-100.

[3] Walter Benjamin, quoted in David Tracy, *Plurality and Ambiguity: Hermeneu-tics, Religion, Hope* (San Francisco: Harper & Row, 1987), 69.

[4] On the irruption of the poor in human history, see especially Gustavo Gutiérrez, *A Theology of Liberation* (Maryknoll, N.Y.: Orbis Books, 1988).

[5] On poststructuralist postmodernism, see, for example, Honi Fern Haber, *Beyond Postmodern Politics: Lyotard, Rorty, Foucault* (New York: Routledge, 1994), esp., 1-8, 113-16; Mark Kline Taylor, *Remembering Esperanza* (Maryknoll, N.Y.: Orbis Books, 1990); Jonathan Arac, ed., *Postmodernism and Politics* (Minneapolis: Uni-versity of Minnesota Press, 1986); Terry Eagleton, *The Ideology of the Aesthetic* (Cam-bridge, Mass.: Basil Blackwell, 1990), esp., 369-401; Jonathan Loesberg, *Aestheti-cism and Deconstruction: Pater, Derrida, and De Man* (Princeton, N.J.: Princeton University Press, 1991); Jürgen Habermas, "Modernity Versus Post-Modernity," *New German Critique* 22 (Winter 1981), 3-14; Hal Foster, "(Post)Modern Polem-ics," *New German Critique* 33 (Fall 1984), 67-78; Seyla Benhabib, "Epistemologies of Postmodernism: A Rejoinder to Jean-François Lyotard," *New German Critique* 33 (Fall 1984), 103-26; David Tracy, *Plurality and Ambiguity: Hermeneutics, Reli-gion, Hope* (San Francisco: Harper & Row, 1987), esp., 47-81; and Fredric Jameson, *Postmodernism, or, The Cultural Logic of Late Capitalism* (Durham, N.C.: Duke Uni-versity Press, 1991); Andrew Ross, ed., *Universal Abandon? The Politics of Postmodernism* (Minneapolis, Minn.: University of Minnesota Press, 1988); Andreas Huyssen, *After the Great Divide: Modernism, Mass Culture, Postmodernism* (Bloomington, Ind.: Indiana University Press, 1986), esp., 179-221.

[6] See, for instance, the Introduction to the revised edition of Gutiérrez, *A The-ology of Liberation*, as well as Gutiérrez's *On Job* (Maryknoll, N.Y.: Orbis Books, 1987) and *We Drink from Our Own Wells* (Maryknoll, N.Y.: Orbis Books, 1984).

[7] For a fuller development of this argument, see Goizueta, *Caminemos con Jesús*, 77-100.

[8] Ibid.

[9] Ibid.

[10] Phillip Berryman, *Stubborn Hope: Religion, Politics, and Revolution in Central America* (Maryknoll, N.Y.: Orbis Books, 1994), 150.

[11] Ibid., 149-50.

[12] See especially Gutiérrez, *On Job*; idem, *The God of Life* (Maryknoll, N.Y.: Orbis Books, 1991), 145-63.

[13] See, for example, Orlando O. Espín, *The Faith of the People: Theological Reflec-tions on Popular Catholicism* (Maryknoll, N.Y.: Orbis Books, 1997); idem, "Tradition and Popular Religion: An Understanding of the *Sensus Fidelium*," in *Frontiers of Hispanic Theology in the United States*, ed. Allan F. Deck (Maryknoll, N.Y.: Orbis Books, 1992); idem, "Popular Catholicism among Latinos," in *Hispanic Catholics in the United States: Issues and Concerns*, ed. Jay Dolan and Allan Figueroa Deck (Notre Dame, Ind.: University of Notre Dame Press, 1994); Jaime Vidal, "Popular Religion

among Hispanics in the General Area of the Archdiocese of Newark," in *Presencia Nueva: A Study of Hispanics in the Archdiocese of Newark* (Newark: Archdiocesan Office of Research and Planning, 1988), 235-352.

[14] See especially, Goizueta, *Caminemos con Jesús,* 89-131.

[15] Rafael Brea and José Millet, "Glossary of Popular Festivals," in *Cuban Festivals: An Illustrated Anthology,* ed. Judith Bettelheim (New York: Garland Publishing, 1993), 116.

[16] Ronald Grimes, *Symbol and Conquest: Public Ritual and Drama in Santa Fe, New Mexico* (Ithaca, N.Y.: Cornell University Press, 1976), 42.

[17] This is reflected in the typical greeting offered by the priest to the young *quinceañera* at the beginning of the liturgical celebration: "The love of God our Father, *source of all life,* the grace of our Lord Jesus Christ, *who gave his life that we might live* . . . We welcome you to this celebration so that the whole community may share in the YES which your parents and godparents pronounced for you in your baptism, and which you now express and affirm yourself—*YES to that life you received through the love of your father and mother, and to the new life you have through baptism in Christ"* (Erevia, *Quinceañera,* 25, emphases added). The response, the yes expressed, is not to life in the abstract but to life in community, a community established and headed by Christ, "who gave his life that we might live." What the *quinceañera* celebrates is not life in general, but *that* life which she has received from God, her parents, and Jesus on the Cross. That life which is celebrated entails, in turn, responsibilities: "Thank you, Lord, for calling me to be, to live, to be an image and likeness of you; thank you for sending your Son to save me, your Holy Spirit to make me holy; to all your goodness and love, I wish to say yes, and with your help I will dedicate myself more and more generously to serve you in my brothers and sisters" (ibid., 29).

[18] Victor Turner, *The Anthropology of Performance* (New York: PAJ Publications, 1986), 128.

[19] Maria Goldwasser, quoted in Turner, *The Anthropology of Performance,* 132.

[20] Turner, *The Anthropology of Performance,* 133.

[21] Ibid., 138.

[22] Grimes, *Symbol and Conquest,* 194.

[23] Felix M. Padilla, *Latino Ethnic Consciousness: The Case of Mexican Americans and Puerto Ricans in Chicago* (Notre Dame, Ind.: University of Notre Dame Press, 1985), 50.

[24] Almudena Ortiz, *Fiesta de Quinceañera: Queen for a Day* (M.A. thesis, University of California at Berkeley, 1992), 62.

[25] Turner, *The Anthropology of Performance,* 101.

[26] Ibid., 102.

[27] Grimes, *Symbol and Conquest,* 66.

[28] Ortiz, *Fiesta de Quinceañera,* 52-55.

[29] Almudena Ortiz recounts the following illustrative anecdote: "I met with a family, who had recently immigrated from Mexico and was living in Oakland, when one of the four daughters was having her *Quinceañera.* At the time of the interview, one of Isabel's older sister [sic] and her mother were the only ones that had jobs and had just been laid off from the cookie factory where they worked. The mother explained to me that even though their financial situation was a desperate one, Isabel was going to have her *Quince Años* as planned. The dress had been made already, it has cost the family from $200 to $250 dollars! . . . it was too late to turn back. Unfortunately this scenario is a common one . . . Some church officials that I spoke to expressed to me their discomfort of families having to spend such incredible amounts of money—subjecting the family to significant

sacrifice so that the females in the family could have their fifteen [sic] birthday celebration. These same officials, also thought that it is not prudent or even realistic to ask the community to do without such a tradition because of a poor financial situation" (ibid., 42-43).

[30] Goizueta, *Caminemos con Jesús*, 32-37.

[31] Kevin Irwin, "Liturgy," in *The New Dictionary of Catholic Spirituality*, ed. Michael Downey (Collegeville, Minn.: The Liturgical Press, 1993), 602.

5

The Bible and U.S. Hispanic American Theological Discourse

Lessons from a Non-Innocent History

❦

JEAN-PIERRE RUIZ

St. John's University, New York

INTRODUCTION: "IT SAYS NOTHING. IT'S EMPTY."

A thousand men sweep the path of the Inca into the great square where the Spaniards wait in hiding. The multitude trembles at the passage of the Beloved Father, the One, the Only, lord of labors and fiestas; the singers fall silent, and the dancers freeze up. In the half light, last light of the day, the crowns and vestments of Atahualpa and his cortege of nobles of the realm gleam with gold and silver . . .

The priest Vicente de Valverde emerges from the shadows and goes to meet Atahualpa. He raises the Bible in one hand and a crucifix in the other, as if exorcising a storm on the high seas, and cries that here is God, the true one, and that all the rest is nonsense. The interpreter translates and Atahualpa, at the head of the throng, asks:

"Who told you that?"

"The Bible says it, the sacred book."

"Give it here, so it can tell me."

A few paces away, Pizarro unsheathes his sword.

Atahualpa looks at the Bible, turns it over in his hand, shakes it to make it talk, and presses it against his ear: "It says nothing. It's empty." And he drops it to the ground.

Pizarro has been waiting for this moment . . . Pizarro yells and pounces. At the signal, the trap is sprung. From the ambush trumpets blare, arquebuses roar, and the cavalry charges the stunned and unarmed crowd.[1]

Eduardo Galeano's chilling dramatization of the November 16, 1532, encounter in Cajamarca Plaza between the *conquistador* Pizarro and the Inca leader Atahualpa provides a disturbingly appropriate point of entry into the question that is the focus of the present essay, namely, the place of the Bible in U.S. Hispanic American[2] theological reflection.[3] More than five hundred years after the *Conquista* brought Spanish Christians and their traditions face to face with the indigenous peoples of the Americas and their traditions, in an encounter of histories and worldviews that was often violent in its unfolding and tragic in its consequences, Atahualpa's struggle to wrest meaning from the book that the Spanish priest singled out as sacred, and the Inca's frustrated conclusion, "It says nothing. It's empty," remain at once haunting and challenging. The irony of his words resounds above the roar of firearms and the charge of Spanish cavalry against the unarmed multitude.[4]

Atahualpa himself was taken prisoner and held for ransom for nine months, during the course of which he learned the language of his Spanish captors. On August 29, 1533, Pizarro publicly garroted Atahualpa, after having him baptized a Christian with his own name, Francisco. However the *conquistadores* themselves may have understood the voice of the deity, whose unique truth their Bible attested, they clearly saw no contradiction between the claims of Bible and crucifix, and the violence they unleashed against the inhabitants of the lands. Their actions spoke in flagrant disregard for the justice of the God to whom they professed allegiance.

In her study of the encounter between Atahualpa and the Spaniards, Patricia Reed notes that this episode constitutes an instance of what structural anthropologist Claude Lévi-Strauss labeled "the writing lesson," an encounter between representatives of literate and nonliterate cultures. In the same breath, Reed hastens to mention Jacques Derrida's critique of Lévi-Strauss

despite Lévi-Strauss's efforts to avoid ethnocentrism, he continued to couple writing with cultural superiority. For example, Lévi-Strauss wrote, "Of all the criteria by which people habitually distinguish civilization from barbarism, this one should at least be retained: that certain peoples write and others do not."[5]

The history of the conquest of the Americas witnesses that neither writing nor reading, not even the reading of the sacred biblical text, prevented barbaric atrocities. While U.S. Hispanic Americans continue to hold aloft the authority of the biblical text, we cannot allow other voices to fall to the ground, whether these voices are inscribed in literary texts or the eloquent sighs of those who suffer at the margins of society.

Centuries after Pizarro and Atahualpa, amid the *mestizaje* and *mulataje* that characterize U.S. Hispanic Americans as descendants and heirs both of the conquerors and of the conquered, we return to the lessons of our own "non-innocent history" to explore the ways in which the Bible has figured and continues to figure in our theological reflection on our complex experience in the past and in the present.[6]

As a participant in the process of *teología de conjunto*, which bears fruit in this volume of explorations in systematic theology, and as one whose training and professional activity is in biblical studies, I am painfully aware that the conversation between biblical scholars and systematic theologians has sometimes been halting, uneasy, and even strained. With practitioners in both areas acquiring new conversation partners within their own disciplinary vernaculars, so to speak, the increasing specialization both in biblical studies and in systematic theology sometimes even threatens to erode the common ground of concern and the common terms of discourse that make productive conversation possible.[7] As a contribution that bears in mind the ground of these essays that claim to speak "from the heart of our people," this effort is deliberately interdisciplinary. Its interest is both historical and hermeneutical, historical insofar as it retrieves a crucial moment in the history of biblical interpretation in the Americas; hermeneutical insofar as it suggests that the trajectories of biblical interpretation begun centuries ago have important implications for religious experience and its interpretation for U.S. Hispanic Americans in the present.[8]

THE BIBLE OF THE *CONQUISTADORES*

From the very beginning of the European encounter with the Americas, the Bible served as a point of departure and as a point of reference, enlisted by pastors and profiteers alike as "faithful ally, and effective weapon."[9] The European discovery of the American continent occasioned an energetic apocalyptic enthusiasm for those who understood it as an opportunity for the fulfillment of the great commission of Matthew 28:19, "Go therefore and make disciples of all nations, baptizing them in the name of the Father and of the Son and of the Holy Spirit."[10] For the missionaries in the Americas and the theologians in Spain, the evangelization of the peoples they encountered was a sign that human history had entered its final, momentous hour, and that the eschatological consummation of all things was on the horizon. Both Columbus and Bartolomé de Las Casas saw the Spanish discovery of America foretold in the prophecy of Isaiah 60:9: "For the coastlands shall wait for me, the ships of Tarshish first, to bring your children from far away, their silver and gold with them," and Columbus sought to ennoble the relentless quest for gold in the Americas as an effort to locate King Solomon's fabled gold mines (1 Kgs 9:28).[11]

With regard to the treatment of the indigenous population by the Spanish invaders, the biblical narrative of the divinely sanctioned destruction of Jericho and the slaughter of its population (Josh 6) was used by the Spaniards to justify their violence against the peoples of the Americas. Luke 14:23 was used to justify the forcible conversion of those who survived sword and plague: "Go out into the roads and lanes, and compel people to come in, so that my house may be filled."[12] On the other hand, in his homily for the Fourth Sunday of Advent in 1510, the Dominican Antonio de Montesinos took up as his own the cry of John the Baptist, "I am the voice of one crying out in the wilderness, make straight the way of the Lord" (Mt 3:3, a citation of Is 40:3) to issue a prophetic denunciation of the oppression of the indigenous peoples by the *encomenderos*.[13] This homily, preached to an audience that included all the notables of Hispaniola (including Columbus's own son, Admiral Diego Colón), echoed across the ocean to Spain itself, where the angry reports of those in attendance that day led to the censure of Montesinos by King Ferdinand V and by his Dominican provincial superior. Despite such turbulent aftershocks, Bartolomé de Las Casas recognized that "after Montesinos's sermon, there was no possibility of invincible ignorance as to the injustice with which the Spanish proceeded."[14]

As for Bartolomé de Las Casas himself, it was Sirach 34:21-27 that provoked his own enlightenment toward the adoption of a stance of advocacy on behalf of the indigenous peoples of the Americas.[15] Emphasizing the particular force of the Vulgate version of the text that Las Casas used, "*Qui offert sacrificium ex substantia pauperum, quasi qui victimat filium in conspectu patris sui*" (One who offers a sacrifice from the substance of the poor is like one who kills a son before the eyes of his father—my translation) (Sir 34:24), Luis N. Rivera notes that *ex substantia pauperum* here "implies that what has been stolen is decisive for the being and existence of the dispossessed poor; their dispossession leads to the death of the oppressed."[16] According to Rivera,

> Las Casas was fully imbued with *the prophetic, biblical and evangelical traditions favoring the poor and denouncing oppressive power.* Las Casas, as the Old Testament prophets, perceives the violence and exploitation suffered by the paupers and the oppressed as a locus of God's presence in the world. Solidarity with the poor and censorship of the powerful, so present in prophetic texts and in the accounts of Jesus, nurtured his passionate spirit.[17]

This reading of the Bible, as the voice of conscience leading to a critical prophetic consciousness that finds its expression in the unambiguous denunciation of injustice, brought Las Casas into direct and heated conflict with others who supported their positions with arguments they also derived from the Christian canon. The polemic between Las Casas and Juan Ginés de Sepúlveda, for instance, involved differences over their opposing interpretations of the biblical accounts of the Israelite conquest of Canaan. Rivera explains that, for Sepúlveda, "the Deuteronomic war code clarifies the transcendent meaning of the armed conquest of the Americas by Spain and justifies it."[18] Thus, he contended, the *conquistadores* were engaged in a holy war that proceeded with God's unfailing blessing. For his part, Las Casas contended that Sepúlveda had "not researched the scriptures with sufficient determination," and therefore that he erred in an "unbending application of the rigid principles of the Old Testament," inappropriate for "this era of grace and piety." This error, Las Casas continued, had awful consequences: "It facilitates the way for the cruel invasion by tyrants and looters, and for the oppression, exploitation, and slavery of innocent nations."[19]

Las Casas was among those friars who employed Matthew 10:16, "See, I am sending you out like sheep into the midst of wolves," with a significant twist. Whereas in the first century this text reminded its hearers and readers of the perils that beset Christian missionaries, in sixteenth-century America, Las Casas writes, "To these meek sheep . . . came the Spaniards who of course were recognized as wolves."[20] Las Casas and others likewise turned to the shepherd imagery of the Hebrew Bible to denounce the abuses of the *conquistadores*, marshalling such texts as Zechariah 11:4-5:

> Thus said the LORD my God: Be a shepherd of the flock doomed to slaughter. Those who buy them kill them and go unpunished; and those who sell them say, "Blessed be the LORD, for I have become rich"; and their own shepherds have no pity on them.

as well as the condemnation in Ezekiel 32 of the shepherds of Israel who feed themselves rather than tending the sheep responsibly.[21]

These examples are suggestive of the extent to which the Bible was tapped as a resource for ethical reflection and debate on the issue of the Spanish conquest itself and on the treatment of the indigenous population by soldiers, *encomenderos*, and missionaries alike. A broad range of texts was brought to bear on an equally broad range of often contradictory ethical stances, with each party setting forth its own biblical evidence against the other. In the instances cited, it is worth noting that the Bible itself was not the direct focus of attention. Instead, for homilist and polemicist, the scriptures served well as a resource mined in order to justify, motivate and challenge, provoke and persuade, convince beyond any doubt, all by virtue of its unique claim to authority as "the sacred book," in the words of Vicente de Valverde. It might therefore be said that the biblical text served as an ideological compass for the paths that Christian Spain charted for itself in the unfamiliar territory of the continent to which it laid claimed for its own sake and for the sake of its God.

A GREAT SIGN APPEARS IN PRINT:
TWO ACCOUNTS OF THE EVENTS AT TEPEYAC

It seems enormously curious that only in 1648, after more than a century had passed since the apparitions of the Virgin Mary to the Nahua neophyte Juan Diego at Tepeyac in December 1531, did the first published account of these events appear. That work, *Imagen de la Virgen María Madre de Dios de Guadalupe milagrosamente aparecida en México: Celebrada en su historia, con la profecía del capítulo doce del Apocalipsis*, came from the pen of the Mexican-born Oratorian priest Miguel Sánchez (1594-1674).[22] Barely six months after the publication of Sánchez's work, a second published account of the events at Tepeyac appeared, entitled *Huey tlamahuiçoltica omonexiti in ilhuicac tlatocacihualpilli Santa Maria totlaçonantzin Guadalupe in nican huey altepenahuac Mexico itocayocan Tepeyacac*, written by the priest Luis Lasso de la Vega, vicar of the *ermita* of Guadalupe.[23] Despite the proximity of their publication dates, the contrast between the two books is enormous, and an attentive comparison of the hermeneutics of the two works is instructive for the purposes of this essay.

When Miguel Sánchez died on March 22, 1674, his obituary testified to the impact of his *Imagen de la Virgen* on the spread of devotion to Our Lady of Guadalupe: "He wrote a learned book about her apparition, which seemingly has been the means by which devotion to this holy image has spread throughout all Christendom."[24] Francisco de la Maza claims that Sánchez "accepts the Guadalupan tradition and develops it by providing it with a theological foundation, without which it would have remained a formless legend."[25] While the latter assertion is highly questionable, the evidence of Sánchez's own contemporaries demonstrates the influence of his work. In a letter to Sánchez, which was published as an appendix to the book itself, Luis Lasso de la Vega describes Sánchez's *Imagen de la Virgen* as an account that he found "fashioned, based on, and concerned with the marvel of the miracle, in the circumstances of her apparition, in the mysteries that her painting signifies, and in the brief mapping of her sanctuary, and which [Sanchez's account as a whole] already speaks in a deciphered manner what came to pass years ago."[26]

The "deciphering" or decoding of which Lasso de la Vega spoke has to do with Sánchez's reading of the hierophany[27] at Tepeyac in the light of Revelation 12. Sánchez prefaces his work with an explanation of his choice of the Apocalypse as the key to understanding the hierophany at Tepeyac and the image that remained as its legacy:

> I chose the revelation of the Apocalypse because in it I discovered the foundation of my subject, which presents as though in code the original, the drawing, the retouching, the painting and the dedication of the sacred image; and also because it comes from the Apocalypse, to which my talents are inclined, bringing divine blessings to those who read it and to those who hear it: "Blessed is the one who reads and who hears the words of this prophecy" (Revelation 1).[28]

Turning to describe the substance of Sánchez's book, the work begins with an introductory exegesis of Revelation 12, followed by an extensive verse-by-verse exposition of correspondences between the biblical text and the Mexican Guadalupe. Next, Sánchez gives an account of the events at Tepeyac, a description of the image, and an elaborately detailed, phrase-by-phrase reading of Revelation 12, which simultaneously renders a "reading" of the hierophany at Tepeyac. Sánchez then recounts the image's relocation from the cathedral to the *ermita* of Guadalupe at Tepeyac, provides a description of that sanctuary, and presents a series of miracle stories associated with the image of Our Lady of Guadalupe. Thus, at great length, Sánchez proposes that the woman clothed with the sun of Revelation 12 corresponds to the image of Our Lady of Guadalupe, and that this chapter of the Apocalypse furnishes the key to understanding the apparitions and the image, and their significance for Mexico.

What did Sánchez aim to accomplish with this work? Stafford Poole writes that Sánchez

> had a messianic view of Mexico city, which he sought to put on a par with the great religious centers of the Catholic world. He compared Zumárraga [*Juan de Zumárraga, the first bishop of Mexico, to whom Juan Diego reported the apparitions of Tepeyac*] to Saint John the Evangelist and Mexico to Patmos . . . and he interpreted Revelation 12 in terms of Mexico and the Spanish empire. The woman clothed with the sun was the city of Mexico. Mary, he asserted, had aided the Spanish conquest, she was the "assistant conquistador." New Spain was her homeland. His emphasis, which took up most of the first part of the work, was that Revelation 12 prefigured Mexico, Guadalupe, and the destiny of the sons of the land.[29]

In this respect, Sánchez's *Imagen de la Virgen* differs more in scale than in substance from the examples mentioned earlier of ways in which the Bible served the *conquistadores*. It is clear that Sánchez sought to advance the *criollo* agenda by means of this work, which recast the traditional account of Guadalupe, directed as it was toward the Nahuatl-speaking people of Mexico, and redirected it on behalf of the Mexican-born descendants of the *conquistadores.*

As for Sánchez's selection of Revelation 12 as the hermeneutical lexicon through which the hierophany at Tepeyac would be read, that choice may have been more than a matter of Sánchez's personal fascination with the Apocalypse, and more than a matter of his participation in the mood of apocalyptic optimism that accompanied the Spanish conquest of the Americas. In her study "Mother of Death, Mother of Rebirth: The Mexican Virgin of Guadalupe," Patricia Harrington calls attention to the constraints that were imposed on painters of religious subjects in Spain and New Spain during the Counter-reformation. In 1649, Francisco Pacheco, an artist who served as inspector of painting for the Inquisition at Seville, published a book entitled *El arte de la pintura: su antigüedad y grandeza.* There he explicitly directed that painters were to employ Revelation 12 as their guide to the representation of the Immaculate Conception.[30] Whether or not the well-educated Sánchez had consulted a work like Pacheco's, there is little doubt that his identification of the Virgin of Guadalupe with the woman of Revelation 12 was strongly influenced by the prescriptive religious aesthetic of the Counter-reformation. Thus, in arguing that the events of Tepeyac were a fulfillment of scripture that confirmed the divine design involved in the Spanish conquest of Mexico, Sánchez simultaneously argued for the hermeneutical sufficiency (and exclusive privilege) of European Christian categories for comprehending and communicating religious experience in the Americas.

As for the particulars of Sánchez's reading of Revelation 12 in the context of the hierophany at Tepeyac, the following examples illustrate his approach. Citing Psalm 121:6 (Vulgate 120:6), "The sun shall not strike you by day," in his comments on Revelation 12:1, Sánchez writes:

> The Virgin Mary, in this image of her as *Amicta Sole,* [is] clothed with the sun, surrounded with the sun as though in a niche, on a throne or in a tabernacle, promising to the earth through the words of David, assurance that the sun will not strike it by day. "By day the sun will not strike you" (Psalm 120 [121]) . . . We have come to know as something evident that naturally this land and this New World were a torrid zone and a region parched by the sun, always presumed to be uninhabitable. Most holy Mary took control of the sun, moderated its rigors, reduced its flames, calmed its fire, tempered its rays.[31]

Here Sánchez moves swiftly from the text of Revelation 12:1, "clothed with the sun," to the image of Our Lady of Guadalupe, and back to a biblical verse that by its mention of the sun brings both the Apocalypse and the image of Guadalupe to bear on the particular Mexican context within which this reading took place. Sánchez's *criollo* agenda lurks just beneath the surface of his fanciful suggestion that it was the Marian intervention that tamed the extremes of the Mexican climate on behalf of her own people. In declaring the New World uninhabitable by virtue of its torrid climate, Sánchez discounts the presence of the indigenous peoples who lived under the Mexican sun that the Spanish found so intolerable.

Where he did make specific reference to the religious beliefs and practices of the indigenous peoples of the Americas, Sánchez did so in order to denounce them as idolatrous. While Sánchez was not alone in this assessment, his *Imagen de la Virgen* is singular in its enlistment of Revelation 12:12 for this purpose, "woe to the earth and the sea, for the devil has come down to you with great wrath." Sánchez comments,

> We depict the dragon with the full likeness, properties and signs of the demon of the idolatry of this land, with its paganism. Finding him now cast down to earth together with his follow demons . . . we proceed in our understanding of these as the many idols which the Indians adore . . . over whom there presides, like another Lucifer, an idol named *Guitzilopusco.*[32]

As for the apparition of the Virgin Mary at Tepeyac, Sánchez drew on Revelation 12:6, "The woman fled into the wilderness, where she has a place prepared by God." For Sánchez, the New World was that wilderness, into which the Virgin Mary came as the New Eve in order to plant the New Paradise:

> To the wilderness, to a place that God has prepared for her, fled the woman who appeared in the heavens, adorned with all the lights that once made her radiant. "The woman fled into the wilderness, where she had a place prepared for her by God." Let us say that the Virgin Mary came to this wilderness of the New World, a land of paganism. She wished to appear and to reveal herself, choosing a fortunate place at the site of the wilderness of Guadalupe, where she demonstrated that it was her intention to establish a new paradise. From the mountain she called to her John. On the mountain sprang up the miraculous flowers that bore fruit in her flowery image.[33]

Here John, the seer on Patmos, becomes Juan Diego at Tepeyac. Guadalupe was the place prepared by God for the Virgin Mary, the woman clothed with the sun. The flowers miraculously sent by Mary as testimony to the bishop recall the Garden of Eden wherein Mary of Guadalupe is the New Eve, and the image itself constitutes lasting testimony to the Virgin's desire to establish the New Paradise in this land. Sánchez dubbed this New Eve the first *criolla.*

Although Sánchez's *Imagen de la Virgen* was "baroque in character, its style ornate and repetitious,"[34] and in spite of the fact that not many copies were printed, its presentation of Our Lady of Guadalupe as a rereading of Revelation 12 established a lasting association between the Virgin of the image and the woman of the text.[35] For instance, the connection between the woman clothed with the sun and the Virgin of Tepeyac first articulated in print by Sánchez recurs in the only sonnet that Sor Juana Inés de la Cruz (1648-95) specifically devoted to Our Lady of Guadalupe:

> This Marvel, composed of flowers,
> Divine American protectress
> who from a rose of Castile,
> is transformed into a Mexican rose;
> She whose proud foot made the dragon
> humbly bend his neck at Patmos.[36]

The allegorical reading of Revelation 12 in connection with Our Lady of Guadalupe took broad and evident hold in seventeenth- and eighteen-century Mexican preaching. In the preface to one such sermon, originally preached on December 12, 1748, by Francisco Javier Carranza, we read: "In Chapter 12 of Revelation, which so truthfully describes the miraculous apparition of our Lady of Guadalupe, following the evangelist's ecstatic vision of this prodigy, the celestial woman . . . "[37]

Six months after the appearance of Sánchez's *Imagen de la Virgen*, Luis Lasso de la Vega, whose letter to Sánchez indicates the high regard in which he held that work, published his own account of the events at Tepeyac. In the introduction to that work, framed as a prayer to the Virgin Mary, Lasso de la Vega explains his purpose:

> The fact has enticed and encouraged me to write in the Nahuatl language the very great miracle by which you revealed yourself to people and have given them your image, [which] is here in your precious home in Tepeyac. May the Indians see there and know in their language all that you have done on their behalf and your love for people.[38]

Lasso de la Vega's *Huey tlamahuiçoltica* (by a great miracle) includes the *Nican mopohua* (here is recounted), an account of the apparitions at Tepeyac written in what almost all commentators recognize as excellent Nahuatl. Though its appearance in Lasso de la Vega's book was the first publication of the *Nican mopohua*, it is highly likely that this printed version reproduces an already familiar account, the composition of which is often dated to the mid-sixteenth century and which has often been attributed to Antonio Valeriano (d. 1605).[39]

There are striking differences between Sánchez's *Imagen de la Virgen* and the *Nican mopohua*. The former, with its elaborate emphasis on bringing the symbolism of Tepeyac into line with the biblical symbolism of Revelation 12, downplays the indigenous Nahua elements of the account. As Poole points out, the *Nican mopohua* recounts Mary's caring and gentle words to Juan Diego as she asks that a church be built:

> I ardently wish and I greatly desire that they build my temple for me here, where I will reveal, I will make known, and I will give to people all my love, my compassion, my aid, and my protection, for I am your compassionate mother. There I will hear their weeping and their sorrows in order to remedy and heal all their various afflictions, their miseries, and their torments.[40]

The corresponding message in Sánchez's *Imagen de la Virgen* is relatively spare:

> I want a house and ermita built for me here, a temple in which to show myself a compassionate mother with you, with yours, with my devotees, with those who seek me in order to remedy their needs.[41]

A similar contrast is found in the accounts the two works provide of Mary's words to Juan Diego about the illness of his uncle, Juan Bernardino. In the *Nican mopohua* she says:

> Know, rest very much assured, my youngest child, let nothing whatever frighten or worry you. Do not be concerned. Do not fear [your uncle's] illness nor any illness or affliction. Am I, your mother, not here? Are you not under my shade and my shadow? Am I not your happiness? Are you not in my lap and my carrying gear? Is there anything more you need? Do not let anything worry you further or upset you. Do not let your uncle's illness worry you. He will not die of what is now upon him. Rest assured, for he is already well.[42]

By comparison with this lavish expression of the Virgin's compassion toward Juan Diego and the caring insistence of her reassuring words, the version found in Sánchez's *Imagen de la Virgen* reads, as Poole quips, with all the "poignancy of the government report":

> He was [not] to fear dangers, fear illnesses, nor be afflicted in his tasks, taking her for his mother, for his health and protection, that the illness of his uncle, who was not to be in danger of death, would

not hinder him, and she assured him from that moment he was completely well.[43]

The differences in tone betray the difference in focus between the two accounts. Whereas the *Nican mopohua* focused on the events at Tepeyac, on the encounters between the Virgin and Juan Diego, with deliberate attention to the indigenous symbolism of the event itself and of the image that testifies to it, Sánchez demonstrated more interest in the Christian biblical text that provided the symbolic lexicon for his interpretation of the hierophany at Tepeyac.

What makes our own attention to the interpretation of Revelation 12 in Sánchez's *Imagen de la Virgen* and our comparison of this work with the *Nican mopohua* more than just a study in the history of biblical interpretation in seventeenth-century Mexico is the abiding power of Our Lady of Guadalupe for Mexicans and, more broadly, for U.S. Hispanic Americans who are not of Mexican descent.[44] U.S. Hispanic American scholars have written much about the place of Our Lady of Guadalupe in the religious experience of Latinas and Latinos today.[45] Yet very seldom have they attended to the symbolic link (first drawn by Sánchez) between Our Lady of Guadalupe and Revelation 12, "reading" the former through the lens of the latter.[46]

With its use of Revelation 12:1-2 as an epigraph, Virgil Elizondo's *Guadalupe: Mother of the New Creation* is a noteworthy exception.[47] This citation notwithstanding, Elizondo emphasizes the Nahuatl symbolism of the hierophany at Tepeyac:

> The story of Our Lady of Guadalupe is the indigenous account of the real new beginnings of the Americas. The story of her appearances and compassion is sacred narrative as remembered by the victim-survivors of the conquest who were equally the first-born of the new creation. The entire Guadalupe event as recorded in the *Nican Mopohua* is a Nahuatl communication par excellence . . . Each detail had special significance for the Nahuatl peoples. The story came from their world, and if we are to discover its regenerative signification, we must seek to understand it through their cosmovision.[48]

For Elizondo, as for other U.S. Hispanic American theologians, it is the narrative of the *Nican mopohua* and not Miguel Sánchez's *Imagen de la Virgen* that furnishes the primary source material for reflection on the significance of Our Lady of Guadalupe. The former appealed to its intended audience by tapping traditional Nahua religious symbolism. The latter wrapped the Mexican Guadalupe in the mantle of the New Testament canon that was familiar to the *conquistadores* and their children. Thus, despite the frequent citations of Revelation 12 since 1648 in connection with Our Lady of Guadalupe, there has been relatively little deliberate reflection on the hermeneutical implications of these "readings" of the Tepeyac hierophany as conscious rereadings of Revelation 12.[49]

Many scholars have noted that Tepeyac was sacred to the Nahua goddess Tonantzin, and the iconographic links between this deity and the Virgin of Guadalupe are underscored:

> She was frequently said to be pregnant or to be carrying a small child on her back or arms. When depicted as pregnant the religious symbol representing the fundamental reconciliation of opposites was placed over her womb . . . She dressed in a particular type of tunic, wore a mantle, and was connected in myth to the serpent high god.[50]

Orlando Espín observes that

> Juan Diego's Mary assumes the symbols that are useful for Christianity but rejects those that could identify her with the old religion [Nahua religion] or that appear to at least condone it. In so doing, the Virgin of Guadalupe followed a long history of Christian appropriation and use of symbols from newly converted peoples.[51]

Elsewhere Espín hastens to explain that

> The Virgin of Guadalupe cannot be simply identified with Tonantzin—not even at the very beginning. But I do not see either how the natives could have simply identified Guadalupe with the Catholic Mary. From the start, it seems that there was an effort (on the part of the Amerindians) at speaking a religious language through culturally understandable religious categories, that would interpret for them the Christian message about God.[52]

The books of Sánchez and of Lasso de la Vega, therefore, represent different directions taken in the same process of recontextualization, of finding a place for the hierophany at Tepeyac in the traditional Nahua religious iconography (Lasso de la Vega) and in traditional Christian biblical language (Sánchez). At the same time, both volumes represent substantial (though divergent) efforts to provide the Guadalupe icon with narrative texts.

What, if anything, is to be made of the 116-year gap between the events at Tepeyac and the publication of accounts of those events? While scholars struggle with the process of investigating the traditional sources that underlie both works, grappling, in that process, with such differences in detail between the two accounts as the chronology, the number of apparitions, and so forth, their appearance *in print* clearly represents a significant development. Without pushing the connection too far, it might be ventured that the move from the (ongoing) oral transmission of popular traditions about the apparitions at Tepeyac to the "canonization" of the accounts in print bears some comparison with the founding dynamics of the gospel, which began with popular traditions in the first century C.E. and only gradually achieved fixed form in texts. At the same time, just as the formation of the New Testament canon by no means put an end to the transmission of the gospel, it must also be recognized that the appearance in print of accounts of the hierophany at Tepeyac, beginning with those of Sánchez and Lasso de la Vega, surely did not bring the oral traditions about those events to an end. In a telling critique of the methodology of Poole's revisionist history, Espín invites us to consider whether

> perhaps Poole's fascination with colonial Mexican *elites* (and their written texts) made him blind to *popular* pneumatology as the foundational epistemology and hermeneutic of the Guadalupe story . . . Poole also unexplainably ignores that the Nahua culture (still very much alive, even after the Spanish conquest) would have transmitted its holiest and most fundamental beliefs and wisdom through oral means too; and especially after Nahuatl became alphabetized, orality remained a viable and frequent means of transmission among the majority of Nahuas.[53]

Thus, the distance of 116 years between the events at Tepeyac and the appearance of the first printed accounts of these events may well indicate that the traditions about the Virgin of Guadalupe had reached an important breadth of diffusion throughout the various ethnic and socioeconomic strata of colonial Mexico, ranging from the indigenous Nahuas, to the *criollos*, to the Spanish-born. While the dynamics of orality *vs.* literacy, the diffusion and social function of printed books in colonial Mexico, and the spread of traditions regarding the Virgin of Guadalupe all warrant closer attention, the particular interest of this essay in the use of the Bible in U.S. Hispanic theological discourse prompts several observations.

First, the application by Sánchez of the canonical text of Revelation 12, so familiar to him, to the otherness of the hierophany at Tepeyac, can be understood as an effort to wrestle with the unfamiliar in the light of European Christian religious categories. The incorporation by Lasso de la Vega of the *Nican mopohua* into his Nahuatl account of the events at Tepeyac represents an explicit effort on his part to appeal to familiar language and symbolism in order to encourage Marian devotion among Nahua audiences. Recalling Elizondo's observations about the *Nican mopohua*—"Each detail had special significance for the Nahuatl peoples. The story came from their world, and if we are to discover its regenerative signification, we must seek to understand it through their cosmovision"[54]—Lasso de la Vega's work capitalized on those details, while Sánchez's *Imagen de la Virgen* explicitly sought to substitute an alternate cosmovision. Both Lasso de la Vega and Sánchez shared a common worldview, and the publication of Lasso de la Vega's letter in Sánchez's *Imagen de la Virgen* suggests that the former took the concerns of the latter into account in the formulation of his own work, deliberately choosing an alternate approach instead of duplicating his colleague's earlier effort. Both works explored the intersection of two worldviews, the European worldview of their authors and the Nahua worldview implicit in the events at Tepeyac (and the century of oral tradition that transmitted them). Despite the differences in the traditional symbolic lexica on which they drew, both publications explained the hierophany at Tepeyac in Christian terms.

CONCLUSIONS:
LESSONS FROM A NON-INNOCENT HISTORY

A letter from indigenous peoples of the Americas to John Paul II on the occasion of a visit by the pope to Latin America provides a striking counterpoint to the story of the encounter between Pizarro and Atahualpa with which this essay began. They wrote:

> We, Indians of the Andes and of America, decided to take advantage of the visit of John Paul II to return to him his Bible, because in five centuries it has given us neither love, peace, nor justice. Please take your Bible back and return it to our oppressors, because they need its moral precepts more than we do. Because ever since the arrival of Christopher Columbus to America the culture, language, religion and European values were imposed by force. The Bible came to us as part of the imposed colonial change. It was the ideological arm of the colonialist assault.[55]

Some five complex centuries after the arrival of the Bible on the shores of the Americas in the hands of the *conquistadores*, what might U.S. Hispanic American theologians learn from the lessons of our history, from the theological discourse of our ancestors, that might serve to situate the Bible in our own theological discourse? After all, we are the heirs of Juan Diego *and* Zumárraga, of Atahualpa *and* Pizarro, of Sánchez *and* Lasso de la Vega. Our struggles to wrest meaning from our own encounters with the same sacred text once held high by the Spanish priest before the Inca crowd must reckon with all that has happened on the shores of the Americas since then, a non-innocent history in which we are deeply implicated. The histories and the narratives that fill the pages of the Bible resonate with our own histories and with the narratives told by our own *abuelas* and *abuelos* (grandmothers and grandfathers), the matriarchs and patriarchs who preserve and hand on our own living traditions.

The *mestizaje* and *mulataje* that characterize U.S. Hispanic Americans as descendants and heirs both of the conquerors and of the conquered are realities that make it impossible (and even undesirable) for us to draw clear lines of division between European culture, language, and religion, and indigenous American culture, language, and tradition. At the same time, our very *mestizaje* and *mulataje* means that we read the Bible very differently today than our ancestors did in the Americas five hundred years ago. The characterization of what the Bible may have been then, the "ideological arm of the colonialist assault," would ring strangely in the ears of participants in a parish Bible study in Brooklyn or in the ears of worshipers in a Pentecostal church in Puerto Rico. They might instead applaud the sentiments of the Reverend Edgar Avitia, "The Bible has been so good to us!"[56]

At this point I will venture a tentative turn from the descriptive to the prescriptive, focusing on the ethics of biblical interpretation. This turn recognizes that no reading of the Bible is either politically or ethically neutral, and insists that to assert otherwise is either naive or deceptive.

On the one hand, U.S. Hispanic American theologians must guard against doing what Sánchez did, if his effort is understood as a matter of expropriating the religious experience of others and objectifying it in religious language alien to those others. Whether the purpose of such objectification is disinterested academic study or inculturated evangelization, the integrity of the other's religious experience and of the other's religious traditions demands respect.

On the other hand, U.S. Hispanic American theologians should not hesitate to engage in the sort of boundary-crossing effort in which Sánchez engaged, entering into bold conversation between the old and the new, comparing the unfamiliar with the familiar. In this effort, where the Bible represents the traditional and the familiar, the theologian must recognize that genuinely contextual readings of the canonical scriptures involve the reciprocal illumination of text and context. New experience can speak in ways that shed light on ancient texts, giving birth to fresh meanings. At the same time, the familiarity of ordinary everyday experience can be challenged by the otherness of the biblical text, an otherness that points beyond the particularity of each community's experience to worlds of meaning and experience distant in time and place from the present and its concerns. If, for the Christian theologian, the Bible is to be an authoritative lens through which religious experience is focused, the optics of the lens itself require close and careful scrutiny.

At the same time, Lasso de la Vega challenges U.S. Hispanic American theologians to be open to new languages and new sources as they grapple with the religious experience of their constituencies. Yet Lasso de la Vega's work also issues a warning, urging us not to assume identities other than our own, identities with which we might clothe ourselves in order to claim to speak on behalf of others. Though not a native Nahuatl speaker himself, Lasso de la Vega wrote in Nahuatl and incorporated traditional materials in order to promote Guadalupan devotion among Nahuas. However noble this intention and approach may have been, beneath both there lurks the potential for ideological manipulation.

A further implication of the present essay has to do with the social location of U.S. Hispanic American theological discourse itself. By virtue of the technologies of their production, the publications of Sánchez and of Lasso de la Vega were both products of cultural elites. Contemporary biblical scholarship has learned, though sometimes only grudgingly, to appreciate the value and significance of popular readings of the Bible. Yet the academic articulation of and critical reflection on such readings often remains distant from and irrelevant to those who are actually engaging in them. Those who actually engage in popular readings of the Bible may not recognize either themselves or their voices in the journal articles that seek to raise such reading strategies to visibility and "respectability" in the academic forum. Thus, we need to be reminded why, as Christians and as theologians, we read the Bible in the first place. The words of Justo L. González offer an apt formulation: "[We read] *not* to understand the Bible better. It is rather to understand *ourselves* better in the light of the Word of God."[57]

The sort of authentic theological reflection that aspires to be *teología de conjunto* and that truly emerges from the heart of our people ought to bear this in mind, resisting the temptation to speak for the people in ways that reduce them to passive objects of our attention. A *teología de conjunto* that seriously engages in critical dialogue with the ancient voices that emerge from the biblical text, voices that testify to the self-disclosing God, must attend respectfully to voices outside the academy, to those who bring their own language and their own experience to their dialogue with the biblical text.

Notes

[1] Eduardo Galeano, *Memory of Fire*, trans. Cedric Belfrage (New York: Pantheon, 1985), 87-88.

[2] Here I am employing the terminology suggested by Fernando F. Segovia in "Aliens in the Promised Land: The Manifest Destiny of U.S. Hispanic American Theology," in *Hispanic/Latino Theology: Challenge and Promise*, ed. Ada María Isasi-Díaz and Fernando F. Segovia (Minneapolis, Minn.: Fortress, 1996), 15-42.

[3] This essay represents a further development of reflections previously articulated in my paper "Biblical Interpretation from a U.S. Hispanic American Perspective: A Reading of the Apocalypse," presented on May 30, 1997, at the confer-

ence *The Hispanic Presence in the U.S. Catholic Church* at the Catholic University of America, Washington, D.C.

⁴ The encounter between Atahualpa and the Spanish *conquistadores* in Cajamarca Plaza in November 1532 occupies a pivotal place in the narratives, past and present, of the conquest of Peru. There has been extensive discussion of whether the book fell from Atahualpa's hand, or, as Galeano's dramatization has it, Atahualpa threw or dropped it. See the insightful literary critical and anthropological analysis by Patricia Reed, "'Failing to Marvel': Atahualapa's Encounter with the Word," *Latin American Research Review* 26 (1991), 7-32.

⁵ Reed, "'Failing to Marvel,'" 8, citing Claude Lévi-Strauss, *Tristes Tropiques* (Paris: Plon, 1955), 291; and Jacques Derrida, "The Violence of the Letter," in *Of Grammatology*, trans. Gayatri Spivak (Baltimore: Johns Hopkins University Press, 1976).

⁶ On the notion of non-innocent history, see Justo L. González, *Mañana: Christian Theology from a Hispanic Perspective* (Nashville, Tenn.: Abingdon, 1985), especially 40, 77-78.

⁷ In his contribution to this volume entitled *"Pueblo* and Church," Gary Riebe-Estrella offers a valuable example of the ways in which the Bible can figure positively in the discourse of U.S. Hispanic/American systematic theology. Riebe-Estrella offers a contextual reading of important traditions in the Hebrew Bible in view of their implications for the construction of a U.S. Hispanic American ecclesiology centering on the church as the People of God.

⁸ In its 1993 instruction, *The Interpretation of the Bible in the Church*, the Pontifical Biblical Commission strongly encouraged conversation and cooperation between biblical exegetes and systematic theologians: "Without being the sole *locus theologicus*, Sacred Scripture provides the privileged foundation of theological studies. In order to interpret Scripture with scholarly accuracy and precision, theologians need the work of exegetes. From their side, exegetes must orientate their research in such fashion that 'the study of Sacred Scripture' can be in reality 'as it were the soul of Theology.' To achieve this, they ought to pay particular attention to the religious content of the biblical writings" (Joseph A. Fitzmyer, *The Biblical Commission's Document, "The Interpretation of the Bible in the Church," Subsidia Biblica* 18 [Rome: Editrice Pontificio Istituto Biblico, 1995], 165). The document itself is also available in *Origins* 23, 29 (January 6, 1994), 497-524; and in pamphlet form as *The Interpretation of the Bible in the Church* (Vatican City: Libreria Editrice Vaticana, 1993).

⁹ The expression is from Fernando F. Segovia, "Hispanic American Theology and the Bible: Effective Weapon and Faithful Ally," in *We Are a People! Initiatives in Hispanic American Theology*, ed. Roberto S. Goizueta (Minneapolis, Minn.: Fortress, 1992), 21-49. On the Bible and the Conquest, see Elsa Tamez, "Quetzalcóatl Challenges the Christian Bible," *Journal of Hispanic/Latino Theology* 4:4 (1997), 6-10.

¹⁰ Unless otherwise noted, biblical translations are from the New Revised Standard Version.

¹¹ Luis N. Rivera, *A Violent Evangelism: The Political and Religious Conquest of the Americas* (Louisville, Ky.: Westminster/John Knox, 1992), 236. Rivera notes Columbus's "keen consciousness of being chosen by God to find the fabulous lands he pursued," and cites Columbus's own words in evidence: "It was our Lord who clearly opened my understanding regarding the need to travel from here to the Indies, and he opened my will so that I would carry it out" (ibid., 55). On Columbus as biblical interpreter, see Hector Avalos, "Columbus as Biblical

Exegete: A Study of the *Libro de las profecías*," in *Religion in the Age of Exploration: The Case of Spain and New Spain*, ed. Bryan F. Le Beau and Menachem Mor (Omaha, Neb.: Creighton University Press, 1996), 59-80.

¹² Ibid., 237.

¹³ Bartolomé de Las Casas was also present, and the specific contents of Montesinos's sermon has come down to us only in the version reported by Las Casas. See Gustavo Gutiérrez, *Las Casas: In Search of the Poor of Jesus Christ*, trans. Robert R. Barr (Maryknoll, N.Y.: Orbis Books, 1993), 27-37.

¹⁴ Ibid., 32. Gutiérrez cites the *Tradado de doce dudas* of Las Casas: "At least since the year 1510, now that, by God's grace, we are in the year 1564, there has never been, nor is there today a person in all the Indies who has ever had good faith."

¹⁵ Gutiérrez, *Las Casas*, 47-51.

¹⁶ Rivera, *A Violent Evangelism*, 238.

¹⁷ Ibid., 240-41.

¹⁸ Ibid., 237. See Juan Ginés de Sepúlveda, *Demócrates segundo o de las justas causas de la guerra contra los indios*, trans. Angel Losada (Madrid: Consejo Superior de Investigaciones Científicas, 1951).

¹⁹ Las Casas, *In Defense of the Indians*, as cited in Rivera, *A Violent Evangelism*, 237. See Vidal Abril-Castelló, "La bipolarización Sepúlveda–Las Casas: la revolución de la duodecima republica," in *La Etica en la conquista de América*, ed. D. Ramos et al. (Corpus Hispanorum de Pace, vol. 25; Madrid: Consejo Superior de Investigaciones Científicas, 1984), 229-88.

²⁰ As cited in Rivera, *A Violent Evangelism*, 238.

²¹ Ibid., 237, 239.

²² Miguel Sánchez, *Imagen de la Virgen María Madre de Dios de Guadalupe milagrosamente aparecida en México: Celebrada en su historia, con la profecía del capitulo doce del Apocalipsis* (Mexico City: Imprenta de la Viuda de Bernardo Calderón, 1648). Reprinted in *Testimonios históricos guadalupanos*, ed. Ernesto de la Torre Villar and Ramiro Navarro de Anda (Mexico City: Fondo de Cultúra Económica, 1982), 153-267.

²³ Luis Lasso de la Vega, *Huey tlamahuiçoltica omonexiti in ilhuicac tlatocacihualpilli Santa Maria totlaçonantzin Guadalupe in nican huey altepenahuac Mexico itocayocan Tepeyacac* (Mexico City: Imprenta de Iuan Ruiz, 1649). Reprinted in *Testimonios históricos guadalupanos*, 282-308.

²⁴ Antonio de Robles, as cited in Stafford Poole, *Our Lady of Guadalupe: The Origins and Sources of a Mexican National Symbol, 1531-1797* (Tucson, Ariz.: University of Arizona Press, 1995), 108.

²⁵ Francisco de la Maza, *El Guadalupanismo mexicano* (Mexico City: Fondo de Cultura Económica, 1981), 50, as cited in Jacques Lafaye, *Quetzalcóatl and Guadalupe: The Formation of Mexican National Consciousness, 1531-1813*, trans. Benjamin Keen (Chicago: University of Chicago Press, 1987), 246.

²⁶ Sánchez, *Imagen de la Virgen*, 264—my translation.

²⁷ Throughout this study, I refer to the events at Tepeyac as a *hierophany*, that is, as a self-manifestation of the sacred. This usage is not employed in contrast to an understanding of these events as Mariophanies, as self-manifestations of the Virgin Mary. It serves instead to allow us to appreciate the impact of the works of Sánchez and Lasso de la Vega on the subsequent understanding of these events *as such* and of the image of Our Lady of Guadalupe, which is venerated as a lasting testimony to what took place in 1531.

²⁸ Sánchez, *Imagen de la Virgen*, 159—my translation. In his letter of approval as one of the two ecclesiastical censors of Sánchez's book, Juan de Poblete recalls

Saint Jerome's observation that the Apocalypse of John contains as many mysteries as it has words (ibid., 154).

[29] Poole, *Our Lady of Guadalupe*, 106-7.

[30] Patricia Harrington, "Mother of Death, Mother of Rebirth: The Mexican Virgin of Guadalupe," *Journal of the American Academy of Religion* 56 (1988), 35-37. Here Harrington refers to Jonathan Brown, *Images and Ideas in Seventeenth Century Spanish Painting* (Princeton, N.J.: Princeton University Press, 1978). On Francisco Pacheco, see Enrique Valdivieso, "Francisco Pacheco," in *The Dictionary of Art*, ed. Jane Turner (New York: Macmillan, 1996), 23:704-6. Valdivieso observes of Pacheco that he "enthusiastically defended iconographic orthodoxy, and this led to a strict and unvarying formula for his compositions and a certain coldness of expression." Valdivieso suggests that the decision to write *Arte de la pintura* probably emerged "from the discussions that took place in Seville among the circle of noblemen, clerics, humanists, artists and literary figures who used to gather in his studio" (ibid., 704, 705).

[31] Sánchez, *Imagen de la Virgen*, 218-19—my translation.

[32] Ibid., 226—my translation.

[33] Ibid., 228—my translation.

[34] Poole, *Our Lady of Guadalupe*, 106.

[35] Beyond its exegetical impact, Sánchez's employment of Revelation 12 in the service of his *criollo* agenda had lasting political and patriotic significance. See Lafaye, *Quetzalcóatl and Guadalupe*, 248-53.

[36] In Sor Juana Inés de la Cruz, *Obras completas*, ed. Alfonso Méndez Plancarte (Mexico City: Fondo de Cultura Económica, 1951), 1:310; Lafaye, *Quetzalcóatl and Guadalupe*, 74.

[37] La transmigración de la iglesia a Guadalupe: Sermon, que el 12 de Diciembre de 1748 años Predicó en el templo de N.S. de Guadalupe de la Ciudad de Santiago de Queretaro, el P. Prefecto Francisco Javier Carranza, Professo de quarto voto de la Sagrada Compañia de Jesús (Mexico City: En el Colegio Real, y Mas Antiguo de S. Ildefonso de Mexico, 1749), as cited in Lafaye, *Quetzalcóatl and Guadalupe*, 245-46.

[38] Translation from Poole, *Our Lady of Guadalupe*, 111.

[39] On the question of the attribution of the *Nican mopohua* to Valeriano, see Poole, *Our Lady of Guadalupe*, 166-69.

[40] As cited in Poole, *Our Lady of Guadalupe*, 107-8.

[41] Ibid., 108.

[42] Ibid.

[43] Ibid.

[44] See Orlando Espín, *The Faith of the People: Theological Reflections on Popular Catholicism* (Maryknoll, N.Y.: Orbis Books, 1997), 73-77. Virgilio Elizondo contends that "If our Lady of Guadalupe had not appeared, the collective struggles of the Mexican people to find meaning in their chaotic existence would have created her. The cultural clash of sixteenth-century Spain and Mexico was reconciled in the brown Lady of Tepeyac in a way no other symbol can rival" ("Our Lady of Guadalupe as a Cultural Symbol: 'The Power of the Powerless,'" in *Liturgy and Cultural Religious Traditions*, ed. Herman Schmidt and David Power, Concilium 102 [New York: Seabury, 1977], 25).

[45] See, for example, Jeanette Rodríguez, *Our Lady of Guadalupe: Faith and Empowerment among Mexican-American Women* (Austin, Tex.: University of Texas Press, 1994); Roberto S. Goizueta, *Caminemos con Jesús: Toward a Hispanic/Latino Theology of Accompaniment* (Maryknoll, N.Y.: Orbis Books, 1995), 37-46. On Guadalupan devotions, see Timothy M. Matovina, "Our Lady of Guadalupe Celebrations in

San Antonio, Texas, 1840-41," *Journal of Hispanic/Latino Theology* 1:1 (1993), 77-96; idem, "Guadalupan Devotion in a Borderlands Community," *Journal of Hispanic/ Latino Theology* 4:1 (1996), 6-26. See also the essays in the August 1997 issue of the *Journal of Hispanic/Latino Theology* (5:1), a special issue on Our Lady of Guadalupe, guest edited by Virgilio P. Elizondo and Timothy M. Matovina. In his essay in this volume, Orlando Espín argues that "if we were to seek out and identify the one symbol within Latino/a popular Catholicism that best explains and expresses the daily relationships that capture experiences of grace and sin, no other symbol would compare to the *Virgen* of Guadalupe (and probably some other *Vírgenes* of Latino/a devotion)" (page 137 herein). On the place of Our Lady of Charity in Cuban and Cuban-American popular Catholicism, see the essay in this volume by Miguel H. Díaz.

[46] Ironically enough, Sánchez's emphasis on Revelation 12 as the lens through which the Virgin of Guadalupe was to be understood did not even survive into the abridged version of his *Imagen de la Virgen* by Mateo de la Cruz, which was published in 1660. In effect, this Jesuit's abridgment amounts to a rewriting of the original work, simplifying its overdone style and attenuating its overt *criollismo*. See *Relación de la milagrosa aparición de la santa imagen de la Virgen de Guadalupe de México, sacada de la historia que compuso el Br. Miguel Sánchez por el P. Mateo de la Cruz* (Puebla de los Angeles: Viuda de Borja, 1660), in de la Torre Villar and Navarro de Anda, *Testimonios históricos guadalupanos*, 267-81.

[47] Virgilio Elizondo, *Guadalupe: Mother of the New Creation* (Maryknoll, N.Y.: Orbis Books, 1997), ix. Elizondo returns to this text at the very end of the book (ibid., 134). The title of the work itself has clear optimistic apocalyptic overtones.

[48] Ibid., xviii. On the notion of cosmovision, see the essay in this volume by Alejandro García-Rivera, "The Whole and the Love of Difference: Latino Metaphysics as Cosmology."

[49] We might also speculate that his omission reflects a certain distaste among many twentieth-century biblical scholars for what they would qualify as "premodern" or "popular" biblical interpretation.

[50] Espín, *The Faith of the People*, 74.

[51] Ibid., 75.

[52] Orlando O. Espín, "Popular Catholicism among Latinos," in *Hispanic Catholic Culture in the U.S.: Issues and Concerns*, ed. Jay P. Doland and Allan Figueroa Deck, Notre Dame History of Hispanic Catholics in the U.S., vol. 3 (Notre Dame, Ind.: University of Notre Dame Press, 1994), 329.

[53] Espín, *The Faith of the People*, 8. At the same time, though, it is important to be cautious about drawing too sharp a distinction between written texts and oral traditions. While it is certainly true that orality remained (and remains) an important vector for the communication of information, traditions, and values, the broadening dissemination of printed texts over the centuries makes it necessary to reckon even with the influence of texts and popular oral traditions on each other.

[54] Elizondo, *Guadalupe: Mother of the New Creation*, xviii.

[55] Cited in Tamez, "Quetzalcóatl Challenges the Christian Bible," 11.

[56] In Justo L. González, *Santa Biblia: The Bible through Hispanic Eyes* (Nashville, Tenn.: Abingdon, 1996), 23; see also González's reflections on Avitia's grateful exclamation (ibid., 115-18).

[57] González, *Mañana*, 86.

6

An Exploration into the Theology of Grace and Sin

❧

ORLANDO O. ESPÍN

University of San Diego

To reflect on grace and sin is to enter one of the most controversial and controverted fields within Christian theology. Indeed, Christianity is not understandable without what we call grace and sin. Few battles in Christian history have been so fierce as those fought over these two subjects. And few theological topics have provoked so much literature and engaged so many brilliant minds throughout the centuries.[1]

It seems, however, that every Christian generation and community is challenged to reflect again on grace and sin. Latino/a Christians are no exception. But only that theology that seriously takes into account the impact of culture, gender, and social position, and which methodologically acknowledges and incorporates the real, daily life situations of Latinos/as, can claim to be Latino/a.

Our people (as all peoples) experience sin in *everyday life*, and certainly not in strictly "religious" contexts. They experience grace too *in daily living*. A discussion of sin without considering its real-life settings would be offensive and ultimately false, because it would hide the existential dimension, and thus the victims, of sin. In other words, it would "sanitize" sin and cover up its horrors. And it would leave the sinner unnamed and uncalled to conversion. The same must be said of grace and salvation. How then to do a theology of sin and grace from the Latino/a perspective?

The sole purpose of this chapter is to suggest new possibilities for Catholic theologizing on grace and sin, specifically from the Latino/a perspective. I first offer some reflections on the role and meaning of culture for

• There's sin experienced in daily life

theology. Then I briefly point to the foundational role of daily life for this theology. And finally I attempt to indicate some elements that might be retrieved for the construction of a systematic reflection on grace and sin from the Latino/a perspective, placing particular emphases on popular Catholicism as context, on a pneumatological reading of the *Virgen* of Guadalupe, and on the (ambivalent) relationship older Latina women have with the *Virgen*.

The reader must understand that the construction of a theology of grace and sin within the scope of a single article is a nearly impossible task. Much of what is presented below would be further elaborated and more thoroughly substantiated were this chapter a book-length work. Space restrictions will not allow me to do as much as I wish. But I intend to suggest possibilities, indicate potentially rich approaches, and emphasize certain criteria for theological reflection. Furthermore, my hope is that the bibliographical and explanatory notes to the text will help the reader realize that the substantiating research is available. This chapter, therefore, should be taken as an exploratory incursion into the theology of grace and sin, as this collective book's subtitle indicates.

THERE IS NO ACULTURAL EXPERIENCE OF GRACE

Scholars argue about the most adequate description or definition of *culture*. They attempt to discover common denominators among diverse, shared "styles of humanness" (or of *praxis*) in living human communities. I understand culture to be the historically shared means and ways through which a people unveils itself (to itself, and only secondarily to others) as *human*. The most basic means and ways for this unveiling are the social construction of reality and the discovery of meaning within and through that socially constructed reality.[2]

This brief description of culture would seem to imply many things. Among others, and as I just mentioned above, there is the implication that no human society and no human individual can even dream of the possibility of existing without culture. We are in culture as in a womb from which there is no birth, because we are already born into it.

Obviously, cultures are not impermeable. They do change, grow, and die. But in the very long history of cultures, individuals and communities never explain or view themselves except through the tools of understanding granted them by culture. These "tools" place certain limits on what can be affirmed as real, as good, as true, as beautiful, as possible, and so on. Although facilitating understanding, these tools also limit it to what is culturally possible.

The church is no exception to this rule of culture.[3] Formed by individuals and communities of the most diverse cultural backgrounds, it would be nonsense to pretend that the cultures of its members have not affected the ways in which the church has understood the gospel and reflected upon it throughout the centuries. Besides being anthropological nonsense, this pretension would imply a denial of what is meant by the Incarnation.

The Christ lived in a specific time period, in a specific land, within a concrete history, and within a single culture. Jesus of Nazareth was a first-century, Palestinian Jew, and there is no way to responsibly understand him by disregarding these historical, geographical, and cultural facts. Modern biblical exegesis has more than sufficiently shown this to be true.

And, after Jesus, all Christians have also lived in historical, geographical, and (especially) cultural milieux. All Christian preaching and sacramental celebrations, all Christian witnessing and living, all Christian theologizing and doctrinal statements, and all shapes of the church throughout history have occurred within specific cultural contexts that have, of necessity, acted as occasions and tools for Christian understanding, doctrine, life, and decision-making. Nothing human in Christianity is acultural. Only that is unlimited by culture in the church which we also find unlimited by Christ's humanness: the God of love and the love of God. This is why the gospel, which Christians believe to be ultimately the message of God, can be preached, believed, and lived in any human culture; being God's, it transcends all cultures.

However, the ones who preach, believe, and live the gospel are human beings, and though the source of the gospel is not limited to culture, Christian human beings and communities are. Therefore, their way of being Christian (and of understanding the reasons for it and the consequences of it) will be necessarily cultural.

This implies many things, but for our purposes here, this centrality of culture means that the way individuals and communities humanize or dehumanize themselves is cultural. The way people are Christian (and the shape their church will take in any given historical period) is also cultural. The role of culture means for Christianity that the way a people or a person experientially perceives the love and grace of God, and the way a people or a person responds to it (faith, conversion, justification), will always be cultural. In other words, *there is no acultural Christianity, just as there is no acultural option for God, love, and salvation.*

Just as humans can dehumanize themselves, so cultures can bear the sinful imprint of the humans that create them. Cultures, all cultures, are also dehumanized and dehumanizing, and in need of the liberating love of God. All cultures need salvation. This leads me to say that, as a consequence, no culture can ever claim to be—of itself, or in comparison with other cultures—better suited to incarnate the Christian message, or better suited to theologically understand it.

Grace as it is in itself—God's eternal, inner self as relational love—might not be bound by culture. But grace as it is for and within us, *which is the only grace we experience*, can only show itself as cultural because *we* are cultural. Traditional Catholic theology used to speak of grace as being "uncreated" *and* "created."[4] In other words, grace—God's eternal, inner self as relational love—is evidently uncreated. And yet grace—God's gift of God's self to humankind, as well as God's actions for and within us—though uncreated in its source, is nevertheless "created" insofar as this self-giving and these actions of God *do occur in real history and culture* and not in some imagined, generic world. Both of the categories (created and uncreated) attempt to define grace as the way God *is*—one in God's eternal self, and the other as God is for us. If God as "grace-in-itself" is eternally transcending history and culture, God as "grace-for-and-within-us" would be utterly meaningless and beyond our perception and experience except as that grace entered our creaturely world, worked through and within our histories and our cultures, and molded itself to our (cultural!) understandings, making it possible for us to "see and touch" the "gracious" actions of the "God-who-is-for-us."[5] *To theologically speak of grace, therefore, means that we speak (and can only speak) about the human experience of grace.* And given the historical, changing character of our cultures, these experiences of God-for-us must in turn be changing, adapting, and molding themselves to our diversity. Thus, what might be perceived as a graced moment or action in one place, at one time, and for one group in human history might be perceived as "disgrace" in or for another.

God's will must include our cultural dimension, since we cannot be human without culture. Or put another way, it must be the will of God that each of us humanizes himself or herself in the manner in which we are human, and that manner is specifically cultural. To trample on the culture of a human group, therefore, might imply a denial and rejection of grace. Furthermore, it could prevent the trampled-on human group from perceiving and responding to the love of God-for-them.

THE "BIRTHING PLACE" OF A LATINO/A THEOLOGY OF GRACE: *LO COTIDIANO*

We can understand how important it is for a theology of grace to acknowledge the existential, cultural soil from which its reflections spring. This is not just a question of authenticity and intellectual honesty, or of methodological concern. It is, above all else, the admission that the *contents and parameters* of the theological reflection are made possible and determined only from within the limits of a particular culture. Any theology of grace is always and exclusively a cultural product and exercise. This does not imply, however, that no legitimate claim can be made beyond the limits of its cultural womb. If a theology is Catholic, then it can and should contribute to the broad mosaic of intuitions and perspectives that enrich and shape the worldwide church. This contribution, however, is not to be construed as claiming universal validity. Universal relevance is not equal to universal validity.[6]

Claims to universal validity usually accompany those theological productions associated with European cultures and with nations that actively participated and/or benefited from the colonial enterprise that followed the bloody conquests. A Latino/a theology of grace must avoid claiming universal validity. A Latino/a theology that is Catholic, however, has a great deal to contribute to the non-Latino/a church—it has universal relevance.

Latino/a Catholics live in this complex U.S. society. Although not all Latinos/as are poor, it seems well documented that most are.[7] Indeed, Latinos/as are (as a group) among the poorest of Americans. They often perceive themselves as powerless vis-à-vis the dominant groups in the country. These facts are not merely lamentable social, economic, and political data. These facts also indicate a perspective, a gender and social location, and a life experience within and from which most Latino/a Catholics understand life and the Christian gospel. It is in the context of poverty and second-class social status that they experience grace and sin, and elaborate their hope for salvation.

Considering that nearly *half of all U.S. Catholics are Latinos/as*, their social perspective cannot be irrelevant for a Catholic theology of grace and sin in the United States. Or, put differently, gone are the days when an authentically *American* theology of grace could be elaborated solely from the European-American perspective, without serious regard for Latino/a Catholicism, culture, and social realities.

Where, then, must we seek the starting point or "birthing place" of an authentically U.S. theology of grace from a Latino/a perspective? I suggest that the experience of *lo cotidiano* is one of the most foundational and richest of potential starting points.

The expression *lo cotidiano* refers to that which occurs and recurs daily. It is everyday reality—with its routines and its surprises, its mysterious depths and its pedestrian quality. *Lo cotidiano* is another way of saying daily life as it actually exists and as it is lived. Thus, it is a rich starting point for a theology of grace, *because* grace is only experienced and known by humans in their real life.

It must be emphasized that real life only exists in lived and living everyday reality, not in humankind's *reflections* (regardless of degree of sophistication, or lack thereof) about real life. Furthermore, *lo cotidiano* is not reducible to the "domestic," the "private," or the "individual." What is experienced and lived within *lo cotidiano* is not just "domestic" or "private"—if by these is meant a sphere somehow secondary to the most significant events and trends within a supposedly more important national or international "public" or "macro" sphere. Employment and unemployment, violence and war, educational systems, famine or plenty, mass media, global economics, information systems, international and national political decisions, etc., etc., all have a very direct impact on the daily realities of families and communities. Indeed, it might be argued that the so-called macro or public sphere only influences people's lives if, when, and to the degree that it existentially affects them at the daily or micro level.

It may be conversely argued that there is *ultimately* no real-life substance or consistency to the macro sphere. Real life exists in the concrete, the local, the familial and communal, the micro. Hence, all macro categories would ultimately be no more than constructs intended to uncover, name, and describe (from within the particular cultural interests and class contexts of specific human groups) common denominators, connections, and trends found among groupings of local (micro) realities. The successful distribution and internalization of these constructs, however, significantly depend on forces and processes—born from within the micro—which are seldom explicit in the disseminated constructs, and which often "cover," "misname," and "proscribe" the objects of the constructs.

If "daily relationships constitute the foundation and image for the totality of social relationships,"[8] then it must be from within daily relationships (that is, from within the micro) that human beings experience and develop their foundational interpretative categories for grace, sin, and salvation—experiences and interpretive categories that are later projected onto the macro sphere. Or put differently, any theology of grace is also dependent on the daily, real-life experience of the theologian *and* of his or her local community (the culturally specific *cotidiano* of the theologian) as its "birthing place."

Since no human experience of grace occurs unmediated by culture and by the everyday, then no human experience of grace occurs outside of contexts or beyond mediations that are limited and (to whatever degree) wounded by the human experience of sin.[9] In other words, the human experience of grace implies and assumes the experience of sin. Now, I am not saying that grace necessitates sin. Nor am I suggesting that the experience of grace requires the experience of sin in some sort of causal relationship. What I am arguing is that for humans to experience grace they *must* experience it as *humans* (since that is what they are, by the will of God at creation), and since nothing human is untouched or unaffected by human sin, then the cultural mediation of the human experience of grace must be understood as affected by sin too, and consequently, the experience of grace (because it is a human experience) must also imply and assume the experience of sin.

These observations must be kept in mind as we now proceed to name and describe authentic Latino/a experiences of grace and sin. We will see that the *same* living mediations (older Latina women and the Guadalupe symbol) uncover and interpret *both* grace and sin.

Grace: Latina Women[10] as Its Living Hermeneutic

The familial, neighborhood, and community relational networks are the bases of *lo cotidiano*, its popular religious mediations and its epistemology. The dynamics of conflict, which so deeply wound and shape our society, also affect Latino/a daily relationships. Indeed, the latter are the "social sacrament" of the former.

Popular Catholicism[11] embodies and epistemologically organizes daily relationships and symbolically expresses their connections to/with the broader social networks—including the "sacred" networks—through the rites, beliefs, objects, and experiences of the people's religion. Latinos/as are convinced, because of experiences mediated by their popular religion, that God is on their side, fighting their battles with them, suffering their pains and humiliations with them, in solidarity with them in their struggles for dignity and justice, and empowering them to overcome the sin that seeks to overwhelm them in society and family. But, on the other hand, the same religious mediation seems to derail the people's solidarity with each other, often blinds them to compassion and social responsibilities, condones domestic violence and the perpetuation of dehumanizing gender and family roles, and seems to perpetuate their "victim-role" self-image. Where are the experiences of grace and sin that may allow us to arrive at these conclusions?

Popular Catholicism exists within the context of *lo cotidiano*. Its various elements intertwine in and are shaped by the public and private spheres that in turn exist (equally intertwined) in *lo cotidiano*. Popular Catholicism is not a parenthesis to real life. It is part, mirror, and hermeneut (interpreter) of daily life. It has been shown that Latino/a popular religion has been and is one of the key bearers (if not *the* key bearer) of Latino/a cultural identity in the United States. Within this religious universe life (all of life) is interpreted and symbolized as nowhere else in the Latino/a cultural milieu.[12]

The people's religion does not refer solely to those relationships or contents that might be typically labeled religious in European-American culture—it refers to *all* human relationships, including the religious ones. Popular Catholicism is like an epistemological womb within which all of daily reality is produced and reproduced. Therefore, any attempt at retrieving and/or authentically constructing a Latino/a (Catholic) theology of grace and sin *must* go to and through popular Catholicism.

But before we can seek an authentically Latino/a reflection on grace and sin, as interpreted and symbolized by the people in and through their

Catholicism, we must consider the daily relationships that are the real-life foundation and content of that which is embodied in popular religion.[13]

If one were to seek out and identify the more crucial Latino/a daily relationships (and indeed the key protagonists in Latino/a popular Catholicism), mature women would easily appear as *the* leaders and interpreters of that religion and, most important, as the ones with whom Latinos/as sustain the most meaningful and deepest of daily relationships. Latina women (and, more specifically, mature women) are typically mothers, married or not, are themselves related to and supported by other older women in similar conditions, and in turn relate to and support younger women.[14]

These mature women have been responsible for the survival and resilience of popular Catholicism. This religion has acted (and continues to act) as a crucial bearer of cultural identity and empowerment within the Latino/a universe *because* mature women play the crucial roles of empowerers and bearers of cultural identity in our daily lives. On the other hand, popular Catholicism suffers from and does not seem to undo many of the consequences of patriarchal society mostly *because* its women leaders and interpreters are themselves victims of that society.[15]

How do most Latinos/as relate to and with the mature women of their daily lives? I believe that the following (acknowledgedly sweeping) descriptive statements would be held as true by most Latino/a women and men. Mature Latina women give us life and nourish it among us (either as heads of single-parent families or as indispensable breadwinners or full-time homemakers in other family settings), teach and counsel us, empower the best in us and forgive our failures, touch our hearts and minds with questions and wisdom, and open hopes and dreams for our lives. They are our refuge in childhood, our co-conspirators in young love, our guides toward responsible adulthood, our steadfast rock in suffering, and the positive validation of our talents and lives.[16]

Mature Latina women (our mothers, grandmothers, aunts, and older sisters) are also our families' wise interpreters of the biblical message and of the heart and mind of God, the teachers of ethics, and the leaders of our prayers, our family's living sacraments of God and the sacred. These women are, above all else, the ones to whom Latinos/as usually relate in the deepest and most meaningful of ways. Among the symbols of popular Catholicism nothing better captures and expresses the mature Latina woman's humanizing contributions and role than the *Virgen* of Guadalupe (and arguably other *Vírgenes* venerated by other Latinos/as). Indeed, it has been shown that Guadalupe is and has been a model for these women.[17]

Are those general elements describing actual experiences of grace? I believe so. Indeed, if, as I said above, the term *grace* labels not a thing but an experience—the human experience of God-for-and-within-us—and if it is true that it is the relational divine being (Trinity) that Christians find in the human experience of grace, and if it is necessary that all experiences of God and of God's grace be culturally mediated in order to be so understood and identified by the human subjects, and if it is true, as Christian revelation claims, that cultural humanness is the most adequate (although still infinitely inadequate) "sacrament" of God's self-outpouring incarnation, then the Latino/a experience of and relations with the mature women of our communities (and with Guadalupe, to the degree that the latter images the former, and vice versa) unveil the underlying mysterious and yet evident pneumatological experiences of the God-for-and-within-us, mediated by these women as authentic cultural forms within our people's daily life.[18]

Is it not an experience of the God-for-and-within-us, mysteriously and truly mediated by culture, to give, nourish, and defend life? Is this not grace, especially within a U.S. social context that threatens Latino/a families and culture, that regards life itself as disposable, and that deems Latino/a children as commodities to be used when convenient and persecuted when not? Doesn't this life-giving, life-nourishing, and life-defending role of mature Latina women reflect (on a human scale) what the God-for-and-within-us does?

Is it not an experience of grace to teach and counsel, to empower and validate us, when the dominant society continues its attempt to keep Latinos/as at the margins? Is it not to do as God does to forgive our failures, touch our hearts and minds with questions and wisdom, and open hopes and dreams for our lives? Is it not grace that inspires Latina women to be refuge and guide, steadfast rock, and affirmation of their people's talents and lives?

Latina women are our families' interpreters of the biblical message and of the heart and mind of God, the teachers of ethics and the leaders of our prayers, our families' living sacraments of God and the sacred. Life and their own observations (shared and affirmed by other women) have taught them wisdom. Reflection and prayer inspired them to trust in the ultimate goodness of God and human life. Their own suffering has often been their best schooling. Mature Latina women might not know the technical language of catechesis and/or theology, but they have experienced what they name through the language and symbols of popular Catholicism and of familial wisdom. Is it not grace to believe in the goodness of God and life when society is dealing Latina women so much pain? Is not such wisdom a sign of the Holy Spirit's active and gracious presence? Is it not grace that has kept the gospel alive and meaningful in and for U.S. Latino/a communities, thanks to the women, in spite of the Christian churches' persistent efforts at deculturalizing and colonizing our people as the unacceptable price to pay for what is our rightful participation in the church of Christ?

Are Latina women not interpreting the experience of grace (that is, the experience of the trinitarian God-for-and-within-us) as the sustained and courageous commitment to give life, and to defend, nourish, and affirm it—especially the life of those deemed disposable by the powerful? Is this interpretation not paralleled in Catholic trinitarian doctrine and, especially, in the Paschal mystery?

A Catholic theology of grace that would dismiss as unimportant these experiences—assuming instead that what makes a theology of grace "solid" is to focus on what theologians or councils have said in the past and on what the contemporary meaning of technical terminology might be—must in turn be unmasked as useless and false. If an authentically Latino/a Catholic theology of grace is to be constructed it *must* start from these and similar experiences as the privileged (and arguably the only) loci of God's grace in *lo cotidiano*.

Sin: Latina Women as Its Living Hermeneutic

To speak of the mature women of the Latino/a communities cannot be limited to their graced, humanizing roles. To regard them as mediators of the experience of grace in our cultural midst (mediated by their leadership and interpretive role in Latino/a communities and in popular Catholicism) cannot hide the other side: women too are victims and protagonists in the opposite movement. All humans and all things human are ambiguous and ambivalent. My emphatic defense of *lo cotidiano* as means of grace is not romantic; I emphatically assert that daily reality is *also* the means of sin.

If daily relationships constitute the foundation and image for the totality of social relationships, then we must also arrive at the conclusion that the daily relationships of Latinos/as must be understood as experiences of sin.

And mature women again appear as the interpreters and arguably as the ones with whom many Latinos/as sustain sinful and dehumanizing daily relationships. Within the context of *lo cotidiano*, women reproduce and hand on to the next generations some of the worst possible assumptions about gender and social roles and about family and community responsibilities. Any generation of women lives by and passes on the daily relationships that constitute the foundation and image for the totality of social relationships. The most terrifying and degrading of these daily relationships are embodied in incidents of and in the attitudes that justify violent domestic abuse.[19] Familial violence is suffered mainly by women and children, and it is perpetrated within and through *lo cotidiano* by adult Latino/a men *and* women who are themselves victims of a society historically built according to the rules and subsequent ideologies of successful abuse and of European/European-American heterosexual male dominance. The equally sinful heritage of Spanish, native and/or African societies, *mestizamente* incorporated into present-day Latino/a cultures, only adds to this situation.

Violent domestic abuse is not exhausted by the physical harm done to its victims. Nor is it simply coextensive with the verbal aggression that often accompanies the bodily violence. Domestic abuse begins to be unmasked at its most degrading level when it is seen as a living, daily web of fears and lies, of self-hating assumptions and self-demeaning attitudes, of raped dreams and hopes, of violated innocence and trust, perhaps in a context of alcohol, drug, and/or gambling abuse, that explode in violent verbal and/or physical assault against others, especially women and children. When the bodily harm and the verbal assault come, as they do within and as a result of that daily web of sin, they further hammer in the nails and provoke the death of the victim(s) of the relationship of abuse. Every instance of abuse, every case, seems to fit the overall pattern of a violence-prone society that often looks the other way, blames the victim, and does little to prevent domestic violence or heal its obsessive fascination with power and abuse of all kinds.

The patterns and webs of physical and/or verbal assault that Latina women and children might encounter at home parallel and display the basic patterns and webs of the physical, verbal, cultural, and/or political assault that Latinos/as (and the poor in general) experience in contemporary U.S. society. Indeed, as María Pilar Aquino so forcefully claims, "daily relationships constitute the foundation and image for the totality of social relationships."[20]

Often taught through popular Catholicism's devotions to the *Virgen* of Guadalupe, mature Latina women have been told that they must endure "like Juan Diego" the abuse, the assaults, and the violence. The call to freedom and to the struggle for justice that many Catholics have heard from Guadalupe (and indeed from the gospel!) is frequently muted here— the call itself being abused and betrayed. Often enough the message that the women (and their children) hear is a call to resignation, to patience, to endurance. Although these may be virtues in other contexts, within the web of domestic violence they are turned into accomplices of sin. The insistent message that Latina women (and, within the broader U.S. society, that most Latinos/as) must be docile and patient—a message so many times mediated and legitimized by popular Catholicism and by the institutional church—depends on sin's masterful inversion of what is meant to be virtuous into what is useful to evil. Frequently there is in the people's religion an inclination to absolutize patience and endurance at the expense of the equally holy and necessary commitments to truth and justice. Idol-making (that is, what occurs when a legitimate sacramental mediation of the divine is adulterated as the symbol overturns the primacy of the symbolized) seems to be another symptom and self-legitimizing tool of the same sinfulness uncovered in Latino/a domestic violence and in U.S. society's treatment of Latinos/as.

Are these not experiences of sin? Are mature Latina women, when they endure abuse or allow their children to be abused, not mediating the experience and perpetuation of sin? Are they not interpreting sin as fundamentally an assault against life at the level of *lo cotidiano*, paralleled by and in the assaults against life at all levels of society (cultural, political, economic)? Are mature Latina women not clearly implying that sin always creates victims? Is not life the most foundational of all divine creations and commandments, and thus is not the assault against *daily* life (which is the only life that exists) *the* foundational sin? A Catholic theology of sin must not avoid serious reflection on these experiences, living hermeneutic, and questions.

POPULAR CATHOLICISM: A SYMBOLIC HOME FOR THE EXPERIENCES OF GRACE AND SIN

The term *grace* labels not a thing but an experience—the experience of God-in-Godself, and the human experience of God-for-and-within-us (that is, uncreated and created grace, respectively, in the best classical Catholic theological terminology). Obviously the experience of God-in-Godself is not available to humans; that we speak of it, even in the vaguest of terms, is due exclusively to revelation. Christians believe, however, that divine revelation allows us to glimpse the being of the one God as lovingly relational (Trinity). And it is this relational God that Christians also and consequently encounter in the human experience of grace. Indeed, the experience of grace is discovered to be the experience of the Trinity, always and necessarily mediated by human culture within daily life.

But to speak of the Trinity and of the experience of grace assumes that the speaker has indeed lived that experience and discovered the One who can be reflected upon under the categories of grace.[21] Since in this chapter I have taken the *experience* of grace to mean the encounter (and consequences of that encounter) with the God-for-and-within-us, especially as hermeneutically mediated by the experience of mature Latina women in *lo cotidiano*, then we may ask if and how do these women, in their daily lives, *explain and express* their experiences of grace. The same questions, *mutatis mutandis*, based on our earlier reflections, must be asked in reference to the mature Latina women's experiences of sin.

I will first try to very briefly explain why I believe that popular Catholicism is the main hermeneutic or symbolic home of the Latino/a experience of grace and sin—its explanation and expression.

Popular Catholicism: Socialization of the Experience of God

Latino/a popular Catholicism is a religion.[22] To speak of it—its experiences, symbols, beliefs, and practices—presumes an understanding of *religion*. However, the term *religion* has been defined in theology and in the social sciences in so many and often contradictory ways that one may wonder if there has been or ever will be a commonly accepted definition.

Religion, in my view, is the *socialization of the experience of the divine*. This definition seems to respect the contributions of both theology and the social sciences, without belonging exclusively to one or another discipline.[23]

By "experience of the divine" I understand an encounter between human beings and some One that is strongly felt, undoubtedly experienced as near, and that (however briefly) grants meaning and fulfillment to the human beings' lives. It seems that this type of experience is available to many, not just to a few especially sensitive people.

The social sciences will and should observe and study the consequences of and the manners through which religious people live and organize religions in society. But what social scientists will not be able to do is judge as true or false human participation in the experience of the divine. In other words, the experience of the divine is beyond the observation of the nonparticipant.[24] The effects of the experience are indeed observable, but not the experience itself or its meaning for believers. Of the experience and its meaning we only have the witness of those who claim to have shared in it.

The experience of the divine always occurs in human culture. But without a prior, explicit acknowledgment that religion is born out of an experience that is perceived by the believers as an encounter with the divine (however the latter is explained), we would not do justice to the faith of the believers nor would we understand that very core which their witness claims as *the most fundamental reason and cause for their belief*. In no way does this acknowledgment impose on the theologian the need to accept anything concerning "God," as explained or intuited by popular Catholicism. What it does is respect the most basic starting point: any religion (including popular Catholicism) exists *because* those who believe in it claim to have encountered the divine. And it is this claim—whose experiential core is unavailable to nonparticipants—that makes a believer out of a human being.

But even after emphasizing that the experience of the divine lies at the core of all religion, and that without this one element there would be no religion, we must also recall that the same testimonies that point to the human encounter with "God" signal precisely that it is an *encounter*. One of the two involved is, by definition, contextualized in a concrete culture, in a concrete society, and in a concrete history. Culture does not exist in a historical vacuum. In a dialectical process, it is born in and of society. Every human society creates culture, and every culture in turn enters the process that creates society.

So, if the experience of the divine can only happen in culture, this also means that it can only occur in society. And just as culture imposes its epistemological, hermeneutic limits on the religious experience, so does society. The "place" of a religious individual or group in society will also shape the language, symbols, and so forth used by that individual or group in the process of interpreting religious experience, thereby also shaping the experience itself as religious and the image(s) of the One encountered as divine. Therefore, not only culture but also social place make possible the diverse interpretations of the religious experiences of humankind.

Experience of God in Culture, Class, and Conflict

The above remarks might not seem important until we recall that in today's urban societies the social place of individuals and groups, and of the cultures and subcultures born in and from them, bears the mark of conflict. Whether we wish consciously to identify or to name the conflict or not, in contemporary U.S. society it is not possible to believe in good conscience that millions of Latinos/as chose to become part of the subaltern in society. It is impossible to argue that there is something genetic or deliberately chosen in the lower social place of U.S. Latinos/as. The fact (and unfortunately it is a fact) that most Latinos/as are at society's bottom has a great deal to do with ongoing conflict. The experiences of the divine culturally and societally available to them bear this mark.

The hegemonic[25] epistemology in U.S. society has managed to keep Latinos/as and their popular Catholicism "in their place." And it is from this place that they claim to have encountered the divine. So, if our preceding observations are correct, the God and the grace experienced by Latinos/as are (necessarily!) culturally and socially contextualized in ways possible to them, and expressive of the language, symbols, understandings, and images of the divine shaped by *their* culture, by *their* social place, and by the *conflict* underlying much of U.S. society. Thus, their religion cannot be like the religion of other Christians whose social place is different, who might not be at the bottom of society's ladder, and/or who benefit from the current configuration of U.S. society.[26]

Any individual or group in society may experience the divine.[27] Important differences among people and groups will not be found so much in the claim to have encountered the divine but in *how* the divine is imaged, in *how* the experience of grace is undergone and interpreted, and so on. And just as it is impossible to conceive of the existence of an event without some prior understanding that would allow it to be labeled as existing, it is equally impossible to speak or conceive of an experience of the divine or of grace without the prior understandings provided by culture, gender, and social place. Therefore, the most important difference among individuals and groups in reference to experiences of the divine will be on which interpretations and images of the divine are presented to the rest of society and how these are received.

In other words, even if it may be true that the divine can be experienced by anyone or any group, the very instant an experience is perceived as "of the divine," or "of grace," the culture, social place, and gender of the individual or group utilize hermeneutic tools made available by that person's or group's standing in society, thereby making any subsequent testimony or report of the experience acceptable and "respectable" in society *in the same manner and degree as are given to the culture, gender, and social place of that individual or group.*[28]

The religious subject will interpret and attempt to remember, symbolize, and live by that which he or she experienced in the encounter with the divine. When this interpretation and these attempts are shared by others who also claim to have met God, however God is imaged, a religion is born. When an individual or group "pours" the experience of the divine into culturally meaningful symbols, images, memories, ethical or doctrinal explanations, and guidelines for living that can be shared by others in society, the experience becomes "socialized."

In theological terms, there is religion only where the experience of God has become truly incarnate in the culture, history, and life of the believing people. And, among other consequences, this implies, for example, that the Catholicism of the hegemonic group and their allies in a society will express itself through the symbols, images, and lifestyles of hegemony, which are not those of the socially marginalized Catholic groups in that same society.[29] But to the degree that the hegemonic religious symbols, images, and lifestyles have penetrated the marginalized, and to the degree that the memory of Christianity's marginal origins have remained among the hegemonic groups, people on both sides of society can claim to participate in the same Catholic religion.[30]

If it is true that Catholicism of its very nature must incarnate and symbolize the social and historical realities of its believers, then *there cannot be one single way of being Catholic or of experiencing grace and sin.*[31] The different ways will reflect the conflicts, social places, classes, cultures, genders, and everything else that are common part and parcel of human societies.[32]

If in the United States the Latino/a communities by and large are discriminated against, the objects of racism and bigotry, and the victims of injustice, then their Catholicism (and their experiences of grace and sin) cannot possibly be understood without further prejudice unless the conflicts and suffering of these communities are admitted as truly *shaping their experiences* of God, of grace and sin, and their socialization of these.

But by the same token, to the degree that other U.S. Catholics (including some communities of U.S. Latino/a Catholics) have benefited by their access to the hegemonic groups and ideologies (whose byproduct has been, among others, the marginalization of most Latinos/as), to that degree *their* Catholicism and *their* experiences of grace and sin are shaped in the likeness of society's victors, and they participate in the hegemonic power and culture that legitimize the marginalization of others.

"Meaning-ful Home" of lo cotidiano—Our Collective, Daily Being

Popular Catholicism has an extraordinary importance in the daily lives—*lo cotidiano*—of Latinos/as. This religious universe, as it has been shown, is *not* mainly or more significantly the sum of devotions, rituals, beliefs, and doctrines that may be retrieved from the people's religion. Popular Catholicism is, arguably, and above all else, an epistemology—a way of knowing and constructing the real by means that are specifically Latino/a.[33] Indeed, it has been shown that popular Catholicism is one of the most foundational (if not *the* most foundational) bearers of Latino/a social and cultural identity. It is the "meaning-ful home" of our collective, daily being.

The people's religion may be compared, no more and no less, to any human family where humanization *and* dehumanization mix in *lo cotidiano*, and where neither dimension alone defines or exhausts it. In its mediation of the experience of grace, popular Catholicism (as human creation), therefore, also mediates the experience of sin. Consequently, it is reasonable to seek within popular Catholicism the signs of the Latino/a experience of grace and of the Latino/a experience of sin.[34] The people's religion is not the source of the experiences of grace and sin, but it is the privileged "sacrament" and repository of their memory, their wisdom, their wounds, and of the most significant daily realities of Latinos/as. That is ultimately why we go to popular Catholicism in order to uncover authentically Latino/a experiences of grace and sin.

Scholars are sometimes inclined to seek long lists of odd rituals or of theologically exotic beliefs when searching for Latino/a popular Catholicism's religious and/or theological "core." This approach assumes and perpetuates the marginalization of our people's real-life faith, casting it into a secondary "folk," "curious," or "popularized" mold vis-à-vis an otherwise (assumed to be) "real and official" Catholicism. Thus, the ecclesiastical institution is held up by many scholars as the witness to "true" Catholicism, while the real-life, daily-life religion of most Catholics is regarded as an adulterated version of the institutional "norm."

I have serious philosophical and theological difficulties with a scholarly method such as the one just described because it studies the outward, sociological, cultural, and even doctrinal forms (necessary as these might be) without a *methodologically* significant regard for the religious *experiences* that ultimately legitimize and sustain the forms. That sort of approach to popular Catholicism misses the main reason for this religion's extraordinary staying power and resilience, it covers up popular Catholicism's more significant threats to dominant culture and its religious doctrinal/institutional forms, and it implies or assumes as self-evident an ecclesiology that is woefully inadequate. As I said above, popular Catholicism is, arguably, and above all else, *an epistemology—a way of knowing and constructing the "real" by means that are culturally specific Latino/a—grounded in an equally culturally specific (and legitimate) experience of God.*

Popular Catholicism exists within the context of *lo cotidiano*. Therefore, its various elements intertwine in and are shaped by the public and private spheres that in turn exist (equally intertwined) in *lo cotidiano*. Popular Catholicism is not a parenthesis to real life. It is part, mirror, and hermeneut of real, daily life. The people's religion does not refer solely to those relationships or contents that might be typically labeled religious in European-American culture—it refers to *all* human relationships. Popular Catholicism is like an epistemological womb within which all of daily reality is produced, reproduced, and lived out.

GUADALUPE: AMBIVALENT SYMBOL OF GRACE AND SIN

If we were to seek out and identify the one symbol within Latino/a popular Catholicism that best explains and expresses the daily relationships that capture experiences of grace and sin, no other symbol would compare to the *Virgen* of Guadalupe (and probably some other *Vírgenes* of Latino/a devotion). Much has been written on Guadalupe in Latino/a religion and culture, and beyond, so I will not repeat here research results readily available elsewhere.[35]

The Virgen of Guadalupe and Pneumatology

Why do I believe that Guadalupe rather than Jesus is the best symbol for grace? If Latino/a Catholicism *is* Christian (and I firmly believe that it is!),[36] how can grace's best symbol not be Jesus? First of all, we must remember that Christians do not believe only in Jesus of Nazareth. Although we might find it easier to explain Christianity christocentrically, we must not forget that Christians (at least mainstream Christians) are *trinitarian*. No mainstream Christian, therefore, believes *only* in Jesus. Theologically that is untenable. And even if it is clear that no intrinsic contradiction or opposition should be found between sound christology and sound trinitarian doctrine, the former cannot be held to be sound without explicit connection to the latter (and vice versa).

Second, it has been suggested by myself and others (with significant evidence to support the suggestion) that Latino/a devotion to the *Virgen* of Guadalupe might not always—in fact, probably seldom—have to do with the historical Mary of Nazareth, the mother of Jesus.[37] Furthermore, some of us have argued that it is time to look again at the Guadalupe apparition story and subsequent devotion from the perspective of *pneumatology*, with a careful analysis of the cultural, historical, and sociopolitical rootings of the symbols involved—including the very appropriation of otherwise Spanish Marian symbols and categories in early colonial Mexico and thereafter. Perhaps it is time to seriously question if Guadalupe is (or has ever been) really Marian *or* is in fact pneumatological for the majority of Latinos/as.[38] I am not suggesting that Mary *is* the Holy Spirit (a theologically impossible affirmation). I am, however, asking whether the *Virgen* of Guadalupe is Mary of Nazareth at all. Indeed, I am proposing that a pneumatological reading of the Guadalupe story and devotion would enrich a Latino/a theology of grace and sin (besides opening up important new vistas in mainstream Christian theologies of the Holy Spirit). Let me explain.

If the majority of Latinos/as (especially mature Latinas) relate to Guadalupe in ways that any mainstream Christian pneumatology would expect with respect to the Holy Spirit,[39] and if the people's expectations, "gifts" received, and explanations surrounding the Guadalupe devotion all seem to fit those that mainstream pneumatologies would associate with the Holy Spirit, is it unreasonable to question whether in fact we might not be dealing in the case of Guadalupe with the Holy Spirit?[40] Must the symbols and language traditionally connected with the Spirit only be those of European cultural and philosophical origins? Couldn't the symbols and language associated with Marian devotions, given the historical, cultural, and sociopolitical events that profoundly rocked early colonial Mexico, have been "transferred" by the recently conquered people to the still new (to them) doctrine of the Holy Spirit?[41] Didn't something similar happen in early christology with Wisdom and Logos thought and language that had historically preceded christological reflection? Haven't feminist scholars clearly shown the processes and consequences of so many of these "transfers" in Christian and Western history?[42] Why couldn't the same process, *mutatis mutandi*, occur again and in connection with the Holy Spirit? I strongly suspect, indeed I am increasingly convinced, that this is what happened in early colonial Mexico, and that once the symbolic "transfer" was made from the traditional mariological to the newly inculturated pneumatological, it gained the depth of understanding and familiarity necessary to explain its holding power and resilience among later generations of Mexicans and Latinos/as. The clergy's later efforts at "mariologizing" Guadalupe have not been as successful as the ecclesiastical institution wants to believe.

Latina Women and Guadalupe: Experience of Grace

If Guadalupe is a Latino/a culturally authentic language and symbol of the Holy Spirit (and, therefore, *not* of Mary of Nazareth), it then has a crucial and legitimate place in the theological reflection on grace. And yet it remains, as all human language and symbols, a cultural creation. Implied in this is the inevitable conclusion that the Guadalupe devotion is humanly limited and thus open to the consequences of sin, as all things human are. Nevertheless, and for that very reason, it also remains open to the possibility of mediating God and God's grace.

Were we to delve into the way mature Latina women relate to Guadalupe, keeping in mind the symbolic, cultural "transference" I pointed to in the last section, we would retrieve very similar results to those suggested by Elizabeth Johnson and Jeanette Rodríguez.[43] Mature Latinas would indeed claim that in and through Guadalupe they encounter and experience the God-who-is-for-us (and, again, not the historical Mary of Nazareth) as mother, as compassion, as power, as active and intimate presence, and as (re)creative/empowering energy. I would add, as further explicitation, that in Guadalupe Latinas also encounter and experience God-for-us as wisdom and understanding.[44] Put briefly, Latinas experience *grace* in and through the *Virgen* of Guadalupe.

Even the most superficial of observations would confirm that Guadalupe is most frequently experienced as mother. The qualities Latino/a cultures expect in the ideal mother can be experienced in Guadalupe—unconditional love and *acogida*, affirming nurture, *acompañamiento*. As specifications and consequences of this maternal role, Guadalupe is also found to be the wise counselor, compassionate with all but especially with the weakest members of the community, empowering the people to continue fighting in the face of adversity, sharing their joys and sorrows, promoting solidarity, encouraging and supporting creative decisions, and making God's active presence and love felt and known within the lives of Latinos/as.

That which can be experienced in and through the *Virgen* of Guadalupe, in other words, is (with the limitations indicated earlier) the God-with-and-for-us—that is, created grace. By engaging Guadalupe and responding to her, Latinos/as participate in the life of God and culturally image the gifts of the Spirit. Mature Latinas certainly encounter the pneumatological reality of the divine (the Holy Spirit) in and through the Guadalupe symbol. Are the Latina women's experience of and relationship with the *Virgen* uncovering actual experiences of grace? I believe so. Indeed if the term *grace* labels not a thing but an experience—the human experience of God-for-and-within-us—and if it is true that it is the relational divine being (Trinity) that Christians find in the human experience of grace, and if it is necessary that all experiences of God and of God's grace be culturally mediated in order to be so understood and identified by the human subjects, and if it is true, as Christian revelation claims, that cultural humanness is the (although still infinitely inadequate) "sacrament" of God's self-outpouring Incarnation, then the Latino/a experience of and relations with the mature women of our communities (and with Guadalupe, to the degree that the latter images the former, and vice versa) unveil the underlying mysterious and yet evident pneumatological experiences of the God-for-and-within-us, mediated by these women as authentic cultural forms within our people's daily life.

What can we deduce about grace from Guadalupe, besides what has already been suggested? If "real life" only exists in lived and living everyday reality, and not in humankind's reflections about real life; and if *lo cotidiano* is not reducible to the domestic, the private, or the individual, then what is experienced and lived within *lo cotidiano* is (also) communal, social, and public. What older Latina women pray for, earnestly share, discuss with, and expect from Guadalupe (the frequent content or "shape" of their relationship with Guadalupe) are very specific, real-life public, social realities experienced in their daily lives: employment, health, housing, family and neighborhood relations, justice, peace, understanding, and so on. Latinas believe that the *Virgen* welcomes these concerns, respects and understands them, and wisely and forcefully empowers them to act.

Guadalupe, as expression and understanding of grace (as experienced by mature Latina women), points to created grace's fundamental reality: God-with-and-for-us who is encountered in daily life through culturally authentic means. Maternal in quality and power, and engaged with and responsive to *lo cotidiano*—that is a decisive interpretation of the grace that emerges from the Latina experience of Guadalupe.

Explanation and Expression of Sin: The Guadalupe Symbol Again

If we were to seek out and identify a symbol within Latino/a popular Catholicism that would express the daily relationships that constitute the foundation of the sinful dimension of social reality, no other symbol would compare to the *Virgen* of Guadalupe (and perhaps other *Vírgenes* of Latino/a devotion). This religious symbol seems at times to derail the people's solidarity with each other, blinding them to compassion and social responsibilities, condoning domestic violence and the perpetuation of dehumanizing gender and family roles, perpetuating their self-image as victim.[45]

If one were to seek out and identify, through popular Catholicism's memory of and devotions to Guadalupe, the more crucial daily relationships (and indeed protagonists in Latino/a popular religion), mature women would again appear as *the* interpreters of that religion and arguably as the ones with whom many Latinos/as sustain a sinful and dehumanizing daily relationship. If daily relationships constitute the foundation and image for the totality of social relationships, then we must also arrive at the conclusion that the daily relationships of Latinos/as must also be understood as experiences of sin.

Within the context of *lo cotidiano* women often reproduce and hand on some of the worst possible assumptions about gender and social roles, and about family and community responsibilities. As I indicated above, violent domestic abuse is not exhausted by the physical harm done to its victims. Nor is it simply coextensive with the verbal aggression that often accompanies the bodily violence. Through popular Catholicism's devotions to the *Virgen* of Guadalupe, Latina mature women have been told that they must endure the abuse, the assaults, and the violence. The call to freedom and to the struggle for justice that many Catholics have heard from Guadalupe is frequently muted here—the call itself being abused and betrayed. These are experiences of sin, even when cloaked under the religious veil of piety.

Mature Latina women mediate the experience and perpetuation of sin. They are interpreting sin as an assault against life at the level of *lo cotidiano*, paralleled by and in the assaults against life at all levels of society (cultural, political, economic). And given that life is the most foundational of all divine creations and commandments, the assault against daily life (which is the only life that exists) is *the* foundational sin. A theological consideration of the *Virgen* of Guadalupe must not be blind to the fact that this symbol of popular Catholicism has often been used (and is all too frequently still used) to justify domestic violence against women and children, and all sorts of other oppressive and alienating behavior.

CONCLUSION

I have insisted in this article that if we were to seek out and identify the more crucial daily relationships (and indeed the key protagonists in Latino/a popular Catholicism), mature women would easily appear as *the* leaders and interpreters of that religion and, most important, as *the ones with whom Latinos/as sustain the most meaningful and deepest of daily relationships.*

These mature women have been responsible for the survival and resilience of popular Catholicism. This religion, as symbolized in Guadalupe, has acted (and continues to act) as the main bearer of cultural identity and empowerment within the Latino/a universe *because* mature women play those same roles in our daily lives. But, on the other hand, popular religion (again, as symbolized in Guadalupe) suffers from and does not seem to undo many of the consequences of patriarchal society mostly *because* its women leaders and interpreters are themselves victims of that society.

A theology of grace and sin, if it were constructed from the Latino/a perspective, cannot ignore the daily realities of Latinos/as or the crucial hermeneutic role still played among us by older women. I am aware of the exploratory character of this essay, and therefore I realize that much has been left unsaid that would have to be discussed in a book-length treatment of grace and sin. But I hope to have shown the importance of *lo cotidiano* for a theology of grace and sin, as well as the potential contributions from popular Catholicism. Based on the premise that daily relationships constitute the foundation and image for the totality of social relationships, I pointed to the relationships of Latinos/as with our communities' older women as a locus where we could uncover the most foundational of daily relationships—grace. The popular symbol of Guadalupe and the manner in which mature Latinas relate in daily life to the *Virgen* have become a means for us to retrieve and to describe some of the elements in a culturally authentic experience of grace and sin.

If a European or European-American mainstream theologian were to seek many of the traditional themes present in theological studies on grace, I am certain that he or she would find them here, albeit under different forms and (often incipient) degrees of elaboration. My intent, however, was not to parallel the traditional theologies of grace. The intent of this chapter was to suggest new possibilities and approaches for Catholic theologizing on grace and sin from the Latino/a perspective. I hope to have done so from the heart of our people.

Notes

[1] For a brief history of the theology of grace, see P. Fransen, "Desarrollo histórico de la doctrina de la gracia," in *Mysterium Salutis*, ed. J. Feiner and M. Löhrer (Madrid: Cristiandad, 1969), 4:2, 611-730.

[2] I reflected on recent literature on culture and culture's impact on religion and religious doctrine in "A 'Multicultural' Church? Theological Reflections from 'Below,'" in *The Multicultural Church: a New Landscape in U.S. Theologies*, ed. W. Cenkner (Mahwah, N.J.: Paulist Press, 1995), 54-71.

[3] See O. Espín, "Inculturación de la fe: planteamiento del problema teológico-pastoral," in *Estudios Sociales* 62 (1985), 1-32; L. J. Luzbetak, *The Church and Cultures* (Maryknoll, N.Y.: Orbis Books, 1988); A. J. Gittins, *Gifts and Strangers* (New York: Paulist Press, 1989); A. Shorter, *Toward a Theology of Inculturation* (Maryknoll, N.Y.: Orbis Books, 1988); C. Geffré, *Le christianisme au risque de l'interpretation: Essais d'herméneutique théologique* (Paris: Ed. du Cerf, 1983); K. Tanner, *Theories of Culture: A New Agenda for Theology* (Minneapolis, Minn.: Fortress Press, 1997); R. Rosaldo, *Culture and Truth: The Remaking of Social Analysis* (Boston: Beacon Press, 1993).

[4] See C. Baumgartner, *La gracia de Cristo* (Barcelona: Herder, 1982), 118-21; Fransen, "Desarrollo histórico de la doctrina de la gracia," 638-56. I hasten to add that I am well aware of shortcomings in some traditional Catholic presentations on grace, especially those that led many Catholics to reify grace into "something" that does not resemble what I suggest in the text. I am here opting, however, for a

theology of grace that I believe represents the best insights from the Catholic tradition. Besides the first two references in this note, see as clear examples of this
better theology L. Boff, *Gracia y liberación del hombre* (Madrid: Ed. Cristiandad,
1978) [in English, *Liberating Grace* (Maryknoll, N.Y.: Orbis Books, 1979)], and M.
de França Miranda, *Libertados para a práxis da justiça: A teologia da graça no atual
contexto latino-americano* (São Paulo: Ed. Loyola, 1980).

[5] See L. Boff, *Gracia y liberación del hombre [Liberating Grace]*, 53-147, 221-36.

[6] By "universal relevance" I mean that a claim may be offered from within a
specific culture to others who may find the claim useful, suggestive, and so forth,
thereby opening for and within the recipients' perspectives (questions and themes,
answers and solutions, practices and approaches, etc.) that had hitherto remained
closed, confusing, or ignored. It might be possible to discover common threads
and denominators among the claims with universal relevance, but the original
claim does not present itself as necessarily applicable or correct for all possible
recipients. The latter must consent to the relevance of the claim that is offered to
them. On the other hand, by "universal validity" I mean that a claim, also from
within a specific culture, is offered to and possibly imposed on the potential recipients because the claim's birthing culture assumes its particular perspectives
(questions and themes, answers and solutions, practices and approaches, etc.) to
be applicable to and correct for all other cultures. The claim to universal validity
usually accompanies power and colonization and is legitimized by them.

[7] Cf. F. D. Bean and M. Tienda, *The Hispanic Population of the United States* (New
York: Russell Sage Foundation, 1990); F. L. Schick and R. Schick, *Statistical Hand-
book on U.S. Hispanics* (Phoenix, Ariz.: Oryx Press, 1991); National Council of La
Raza, *Poverty Project Fact Sheet: Hispanics, AFDC, and JOBS* (Washington, D.C.:
National Council of La Raza, 1995).

[8] M. P. Aquino, *Nuestro clamor por la vida* (San José: DEI, 1992), 75. In English,
Our Cry for Life (Maryknoll, N.Y.: Orbis Books, 1993).

[9] It is important to note that I am referring here to the *human* experience of
grace and its mediations, and not to grace in itself.

[10] The reader must recall that I am writing from the Latino/a perspective; therefore, I refer only to *Latina* women throughout this essay. This should not be interpreted to imply that Latinas are the only women who could be understood as
living hermeneuts (that is, interpreters) of grace and sin. Nor should the reader
assume that Latinas are more graced or sinful than other women and men. See
my comments on claims of universal relevance (in note 6, above).

[11] For a more thorough discussion of Latino/a popular Catholicism, and abun-
dant bibliographical references to its study, see Orlando O. Espín, *The Faith of the
People: Theological Reflections on Popular Catholicism* (Maryknoll, N.Y.: Orbis Books,
1997); idem, "Religiosidad popular: Un aporte para su definición y hermenéutica,"
Estudios Sociales 58 (1984), 41-57. The reader must have noticed that, in the text, I
have just said that popular Catholicism embodies, epistemologically organizes,
and symbolically expresses daily relationships and their broader networks and
connections. From this it must *not* be deduced that popular Catholicism is the
only Latino/a cultural creation that embodies, organizes, and expresses daily relationships and their networks within and for the Latino/a milieu. What should
be understood, nevertheless, is that popular Catholicism is an extraordinarily
important, culturally authentic manner for those tasks.

[12] Espín, *The Faith of the People*, 63-103.

[13] It will become apparent to the reader that most of the sources used and cited
in this article are on Chicanas/Mexican-American women and their families. I
am convinced that much of what I say in reference to older Mexican-American

women could be said—*mutatis mutandi*—about Puerto Rican, Cuban-American, Dominican-American, and Central-American older women too. Because Mexican Americans comprise over half of all U.S. Latinos/as, I have chosen to discuss Guadalupe in this article and to focus on Mexican-American realities. But the reader should be aware of my comments in notes 38 and 40, below.

¹⁴ I am in no way implying that *all* Latina women fit this description (see also the preceding note). Indeed, younger generations of Latinas are creating new roles for themselves that will of necessity expand or overturn this description in due time. Nor am I assuming either that the family is the only or best context for understanding Latinas or that it is where they may be better "found." Not at all. Indeed, it has been convincingly argued that the benefits Latino/a families have derived from their women members have usually been at the expense of Latinas' own self-worth, talents, and personhood. Latinas often feel guiltridden (and are made to feel so by Latino/a cultures) if they do not conform to a family context (and role within that context) that frequently suffocates and unduly sacrifices them for the "good" of the adult men and children in the family. What should not be, however, does not erase the reality of what has been. In other words, the self-sacrifice of Latinas—which must be questioned and challenged on many grounds—does not cancel the extraordinary services they have in fact performed (and, frequently the older women, continue to perform) to benefit their families. For research on Latina women and Latino/a families, and thus for all said about them in this article, see B. García-Bahne, "La Chicana and the Chicano Family," in *Essays on la Mujer*, ed. R. Sánchez and R. Martínez Cruz (Los Angeles: University of California Press/Chicano Studies Center Publications, 1977); J. Rodríguez, *Our Lady of Guadalupe: Faith and Empowerment among Mexican American Women* (Austin, Tex.: University of Texas Press, 1994); A. M. Díaz-Stevens, "Latinas and the Church," in *Hispanic Catholic Culture in the U.S.*, ed. J. Dolan and A. F. Deck, (Notre Dame, Ind.: University of Notre Dame Press, 1994), 240-77; N. Alarcón, "What Kind of Lover Have You Made Me, Mother?," in *Women of Color: Perspectives on Feminism and Identity*, ed. A. T. McCluskey, Women's Studies Program Papers Series no. 1 (Bloomington, Ind.: Indiana University Press, 1985); S. J. Andrade, "Social Science Stereotypes of the Mexican American Woman: Policy Implications for Research," *Hispanic Journal of Behavioral Sciences* 4:2 (1982), 233-44; G. Anzaldúa, *Borderlands: The New Mestiza* (San Francisco: Aunt Lute Book Co., 1987); M. Baca Zinn, "Political Familism toward Sex Role Equality in Chicano Families," *Aztlán: International Journal of Chicano Studies* 6 (1975), 13-27; idem, "Chicanos: Power and Control in the Domestic Sphere," *De Colores* 2 (1976), 19-44; idem, "Chicano Family Research: Conceptual Distortions and Alternative Directions," *Journal of Ethnic Studies* 7 (1979), 59-71; idem, "Employment and Education of Mexican American Women: The Interplay of Modernity and Ethnicity in Eight Families," *Harvard Educational Review* 50 (1980), 47-62; G. Bernal and A. I. Alvarez, "Culture and Class in the Study of Families," in *Cultural Perspectives in Family Therapy*, ed. J. C. Hansen and C. J. Falicov (Rockville, Md.: Aspen Systems, 1983), 33-50; I. I. Blea, *La Chicana and the Intersection of Race, Class, and Gender* (New York: Praeger, 1992); O. O. Espín, "Cultural and Historical Influences on Sexuality in Hispanic/Latin Women: Implications for Psychotherapy," in *Race, Class, and Gender: An Anthology*, ed. M. L. Anderson and P. H. Collins (Belmont, Calif.: Wadsworth Publishing, 1990), 141-46; C. J. Falicov and B. M. Karrer, "Cultural Variations in the Family Life Cycle: The Mexican American Family," in *The Family Life Cycle*, ed. E. A. Carter and M. McGoldrick (New York: Gardner Press, 1980), 383-425; P. Gándara, "Passing through the Eye of the Needle: High-Achieving

Chicanas," *Hispanic Journal of Behavioral Sciences* 4:2 (1982), 167-69; S. González, "La Chicana: Guadalupe or Malinche," in *Comparative Perspectives of Third World Women: The Impact of Race, Sex, and Class*, ed. B. Lindsay (New York: Praeger Press, 1980), 229-50; A. M. Isasi-Díaz and Y. Tarango, *Hispanic Women: Prophetic Voice in the Church* (San Francisco: Harper & Row, 1988); S. Keefe and A. Padilla, *Chicano Ethnicity* (Albuquerque, N.Mex.: University of New Mexico Press, 1987); idem, "The Mexican American Extended Family as an Emotional Support System," in *Family and Mental Health in the Mexican American Community*, ed. J. M. Casas and S. Keefe (Los Angeles: University of California Press/Chicano Mental Health Research Center, 1978), 49-67; M. B. Melville, *Twice a Minority: Mexican American Women* (St. Louis: C.V. Mosby Co., 1980); A. Mirandé and E. Enríquez, *La Chicana: The Mexican American Female* (Chicago: University of Chicago Press, 1979); A. Del Castillo, *Between Borders: Essays on Mexicana/Chicana History* (Encino, Calif.: Floricanto Press, 1990); A. Castillo, *Massacre of the Dreamers: Essays on Xicanisma* (New York: Plume/Penguin, 1995); E. L. Vásquez, "The Mexican American Woman," in *Sisterhood Is Powerful*, ed. R. Morgan (New York: Vintage Books, 1970); T. Córdova et al., eds., *Chicana Voices: Intersections of Class, Race, and Gender* (Austin, Tex.: University of Texas Press, 1986); N. Williams, "Role Making among Married Mexican American Women: Issues of Class and Ethnicity," *Journal of Applied Behavioral Science* 24 (1988), 203-17; idem, *The Mexican American Family: Tradition and Change* (Dix Hills, N.Y.: General Hall, 1990); L. Ybarra, "When Wives Work: The Impact on the Chicano Family," *Journal of Marriage and the Family* 2 (1982), 169-78; and P. Zavella, *Women's Work and Chicano Families* (Ithaca, N.Y.: Cornell University Press, 1987); R. A. Alvarez, *Familia: Migration and Adaptation in Baja and Alta California, 1800-1975* (Berkeley and Los Angeles: University of California Press, 1987); R. Griswold del Castillo, *La Familia: Chicano Families in the Urban Southwest, 1848 to the Present* (Notre Dame, Ind.: University of Notre Dame Press, 1984); M. P. Aquino and A. M. Tepedino, eds., *Entre la indignación y la esperanza: Teología feminista latinoamericana* (Bogotá: Indo-American Press, 1998).

[15] I am not attempting to romanticize the role of mature women in Latino/a culture and religion, or to "freeze" or stereotype it in time. As I suggested in the preceding note, it is true that there is no guarantee that future generations of Latinas will preserve or continue the role that mature Latinas have had and currently have among us (as described in the text). Reason clearly suggests that there will be changes as more and more women become professionals and enter the job market and consequently the urban middle class, and as the stresses and realities of family life in the United States affect Latina women's self-definition. The impact of the dominant culture, inevitably, will be felt on the cultural role of mature Latinas. But whatever the changes, it is very important to remember that these will happen *from* the current situation, as this situation was itself molded from past circumstances. To understand the present cultural status of mature Latinas is an essential step in preparing for and understanding their future. On issues relating to popular Catholicism, see Espín, *The Faith of the People*, especially chaps. 3, 4, 6.

[16] These descriptive statements, as we will see, echo very closely the mature Latinas' own relationship with and expectations about the *Virgen* of Guadalupe. The statements also clearly resemble the traditional Catholic understanding of the gifts bestowed by the Holy Spirit to the believers. We should not forget these similarities, which are not coincidental. See also the important clarification in note 10 above.

¹⁷ See, as a good but certainly not the only example, Rodríguez, *Our Lady of Guadalupe*.

¹⁸ It might seem strange that I do not reflect on men (including the ordained clergy) in this article. I am not implying that individual males cannot be legitimate hermeneuts of grace (or of sin) in specific Latino/a contexts. There are plentiful examples to indicate that this can indeed be the case. But since mature Latinas are sociologically and anthropologically at the center of Latino/a Catholicism and families, and are thus the *privileged* hermeneuts of grace and sin in our culture, theological reflection cannot ignore them as it has frequently done. We must focus on Latina women when understanding the experiences of grace and sin (as men have been the focus for reflections on grace and sin among other peoples), if we really want a theology born from the Latino/a perspective.

¹⁹ Readers will remember that sin, in myriad ways and forms, expresses itself in *every* human community. Therefore, Latino/a communities are not alone in displaying the horrors and consequences of sin. Furthermore, the specific situations I mention in the text are not exclusively, mainly, or especially present among Latinos/as. Indeed, it would be a sign of sin to engage in such biased reading of Latino/a suffering.

²⁰ Aquino, *Nuestro clamor por la vida*, 75 [in English, *Our Cry for Life*]; see also Aquino and Tepedino, *Entre la indignación y la esperanza*; and, on domestic violence as it affects Latina women, see M. N. Zambrano, *¡No más! Guía para la mujer golpeada* (Seattle, Wash.: Seal Press, 1994).

²¹ I admit that sometimes the experience and discovery I am referring to here require approximation by analogy. In other words, it is possible for me to *reflect* upon someone else's experience of grace without having first experienced grace *within that other person's cultural context*. But my reflection on the other's experience of grace will ultimately prove insufficient and inadequate unless I can approximate the neighbor's *experience* on which I reflect. This, in turn, requires my delving into *my own culturally contextualized experience of grace*. Description of the neighbor's experience of grace will not suffice as "material" for *my* reflection. As a Latino male theologian writing on Latinas, I am fully aware of the limitations inherent in my reflection, even though I benefit from the cultural context I share with Latina women.

²² I will not provide here exhaustive bibliographical references to popular Catholicism and its crucial importance in Latino/a cultures and theology. Most of the more recent literature, at least as it applies to theological reflection, is referenced in my *The Faith of the People*, and my articles "Religiosidad popular"; "The Vanquished, Faithful Solidarity and the Marian Symbol: A Hispanic Perspective on Providence," in *On Keeping Providence*, ed. B. Doherty and J. Coultas (Terre Haute, Ind.: St. Mary of the Woods College Press, 1991), 84-101; "Grace and Humanness: A Hispanic Perspective," in *We Are a People! Initiatives in Hispanic American Theology*, ed. R. S. Goizueta (Minneapolis, Minn.: Fortress Press, 1992), 133-64; "Pentecostalism and Popular Catholicism: The Poor and *Traditio*," *Journal of Hispanic/Latino Theology* 3:2 (1995), 14-43; with S. García, "Lilies of the Field: A Hispanic Theology of Providence and Human Responsibility," *Proceedings of the Catholic Theological Society of America* 44 (1989), 70-90; and again with S. García, "Sources of Hispanic Theology," *Proceedings of the Catholic Theological Society of America* 43 (1988), 122-25. For more bibliographical references, see also A. M. Stevens-Arroyo and S. Pantoja, *Discovering Latino Religion: A Comprehensive Social Science Bibliography* (New York: CUNY Press, 1995); Rodríguez, *Our Lady of Guadalupe*; R. S. Goizueta, *Caminemos con Jesús: Toward a Hispanic/Latino Theology of Accompaniment* (Maryknoll, N.Y.: Orbis Books, 1995); E. Dussel, "Popular Religion as Op-

pression and Liberation: Hypotheses on Its Past and Present in Latin America," in *Popular Religion*, ed. N. Greinacher and N. Mette (Edinburgh: T. and T. Clark, 1986); T. A. Tweed, "Identity and Authority at a Cuban Shrine in Miami: Santería, Catholicism, and Struggles for Religious Identity," *Journal of Hispanic/Latino Theology* 4:1 (1996), 27-48; V. Elizondo, "Popular Religion as Support of Identity," in Greinacher and Mette, *Popular Religion*; L. Maldonado, *Génesis del catolicismo popular* (Madrid: Cristiandad, 1979); and A. Bañuelas, "U.S. Latino/a Theological Bibliography," in *Mestizo Christianity: Theology from the Latino Perspective*, ed. A. Bañuelas (Maryknoll, N.Y.: Orbis Books, 1995), 261-70. The bibliography on Catholic systematics, put together for the present volume by Arturo Bañuelas, also includes a significant number of pertinent entries.

[23] Since *socialization* by definition implies cultural, social settings, and processes, it is impossible to have a "religion of one." There is an element of *communal* reception at the start and throughout the development of all religion. The "experience of the divine" may be had by individuals, but there is no religion after that experience alone. There is religion only when the experience of the divine is socialized; that is, when it is "poured" into the cultural and social contexts of the community that holds the experience to be true and significant.

[24] This point—that the *experience* of the divine in a religion is beyond the observation of the nonparticipant—is frequently forgotten by scholars and also by pastoral agents who work with Latino/a popular Catholicism. This "forgetfulness" is usually the unnecessary cause of negative and often painful pastoral and human consequences. The same point might be considered by our Protestant interlocutors in the intra-Latino/a ecumenical dialogue.

[25] I am using *hegemony* in the Gramscian sense. See L. Gruppi, *O conceito de hegemonia em Gramsci*, 2d ed. (Rio de Janeiro: Ed. Graal, 1978); H. Portelli, *Gramsci et le bloc historique* (Paris: Presses Universitaires de France, 1972).

[26] Although I am referring to the U.S. Roman Catholic Church in this chapter, I believe that, *mutatis mutandi*, my remarks are probably applicable to mainline Protestant churches as well. Furthermore, we must not forget that many members of U.S. Catholic and Protestant denominations have individually and socially benefited, and continue to benefit, from biases and discriminatory practices against Latinos/as. Indeed, many U.S. Catholics do not see the moral issues raised (for *their* consciences!) by their support of clearly anti-Latino/a legislation.

[27] Max Weber seemed inclined to think that religious "virtuosi" were the most apt to experience the divine. It appears that Weber assumed that the creation of religious symbols and so forth (the sphere of the "virtuosi") was the identifying criterion of those capable of the experience. Obviously, this assumption is not self-evident (see M. Weber, *The Sociology of Religion* [London: Meuthen, 1966]).

[28] On this, see Orlando O. Espín, "A 'Multicultural' Church? Theological Reflections from 'Below,'" in Cenkner, *The Multicultural Church*; see also L. Alcoff and E. Potter, eds., *Feminist Epistemologies* (New York: Routledge, 1993); and K. Lennon and M. Whitford, eds., *Knowing the Difference: Feminist Perspectives in Epistemology* (New York: Routledge, 1994).

[29] Cf. H. Portelli, *Gramsci et la question religieuse* (Paris: Anthropos, 1974), 141-62.

[30] Ibid., 43-94.

[31] I found stimulating, concerning this premise of Catholicism's "sacramental ethos" and the "catholicity" it entails, the sequential reading of D. Tracy, *The Analogical Imagination* (New York: Crossroad, 1986); A. M. Greeley, *The Catholic Myth* (New York: Charles Scribner's Sons, 1990); and W. G. Jeanrond and J. L. Rike, eds., *Radical Pluralism and Truth: David Tracy and the Hermeneutics of Religion* (New York: Crossroad, 1991).

³² Cf. F. Houtart, "Religion et champ politique: cadre théorique pour l'étude des sociétés capitalistes périphériques," *Social Compass* 24:2-3 (1977), 265-72; idem, "Weberian Theory and the Ideological Function of Religion," *Social Compass* 23:4 (1976), 345-54.

³³ See Orlando O. Espín, "Popular Catholicism as an Epistemology (of Suffering)," *Journal of Hispanic/Latino Theology* 2:2 (1994), 55-78 (included as chapter 6 in *The Faith of the People*).

³⁴ What is said here in reference to and as a consequence of Latino/a popular Catholicism is by no means limited to the Latino/a Catholic communities. I believe our construction is applicable, *mutatis mutandi*, to the vast majority of Catholic communities across the country—not by way of claiming universal validity for the Latino/a experience or expressions, but because very similar daily life realities are found in other cultural and social contexts. As a prime example of this, it is important to note that practically all Catholic communities in the country (and across the world) have access to one or another version of Catholicism that is not coextensive or synonymous with "official Roman Catholicism." For most Catholics worldwide, their religion is this real, daily life symbolic, ethical, epistemologic universe. It is self-consciously "Catholic" (in the Tradition's sense), but it often sees little need to justify or legitimize itself ecclesiastically. Most European and European-American popular Catholicisms are the complex result of Tridentine reforms, baroque piety, and modernity's assumptions. But there are exceptions to this general statement—for example, southern Italian (and Italian-American) popular Catholicism has drunk less from the wells of modernity and of the baroque period than from its medieval past (although this in no way implies the absence of modern and baroque influences). Latino/a and Latin American popular Catholicisms have been less influenced by Trent (and thus are more "pre-Tridentine," emphatically laity-led, and internally diverse) than by the horrors of conquest and colonialism, and the ambivalent/ambiguous experience of *mestizaje*. As in the case of most European and European-American popular Catholicisms, the Latino/a and Latin American versions are also self-consciously "Catholic" and find little need to justify or legitimize themselves ecclesiastically. Now, if it is true (and I believe it is) that most Catholics worldwide are Catholic in and through their local tradition of popular Catholicism, *and* if it is true that this religious universe has little need to justify or legitimize itself ecclesiastically (even when some varieties of popular Catholicism might seem close to the "official" religion—usually for historical, cultural, and/or national identity purposes, as possibly in the cases of Irish and Polish Catholics), then all sorts of very serious theological, pastoral questions need to be raised, most emphatically those arising from the ecclesiological doctrines concerning the nature and dynamics of Tradition, "reception," magisterium, and the *sensus fidelium*.

³⁵ See, from a very vast bibliography, Rodríguez, *Our Lady of Guadalupe*; the five articles by J. Traslosheros, T. Matovina, M. Engh, J. Rodríguez, and V. Elizondo in the recent special issue on Guadalupe in the *Journal of Hispanic/Latino Theology* 5:1 (1997); V. Elizondo, *Mary: Prophetess and Model of Freedom for Responsibility* (San Antonio, Tex.: Mexican American Cultural Center, 1972); idem, "La Virgen de Guadalupe como símbolo: El poder de los impotentes," *Concilium* 122 (1977), 149-60; idem, *La morenita: Evangelizer of the Americas* (San Antonio: Mexican American Cultural Center, 1980); idem, *Guadalupe: Mother of the New Creation* (Maryknoll, N.Y.: Orbis Books, 1997); S. Poole, *Our Lady of Guadalupe: The Origins and Sources of a Mexican National Symbol, 1531-1797* (Tucson, Ariz.: University of Arizona Press, 1995); R. Nebel, *Santa María Tonantzin Virgen de Guadalupe: Continuidad y transformación religiosa en México* (Mexico City: Fondo de Cultura Económica, 1995);

X. Noguez, *Documentos guadalupanos: Un estudio sobre las fuentes de información tempranas en torno a las mariofanías en el Tepeyac* (Mexico City: Fondo de Cultura Económica, 1993); J. L. G. Guerrero, *El Nican Mopohua: Un intento de exégesis,* vol. 1 (Mexico City: Universidad Pontificia de México, 1996); J. I. Echegaray, ed., *Album conmemorativo del 450 aniversario de las apariciones de Nuestra Señora de Guadalupe* (Mexico City: Buena Nueva, 1981); E. Burrus, *The Oldest Copy of the Nican Mopohua* (Washington, D.C.: CARA, 1981); idem, *The Basic Bibliography of the Guadalupan Apparitions, 1531-1723* (Washington, D.C.: CARA, 1983); idem, *Juan Diego and Other Native Benefactors in the Light of Boturini's Research* (Washington, D.C.: CARA, 1984); Centro de Estudios Guadalupanos, *Documentario guadalupano, 1531-1768,* Monumenta Histórica Guadalupana Series no. 3 (Mexico City: Centro de Estudios Guadalupanos. 3, 1980); M. DeCock, "Our Lady of Guadalupe: Symbol of Liberation?," in *Mary according to Women,* ed. C. F. Jegen (Kansas City, Mo.: Leaven Press, 1985); E. de la Torre Villar and R. Navarro de Anda, *Testimonios históricos guadalupanos. Compilación, prólogo, notas bibliográficas e índices* (Mexico City: Fondo de Cultura Económica, 1982); R. R. Dri, "El mensaje liberador guadalupano," *Servir* 17 (1981), 355-76; S. González, "La Chicana: Guadalupe or Malinche?," in *Comparative Perspectives of Third World Women: The Impact of Race, Sex, and Class,* ed. B. Lindsay (New York: Praeger, 1980), 229-50; A. Guerrero, *A Chicano Theology* (Maryknoll, N.Y.: Orbis Books, 1987); P. Harrington, "Mother of Death, Mother of Rebirth: The Mexican Virgin of Guadalupe," in *Journal of the American Academy of Religion* 55 (1988), 25-50; D. Kurtz, "The Virgin of Guadalupe and the Politics of Becoming Human," *Journal of Anthropological Research* 38 (1982), 194-210; J. Lafaye, *Quetzalcóatl and Guadalupe: The Formation of Mexican National Consciousness, 1531-1813* (Chicago: University of Chicago Press, 1987); B. López Bucio, "Catolicismo guadalupano," in *Servir* 17 (1981), 333-54; A. Ramírez Jasso, *La religiosidad popular en México* (Mexico City: Paulinas, 1975); B. Bravo, ed., *Diccionario de religiosidad popular* (Mexico City: Lib. Parroquial, 1992); M. Rojas, *Nican Mopohua: Traducción del náhuatl al castellano* (Huejutla/Mexico City: Librería Parroquial, 1978); C. L. Siller Acuña, "Anotaciones y comentarios al Nican Mopohua," *Estudios Indígenas* 8:2 (1981), 217-74; idem, "El método de la evangelización en el Nican Mopohua," *Servir* 17 (1981), 255-93; idem, *Flor y canto del Tepeyac: Historia de las apariciones de Santa María de Guadalupe: Texto y comentario* (Xalapa, Ver.: Publicaciones Servir, 1981); idem, *Para comprender el mensaje de María de Guadalupe* (Buenos Aires: Ed. Guadalupe, 1989); E. R. Wolf, "The Virgin of Guadalupe: A Mexican National Symbol," in *Reader in Comparative Religion: An Anthropological Approach,* ed. W. A. Lessa and E. Z. Vogt (New York: Harper & Row, 1968), 226-30. Most entries in this bibliography also retell and explain the story of the Guadalupe apparitions and the subsequent devotion.

[36] See Orlando O. Espín, "Tradition and Popular Religion: An Understanding of the *Sensus Fidelium,*" in *Frontiers of Hispanic Theology in the United States,* ed. A. F. Deck (Maryknoll, N.Y.: Orbis Books, 1992), 62-87. Other Latino/a Catholic theologians (Goizueta, Díaz, García-Rivera, Isasi-Díaz, Rodríguez-Holguín, etc.) have argued for the "Christian" quality and content of popular Catholicism. However, Justo González's article in the present volume raises some very important issues (from his Protestant perspective) that Latino/a Catholic systematicians *must* sooner or later address. I do not believe that Professor González's questions imply or indicate insurmountable difficulties in the intra-Latino/a ecumenical dialogue. But he does place some issues on the table that Catholics cannot avoid or disregard. As a first response to some of González's concerns, I suggest that the pneumatological reading of Guadalupe (as well as a "re-pneumatologized" christology and ecclesiology) might very well be the bridge needed in the intra-

Latino/a ecumenical conversation. Nothing has separated Latino/a Catholics and Protestants more than Mary (at the street if not always at the academic levels). What if, I ask Professor González, Protestants and Catholics were to discover that Guadalupe is in fact an authentic cultural way of doctrinally expressing and existentially experiencing the Holy Spirit? What if they were to agree that this "Mary" is not Mary but the Spirit? I suspect that new ecumenical perspectives can and would open as a consequence. Very serious obstacles (ecclesiological, especially) would remain, unfortunately, but a huge step would have been taken in the right direction. Nevertheless, Catholic theologians should carefully consider the issues raised by González, the most crucial of which (if I interpret Professor González correctly) is our focus on popular Catholicism as the theological starting point. For another possible contribution to the intra-Latino ecumenical dialogue, also from a theology of popular Catholicism, see Orlando O. Espín, "Pentecostalism and Popular Catholicism: The Poor and *Traditio*," *Journal of Hispanic/Latino Theology* 3:2 (1995), 14-43.

[37] From a growing bibliography, see Espín, *Faith of the People*, 7-10; Isasi-Díaz and Tarango, *Hispanic Women*; Lafaye, *Quetzalcóatl and Guadalupe*; F. González-Crussi, "The Anatomy of a Virgin," in *Goddess of the Americas: Writings on the Virgin of Guadalupe*, ed. A. Castillo (New York: Riverhead Books, 1996), 1-14; and Nebel, *Santa María Tonantzin Virgen de Guadalupe*. Although Professor Elizabeth Johnson does not write explicitly on Guadalupe, three of her articles on Mary are quite pertinent here and throughout this chapter: "Mary and the Image of God" and "Reconstructing a Theology of Mary," in *Mary, Woman of Nazareth: Biblical and Theological Perspectives*, ed. D. Donnelly (New York: Paulist Press, 1987), 25-68 and 69-91; and, "Mary and the Female Face of God," *Theological Studies* 50 (1989), 501-26.

[38] The *Virgen* of Guadalupe is arguably unique among all other Latino/a and Latin American *Vírgenes*. Further research will indicate if the pneumatological interpretation, which I regard as already valid in the case of Guadalupe, can be extended to other *Vírgenes*, although Yves Congar, Elizabeth Johnson, Leonardo Boff, and others seem inclined to discover a pneumatological dimension in *all* Marian devotions. However, not all devotional relationships with the *Vírgenes* are alike, thus creating considerable difficulties for the extension of the pneumatological interpretation. Indeed, one must first ask whether a given "Marian" devotion in fact refers to Mary. I have often thought that there are at least three types of devotional relationships to *Vírgenes* among Latinos/as and Latin Americans: (1) the traditional type, which presents the *Vírgenes* in typical Mediterranean Catholic fashion, always and exclusively identified with Mary, for example, Our Lady of San Juan de los Lagos; (2) the syncretic type, which, although apparently venerating the *Vírgenes* according to Catholic piety, often integrates at the popular level (in spite of strong ecclesiastical opposition) interpretations of the *Vírgenes* from evidently non-Christian sources, for example, Our Lady of Charity of El Cobre, often associated with (and frequently a cover for) Oshún, the Yoruba *orisha* (it should be added, however, that the veneration of Our Lady of Charity—and of other similar *Vírgenes*—does not necessarily lead to syncretic interpretations, in which case the devotion could then be of the traditional type); and (3) the pneumatological type, which refers to the one *Virgen* we are discussing here. Only Guadalupe, in my view, stands out as uniquely pneumatological among the other Latino/a and Latin American devotions. This typology, *mutatis mutandi*, might prove useful in other contexts beyond the Latino/a and Latin American religious milieu.

[39] See, for example, C. M. LaCugna, *God for Us: The Trinity and Christian Life* (San Francisco: Harper Collins, 1992); E. A. Johnson, *She Who Is: The Mystery of God in Feminist Theological Discourse* (New York: Crossroad, 1992), and the three articles by Johnson cited in note 37, above; V. Codina, *Creo en el Espíritu Santo: Pneumatología narrativa* (Santander: Sal Terrae, 1994); W. Kasper, *The God of Jesus Christ* (New York: Crossroad, 1984). See also *Catechism of the Catholic Church*, nos. 683-93, 733-41, 1810-32; *Medellín Conclusions* 1:4, 8:6; *Puebla Document*, nos. 23, 27, 200-204, 208, 219, 638, 755, 1128, 1294; *Santo Domingo Document*, no. 65. An indispensable contribution to the theological study of the relationship among Mary, Marian symbols, and the Holy Spirit throughout Christian history is Y. Congar, *I Believe in the Holy Spirit* (London: G. Chapman, 1983), vols. 1-3, but esp. vol. 1, where Congar explicitly addresses the relationship.

[40] It is important to emphasize that Guadalupe is unique in Christian history. Pneumatological readings of the event and of the subsequent devotion are possible because of a historical "fluke." The cultural, symbolic, doctrinal, and historical circumstances that occurred as context for Guadalupe (in sixteenth-century Mexico and beyond) did not have to happen. In fact, these circumstances do not seem to have repeated themselves in the case of other colonial or modern *Vírgenes*.

[41] For extensive bibliographies on early colonial Mexico and the possibilities (and reality) of symbolic, religious "transfers" there, see Orlando O. Espín, "Trinitarian Monotheism and the Birth of Popular Catholicism: The Case of Sixteenth-Century Mexico," *Missiology* 20:2 (1992), 177-204; as well as idem, "Popular Catholicism among Latinos," in Dolan and Deck, *Hispanic Catholic Culture in the U.S.*, 308-59. See also F. W. Dillistone, *The Power of Symbols in Religion and Culture* (New York: Crossroad, 1986). Three indispensable works on symbolic and doctrinal "transfers" in colonial Mexico are S. Gruzinski, *La guerra de las imágenes* (Mexico City: Fondo de Cultura Económica, 1995); idem, *La colonización de lo imaginario: Sociedades indígenas y occidentalización en el México español: Siglos XVI-XVIII* (Mexico City: Fondo de Cultura Económica, 1995); and L. M. Burkhart, *The Slippery Earth: Nahua-Christian Moral Dialogue in Sixteenth-Century Mexico* (Tucson, Ariz.: University of Arizona Press, 1989). Although not explicitly on Guadalupe, these three works painstakingly describe how other doctrinal and symbolic "transfers" did occur in colonial Mexico.

[42] Three evident scholarly works come to mind: Elizabeth Schüssler Fiorenza, *In Memory of Her: A Feminist Theological Reconstruction of Christian Origins* (New York: Crossroad, 1986); Anne E. Carr, *Transforming Grace: Christian Tradition and Women's Experience* (San Francisco: Harper & Row, 1988); and Johnson, *She Who Is*. Other pertinent titles have been cited throughout the present article.

[43] See E. Johnson, "Mary and the Female Face of God," *Theological Studies* 50 (1989), 501-26; J. Rodríguez, "Guadalupe: The Feminine Face of God," in Castillo, *Goddess of the Americas*. See also idem, *Our Lady of Guadalupe*, 105-13.

[44] God as grace-for-and-within-us would be utterly meaningless and beyond our perception and experience except as that grace entered our creaturely world, worked through and within our histories and our cultures, and molded itself to our cultural understandings, making it possible for us to "see and touch" the gracious actions of the God-who-is-for-us. To theologically speak of grace, therefore, means that we speak (and can only speak) from and about the human experience of grace.

[45] We should remember that Guadalupe is a human symbol, even if it is for the Holy Spirit. When the symbol (*not* the symbolized) is derailed from its humanizing, graced, liberative character we may speak of Guadalupe as expressive of sin.

Human history is unfortunately filled with other examples of religious symbols and beliefs that have been and are abused or prostituted by explanations, relationships, and usages that were certainly not initially intended (or are necessitated) by those symbols and beliefs. All human religious language is evidently human, and hence ultimately and constantly ambivalent. This ambivalence (or perhaps, plurivalence), furthermore, cannot be erased or ignored. Although not directly on Guadalupe, see, for example C. R. Boxer, *Mary and Misogyny: Women in Iberian Expansion Overseas, 1415-1815* (London: G. Duckworth, 1975), especially 97-112.

7

Dime con quién andas y te diré quién eres
(Tell me with whom you walk, and I will tell you who you are)

We Walk-with Our Lady of Charity

❧

MIGUEL H. DÍAZ

St. Vincent de Paul Regional Seminary

The chapter title, an oft-cited aphorism among U.S. Hispanics, expresses the importance of relationships in constituting who one is. Aphorisms are wisdom phrases "frequently used in daily life to explain circumstances, to communicate meaning, to teach values and expected behavior, and in general to share among the members of a community the wisdom of living learned by many generations."[1] While such aphorisms are not the exclusive creation of any community, their uniqueness lies in their ability to reflect and transmit specific communal convictions concerning the nature of persons. Because they emerge within particular linguistic and cultural contexts, they are often valuable sources for gaining communal self-understanding.[2]

The aphorism *Dime con quién andas y te diré quién eres* affirms that particular relationships (not simply *relationship* in the abstract) constitute persons, and that the specific persons with whom we relate mediate self-understanding.[3] The active sense of the expression *andar-con* (to walk-with) suggests an understanding of what is human, defined not so much as static presence but, rather, as a dynamic being-with others.[4] Moreover, since "walking-with" others presupposes an embodied anthropology,[5] we accompany persons within spatial and cultural landscapes. Consequently, implicit in this aphorism is not only "who" mediates self-understanding, but also "where" and "how" such mediation occurs. The wisdom of this aphorism will guide the theological reflections of this essay.

Were we to consider theologically, *from the heart of our people*, particular persons who reveal this anthropology, we would have to recognize (beyond the crucified Christ[6] and specific saints that accompany U.S. Hispanics[7]) the "Marys" of U.S. Hispanic popular Catholicism.[8] As Orlando Espín notes, "Under different names, in different locations, and with different external appearance, the veneration of Mary is so pervasive in Hispanic popular religion and daily life that it would be practically impossible to understand U.S. Hispanic cultures without the Marian symbol."[9] Mary, Espín goes on to emphasize, says more about the persons she accompanies than about the New Testament figure identified as the mother of Jesus. In her accompaniment of U.S. Hispanic communities, I will argue, Mary provides a central locus from which to construct U.S. Hispanic theological anthropologies.

Upon close examination of any U.S. Hispanic popular devotion to Mary (for instance, Our Lady of Guadalupe, or Our Lady of Charity, or Our Lady of Monserrat),[10] one realizes how each of these devotions reveals not only a specific community of persons (i.e., Mexican-Americans, Cuban-Americans, Puerto Ricans, etc.), but also the distinctive cultural nature of her accompaniment. In other words, Mary walks-with persons who have been culturally marginalized. As she looks at, welcomes, and assumes the cultural face of those who have been rejected, forgotten, and oppressed, they are welcomed, remembered, and resurrected.

The present essay will highlight the story of Our Lady of Charity. This story, as all other Marian stories, emerges from and reflects local communal experiences.[11] Building upon U.S. Hispanic precedents, we understand the story of Our Lady of Charity as a popular faith expression. Its widespread appeal among Cubans and Cuban-Americans does not necessarily make this story popular. Rather, the popular element of this story derives from its association with communities who have been or continue to be marginalized.[12]

Retrieving a popular story as a source for theological reflection may not be universally accepted. To associate any kind of normativity, let alone to attribute theological wisdom, to a popular faith expression has been generally uncommon for theologians, especially after changes brought about in post-Tridentine Christianity.[13] Indeed, "for a long time popular religion was by and large denigrated by theologians as a way of expressing faith that needed to be overcome sooner or later by a more sophisticated understanding of the gospel."[14] Notwithstanding this trend, some

of the most respected theological voices of our times have recognized popular religion as essential for Christian theological reflection. For instance,
the late Karl Rahner notes:

> If the Church, despite its institutional character and hierarchical or-
> ganization, is the Church of the "People of God," a pilgrim Church,
> in which everyone not only receives but also gives and serves, is
> "popular religion" then not a *constitutive moment of this Church of the
> one and entire people of God, whose faith is the point of reference for theol-
> ogy and the real object of its reflection?* We would then still have to
> determine within this one Church as the People of God the precise
> relation, one to another, of the magisterium, official church doctrine,
> the life of faith, popular religion, and so on. But it would be impos-
> sible to deny that popular religion has a fundamental importance
> for theology (and not just the other way round).[15]

Recognizing the importance of popular religion as an indispensable source
in theological reflection and as a constitutive moment in the life of U.S.
Hispanic communities, this essay explores the story of Our Lady of Charity as *a* locus in theological anthropology.

The story of Our Lady of Charity, like other U.S. Hispanic Marian stories, has been primarily transmitted by and as an oral tradition.[16] A comprehensive theological study would require listening to and document-
ing the varying voices that make up and embody this tradition.[17] Such a
task lies beyond the scope of this essay. Instead, we will highlight the
recently discovered testimony of Juan Moreno as a key theological source
within the oral tradition.[18]

This *locus theologicus* makes sense for four reasons. First, Moreno was
an African slave who in storylike form recalled how he, along with two
Amerindians,[19] found the statue of Our Lady of Charity and witnessed
thereafter some of the key events that constitute the tradition.[20] Second, as
a story of someone who could not read or write,[21] his testimony reflects
the oral basis of this tradition. Third, as a representative of an enslaved
community he witnesses the popular nature of this devotion. Indeed, the
devotion is popular because it emerged from and flourished within the
heart of a marginalized copper-mining community.[22] And fourth, Moreno's
story is consistent with the Christian oral testimony that has kept alive the
memory of Our Lady of Charity.[23]

In what follows, we will first briefly examine the anthropological nature of stories and then summarize Moreno's account of Our Lady of Charity. Second, we will discuss how this story reflects a Christian understanding of what it means to be human: to be a human person in the image of
God means to be relational as God is relational.[24] To image how God is
relational is to walk preferentially with marginalized persons within their

specific sociocultural landscape. Similar to Jesus' accompaniment of the marginalized, the poor, the suffering and the oppressed, Our Lady of Charity walks-with enslaved Amerindian and African slaves in their struggle to overcome sociocultural marginalization. Finally, we will discuss how this story speaks to the reality of Latinos/as in the United States today.

DIME LO QUE CUENTAS Y TE DIRÉ QUIÉN ERES
(Tell me your stories, and I will tell you who you are)
STORIES GIVE RISE TO HUMAN IDENTITY

Our culture is a culture of stories. We live our stories.[25] Generally speaking, stories give rise to human identity. They suggest how persons act and are acted upon in the world. They describe relationships that influence and partly determine who persons become. And they offer Latino/a communities an alternative to modern and postmodern distortions of the human person.[26] Stories resist the temptation to abstract persons from their social location because "neither disembodied minds nor mindless bodies can appear in stories. There the self is given whole, as an activity i.1 time."[27] Stories often recall a "dangerous memory," foster communal solidarity, and evoke human liberation.[28] Stories, argues contemporary theologian Terrence Tilley, come in different genres: myths, parables, and actions.[29]

Myths are stories that create worldviews. They foster traditions that address the origins of a people. Myths often legitimize established authorities, symbol systems, and the like, and attempt to give persons within a particular social structure a sense of belonging. Conversely, parables are stories that upset and overturn the worldviews created by myths. Parables work within a mythic worldview to subvert such a view. Finally, actions refer to stories that simply explore human experiences in the world. Actions describe *either fictionally or factually* specific world events.

The story of Juan Moreno is primarily an action that describes the relationship between the slaves living and working in the easternmost province of Cuba in the seventeenth century and a religious object—the statue of Our Lady of Charity.[30] This statue mediates, in a sacramental fashion, for this community what it means to be human. The miracles associated with Our Lady of Charity function parabolically to upset expected patterns of relationships.[31] Who, where, and how she accompanies the community, and consequently, who and what she saves, reveal the parabolic nature of these sacramental relationships. Her miracles challenge, from the perspective of the marginalized, the "normative" ways of conceiving answers to the question of what it means to be human.

We will now proceed to a summary of Moreno's story of Our Lady of Charity and some theological reflections on the nature of her accompaniment.

THE STORY OF JUAN MORENO

Juan Moreno recounts how, as a ten-year-old child, he went along with Rodrigo de Hoyos and Juan de Hoyos (two Amerindian brothers) in search of salt. They spent some time on a cay located in the middle of the Bay of Nipe (in the northeastern part of Cuba), waiting for good weather before heading out on their mission. With the arrival of calm waters, they began to row, and then they noticed a floating object. Upon close examination, they realized that it was a statue, recognized by the Amerindian brothers to be that of the Virgin with the Child Jesus in her arms. They were surprised to discover that her clothes were not wet.[32]

Rodrigo de Hoyos read the following inscription on the base of the statue: *Yo soy la Virgen de la Caridad* (I am the Virgin of Charity). They brought the image into their boat, took it ashore, and notified the appropriate Spanish authorities of their find. While they waited for the news of this event to reach Sánchez de Moya, the administrator of the local copper mines,[33] the statue of Our Lady of Charity was placed on an altar within the living quarters of their settlement.[34] Rodrigo was charged with the responsibility of always keeping her lamp lit.

Numerous miracles began to be associated with the *Virgen de la Caridad*. For instance, Moreno notes in his testimony how Rodrigo de Hoyos and Matías Olivera, a local lay hermit, witnessed on various occasions the disappearance and reappearance of the statue from her shrine. Each time she returned wearing wet clothes.[35] Moreno also recalls how various persons who worked the mines would hear Olivera addressing the following questions to Our Lady of Charity: "Where do you come from, Lady? Why do you leave me alone? Why do you dirty your clothes if you know that you do not have any others, nor any money to buy some more? How is it that you bring them wet? From where do you come wet?"[36]

Moreno relates that the site for a shrine to Our Lady of Charity was determined by miraculous lights seen on top of a copper hill, and that Olivera was saved by bystanders when he fell into a mine shaft located near that same hill.[37] According to the Moreno testimony, Matías Olivera was heard to say that on one occasion the oil for the lamp of Our Lady of Charity was not consumed for two consecutive days until supplies of lard arrived.[38] Finally, Moreno recalls that upon prayerfully processing with the statue of Our Lady of Charity, her miraculous intervention ended a severe drought.[39]

DIME CON QUIÉN, DÓNDE Y CÓMO ANDAS Y TE DIRÉ QUIÉN ERES
(Tell me with whom, where, and how you walk, and I will tell you who you are)
OUR LADY OF CHARITY
AND THE NATURE OF HER ACCOMPANIMENT

Moreno's story highlights sacramental interactions between the various members of this copper-mining community and the statue of Our Lady of Charity. These interactions reveal not only who the *Virgen de la Caridad* accompanies, but also where and how she accompanies these members. While these interactions suggest affirming relationships—persons care for her, abide with her, converse with her, and even disagree with some of her actions (for example, her unexplained disappearances)—the story also witnesses less affirming relationships. The vanquishment of the members of this copper-mining community and the pillaging of the land they abide in reveal the kind of oppressive relationships challenged by the *Virgen de la Caridad*. The following five points explore the preferential nature of her accompaniment.

Our Lady of Charity walks preferentially with marginalized persons who struggle to survive.

The most obvious example comes from her accompaniment of Juan Moreno, Rodrigo de Hoyos, and Juan de Hoyos. Those who first encounter this image are members of an enslaved copper-mining community. Similar to Jesus, who begins his public ministry among the poor and outcast (Lk 4:16-19), Our Lady of Charity begins her public ministry, if you will, among "representatives of Cuba's most exploited and poor classes: two indians and a black slave, whom she fills with the joy of her presence."[40]

She also accompanies others in the community who struggle to survive. Recall for instance, how Matías Olivera was miraculously saved after falling into a mine shaft. Although Moreno describes him as a big man, he is able to hold onto a branch of a maguey tree. From there, he invokes the *Virgen de la Caridad* and calls for assistance. She answers his prayer. The branch does not collapse, and those nearby rescue him by using ropes.

There is nothing unique in the miraculous intervention of Mary to save persons. For instance, Our Lady of Charity in Castile, Spain—a Marian image some have associated with the Cuban *Virgen de la Caridad*—was also known for its numerous cures and miraculous interventions.[41] What is significant is the parabolic nature and social location of this relationship.

For example, Olivera's "salvation" comes as a result of his accompanying a community. In all likelihood Olivera was a Spanish religious, charged with the care and evangelization of the African slaves at this copper-mining community.[42] His presence among (his "being-with") the marginalized mine workers saved him.[43] An unexpected parable-like miracle occurred: the branch that held a strong body (Olivera's) did not collapse, and the community of weak bodies (the mining slaves)—who struggle to survive—bestow life upon a representative of the very community that exercises enslaving power over them. In other words, in this story the lives of persons who marginalize others are related intrinsically to the lives of those who are marginalized. The story invites the reader to realize that oppressive relationships affect all persons within a given community. Those who marginalize are also deprived of their humanity. Indeed, as Martin Luther King Jr. observed:

> whatever affects one directly affects all indirectly. I can never be what I ought to be until you are what you ought to be, and you can never be what you ought to be until I am what I ought to be. This is the interrelated structure of reality.[44]

Our Lady of Charity walks with persons in ways that recall their marginalized cultural identity.

Religious expressions reveal cultural identity and vice versa.[45] The miracle associated with how the statue of the *Virgen de la Caridad* was found at sea wearing dry clothing, her various reappearances on land while wearing wet clothes, and the lights seen on top of the copper hill may suggest how her presence could have evoked the memory of the suppressed Taíno culture.[46] The dryness of the statue at sea as well as its wetness on land resonate well with Taíno cosmology. As some have noted, characteristic of Taíno metaphysics is the dual nature of all reality and the ability of "inanimate objects to move and glow."[47]

Moreover, given the materials from which the statue of Our Lady of Charity is made, and her association with water, she probably mediated for Juan de Hoyos, Rodrigo de Hoyos, and the other remaining Taínos of this copper-mining community the cultural memory of their *zemí*, Atabex.[48] Similar to Atabex, who was the mother of Yúcahu (the Lord of the all-important cassava plant), Our Lady of Charity is, for Christians, the mother of a Son who is confessed to be Lord of all creation. Again in a way similar to Atabex, Taíno goddess of the waters, the *Virgen de la Caridad* has always been associated with waters.[49]

The ability of religious objects to mediate cultural meaning has been amply explored. As William Christian has argued persuasively, images communicate cultural values because,

> as symbols for social identities, as measures of belonging, as cultural boundary markers, they have a function that is primeval. They are

virtually totem objects, embodying in some way the essence of the
humanity of their devotees.[50]

Seen from a theological perspective, Our Lady of Charity invokes a thoroughly "incarnational" understanding of what is human. Were we to agree
that in Jesus Christ, God embodies a specific marginalized cultural reality, namely, that of a Galilean Jew,[51] we could perhaps embrace the symbolic accompaniment of Our Lady of Charity as an ongoing expression of
how the Christian God identifies with marginalized persons and assumes
their marginalized cultural reality.

Seen from a "New World" Christian perspective, what the *Virgen de la
Caridad* accomplishes is in continuity with "Old World" Christian traditions. There is nothing new about bridging cultural and religious traditions and birthing forth persons who live, as we could colloquially say,
con un pie de cada lado (with a foot on each side). At the heart of the Christian story is a theology that affirms how God, in Jesus Christ, bridges two
realities—what is human and what is divine—without in any way undermining either of these. At the heart of Our Lady of Charity's story is an
anthropology that affirms how persons can bridge cultural worlds so as
not to subordinate or sacrifice an essential part of their humanity. In the
Virgen de la Caridad, what is Spanish does not subordinate what is Taíno
(or what is African).[52] Rather, in her person cultural and religious expressions accompany one another.

Our Lady of Charity walks in a marginalized landscape.

She walks in places where the marginalized live and work—namely,
the copper-mining settlement's living quarters and the hill above the mines.
Moreover, her accompaniment of this community, in both the private and
the public places (the living quarters and the mines), suggests the direct
relationship that exists between these two aspects of a person's life. Persons marginalized privately also generally experience public marginalization, and vice versa.[53]

The relationship between the natural landscape and the persons who
inhabited and worked that land is also striking. The pillaged land that
had supplied the raw materials to make the Spanish artillery became the
place where Our Lady of Charity dwelled. The miracle of the lights became the sign that indicated to this copper-mining community where she
would reside. They placed her on a hill on top of the mine, directly above
the place where the slaves worked.[54] While it is commonly assumed that
the statue of the *Virgen de la Caridad* was immediately placed in the main
Spanish shrine of Cobre Hill (the hill of the copper mines),[55] some recent
scholarship suggests that the statue may have been placed "in the chapel

of the hospital for slaves, which was adjacent to the shrine in El Cobre."[56] This is no minor detail. Our Lady of Charity's first shrine implies a preferential relationship consistent with those who first encountered her. She is to be found in the place where persons struggle to survive.

This preferential relationship between the *Virgen de la Caridad* and the marginalized land can be further exemplified in the miracle that ends the drought (according to Moreno's testimony). Matías Olivera, the lay hermit, literally walks-with Our Lady of Charity, prayerfully expecting that life-sustaining waters will overcome a severe drought. Olivera takes the statue out in procession, and Moreno tells us that in this very act that which had been made lifeless (the exploited land) returned to new life ("and in an instant the river grew and the drought ceased").[57]

The barrenness of the river and of the land suggested the marginalization of all creatures, while their resurrection implied a new way of relating for all creatures that lived in this copper-mining community. The new life and power of nature ("and the rain began to come down so heavy")[58] mirrored the new life and empowerment offered by Our Lady of Charity to the copper-mining community. The copper miners "dwelled-in" the landscape, and the landscape "dwelled-in" them. This connection between the land and its people should not surprise us.[59] As Sallie McFague has noted:

> The link between justice and ecological issues becomes especially evident in light of the dualistic, hierarchical mode of Western thought in which a superior and an inferior are correlated: male-female, white people-people of color, heterosexual-homosexual, able bodies-physically challenged, culture-nature, mind-body, human-nonhuman. These correlated terms—most often normatively ranked—reveal clearly that domination and destruction of the natural world is inexorably linked with the domination and oppression of the poor, people of color, and all others that fall on the "inferior" side of the correlation. Nowhere is this more apparent than in the ancient and deep identification of women and nature, an identification so profound that it touches the very marrow of our being: our birth from the bodies of our mothers and our nourishment from the body of the earth.[60]

Our Lady of Charity walks in solidarity with marginalized persons.

Charity as solidarity among the oppressed is the primary meaning of this narrative.[61] God's solidarity with this copper-mining community manifests itself through the expression of a Marian symbol that empowers this community to recall a dangerous memory. "To reduce someone to the status of a non-person, to keep someone quietly in the situation of bondage, a dominating power must take away the memory of an individual's personal history, ancestors, and traditions."[62] As we have seen, however, Our Lady of Charity saves, frees, and evokes the traditions of persons within the community. The landscape and its people reveal her solidarity.

The *names of Juan Moreno, Rodrigo de Hoyos, and Juan de Hoyos reveal their religious and social marginalization.* Names recall relational, cultural, religious, and geographical origins. Names often reveal social and political status. The names of Juan Moreno, Rodrigo de Hoyos, and Juan de Hoyos reveal not only their post-baptismal Christian identity, but also their subordinate status. Their names suggest cultural and religious marginalization, since names often reveal the power of one person over an other.[63] While their baptism signified that they were considered human (as opposed to being "a little less than human"), to Spanish authorities they were still seen as natural children with only a mind *in potentia.*[64] In other words, they were subordinate creatures, subject to the "rational" authority of figures such as Sánchez de Moya, the Spanish administrator of the copper mines.

Our Lady of Charity's accompaniment of this marginalized copper-mining community suggests an embodied anthropology.

As mentioned in the beginning of this essay, "walking-with" or "being-with" others presupposes an embodied relationship. The members of the copper-mining community relate sacramentally to Our Lady of Charity as an embodied person. They relate to her in ways that implicitly or explicitly acknowledge one or more of the five senses. For instance, Juan Moreno, Juan de Hoyos, and Rodrigo de Hoyos encounter the *Virgen de la Caridad* while searching for salt. Salt was used both as a flavoring substance and as a food preservative. Moreover, upon seeing her, they carried her into the boat. Recall too, how Matías Olivera questioned Our Lady of Charity, expecting to hear answers regarding her unusual disappearances. Finally, her lamp oil, or more precisely her lard (*manteca*), was said to be "a remedy for all illnesses."[65] Oil used as a remedy suggested the sacramental practice of anointing vanquished bodies—a practice that is both healing and fragrant.

In summary, as a woman, the *Virgen de la Caridad* favors and assumes the reality of the poor and marginalized. She reveals their identity as much as they reveal hers. She walked-with Juan Moreno, Juan de Hoyos, and Rodrigo de Hoyos, names that may have evoked the memory of other marginalized persons in the Christian tradition.[66] In so doing, Our Lady of Charity imaged who God is and called human persons to do the same. She was a symbol of God's ongoing solidarity with persons who struggled to overcome various sociocultural forms of marginalization. In her solidarity, she witnessed what it meant to be created in the image of God. Being like God means walking-with others, especially and preferentially the socioculturally marginalized persons as they struggle to survive.

DIME CON QUIÉN ANDAS Y TE DIRÉ QUIÉN ERES
SOME PRACTICAL IMPLICATIONS
WITHIN THE CONTEMPORARY REALITY OF U.S. HISPANICS

As stories are told again and again, they have the potential to be reinterpreted and appropriated so as to influence the lives of many peoples. This is precisely why the gospel stories never cease to challenge, subvert, and reenvision patterns of relationships. The story of Our Lady of Charity can speak to contemporary U.S. Hispanic reality. To walk-with the *Virgen de la Caridad* and with those who today are like the marginalized of the copper-mining community, requires us to be-with the culturally marginalized of our contemporary U.S. landscape and to walk in the places where they abide.[67]

The story of Our Lady of Charity strikes a chord primarily among Cuban-Americans. As Thomas Tweed's recent study has pointed out, Cuban-Americans continue to live this story, especially within the physical landscape of the shrine of Our Lady of Charity in Miami.[68] One can see why faith-filled Cubans find religious significance in the ongoing experience of exiles saved at open sea by ropes thrown to their rafts. Associated with water and the salvation of persons, the *Virgen de la Caridad* serves as a symbol of hope for such exiles who, like Matías Olivera, find themselves crying out for help as they face life-threatening experiences.

Yet, it is precisely the association of Our Lady of Charity with exiles that makes this Marian devotion capable of speaking to the reality of other U.S. Hispanics. U.S. Hispanic "exiles" come to this land not only on rafts that cross the Florida Straits but also on rafts that cross the Rio Grande. Indeed, the *Virgen de la Caridad* can be fittingly characterized as Our Lady of the Exile. Exile is our most basic shared U.S. Hispanic experience.

Some of us came to the U.S. fleeing various oppressive sociocultural conditions in our native lands, while others were "exiled" from their own lands and cultural heritage as a result of U.S. expansionist policies.[69] For most of us, exile has come to be identified more and more with the reality of sociocultural marginalization. The landscape where we live and the persons who rule it have not always been receptive to our cultural identity and our religious traditions.

There are three signposts that highlight this marginalization: (1) the experience of "naming" U.S. Hispanics, (2) the reception of U.S. Hispanic religious expressions within ecclesial and educational institutions, and (3) the places where U.S. Latinos/as live and work.

As we have seen, naming implies power over an "other." In ways that parallel Juan Moreno, Juan de Hoyos, and Rodrigo de Hoyos, U.S. Hispanics[70] have been subjected to name changes. Take, for instance, the label *Hispanic*, a name given to us by the U.S. Census Bureau. Most of us, however, prefer a name that relates us to our own or our family's country of origin (Cuban-American, Mexican-American, Puerto Rican, and so on). While many of us have increasingly embraced umbrella terms such as Hispanic or Latino/a, we need to remember the cultural limitations of these labels. These terms can "melt" away human differences and thereby marginalize the specific cultural identity of our peoples.

Perhaps more than ever, mutual relationships, common interests, and recent issues within the U.S. landscape (immigration policies, affirmative action, and various educational propositions) have prompted us to recall shared linguistic, cultural, and religious Catholic roots, and to create common ways by which to name ourselves as a whole. Without in any way undermining the importance of the present as a community-building moment among Latinos/as in this country, it is equally important not to allow names—or those who exercise the power to name and describe us—to suppress our particular cultural heritage. A U.S. Latino/a with Cuban roots is not the same as a U.S. Latino/a with Mexican roots. The "melting pot" theory, in all of its manifestations, must be resisted. Put religiously, there are many similarities between Our Lady of Charity and Our Lady of Guadalupe, but each assumes, reveals, and preserves the cultural identity of persons situated in distinctive spatial and cultural locations.

The reception of U.S. Hispanic religious expressions within ecclesial and educational institutions also reflects cultural marginalization. I recall being in a Midwestern parish where an image to Our Lady of Guadalupe had been placed near the left side of the main altar. One Sunday, as my wife and I walked into church, we realized that the image had been removed from center stage and placed in a side chapel. A white carved statue of a European madonna had taken its place. While no harm was intended, we could not fail to speculate on the sacramental implications of this move. The implicit yet subtle message for Latinos/as in that parish was clear to us: European culture and religion is better than brown *mestizo* culture and religion. And, yes, sacramental actions do mirror communal experiences.

The story of Our Lady of Charity resists the temptation to subordinate one form of religious or cultural expression to another. The story challenges anthropological and religious marginalization. The *Virgen de la Caridad* accompanied members of a marginalized copper-mining community in ways that recalled and affirmed their cultural/religious identity.

Similarly, those who accompany U.S. Hispanics (that is, persons in ecclesial and educational positions of leadership) should do the same.

Since religious expressions and human identity are intertwined, marginalizing the former often implies human marginalization. The present marginalization of U.S. Hispanic religious experiences in places with significant numbers of Latinos/as, such as parishes and educational institutions, exemplifies the point. The failure of pastoral leaders, religious educators, and non-Latino/a theologians to incorporate these experiences into overall liturgical life, educational programs, and theological reflection mirrors the concrete marginalization of bodies within locations that often claim—rather uncritically—a "catholic" identity. In many of these places, Latinos/as are under-represented in occupational and leadership roles.

Finally, as we have seen exemplified in the story of Our Lady of Charity, what is of God does not discriminate among the various sectors of the profane. Indeed, what is of God is intrinsically related with the profane, especially with those places where marginalized persons live and work.[71] In ways parallel to the copper-mining community of the *Caridad* story, marginalization characterizes the places where large numbers of U.S. Hispanics live and work. While the oft-heard accounts of sweat shops and migrant camps have brought this issue to the forefront, we need to be mindful of other less visible but equally oppressive experiences. Many instances of labor injustice, long hours of low-paying work, mandatory overtime in places with a surplus of documented or undocumented bodies, linguistic barriers, the presence of Latinos/as in urban areas often neglected and plagued with violence—these instances and too many others also exemplify Latino/a marginalization in the United States. Given these experiences the challenge that Our Lady of Charity presents is clear: to walk in solidarity with persons who live and work within such places, so as to mediate God's saving grace.

CONCLUDING REMARKS

This essay provided an exploration in U.S. Latino/a theological anthropology. It has done so mindful of this volume's efforts to reflect methodologically and theologically the *heart of our people*. A number of other loci could have easily served our purpose. Given the present limitations, I chose a devotion that resonates well with my specific cultural background and ecclesial experience—the devotion to Our Lady of Charity. As the essay's argument and footnotes witness, however, this article attempted to remain faithful to some of the leading insights emerging in U.S. Hispanic theological anthropology.

La Virgen de la Caridad offers a praxis for imaging who God is. Her lamp oil can become, to paraphrase the testimony of Juan Moreno, a "remedy" for social diseases that afflict marginalized persons in our time. And unlike those who walked the road of Emmaus with Jesus (who neither knew him nor the purpose of his accompaniment), we can accept the invitation to know whom and what she represents by walking-with persons within her landscape. By walking-with Our Lady of Charity we affirm and reveal the popular wisdom of the aphorism *Dime con quién andas y te diré quién eres.* And in so doing, we become more God-like, truly "catholic," because we lift the lowly, depose the mighty, and feed the hungry—thereby fulfilling the promises God made to all our ancestors now and forever (Lk 1:46-55).

Notes

[1] Sixto J. García and Orlando O. Espín, "'Lilies of the Field': A Hispanic Theology of Providence and Human Responsibility," *Proceedings of the Catholic Theological Society of America* 44 (1989), 76. See also J. A. Cruz Brache, *Cinco mil seiscientos refranes y frases de uso común entre los dominicanos* (Santo Domingo: Galaxia, 1978); José Sánchez-Boudy, *¡Guante sin grasa, no coge bola!: El refranero popular cubano* (Miami: Ediciones Universal, 1993); and Germán Diez Barrio, *Los refranes en la sabiduría popular* (Valladolid: Ed. Monte de Piedad, 1985).

[2] See Stephen B. Bevans, *Models of Contextual Theology* (Maryknoll, N.Y.: Orbis Books, 1992), 12; and, J. G. Healey, "Proverbs and Sayings—A Window into African Christian World View," *Service* 3 (1988), 1-35.

[3] This proposed interpretation is more concerned with anthropology and less with morality. While undoubtedly every relationship has a moral dimension, the wisdom phrase simply affirms relationship as constitutive and revelatory of persons without prejudging the moral character of these relationships. See Virgilio Elizondo, *Mestizaje: The Dialectic of Cultural Birth and the Gospel* (San Antonio, Tex.: Mexican American Cultural Center, 1978), 348.

[4] In this essay we will use the expressions "walking-with" and "being-with" interchangeably. While the former connotes more explicitly the dynamic understanding of "person" we propose here, the latter resonates well with the ontologies of "person" in the West. Note, however, that by using the expression "being-with" we do not mean a mere standing next to an "other." Rather, for us, "being-with" presupposes participating in, and sharing the condition of another person. For instance, when we say in Spanish *"estoy contigo"* (I am with you), we do not mean that we are merely standing next to someone. What we mean is that we stand *in solidarity with* another person, sharing his or her experiences to the degree humanly possible. Moreover, note too how in Spanish the verb *estar* ("to be"), as opposed to *ser* (also "to be"), connotes the dynamic nature of persons we propose here. For a philosophical discussion of *estar*, see Juan Carlos Scannone, "Un nuevo punto de partida en la filosofía latinoamericana," in *Stromata* 36 (1980), 35-41.

[5] See Roberto S. Goizueta, *Caminemos con Jesús: Toward a Hispanic/Latino Theology of Accompaniment* (Maryknoll, N.Y.: Orbis Books, 1995), 68.

[6] See ibid., 65-76.

[7] See Alex García-Rivera, *St. Martín de Porres: The "Little Stories" and the Semiotics of Culture* (Maryknoll, N.Y.: Orbis Books, 1995), esp. 97-105.

[8] As a result of cultural, racial, and religious relationships that have yielded various *mestizo* and *mulato* religious expressions, it would be incorrect to *simply* identify any "Mary" of U.S. Hispanic popular Catholicism with Mary, the mother of Jesus. For instance, as we will later see, Hispanic expressions of Mary (such as Our Lady of Charity) are loci of cross-cultural and religious expressions. But since the present essay is written from a Christian perspective, we will use the name Mary (or the adjective Marian) even though we remain keenly aware of the theological complexity of this use within U.S. Hispanic culture.

[9] Orlando O. Espín, "The Vanquished, Faithful Solidarity and the Marian Symbol: A Hispanic Perspective on Providence," in *On Keeping Providence*, ed. B. Doherty and J. Coultas (Terre Haute, Ind.: St. Mary of the Woods College Press, 1991), 89.

[10] For a brief description of U.S. Hispanic "Marys," see Stephen Holler, "The Origins of Marian Devotion in Latin American Cultures in the United States," *Marian Studies* 46 (1995), 108-27.

[11] On the communal sociohistorical grounding of Marian devotions, see Sandra L. Zimdars-Swartz, *Encountering Mary: From La Salette to Medjugorje* (Princeton, N.J.: Princeton University Press, 1991).

[12] For U.S. Hispanic understandings of the popular element in popular religion, see Orlando O. Espín, "Popular Religion as an Epistemology (of Suffering)," *Journal of Hispanic/Latino Theology* 2:2 (1994), 65-66; Goizueta, *Caminemos con Jesús*, 21-22; and García-Rivera, *St. Martín de Porres*, 16-18. For an alternative view, see Robert E. Wright, "If It's Official, It Can't Be Popular? Reflections on Popular and Folk Religion," *Journal of Hispanic/Latino Theology* 1:3 (1994), 47-67. For a Latin American perspective on this issue, see Cristián Parker, *Popular Religion and Modernization in Latin America: A Different Logic* (Maryknoll, N.Y.: Orbis Books, 1996), 35-38.

[13] See Espín's work on medieval and pre-Tridentine Christianity. Among other things, Espín's work highlights the normative role of popular expressions of faith. Of special interest is his argument that as a result of Claude LeJay's distinction at the Council of Trent between *traditiones quae ad fidem pertinent* (traditions that pertain to faith) and the *traditiones ecclesiae* (traditions of the Church), post-Tridentine theology witnessed the "separation between received, unchanging doctrine *(Traditio,* now with a capital T) and other (equally received) reformable traditions *(traditiones,* now with lower-case t)." Thus, Espín continues, "revelation came to be viewed as 'doctrinal,' and the rest of Christian living (spirituality, worship, the ethical life of communities and individuals) became dangerously demoted to reformable traditions" (see Orlando O. Espín, "Popular Catholicism among Latinos," in *Hispanic Catholic Culture in the U.S.: Issues and Concerns*, ed. J. Dolan and A. Figueroa Deck (Notre Dame, Ind.: University of Notre Dame Press, 1994), 318.

[14] Robert J. Schreiter, *Constructing Local Theologies* (Maryknoll, N.Y.: Orbis Books, 1995), 122.

[15] Karl Rahner, "The Relation between Theology and Popular Religion," *Theological Investigations, XXII* (New York: Crossroad, 1974), 142. Emphasis added.

[16] Written accounts are available, but such accounts are not the primary means through which this tradition has been communicated. For instance, see Onofre de Fonseca, *Historia de la aparición milagrosa de Nuestra Señora de la Caridad del Cobre* (Santiago de Cuba: Impr. del Real Consulado de Santiago de Cuba, por Loreto Espinel, 1830); Ismael Testé, *Historia eclesiástica de Cuba* (Burgos: Editorial El Monte Carmelo, 1969), 3:346-412; Leví Marrero, *Los esclavos y la Virgen del Cobre. Dos*

siglos de lucha por la libertad de Cuba (Miami: Ediciones Universal, 1980); Irene A. Wright, "Our Lady of Charity: Nuestra Señora de la Caridad del Cobre (Santiago de Cuba), Nuestra Señora de la Caridad de Illescas (Castilla, Spain)," *Hispanic American Historical Review* 5 (1922), 709-17; and, most recently, Olga Portuondo Zúñiga, *La Virgen de la Caridad del Cobre: Símbolo de cubanía* (Santiago de Cuba: Editorial Oriente, 1995).

[17] The recent ethnographic study by Thomas A. Tweed in relation to the impact of this tradition on Cuban-Americans, as well as the historical study of this tradition by Cuban historian Olga Portuondo Zúñiga, provide helpful signposts for undertaking this task. See T. A. Tweed, *Our Lady of the Exile: Diasporic Religion at a Cuban Catholic Shrine in Miami* (New York: Oxford University Press, 1997); Zúñiga, *La Virgen de la Caridad del Cobre.*

[18] The testimony of Juan Moreno was discovered in 1973 by Cuban historian Leví Marrero in the Archives of the Indies, in Seville. See Archivo General de Indias, Audiencia de Santo Domingo, *legajo* 363. This document has been transcribed and printed in several places. Throughout this essay we will be using and referring to the complete transcription published in Mario Vizcaíno, *La Virgen de la Caridad, Patrona de Cuba* (Miami: Instituto Pastoral del Sureste, 1981), 10-27.

[19] See Glossary.

[20] According to Juan Moreno, the events took place around 1612. In the Spanish inquiry, Moreno says that he was (at the time of the inquiry) eighty-five years old, and that he was ten years old when the image of Our Lady of Charity was found. Subtracting 85 from 1687 (the year the Spanish inquiry took place) and adding 10 yields the year 1612. See Vizcaíno, *La Virgen de la Caridad*, 23.

[21] Moreno infers in the declaration that he could not read and explicitly states that he could not write. See Vizcaíno, *La Virgen de la Caridad*, 23, 27.

[22] See Tweed, *Our Lady of the Exile*, 22-23.

[23] We say "Christian" because there are various counter voices that have provided a different interpretation of this narrative from the perspective of Yoruban religion. For instance, see Raúl Cañizares, *Walking with the Night: The Afro-Cuban World of Santería* (Burlington, Vt.: Destiny Books, 1993), 65-66.

[24] See Catherine M. LaCugna, "The Practical Trinity," *The Christian Century* 109 (1992), 681-82.

[25] Jeanette Rodríguez, *Stories We Live, Cuentos que vivimos: Hispanic Women's Spirituality* (New York: Paulist Press, 1996), 7, 15.

[26] On the anthropological presuppositions of modernism and postmodernism see Roberto Goizueta's essay in this volume.

[27] See Stephen Crites, "The Narrative Quality of Experience," in *Why Narrative: Readings in Narrative Theology*, ed. Stanley Hauerwas and L. Gregory Jones (Grand Rapids, Mich.: W. Eerdmans Publishing Company, 1989), 85.

[28] See Johann Baptist Metz, *Faith in History and Society: Toward a Practical Fundamental Theology* (New York: Seabury Press, 1980), 184-237.

[29] For what follows, see Terrence W. Tilley, *Story Theology* (Collegeville, Minn.: Liturgical Press, 1990),18-54. Tilley now recognizes that sagas also usually function as myths (personal communication, 21 July 1997).

[30] For a brief history of this community, see Marrero, *Los esclavos y la Virgen del Cobre: Dos siglos de lucha por la libertad de Cuba.*

[31] In many ways, Jesus' miracles can also be characterized as parabolic actions. Because they are often directed at persons considered to be "unclean," Jesus' miracles shatter common expectations and upset expected patterns of relationships. See Paul W. Hollenbach, "Jesus, Demoniacs, and Public Authorities: A Socio-

Historical Study," *The Journal of the American Academy of Religion* 49:4 (1981), 567-85.

[32] See Vizcaíno, *La Virgen de la Caridad*, 23.

[33] In 1597 King Philip II of Spain charged Sánchez de Moya with the responsibility of administering the copper deposits in Cuba. He was given the official title of captain of artillery for Cuba. He administered the mines until 1620. See Wright, "Our Lady of Charity," 710; and J. J. Arrom, *Certidumbre de América: Estudios de Letras, Folklore y Cultura* (Madrid: Editorial Gredes, 1971), 202-3.

[34] Vizcaíno, *La Virgen de la Caridad*, 23-24.

[35] Ibid., 24.

[36] Ibid., 26.

[37] Ibid., 25.

[38] Ibid., 26.

[39] Ibid.

[40] See *Encuentro nacional eclesial cubano: Documento final e instrucción pastoral de los obispos* (Havana: Publications of the Cuban Episcopal Conference, 1987), 44, my translation.

[41] See William A. Christian, *Local Religion in Sixteenth-Century Spain* (Princeton, N.J.: Princeton University Press, 1981), 84-87. On the relationship between the Cuban and Spanish devotions to Our Lady of Charity, see Wright, "Our Lady of Charity." See also Tweed, *Our Lady of the Exile*, 20-21.

[42] In a document entitled "Declaration of Agustín Quiala," a sixty-year-old slave of the copper mines tells how black slaves who worked in the mines would hear the lay brother speak to the Virgin. Note how the close association of a religious brother with African slaves is in continuity with the Spanish royal edict of 1577, which gave specific evangelizing instructions to religious for the care and evangelization of African slaves. For Quiala's story, see Vizcaíno, *La Virgen de la Caridad*, 68.

[43] Note how Moreno's story explicitly confirms that it was copper miners who heard him question Our Lady of Charity. See Vizcaíno, *La Virgen de la Caridad*, 26.

[44] Martin Luther King Jr., *Strength to Love* (Philadelphia: Fortress Press, 1963), 72.

[45] For instance, Orlando Espín argues that there is no such thing as an "acultural Christianity." He further argues that the way "a people experientially perceive the love of God, and the way they respond to it, will always be cultural." See Orlando O. Espín, "Grace and Humanness," in *We Are a People!: Initiatives in Hispanic American Theology*, ed. Roberto S. Goizueta (Minneapolis, Minn.: Fortress Press, 1992), 145.

[46] The Taínos were the Amerindians who inhabited most of Cuba. They were quickly exterminated as a result of the Spanish conquest. See Irving Rouse, *The Taínos: Rise and Decline of the People Who Greeted Columbus* (New Haven, Conn.: Yale University Press, 1992), 1-25.

[47] For instance, see Anthony M. Stevens-Arroyo, "The Persistence of Religious Cosmovision in an Alien World," in *Enigmatic Powers: Syncretism with African and Indigenous Peoples' Religions among Latinos*, ed. A. M. Stevens-Arroyo and A. I. Pérez (New York: CUNY Press/Bildner Center for Western Hemispheric Studies, 1995), 130-31.

[48] The *zemís* were divinities as well as their representations in religious objects made of wood, stone, bone, shell, or pottery. See Rouse, *The Taínos*, 13.

[49] On the relationship between Atabex and Our Lady of Charity, see Salvador Larrúa Guedes, "La aparición de Nuestra Señora de la Caridad del Cobre. Tres

hipótesis," *Palabra* 50 (1996), 6. Note too how Guedes mentions an incident, re-corded by Cuban historian Ramírez, of a Cuban Taíno chief who attributed his victories to a Marian statue, and of how on one occasion the chief threw the statue into the sea for fear that his opponents would steal it. On the relationship be-tween Atabex and Yúcahu, see Rouse, *The Taínos*, 13.

⁵⁰ William A. Christian, *Person and God in a Spanish Valley* (New York: Seminar Press, 1972), 100.

⁵¹ On the Galilean identity of Jesus, see Virgilio Elizondo, *Galilean Journey: The Mexican-American Promise* (Maryknoll, N.Y.: Orbis Books, 1994), 49-66.

⁵² Note that while our arguments have been primarily concerned with Taíno culture, a similar process probably occurred with the early African slaves. In-deed, as later eighteenth- and nineteenth-century Lucumí associations between Our Lady of Charity and the Yoruba *orisha* Ochún witness, Our Lady of Charity also walks-with Afro-Cubans in ways that assume their cultural roots. (The Lucumí are the Yoruba in Cuba.)

⁵³ On the anthropological relationship between public and private places, see Goizueta, *Caminemos con Jesús*, 191-211.

⁵⁴ See Vizcaíno, *La Virgen de la Caridad*, 26.

⁵⁵ *Cobre* means "copper" in Spanish.

⁵⁶ See Tweed, *Our Lady of the Exile*, 22.

⁵⁷ See Vizcaíno, *La Virgen de la Caridad*, 26.

⁵⁸ Ibid.

⁵⁹ See Jeanette Rodríguez's essay in this volume.

⁶⁰ Sallie McFague, "An Earthly Theological Agenda," in *Ecofeminism and the Sacred*, ed. Carol J. Adams (New York: Continuum, 1993), 85.

⁶¹ For a discussion of charity as solidarity, see the work of Cuban-American ethicist Ada M. Isasi-Díaz, "Solidarity: Love of Neighbor in the Twenty-First Cen-tury," in *Mujerista Theology: A Theology for the Twenty-First Century* (Maryknoll, N.Y.: Orbis Books, 1996), 87-88.

⁶² Elizabeth Johnson, "Reconstructing a Theology of Mary," in *Mary, Woman of Nazareth: Biblical and Theological Perspectives*, ed. Doris Donnelly (New York: Paulist Press, 1989), 71.

⁶³ For the biblical implications of "naming," see, for example, Phyllis Trible, *God and the Rhetoric of Sexuality* (Philadelphia: Fortress Press, 1985), 99-105 and 133-35.

⁶⁴ For a discussion of these anthropological categories as they emerged in the Valladolid debate of 1550, see García-Rivera, *St. Martín de Porres*, 97-98.

⁶⁵ Ibid.

⁶⁶ Take, for instance, the "beloved disciple" traditionally identified as John, who stood with Jesus at the climactic moment of his marginalization, and Juan Diego, the marginalized protagonist of the *Nican mopohua*. Note that in colonial Spanish texts "Rodrigo" was often confused for "Diego."

⁶⁷ For this insight I am indebted to Roberto Goizueta (see his *Caminemos con Jesús*, 191).

⁶⁸ See Tweed, *Our Lady of the Exile*, esp. 99-133.

⁶⁹ See Justo González, *Mañana: Christian Theology from a Hispanic Perspective* (Nashville, Tenn.: Abingdon Press, 1990), 41-42.

⁷⁰ See Glossary.

⁷¹ See Karl Rahner, "History of the World and Salvation History," in *Theologi-cal Investigations, V* (Baltimore: Helicon, 1966), 97-114. More specifically related to Our Lady of Charity, note Teok Carrasco's mural behind the altar at the shrine in

Miami. This mural weaves the ecclesial and national history of the Cuban people. At the center is an image of Our Lady of Charity surrounded by Cuban history's main ecclesial and political figures. As Carrasco observed in his description of this mural, "the Cuban community, *el pueblo cubano*, encounters its salvation in the arms of the Virgin of Charity" (see Tweed, *Our Lady of the Exile,* 107).

8

Pueblo and Church

❧

GARY RIEBE-ESTRELLA, S.V.D.
Catholic Theological Union

INTRODUCTION

Little sustained reflection on ecclesiology has been done in U.S. Latino Catholic theology.[1] This essay attempts to chart, in broad strokes, some of the directions that reflection might take. The need for this type of reflection has become increasingly clear. As U.S. Latino theology more pointedly voices its claim to be engaged in a theological inquiry that is relevant to and valid for the whole theological enterprise, not simply in one that pertains only to Latinos, it must engage those larger and more traditional theological themes that have served as foci of so much of North Atlantic theology. If we pursue only themes that can be identified with the particularity of Latino praxis, no matter how significant these themes may be in themselves and for our peoples, we Latino theologians run the risk of marginalizing ourselves as "ethnic theologians."

At the same time, as we engage these traditional themes we must do so with fidelity to the methodological presuppositions that we claim characterize U.S. Latino theology, particularly our commitment to theologize out of the praxis of our peoples.[2] In pursuing this task, the clarity with which we articulate our starting point often differs from that of many non-Latino theologians, whose theological reflections rarely mention the historical and cultural contexts out of which they come, but rather, precisely by the omission of the mention of the context, pretend to universalism.

Ecclesiology from a U.S. Latino perspective must be, therefore, a reflection rooted in our peoples' experience of church. And perhaps no part of our experience of church in the recent history of our presence in the United

172

States has received more attention than the *Encuentro* process.[3] The first *Encuentro* in 1972 was a meeting of Latino leaders. By the time of the second *Encuentro*, in 1977, the process had developed to involve mainly the grassroots folk. The theme chosen during this second *Encuentro* was *Pueblo de Dios en Marcha*. Subsequently, the third *Encuentro* took up the theme, "Prophetic Voices." Each of the third *Encuentro*'s "Prophetic Pastoral Guidelines," which give direction for pastoral action by Latinos and embody this last *Encuentro*'s theme, begins with the phrase "*Nosotros, como pueblo hispano.*"[4] What becomes clear in this *Encuentro* process is that when Latino Catholics in the United States have gathered together to reflect on their ecclesial identity and to set priorities for pastoral action, we have used the term *pueblo* as one of our defining characteristics. And this should not be surprising, because *pueblo* reflects a fundamental category in Latino self-identity.

A SOCIOCENTRIC ORGANIC CULTURE

Latino cultures, by and large, are "sociocentric organic" in nature.[5] In other words, the fundamental unit of society is envisioned as a group, primarily the family. The identity of an individual emerges from his or her membership in the group. In this cultural perspective, human persons mature by recognizing their place within the group and by refining to some extent the mutual obligations and rights which that place entails. But who they are is always bounded by the group.[6]

In counterdistinction to this cultural perspective is that found in mainstream U.S. culture, which might be characterized as "egocentric contractual." In other words, the fundamental unit of society is envisioned as the individual. In the process of individuation, human persons mature by distancing themselves from others in order to discover their own strengths and weaknesses, that is, their identity. When this identity has achieved sufficient strength and form, the individual freely associates with others for mutual benefit in the lifelong developmental task of intimacy. The relationship of the individual to other individuals or groups and to society at large is contractual, dependent on the mutual consent of the parties. Consequently, one freely chooses or dissociates relationship.[7]

The use of names in self-identification exemplifies how these two cultural perspectives differ in their understanding of the human person. When meeting young people from the dominant culture of the United States, they will ordinarily introduce themselves by using their first name: "Hi, I'm Fred." When you meet a Latino/a, you're given a whole string of last names as the person attempts to identify for you who she or he is: "Soy Josefina González Obregón." The Latino use of two last names (*el doble apellido*) is a way by which persons identify the two primary groups of belonging which found their identity, that is, their father's family and their mother's family. When Josefina marries, she takes on the last name of her husband's family, which is prefaced with a "de": "Josefina González de Chávez, a sus órdenes."[8] While the young North American has situated his uniqueness, his personal identity, in his first name, the name that differentiates him from the rest of the members of his family, the Latina lays out a shortened version of her family tree since her uniqueness, her identity, is determined precisely by the intersection of the primary groups to which she belongs.

Another instance of these two very different understandings of the human person can be found in the exchange that often follows self-introductions. The non-Latino will often lead with the question, "So, what do you do?" The Latino/a might say, "Oh, you're an Obregon. Is your family from Jalisco?" While the Latino/a pursues relationship as the source of the other's identity, the dominant culture centers on how the individual chooses to relate to society; that is, how that person constitutes his or her identity by contributing to the productivity of society.[9]

The Latino group-oriented world of relationships is organic. The identity of persons within a group changes upon being grafted into other groups. Latinos/as are not free to choose which members of these additional groups they will have a relationship with and which they will not. The link among the groups itself determines that all the original members of each of the newly interconnected groups have a relationship with all the other members, a relationship embodied in a series of obligations and rights. The most usual ways for a Latino's primary group, the family, to grow are through marriage and *compadrazgo*. Through marriage, the already extended family extends its network of relationships throughout another extended primary group, so that the original definitions of familial terms like *tía/o* (aunt/uncle) and *prima/o* (cousin), which were fairly narrow in scope, now can be used of persons that one will never meet but the invocation of whose name can demand generous behavior to relatives of relatives' relatives.[10]

The use of *compadrazgo* presents an even more interesting picture of the significance of the growth of familial relationships.[11] Parents choose *padrinos* for their child in baptism. As *padrinos*, these people take on the role of godparents; that is, they take on a role of responsibility for the child. But the more significant new relationship is not that of the *padrinos* with the child but the relationship they now have with the child's parents in which they become *compadres*. As "co-parents," they become members of the family. In addition, most often their families now are considered related to the child's family. *Compadres* are chosen with an eye to the advantages this new link among primary groups will bring to the members of each of the groups involved. Once this link occurs, the individual members are expected to recognize the new set of relationships without regard to their personal opinion of the merits of the other group(s) or individuals.

Among sociocentric organic Latinos, all relationships use family as their paradigm. Friends really become family members. First of all, once true friendships are developed, the persons involved can call on one another for assistance as members of a family might, with full expectation that that assistance will be forthcoming and reciprocated. Second, the friendship is not simply with an individual member of the family, but, because that member's identity is founded precisely on his or her membership in a family, by organic association the "friend" is now subsumed into those family relationships. It is not by chance that relationships that are not biologically familial are often referred to among Latinos by the use of familial terms such as *mano* (*hermano*) or *tío/a*. The expectations of rights and responsibilities as they affect friends are on a par with those of family members.

Although the sociocentric nature of Latino cultures is quite distinct from the egocentric perspective of the dominant culture in the United States, it is important to note that the process of acculturation experienced by Latinos in the United States appears to have little effect on this fundamental characteristic of our self-understanding. A growing number of cultural anthropologists today affirm that the single continuum model of acculturation does not exhibit a sensitivity to the very complex nature of this encounter between cultural worlds. Whereas the single continuum model would hypothesize that a Latino/a, through constant contact with the dominant culture, would gradually move from a state of being unacculturated (primarily Mexican, for instance) to that of being acculturated (primarily reflective of dominant U.S. culture), in fact, it appears that acculturation takes place at different rates for different cultural traits.[12] This multidimensional model of acculturation allows us to see that, for example, while language may be the trait for which acculturation happens most quickly, other cultural traits show little significant change even after prolonged interaction with the dominant culture. The sociocentric understanding of family and the strength of family relationships for Latinos are strengthened in Latinos' continued contact with the dominant culture.[13]

This use of the familial as the fundamental paradigm for understanding all relationships is played out on a larger scale in the meaning of the term *pueblo*. The fact that in Spanish the word *pueblo* means both "town" and "people" is quite suggestive. The realities to which the word points to have been interchangeable, particularly in the countries of origins of Latinos. The *town* is composed of a network of families, most, if not all, of whom are related to one another through blood, *compadrazgo,* or friendship. The geographic confines of the physical location of these primary groups incarnates the network of family relationships that founds the identity of the members. Thus, Latinos often identify themselves by the town which has been home to the families that bound their identity. By extension, then, the term *pueblo* evokes for Latinos the concrete and embodied relationships that define who they are.

The experience of *pueblo* as "town/people" also commonly has a religious dimension in that rural communities in Latinos' countries of origin often coincided with the geographic boundaries of a parish and were frequently organized physically around the church building that held a prominent place in the central plaza of the town. For Latinos, then, it is not only a somewhat natural move to use the term *pueblo* to designate their identity as church, but the term brings with it all the cultural assumptions about identity that are typical of sociocentric organic cultures.

For our purposes here, the following points can then be made: (1) the Latino understanding of all relationships is modeled on familial relationships; (2) these relationships can be extended through the inclusion of other groups (as is done analogously in the dynamics of *compadrazgo*); (3) these relationships become stronger rather than weaker in the Latino community's prolonged contact with North American culture; (4) being part of one's primary group and its interrelationships with other groups, resulting in a sense of *pueblo*, is not a matter of choice but is experienced by Latinos as a given; (5) individuals are free to refine these identity-founding relationships but are not free to dissociate themselves entirely from them without risking the loss of personal identity; and (6) when the relationships involved in being church are summed up in the term *pueblo*, the term is understood by Latinos within the cultural perspective of a sociocentric organic culture.

A CONTRASTING SENSE OF PEOPLEHOOD

As I have noted above, persons from the dominant U.S. culture bear a quite distinct cultural understanding of what it means to be a people and of the individual's relationship to that people. As Shweder and Bourne note, the first characteristic of this cultural world is egocentrism.

A kind of sacred personalized self is developed and the individual qua individual is seen as inviolate, a supreme value in and of itself. The "self" becomes an object of interest *per se*. Free to undertake projects of personal expression, personal narratives, autobiographies, diaries, mirrors, separate rooms, early separation from bed, body, and breast of mother, personal space—the autonomous individual imagines the incredible, that he lives within an inviolate protected region (the extended boundaries of the self) where he is "free to choose" . . . where what he does "is his own business."[14]

Both the private and the public lives of members of the dominant U.S. culture are characterized by individualism.[15]

The second characteristic of this cultural world is its contractual nature. The relationships that have meaning for an individual are those this autonomous self freely chooses and from which disassociation is equally possible. Even family is often seen less as that group to which one belongs than as something that exists at the service of the individual.[16] Religious affiliation, which in earlier times was understood as a defining characteristic of the person, is now submitted to the same criterion of personal benefit.

> The issue, both for the local parish and for the national or international church, is whether membership is accepted as having a formative claim on one's very sense of self, as involving loyalty that can persist through difficulties, or whether membership is merely instrumental of individual self-fulfillment and, like some current conceptions of marriage, can be abandoned as soon as it "doesn't meet my needs."[17]

Given this distinct starting point in understanding the identity of the individual, peoplehood, whether looked at in a political or religious framework, is not fundamentally linked to biology; it is in no sense a given. Rather, peoplehood in egocentric cultural contexts is created as a voluntary association of free individuals who bind themselves together for mutual benefit and who, in light of their fundamental autonomy, reserve the right to dissociate when that mutual benefit is no longer served. In referring to North American Catholics' understanding of themselves as church, T. Howland Sanks presses the influence that the individualistic emphasis of this cultural world has on their sense of community and peoplehood.

> This cultural individualism, deeply embedded in the tradition, makes it difficult to think about or place high priority on community as such. Community is not something that is taken for granted in our society; it is something that must be striven for, something to be achieved. For many reasons, we do not assume that we *belong* to a community; rather, we have to construct one. The problem is on what basis are we to construct such a community.[18]

The political reality of the United States is built precisely on this fundamental principle of free association. No determinative, intrinsic relationship is allowed to exist in the political arena. The colonists were free to sever their ties with England, for those ties depended solely on the free decision of the governed, who had entered into this contract for mutual benefit. When those benefits were no longer forthcoming, the colonists deemed themselves free to dissociate and form a new association with each other.[19]

THE HISTORICAL COORDINATES OF "EL PUEBLO HISPANO"

One of the great advances in ecclesiology promoted by the Second Vatican Council is its use of "People of God" as the primary image for its understanding of church. But it should also be clear that how this image is understood depends in great part on the "geo-theological" contexts in which the image is used.[20] For example, in his book on the contours of ecclesiology in Latin American liberation theology, Alvaro Quiroz Magaña emphasizes that the socioeconomic categories in Latin America have determined the direction of the reflections these theologians have made on their self-understanding as People of God and on the particular role in church that Latin American Catholics are called upon to play. He posits that there are core facets to the concept of church as the People of God: (1) the priority of Christian existence over the organization; (2) the pilgrim people, sacrament of God's Reign; and (3) church as called to be a permanent historical incarnation.[21] However, how these core facets are understood is determined by those situations of massive poverty and structural oppression that constitute the reality of most Latin American countries.

The history of Latinos in the United States has been primarily one of cultural oppression. While it is true that some 30 percent of Latinos in the United States fall below the poverty line as established by the federal government, a number substantially higher than that for the white population or the population as a whole, the most pervasive kind of marginalization that Latinos have suffered is cultural, not economic. The 70 percent of Latinos whose income is above the poverty line do not find that their economic status guarantees them a place within mainstream American society. Rather, we are disproportionately represented in service industries and factory work, while our presence in white-collar positions is far below our presence in the U.S. population as a whole.[22] The number of Latinos enrolled in institutions of higher education has become proportionately lower, even though our percentage within the overall U.S. population has increased.[23] The number of U.S.-born Latino priests in the Catholic church in the United States has remained constant at about two hundred.[24] In area after area of our lives, we find ourselves living on the periphery of U.S. society.

Nor is this marginalization an accident. We entered the pages of U.S. history not as equals but as the conquered. Whether it was due to the Mexican-American War or the Spanish-American War, we found ourselves and our lands incorporated into the United States not by our choice but as the spoils of conquest. Despite the current myth in American society that the Latino presence is the result of a brown invasion across the southern border, our presence in this country historically happened not because we crossed the border, but rather because the border crossed us.[25]

As the victims of conquest, it has been important that we be portrayed in the American psyche as deserving of that conquest. As Justo González has so convincingly demonstrated, the United States, like most countries, has written an "innocent history" of its geographic expansion in the northern hemisphere. In such an "innocent history" the victors are lauded while the losers are unmentioned.

> Then the revolutionary "fathers" sued for independence, mostly in the name of freedom. That this was to a great degree the freedom to make money and to take lands from the Indians is again mentioned but is not allowed to play more than a secondary role in our understanding of the "revolutionary" war . . . We seldom hear of the degree to which the leaders of the movement for independence lusted for Indian lands that the British would not allow them to possess . . . The West was "won," we are told. But how, and who "lost" it, is not part of our national consciousness.[26]

When Latinos do appear in this "innocent history" we are described as having any number of unsavory characteristics which "prove" the wisdom and merit of our subjugation. Our possession of these cultural traits is used to justify our historical marginalization within U.S. society and, by implication, our continued location on the periphery.[27]

Ultimately, our exclusion is not the result of racism in the narrow sense. Though things were different in the Southwest, in the urban north of the United States neither we Latinos nor persons from the dominant culture saw our difference as primarily racial.[28] In fact, up until the 1980 census, Latinos were considered Caucasians on federal government forms.[29] Peter Skerry would argue that it was only in the 1950s and 1960s, with the success of Black Americans in their successful fight for the passage of civil-rights legislation, that Latinos/as began to identify themselves as racially different from the majority of Americans. And that identification had neither an anthropological nor a philosophical basis but was developed as a strategy to ensure that Latinos would benefit from the civil-rights legislation designed to fight racial discrimination. To be considered non-white would guarantee Latinos the same rights in politics and in the workplace as were now guaranteed to blacks.[30]

In a sense, the complex dynamics of this "second *mestizaje*" (Latinos' immersion into dominant U.S. society and culture) have been as formative of the identity of U.S. Latinos as was the first *mestizaje* in our countries of origin.[31] If the first *mestizaje* birthed our peoples in all their diversity out of the violence of the Spanish conquest of the indigenous of the Americas, the second is forcing us to overcome that diversity in order to present a united front in the face of a hostile environment that excludes us because of our cultural difference. Though we identify ourselves with each other by country of origin (that is, Cubans, Mexicans, Colombians, Mexican-Americans), in view of the larger society, which discriminates against us, we speak of ourselves as Latinos/as.[32] It is the common characteristic of the sociocentric nature of our cultures and this common history of our marginalization within U.S. society that come together as the major determinants of our experience as *pueblo*. As such, they form the geo-theological context for our reflection on ourselves as *Pueblo de Dios*, the People of God, the church.

THE PROBLEMATIC OF LATINOS AS *PUEBLO DE DIOS*

The Old Testament roots, seen as the beginning of our understanding of church as the People of God, can be read by Latinos/as as fairly congruous with both these major determinants of Latinos' identity.[33] The first creation story of Genesis, in its portrayal of the simultaneous creation of male and female (Gn 1:27), resonates with Latinos' sociocentric perspective of the group as the fundamental unit of society. It is not the individual human being who is created in the image of God but rather the couple. This couple is immediately charged with multiplying and filling the earth; that is, they are charged with becoming a primary group, a family. The killing of Abel by Cain is particularly heinous because it is a crime of brother against brother. Cain's punishment is banishment from the group, from the source of his identity (Gn 4:12). The "family origin" of humanity undergirds for sociocentric Latinos/as what will later become the theme of the brotherhood and sisterhood of all as announced by Jesus.

From a Latino perspective, one might say that there are two movements in the history of Israel as portrayed in the Old Testament. The first is the history of this original family's development as it is refounded in Noah, with the attendant prohibition against breaking the family bonds as Cain did (Gn 9:5-6), and as one branch becomes central in the blessing given to Abraham to be the father of a great nation (Gn 12:2). The stories of the patriarchs are family stories of sons and fathers, of barren women becoming mothers, of a single family's development into branches, and of the extension of the primary group through marriage. The branches of the family slowly gather in Egypt until, faced with oppression by the other (the non-family), they coalesce into the identity of a people whose distant roots are to be found in the story of the creation of the original group and whose more recent roots are situated in the patriarchal stories of God's relationship with Abraham, Isaac, and Jacob. The second movement of the Old Testament details the history of the family's encounter with the other, its attempt to preserve its identity in the face of dominant groups that are not part of the family, its aspirations to power and importance, and the influences that outsiders have on the identity of the members of the group and ultimately on the identity of the group itself. Particularly because of its constant encounter with the other, family-oriented Israel focuses its stories on itself, on its development and disintegration. That is, Israel's sociocentric cultural bias, which on the positive side acts as a sound basis for its self-identity, tends, when placed in conflictual relationship with the other, to concentrate attention on the group in a fairly defensive posture vis-à-vis the outsider. The function of Israel as God's people becomes that of protecting the divine call, preserving its integrity, and, through its own living out of the covenant, acting in some fashion as a witness and light to other nations.

The formation and history of Israel as a people can be read as reflecting the cultural and historical dynamics that have been at work among Latinos in our formation as a people in the United States. The centrality of our identity in the extended family, linked in a network of relationships to other families, allows us a stable foundation for our sense of peoplehood, even though that is usually first demarcated by criteria of country of origin and a much more specific geographic location within that country. Our constant conflictual encounter with the dominant culture of the United States has encouraged a growing sense of peoplehood founded first not on our internal identity (that is, our family relationships) but on our difference from the aggressive other. When linked to the group perspective, which is fundamental to our cultural world, it creates a fertile ground for a sense of *latinidad* and for a less biological and more analogous sense of *pueblo*. This expanded sense of *pueblo* undergirds our understanding of ourselves as church when we use the image *Pueblo de Dios*.[34]

In light of the above, I suggest that it is not by accident that the conclusions of the three *Encuentros* revolve around the needs of Latinos in the church in the United States and are a call to the rest of the church in this country to address the needs of the Latino membership. Though the four specific dimensions of the *National Pastoral Plan for Hispanic Ministry* also include guidelines for the pastoral action by Latinos/as within the church, by and large the objects of this pastoral care are Latino Catholics.[35] The

Plan's call for the use of a *pastoral de conjunto* focuses on providing ways for Latinos/as to have a more significant voice in ecclesial decision making. Evangelization centers on the formation of small communities that are "effective instruments of evangelization for the Hispanic people." The missionary thrust of the third specific dimension is directed at *Hispanic* families, women, and youth. Only the fourth specific dimension has a more outward thrust:

> To provide leadership formation adapted to the Hispanic culture in the United States that will help people to live and promote a style of Church which will be a leaven of the Kingdom of God in society.[36]

Like the Israel of old, the Latino *Pueblo de Dios* tends to concentrate on itself; its ecclesial reflections tend to be oriented to what others can do for us or what we can do for other Latinos. The very positive value is that our sense of being a people is a given, and so the reality of church can also be proposed not so much as an organization with which one associates or dissociates freely, but rather, as an analogous kind of peoplehood, a membership that touches the depths of one's identity. That is, being church is not so much something that needs to be constructed but something which flows "naturally" out of our relationships. However, the limitations of the sociocentric perspective also have their play, as the sense of church is rather narrowly restricted to the *Pueblo de Dios en Marcha* (the Latino segment of the church in the United States), or to the local parish, to which there is often a high sense of allegiance, or even more narrowly to the groups of families within the parish to which one is related. The often-present divisions in Latino parishes of family versus family and the pastoral difficulty of getting Latinos/as to work together for a common good in the parish or neighborhood that is larger than that bounded by their concrete family relationships exemplify this narrowing dynamic, which might be called the downside of the concreteness of the Latino experience of peoplehood in church.

CHURCH AS ICON OF HUMANITY AND ICON OF GOD

Jesus expands the notion of People of God by making membership depend on a positive response to the announcement of the coming of God's reign and not simply on familial relationships, whether narrowly or broadly understood (Mk 3:31-35). Membership in the people of Israel no longer carries with it any surety of membership in the new People of God (Jn 8:39). Nevertheless, this qualitative move to the primacy of personal response as the criterion and sign of membership remains ambiguous in the ministry of Jesus. In fact, a fundamental struggle of the apostolic community is precisely this question of the growing understanding of the defining characteristic(s) of membership in God's People. David Stanley argues quite convincingly that this struggle took the form of a gradual process, moved forward both by revelation and historical circumstance. Stephen comes to a faith in the centrality of Jesus; Peter is told to disregard the dietary laws that served as markers of faithful adherence to the faith of Israel; Paul discerns the need to witness to common table fellowship with Gentiles; the Council of Jerusalem removes the heretofore binding sign of participation in the covenant; the evangelization efforts among the Gentiles meet with astounding success; and the destruction of Jerusalem signals the end of the possibility of a primarily Jewish Christianity.[37]

People of God now becomes the result of personal commitment, yet it is a commitment to a reality that predates the commitment of every individual. For the church as the People of God is to be understood in its function as sign and instrument (*Lumen gentium*, no. 1). The way this people lives out with each other the mystery of costly love, embodied in Jesus' death and resurrection, becomes revelatory of the vocation of all humanity to form a single people who live in sisterhood and brotherhood with one another.[38] However, this sisterhood and brotherhood of humanity is neither created nor constituted by the free choice of individuals. Rather, this relationship mirrors how humanity was originally created—not as unrelated individuals but as family (Gn 1:27-28). This relationship constitutes the fundamental identity of each human person.

In addition, as family, the creation of humanity images who God is. The peoplehood of humanity, which is signified in the People of God, is revelatory of the communitarian nature of God. In this sense the church as the People of God is an icon of the divine. And, like the communitarian nature of God, which is not constituted by the free choice of individuals but speaks to us of the fundamental nature of reality at its depth,[39] so the peoplehood of humanity is a given of human existence. The personal commitment involved in membership in the People of God as church is a choice to live out who we already are with each other so as to image God.

THE CHALLENGE TO *PUEBLO DE DIOS*

As I have mentioned earlier in this essay, both the sociocentric nature of Latino cultures and the conflictual nature of the second *mestizaje* have produced, in my opinion, an excessively narrow understanding of our reality as church. In the three *Encuentros* that have constituted our most intentional efforts to reflect on our reality as church, we have tended to focus on our needs as a people. One might say that the ecclesial question we have been asking is: What should the church in the United States do for its Latino members?

The very same characteristics, however, that have defined those reflections on our reality as church bear within themselves a radically different question. The very sociocentric and organic nature of our experience as *pueblo* grounds us in appreciating the concreteness of peoplehood, and moreover, the fact that peoplehood is a given and is not constituted on its deepest level by the choice of individuals conceived as having no intrinsic relationship to each other. Yet, both realizations need to be challenged by an understanding of the sign function of church as the People of God. If we continue to limit the concreteness and the givenness of peoplehood to family networks, even broadly conceived, we will not uncover their revelatory nature. For it is precisely these two characteristics that are fundamental to a true appreciation of the function of the church as the People of God.

First, as in the case of our use of family as the paradigm for all relationships, church as the People of God witnesses to the fact that the relationship of all human beings to one another is that of members of a single family with God as its origin and end. Second, church as the People of God witnesses to the fact that this familial relationship of humanity is a given and does not depend on the choice of individuals or on the employment of any criteria of similarity or difference. In a real sense, we need to reverse the terms of the ecclesial question we have been asking. It should read: What does the Latino experience of peoplehood have to say to the way church is lived out by all Catholics in the United States?

THE CHALLENGE OF *PUEBLO DE DIOS*

The answer to that newly structured question would entail at least two points. First, the Latino sense of *pueblo* pushes the egocentric understanding of U.S. society toward a sense of the givenness of the mutual relationships of the members of our society. While it might not challenge the political *theory* that undergirds the formation of U.S. society, it does challenge the validity of the current experience of North Americans—that we have lost a sense of the common good and are divided into economic groups, each competing with the other for a larger share of the economic pie.[40] This lack of appreciation for what we have in common makes impossible intelligible discussions of, much less finding solutions to, the major issues which confront us.[41] Only a renewed understanding of who we are can allow us the possibility of dealing constructively with these contemporary problems.

Second, a more sociocentric understanding of the interrelatedness of all people would necessitate a rewriting of our national history. We can no longer make pretensions to an innocent reading of our expansion across this continent, our use of slavery for economic benefit, our dominating relationship to our neighbors to the south. If we can right the historical record, we will go a long way to unmasking our need for the social construction of race, which serves as a justification for some of the more sordid pages of the history of our country.

CONCLUSION

This essay has dealt in broad strokes with the content of a Latino understanding of church and the challenges it offers to the more egocentric understanding of church typical of the majority of U.S. Catholics. But, as much as this essay has dealt with content, it has been an exercise in method. It began with the concrete self-interpretation of church used by Latino Catholics and traced the anthropological and historical sources of that self-interpretation. It then placed the analysis of that experience in dialogue with the Christian tradition to see where the tradition supports our experience and understanding and where the tradition challenges that experience. Lastly, on the basis of this theological reflection, I have tried to map out the implications for a living out of the reality of church by Latinos/as and by non-Latinos in the United States. I contend that, more than the fact that the content of this essay deals with Latinos/as, it is the (1) conscious employment of a method that begins with praxis, turns to reflection, and returns to praxis, and (2) the forthright attention to the cultural context that make this essay an exploration in systematic theology done *latinamente*.

It would be fascinating to attempt the same kind of reflection using the other two major Pauline images of church, Body of Christ and Creation of the Spirit. Body of Christ would seem to speak forcefully of the corporeality of church, refusing to allow the reality of church to be spiritualized, but emphasizing its grounding in human experience. This may be reflective of the Latino insistence on a holistic understanding of the human person, in which bodiliness (affectivity, sensation, sexuality) is an intrinsic feature of the fully human. Creation of the Spirit balances the rootedness of corporeality with the new and the creative. The Latino experience of adaptiveness to changing historical situations, which is evident in the repeated phenomenon of *mestizaje*, in which the new is birthed, may be able to serve as the focusing lens for that reflection. Unfortunately, due to the constraints of space and of time, the development of those reflections will have to wait for another moment.

Notes

[1] Roberto Goizueta's book *Caminemos con Jesús* probably comes closest to sustaining an ecclesiological reflection, particularly his chapter "Hacia Una Teologia de Acompañamiento," but even here the emphasis is on possible functions of church rather than an explicit reflection on its nature. Obviously too, Orlando

Espín's work on the *sensus fidelium* presupposes an ecclesiology, although this theme is rarely the explicit focus of his reflections. See Arturo Bañuelas's updated bibliography of works published by Latino Catholic theologians at the end of this volume.

² Gary Riebe-Estrella, "Latinos and Theological Education," *Journal of Hispanic/ Latino Theology* 4:3 (1997), 6-7.

³ For an overview of this process, see Moisés Sandoval, "Organization of a Church," in *Hispanic Catholic Culture in the U.S.: Issues and Concerns*, ed. Jay P. Dolan and Allan Figueroa Deck (Notre Dame, Ind.: University of Notre Dame Press, 1994), 143-44.

⁴ Secretariado de Asuntos Hispanos, United States Catholic Conference, National Conference of Catholic Bishops, *Voces Proféticas: El Documento del Proceso del III Encuentro Nacional Hispano de Pastoral* (Washington, D.C.: United States Catholic Conference, 1986), 6.

⁵ For a comparison of sociocentric and egocentric cultural worlds, see Richard A. Shweder and Edmund J. Bourne, "Does the Concept of the Person Vary Cross-Culturally?" in *Culture Theory: Essays on Mind, Self and Emotion*, ed. Richard Shweder and Edmund Bourne (Cambridge: Cambridge University Press, 1984), 188-95.

⁶ The centrality of this cultural perspective for Latinos/as is underlined in the essays in this volume by Miguel Díaz and Roberto Goizueta, each of which, from a different sector of Latino praxis, develops a Latino theological anthropology that is decidedly sociocentric in nature.

⁷ The many times I have presented this framework for understanding some of the differences between Latino and mainstream U.S. cultures have taught me that within many non-Latinos in the United States the distinction is not so clear-cut. Those non-Latinos from Mediterranean backgrounds or who are second or third generation in families that emigrated from predominantly rural societies in Europe see the vibrant presence of some aspects of a sociocentric cultural perspective in their lives, even though these are by and large reflective of the egocentric perspective of mainstream U.S. culture.

⁸ The fact that she loses the last name of her mother's family in the process exhibits the prejudice of male domination in the marriage tradition of Latinos/as.

⁹ For a more extensive exploration of the impact of this anthropology of the person as "maker," see the essay of Roberto Goizueta in this volume, "Fiesta: Life in the Subjunctive," particularly the section "The Self in Modernity and Postmodernity."

¹⁰ An expanded use of the familial term *tío/a* is applied to very close friends who are often introduced to children with this honorific title even though there exists between them no biological relationship.

¹¹ *Compadrazgo* exists in the context of a number of sacraments (baptism, confirmation, marriage), but the baptismal context is the one that most shapes new family configurations (see Virgilio P. Elizondo, *Christianity and Culture* [Huntington, Ind.: Our Sunday Visitor, 1975], 161-62).

¹² Susan E. Keefe and Amado M. Padilla, *Chicano Ethnicity* (Albuquerque, N.Mex.: University of New Mexico Press, 1987), 14-18.

¹³ Ibid., 141-42.

¹⁴ Shweder and Bourne, "Does the Concept of the Person Vary Cross-Culturally?" 191-92.

¹⁵ Robert N. Bellah et al., eds., *Habits of the Heart: Individualism and Commitment in American Life* (New York: Harper & Row, 1985), chap. 2.

[16] Robert Bellah et al., eds., *The Good Society* (New York: Alfred A. Knopf, 1991), 46.

[17] Ibid., 184.

[18] T. Howland Sanks, *Salt, Leaven, and Light: The Community Called Church* (New York: Crossroad, 1992), 19.

[19] It is interesting that when, in the mid-1800s, the southern states attempted to use this same argument for secession, it was not accepted as valid by the federal government.

[20] Alvaro Quiroz Magaña, *Eclesiología en la teología de la liberación* (Salamanca: Ediciones Sígueme, 1983), 159.

[21] Ibid., 155-59.

[22] National Council of La Raza, *The State of America 1991: An Overview* (Washington, D.C.: National Council of La Raza, 1992), 5.

[23] Jean Merl, "Latinos Lagging on Every School Level, Study Finds," *Los Angeles Times,* 25 January 1991, sec. A.

[24] Moises Sandoval, *On the Move: A History of the Hispanic Church in the United States* (Maryknoll, N.Y.: Orbis Books, 1990), 89.

[25] Virgilio Elizondo, "*Mestizaje* as a Locus of Theological Reflection," in *Mestizo Christianity: Theology from the Latino Perspective,* ed. Arturo J. Bañuelas (Maryknoll, N.Y.: Orbis Books, 1995), 9.

[26] Justo González, *Mañana: Christian Theology from a Hispanic Perspective* (Nashville, Tenn.: Abingdon Press, 1990), 39.

[27] For a fuller treatment of this pathology to make the conquered deserving of their conquest, see Gary Riebe-Estrella, "From Monocultural to Multicultural Congregations," *Review for Religious* 55/5 (September-October 1996), 508-12.

[28] John McGreevey, *Parish Boundaries: The Catholic Encounter with Race in the Twentieth-Century Urban North* (Chicago: The University of Chicago Press, 1996), 104.

[29] Marta Tienda and Frank Bean, *The Hispanic Population of the United States* (New York: Russel Sage Foundation, 1987), 48-49.

[30] Peter Skerry, *Mexican-Americans: The Ambivalent Minority* (New York: The Free Press, 1993), 16-31.

[31] For a fuller discussion of the meaning and function of *mestizaje* in the formation of Latinos, see Virgilio Elizondo, *The Future Is Mestizo: Life Where Cultures Meet* (Bloomington, Ind.: Meyer Stone Books, 1988).

[32] Admittedly there is no mutually agreed upon generic term that is used by people of Latin American descent to describe this larger non-white community. Some prefer *Latino,* others *Hispanic,* still others *Spanish-speaking.* Nevertheless, there is a growing sense of common identity vis-à-vis dominant U.S. culture that is not present among us when we are in our Latin American and Caribbean countries of origin.

[33] See Justo González's idea of "reading the Bible in Spanish," in *Mañana,* 75-87.

[34] Some Latino theologians, such as Justo González, prefer to use the metaphor of family as representative of Latinos/as' understanding of themselves as church. I take issue with that approach for two reasons. First of all, Latino *Catholics* themselves have chosen *pueblo* as their metaphor, as I mentioned in the introduction to the essay. Second, for sociocentrics, *family* is that into which others (non-family) enter, in many ways, into which they are assimilated. That is, the metaphor of family does not allow the other to remain other in any sense but establishes that person's identity on the basis of how he or she is related to "us."

As I note later in this article, the challenge of church as *pueblo* for Latinos/as is precisely to move beyond this narrow sense of identity for the self and for the other.

35 National Conference of Catholic Bishops, *National Pastoral Plan for Hispanic Ministry* (Washington, D.C.: United States Catholic Conference, 1988), nos. 19-84.

36 Ibid., no. 69.

37 David Stanley, "Kingdom to Church: The Structural Development of Apostolic Christianity in the New Testament," *Theological Studies* 16 (1955), 1-29. There are other schema for the development of church used in the New Testament. Stanley's analysis is drawn solely from Acts.

38 Juan Luis Segundo, *The Community Called Church*, trans. John Drury (Maryknoll, N.Y.: Orbis Books, 1973), especially chap. 3.

39 González, *Mañana*, 114.

40 Bellah et al., *The Good Society*, 66-81.

41 Ibid. See also chap. 4, "Government, Law, and Politics." This chapter contains a fascinating discussion of how this loss of the common good carries implications relative to the analysis and resolution of some of the more significant contemporary issues before the country.

9

La Tierra

Home, Identity, and Destiny

❦

JEANETTE RODRÍGUEZ-HOLGUÍN

Seattle University

My bare feet felt the throbbing earth and my body trembled with excitement. Time stood still and it shared with me all that had been and all that was to come.

—RUDOLFO ANAYA, BLESS ME, ULTIMA

INTRODUCTION

An exciting, developing theme is that of ecotheology. I am particularly interested in entering this dialogue as a Latina theologian. The pages that follow, however, are just the beginning, a reflection that may later lead to a more formal systematization.

Hispanic theology emerges out of the experience and context of Latinos/as living in the United States. This perspective recognizes itself as committed to liberation—whether historical, political, social, cultural, religious, or ecological. In particular, I draw my inspiration from both Latin American liberation and feminist theologies and from their spirituality.

In this chapter I enter the dialogue of ecotheology by drawing from my own cultural tradition, focusing on the concept of *la tierra* as it is expressed within the notions of home, identity, and destiny. Relying on the insights of María Pilar Aquino, I too acknowledge that theology done by women—

and in particular by Latina women—must include women in the production and making of knowledge, in the creation of a new and liberating
reality.[1] This brings with it a new way of reflection.

For Latinas, religious views and the experience of faith—mediated
through our culture—have played a primary role in our lives and in the
lives of our families. It is in our faith that we have found the criteria with
which to recognize our values, develop our self-esteem, and resist the
aggressive processes of religious, spiritual, and cultural colonization. Despite the overwhelming pressures of domination and assimilation, Latina
women seek to transform structures of oppression into dynamic patterns
of faith and hope.

As María Pilar Aquino reminds us, the theology that women develop
has to do with the real world, "vital physical and spiritual needs, [incor-
porating] the integrity of the body, as well as the expansion of the spirit
within the limits and possibilities of daily life."[2] The theology that women
develop integrates human and social reality as it presents itself in its unity
and diversity. This human and social reality, however, is lived out within
a larger context shared by all human beings: the earth.

I focus on the term *la tierra* as it is expressed in the wisdom and
worldview of *flor y canto* (flower and song). This pre-Columbian Nahuatl
philosophical thought is expressed by León-Portilla as

> an aesthetic conception of the universe and life, for art "made things
> divine," and only the divine was true. To know the truth was to un-
> derstand the hidden meanings of things through "flower and song,"
> a power emanating from the deified heart.[3]

Flower and song is an example of *disfrasismo*. The Nahuatl language used
disfrasismos to connote a complementary union of two words or symbols
to express one meaning. *Disfrasismo* is used to communicate and express
the most profound thought or feeling.[4] The phrase *flor y canto* is not only a
metaphor for poetry; it is a means by which to express a worldview. The
Nahuas believed that only through "flower and song" could truth be
grasped. Truth intuited through poetry derives from a particular kind of
knowledge. It is a knowledge that is a consequence of "the fruit of authentic inner experience—the result of intuition."[5]

> Poetry is . . . a creative and profound expression which, through
> symbol and metaphor, allows man to discover himself and then to
> talk about what he has intuitively and mysteriously perceived . . .
> Poetry enraptures . . . and by intensifying . . . emotions and per-
> ceptive powers . . . enables him to perceive what he ordinarily could
> not.[6]

The wise men did not believe that they could form rational images of what is beyond, but they were convinced that through metaphors . . . truth was attainable . . . The Nahuatl language allowed the *tlamatinime* [wise men] to embody in their poetry the only truth on earth. Only through metaphor and poetry could they utter some truth about, and thus communicate with, the Divine.[7]

The subject or seeker of this "truth on earth" is mediated through the cultural constructs of the community as understood by the individual. Among the Nahuas the concept of the individual is manifested through the expression *rostro y corazón* (face and heart). Understanding the language and the affectivity of the heart is paramount in this worldview.

To surrender one's heart to something meant to pursue something. The inference is that the word "heart" . . . signified man's dynamism; it was the active searcher of the self.[8]

The goal of the philosophers was to teach their students how to "assume a face" and "to humanize their will." Because it is only through these processes that one can arrive not only at one's own truth but also find the path that leads to the "only truth on earth." "At the end of this path he might find the answer to that which only 'flower and song' could solve: the mystery of human life."[9]

This concept of the individual *rostro y corazón*, pursuing the mysteries of life through "flower and song," reflects the emphasis on the intuitive nature of thinking in Nahuatl philosophy. It is not an understanding based on cold rationalization; rather, it is dynamic, fluid, open, creative, and searching.

The task of U.S. Latino/a theology, similarly, is not simply to interpret symbols but to imagine new and hopeful ways of thinking and feeling in the light of existing needs in the present.[10] What is needed is a way of thinking and being in the world that is inclusive. According to Jay McDaniel:

It is a disposition to recognize and appreciate a plurality of life's paths, lifestyles and life orientations . . . We must foster life orientations that promote the well being of women as well as men, African as well as Asian, and Latin American as well as North American, rural as well as urban, heterosexual as well as homosexual, all forms of life.[11]

What is paramount in this set of values is that it excludes no one and calls for openness to the other, not just acknowledgment of the other's existence, but the possibility of being influenced by the other to be changed by him or her. "The consequences of such openness is a hunger for justice."[12]

One of the dualisms addressed most profoundly by both Latino/a and feminist theologians has been the distinction between thinking and feeling. Until recently in the West, reason has been perceived solely as a cognitive activity independent of feeling. It was presumed that rational thought was a non-affective activity, devoid of passion, in which feelings and emotions were viewed as having no cognitive content. This "turn to modernity," characterized by Rene Descartes's *cogito*, distances us from the "blood that informs the intellect."[13] This break from the "blood flow" dichotomizes human existence from the land and its creatures.

Reflecting on the lives of Latina women reconnects us with the power and wisdom of *flor y canto*. We can learn something from the way women live and relate to the concrete experiences of daily life. Bread, water, shelter, land, belonging, relationships—these are the elements of daily significance. Women's theological work is done with the body, the heart, and the hands, as well as with the head.[14] While women have been successful in doing theology from the Western European perspective, they have discovered that they can also do theology using a different set of tools, methods, and starting points. My work is to discover the insights expressed through affect-laden images found in poetry, song, literature, and symbol. These forms become an appropriate way, then, of expressing the understanding and wisdom of the faith. This is an opportunity to grasp the deepest and most authentic desires of the human heart. I will use these tools to formulate one Latina theologian's contribution to ecotheology.

LA TIERRA

Each of us has a place where we feel a special relationship with the land. All of us are profoundly affected, sometimes without even being aware of it, by the many places in which we have spent our lives. Often this relationship with the land bursts forth in special places: the desert, the ocean, a mountain, a field. This focus on relationship is key to any spirituality. Latino/a spirituality is an example of a spirituality especially conscious of a relationship with the land. This relationship with the land, however, cannot be separated from one's relationship with family, community, and even the cosmos.

Let me very briefly present two examples of Latino/a reflection on our relationship with the land. These two examples will serve as an introduction to my own reflections on the subject.

Luis Valdez, a well-known Chicano film maker, insists that he has never "read a single poem by an Azteca, Tolteca, Maya or Yaqui atheist."[15] Valdez captures the Chicano/a imagination when, in a poem, he speaks about an integral epistemology:

> MOVE
> *con el* MOVEMENT
> of the Cosmos
> with the *Nahui ollin,*
> *el quinto sol,*
> SOL DE MOVIMIENTO.
>
> It must move with the
> EARTH. *LA TIERRA,*
> It must move with the
> MORNING STAR, VENUS
> Quetzalcoatl, *Jesucristo,*
> it must move with God.
>
> RELIGION (re-ligion)
> is nothing more than the
> tying back
> *RE-LIGARE*
> with the cosmic center . . . [16]

Relationships that Latinos/as are capable of appear to go beyond the individual/interpersonal level to a broader field of relating that includes family, land/place, and ancestors. This broader field of relating may include animate and inanimate things—or anything that reminds us or connects us to where we come from or to whom we belong. This understanding and spirit have been our legacy.

Before reading and writing developed, there existed a knowledge that our ancestors carried, formed by their experience and relationships with all that lived and moved. They understood the human as one who needed to be grateful for every day of life, to respect the gifts of life provided by nature, and thus respect nature. Modernity makes an essential separation between nature and human beings. Indigenous peoples, however, are sensitive to the human role of harmony and balance in the world.

In 1991, the International Organization of Indigenous Women echoed the wisdom of our ancestors at the "Women for Our Healthy Planet" Conference:

> As women of the indigenous peoples, our lives are interwoven with the natural world. Our myths of creation tell of our emergence from

birthing lands that still nourish us, and which remain the reason for our existence. We are inseparable from the land from which we were created.

As indigenous peoples, we have lived in these lands for thousands of years, in harmony and equilibrium with Nature. We believe that all living beings were given life by the Creator and, therefore, that we are all participants in the gifts of our Sacred Mother Earth. We depend on her for our sustenance. We depend on each other for the development of our lives; we are physically and spiritually inter-related. As human beings, it is our responsibility to take care of each other, and to care for Nature with the same love the Creator showed us by giving us life.[17]

This statement, articulated by indigenous women, makes clear that our lives are intertwined with the breathing pulse of all living things. It demonstrates gratitude for and understanding of the inseparability that exists between the land and ourselves. The statement acknowledges our creaturehood and our dependence on the Creator, the giver of life, for whom we live.

Having briefly presented our legacy of *flor y canto* through the two introductory examples, I can now move to my main theme. While I hope to reflect accurately what lives in the hearts of the people, I must acknowledge that the categories are mine.

LA TIERRA AS HOME

Earth is our first, our oldest home. Yet many in contemporary society experience a homeless feeling often articulated as not belonging. At times this "homeless feeling" is concrete. Many people in third-world countries, as well as in so-called developed countries, have literally lost their homes. Indigenous people, the poor, and women have been displaced from their homes.

The term *ecology* derives from two Greek words: *oikos*, which means "house" or "home," and *logos*, meaning "reflection" or "study." Home/habitat/*oikos* is made of living beings, matter, energy, bodies, and forces in relationship to one another. A hundred years ago ecology, for Ernest Hacekel (a German biologist), was a branch of biology. Today, Leonardo Boff explains, ecology represents for us not only a global interest, but a question of life and death not only for humanity but for the whole planetary system.[18]

Larry L. Rasmussen writes that *"oikos,* as the experience of belonging somewhere intimate to one's bones, eludes most moderns."[19] It is a condition that accompanies development and modernization. Rasmussen writes:

Even apart from homelessness as a matter of mind, it is quite literally displacement of one kind or another. The highly mobile rich, living from hotel to suburbia lot to condo and hotel again hardly have an enduring community they consider their own, even less a binding commitment to a neighborhood. Many advertisements of job descriptions . . . declare the world their "oyster." Every locale is at their disposal, but no particular locale is home in a deep, settled sense.[20]

In the last few years, my own experience as a teacher confirms that many students seem to experience a deep sense of aloneness in the world.

Would a reclaiming of the knowledge that earth is in fact our first and oldest home have an impact on the experience of displacement and aloneness that earthlings feel? I believe this ancestral knowledge is deep within us in our collective memory. If we are to recall the wisdom of that memory, we must be able to stand firmly on the earth and in reverential silence recall the interdependence and intricate relationship we have, not just with the world, the earth, the land, but with the entire universe. As Teilhard de Chardin reminds us, "We are the universe reflecting on itself."[21] I find that the consciousness and awareness of our common "birth home" is a starting point for that reflection.

Awareness of our common birth home initiates our understanding that this sacred place on which we stand, and on which we make our habitat, holds for us the secret of our relationships. In other words, *our relationship with the earth is the context of all contexts.* Many of us do not begin with this global insight, but with our particular, culturally conditioned experience of home.

The classic Chicano writer Rudolfo Anaya recognizes as self-knowledge the truth contained in the expression "my homeland flows through my blood." He argues that "it was indigenous America that held the tap root of our history; its mythology was the mirror by which to know ourselves."[22]

A classic "home" myth in Chicano/a (and earlier Nahuatl) literature tells us of Aztlan.[23] Aztlan is that place somewhere in the Southwest where migrating groups of natives came together in the process of becoming indigenous Americans.

There they evolved new levels of spiritual orientation to cosmos, the earth, and community . . . Somewhere in the desert and mountains of what we now call the Southwest, they created a covenant with their gods and from there they moved south to Mexico to complete the prophecy.[24]

In the religious psyche of many Chicanos/as there is a desire to return to Aztlan, to return to the homeland.[25] I concur with Anaya, who argues that the need for homeland is inherent in the collective memory of any group. It is a covenant with the tribal gods, an encompassing spiritual yearning for homeland.[26]

Indo-Hispano/a religious sensibility was deeply influenced by a great respect for the earth. "The recognition of the earth as . . . *la sagrada tierra* permeated the spiritual life of the Hispanic villages, and the process of synthesis fused Spanish Catholicism and Native American thought."[27] The worldview of these indigenous tribes held all things in relationship with one another. In this understanding we are part of the web of life and dependent on each other not just for survival but as a hope for our community. These principles—and the wisdom of the indigenous—continue to emerge from our contemporary writers. Anaya, in his discussion about Aztlan, reaffirms the indigenous values in his description of the Chicanos/as' home of Aztlan:

> The true guardians of Aztlan have been the Rio Grande Pueblo people, and the knowledge and love for their homeland has kept their spiritual thought alive in the face of overwhelming odds. They have kept themselves centered with the earth, and that has provided their communities a spiritual and psychological center . . . In a world so in need of ecological and spiritual awareness which would allow us to save the earth and practice democratic principles of love and sharing, these ties to the earth . . . provide hope for our community.[28]

The myths surrounding Aztlan manifest a people's affective ties with their environment and, in this case, the land. Difficult to express are the feelings we have toward a place—because it is home, or the locus of memory, or the expression of a prophecy, a dream, or of Utopia. Reflections about Aztlan and homeland are compelling. They are the carriers of emotionally charged events and situations raised to the level of symbol. They carry the aspirations and hopes of a people.

LA TIERRA AS IDENTITY

Music has provided a great source for reflection in my work with *campesinos* (farm workers) both in the United States and in Mexico. Through music, a people's sufferings, hopes, and aspirations are revealed. One song from the diocese of Cuernavaca, entitled *Cuando tenga la tierra*, serves as an example. Because this song is very difficult to translate, I provide an excerpt from the text as it appears in Spanish followed by a summary of the main themes:

> Campesino,
> cuando tenga la tierra,
> corazón de mi mundo, desde atrás de todo olvido
> secaré con mis lágrimas todo el horror de la lástima,
> y por fin te veré.
>
> Campesino, campesino,
> campesino, dueño de mirar la noche,
> en que nos acostamos para hacer los hijos.
>
> Campesino,
> cuando tenga la tierra, me pondré la luna en el bolsillo
> y saldré a pasear con los árboles y el silencio,
> y los hombres y las mujeres conmigo.[29]

Addressing the *campesino*, the songwriter promises that the land will belong to those who have fought for her, who have struggled with her. The song speaks of the land not only as a resource but tied into one's very identity and personhood. The song concludes with the great joy that will follow when one reclaims the land.

> Land is not conceived of as just a marketable good. There is a much deeper connection with the land. It is an indispensable productive resource that forms part of the inherited culture. It is the land of the ancestors, in which they are now resting.[30]

The songwriter promises that when the *campesinos* reclaim the land, the heart of our world will be brought forth from the past with all its pain and suffering and brought to great healing. When the *campesinos* reclaim the land, they will be able to put "the moon in their pocket and walk with the trees and silence, accompanied by men and women." The song is a song of liberation and Utopia. It speaks of the healing and wholeness one achieves through reclaiming one's land. This reclaiming of the land is connected to the reclaiming of one's personhood and place in the world.

In a recent visit to *comunidades de base* in Chiapas, Mexico, I was impressed to hear at a Mass a somewhat different *Sanctus*. It was not the traditional "Santo, Santo, Santo" we are accustomed to; rather, it was a "santo de la tierra" (holy of the land). The words are as follows, and they suffice as reflection:

Cantemos todos juntos	Let us sing together
a nuestro Dios creador.	to our Creator God.
El hizo maravillas,	He has done marvels,
eterno es su amor.	eternal is his love.
Santo, santo, santo,	Holy, holy, holy,
santo es el Señor.	holy is the Lord.
Bendito el que viene	Blessed is the one coming
en nombre del Señor.	in the name of the Lord.
Cantemos por la tierra	Let us sing for the earth
que nos da de comer.	that gives us to eat.
Si ella es nuestra madre,	If she is our mother,
de todos debe ser.	everyone else's she must be.
Santo, santo, santo,	Holy, holy, holy,
santo es el Señor.	holy is the Lord.
Hosana en las alturas,	Hosanna in the highest,
oh Dios libertador.	O Liberator God.

Literature offers yet another source for understanding the connection between land and nature (or landscapes). For example, the classic Chicano/a novel *Bless Me, Ultima* by Rudolfo Anaya[31] contains a number of religious dimensions characteristic of the Chicano/a experience. David Carrasco identifies the two religious dimensions of Chicano/a life reflected in the novel as the dimensions of sacred landscape and of the sacred human being. Carrasco calls our attention to such details as the following: the name of the protagonist, Antonio Luna y Mares; the presence of the river; the golden carp; and the relationship between Antonio and the *curandera* Ultima, who teaches him about the world of sacrality. The setting for Antonio's maturation is a magical landscape.

He is Luna y Mares, moon and sea. Anaya's portrayal of these names shows that the Chicanos in the story do not regard them as simple, natural objects but as powers that influence the boy's life from birth. From one side he descends from the people of the "earthly sea," "people who hold wind as brother," and his character is full of the spirits of the sea. From the other side he carries the blood and the spirits of the people of El Puerto who are "steady, settled" and "hold the earth as brother."[32]

Antonio Luna y Mares's name suggests something sacred. Sacred places, such as the river, appear repeatedly throughout the novel. "The river flowing through Antonio's world is not just a water source, but a presence, a manifestation of some 'other' power."[33]

Anaya develops in the novel the character of Ultima, the *curandera*, who opens up for Antonio not just the "beauty of the land, the songs of the river, the mystery of the earth, but the magical force within the human being."[34] The magical force that lies within the human being is summed up in the sentence, "The tragic consequences of life can be overcome by the magical strength that resides in the human heart."[35]

These examples illustrate similar themes developed in other Latino/a poems, songs, and novels. These sources demonstrate intelligent affectivity: a deep awareness and understanding of God's love expressed in place, and the importance of a broader network of relationships. The language of poetry, song, and novel reveals that a *la tierra* theology is, in essence, aesthetics. Given these sources, one cannot but approach aesthetics as a wisdom from the heart.[36]

The vision of spirituality around the world, and in particular Indo-Hispano/a spirituality, focuses on relationships—relationships that include the whole of creation. Many indigenous people call the earth "our Mother." All living creatures are related and are made reference to as brothers and sisters. Indigenous words for the earth indicate sharing and belonging, as opposed to possessing or owning. This deep love and connection to the land is beautifully reflected in the words of Buffalo Woman, a Hidatsa of the Missouri area:

I am an old woman now. The buffaloes and blacktail deer are gone, and our Indian ways are almost gone. Sometimes I find it hard to believe that I ever lived then.

My little son grew up in the white man's school. He can read books, and he owns cattle and has a farm. He is a leader among our Hidatsa people, helping them to follow the white man's road. He is kind to me. We no longer live in an earth lodge, but in a house with chimneys; and my son's wife cooks by a stove.

But for me, I cannot forget our old ways.

Often in summer I rise at daybreak and steal out to the cornfields; and as I hoe the corn I sing to it, as we did when I was young. No one cares for our corn songs now.

Sometimes at evening I sit, looking back on the big Missouri. The sun sets, and dusk steals over the water. In the shadows I seem again to see our Indian village, with smoke curling upward from earth lodges, and in the river roar I hear the yells of the warriors, the laughter of little children as of old. It is but an old woman's dream. Again

I see but shadows and hear only the roar of the river; and tears come into my eyes. Our Indian life, I know, is gone forever.[37]

When I was a young girl, my mother told me a story regarding her migration to the United States from Quito, Ecuador. She told me of her fifteen-hour flight at a time when airplanes consisted of bleachers on either side. There were no snacks or frills. She told me that as she came down the steps of the plane, she sensed herself feeling weak in the knees, and that by the time she had placed her foot on this land, she felt that *all the blood had drained from her body.* This image of being drained of one's life blood symbolizes the consequence of being removed from the land that gives one meaning and identity. It recalls the words of Buffalo Woman, the sense that "our . . . life is gone"—gone because of the forgotten songs, ruptured from the natural and familiar rhythms of the land.

As a Christian, I ground myself in the premise that we are part of creation, formed out of the dust of the earth and the "breath of God"; anchored in our embodied life; grounded to the earth. Our *latinidad*—our identity as Latinos/as—rests upon our Catholicism. And within our Catholic tradition we recognize the goodness of all God's creation. We believe that God's wisdom, power, and love are ever present. It is a creative love, unfolding in creation. It is because we are the creation of a loving and relational God that *la tierra* becomes a gift to all creatures.

When we forget our identity, place, and inherited relationships, God—in God's goodness—sends us prophets, artists, "ordinary" saints, and mystics to remind us of our communal relationship with all creation. Benedict, Hildegard, and Francis, among others, have given us a language in which to nurture and sustain our relationship with "Brother Sun and Sister Moon." Latin American theologian Leonardo Boff comments: "None of these masters believed that knowledge was a form of appropriation or of domination of things, but rather a form of love and of communion with things."[38] Thomas Berry invites us to move from being a collection of objects to a communion of subjects. It is through our embodied selves, in the context of being a part of creation, that we experience God. And the Catholic bishops of the United States remind us that "earth, a very small blessed corner of the universe, gifted with unique natural blessings, is humanity's home and humans are never so much at home as when God dwells with them."[39]

LA TIERRA AS DESTINY

Ecology has to do with the interaction, relation, and dialogue of all living creatures, which includes not only nature but culture and society as well. From an ecological viewpoint, *everything that exists coexists.* This co-existence is not devoid of struggle, death, and disharmony. Ecologists and social ecologists have clashed around the issue of setting the human person apart from the environment. The former speak ideally about the "communion of subjects," understood as the fundamental equality of every living thing. However, the social ecologists would argue, since the human subject is the only one who creates, transmits, and adapts culture, the human is ultimately responsible for the balance of the biosphere. This functional separateness of the human person does not alter our need to understand the interrelationship and interdependence of all of creation.

People all over the globe are coming to understand that we cannot continue to use without limit the resources of the earth. I add my voice to the ecological dialogue already underway globally and within our churches.

There are two fundamental questions for me as a Latina and a Catholic: How can we move beyond our own ethnocentric boundaries and at the same time celebrate the distinctiveness we bring as a people? What does our tradition offer in terms of understanding our commitment to justice?

> The argument of survival in our modern world seems to urge us toward the common center of our humanity. When we established our rights to the homeland of Aztlan, we understood that this right belongs to every group or nation, and we understood how we share in all the homelands of world mythology. The children of Aztlan are citizens of the world. We must move beyond the limitations of ethnicity to create a world without borders. Each community rising to its new level of awareness creates respect for self and for others, and we are in need of this awareness before we destroy the Earth and each other.[40]

Alone I cannot surrender myself to the "common center of our humanity." This commitment must be communally engaged on global and interdenominational levels.

A major cultural critique of the dominant culture's way of thinking and living has come from feminist thought. The ecological movement and the feminist movement have joined together to work for justice and peace, and for the integrity of all of creation. Chung Hyun Kyung insists that a reintegration of the wisdom of the First Peoples and what I call *la tierra* theology will add to a more holistic spirituality. Indigenous wisdom will restore that which has been breached by the development of institutionalized patriarchal systems:

> The spirituality of the indigenous peoples in Asia, Africa and North America gives full value to creation as a dynamic, and highly integrated web of life. It exudes life-giving values: sacredness of the land, reverence for all creatures, judicial use and conservation of the earth's

resources, and compassion for the weak, oppressed and marginalized.[41]

Although much contemporary rhetoric espouses "value language," we need to remember the *meaning* that incarnates these values. For example, the modern value of *land* is either neutral or reduced to an economic or functional value. Native spirituality recognizes the intrinsic sacrality of *la tierra*. This meaning and sense of the sacred are not confirmed by humanity but revealed to us in the created and formational interplay with *la tierra*. This heartfelt *meaning* is foundational to the values that we must nurture and/or regain if we are to continue to contribute to the web of life.

All great religious traditions recognize and acknowledge that life is a sacred gift. Ecologists, scientists, and theologians are asking how we can live with our Mother Earth, Pachamama,[42] in a way that promotes sustainability. As we may learn from *la tierra* theology, the concept of Pachamama is integral to the identity and culture of the people. For the Quechua and Aymara peoples of Peru, the land they inhabit is not a commodity to be bought and sold. The earth is in danger, and it is very possible that the next generation of human beings will not have a livable earth to inherit. Thus today, through Peruvian land-reform laws, the Quechuas and the Aymaras are reclaiming the land of their ancestors as their birthright.

Abuse of our ecobalance (interpersonally and naturally) has a devastating effect upon the world, but in particular on the most vulnerable members of the world: women, children, and third-world peoples. Deforestation, acid rain, soil erosion, and the indiscriminate use of fertilizers and pesticides lead to the breakdown of the local subsistence economy on which most women and children depend.[43] The poor, the marginalized, the powerless bear the brunt of the current environmental crisis. Their lands and their neighborhoods are more likely to be polluted. The expression "environmental justice" has received much attention in recent years because it refers to the inequitable distribution of environmental hazards. Not surprisingly, higher levels of toxic chemicals are found in poor and minority communities.

Here in the United States the civil-rights movement made explicit the connections among race, poverty, and pollution. Activists in poor and minority communities are not only focusing on how the environment and our people are affected by such things as toxic wastes and the larger global issues of deforestation, acid rain, and so on, but more and more activists are articulating and demonstrating the impact that environmental issues have on the very health and overall quality of people's lives.

A 1993 report from the Center for Policy Alternatives warned that "people of color were forty-seven percent more likely than whites to live near a commercial hazardous-waste facility."[44] It is in their neighborhoods that toxic wastes are dumped. In their communities the poor and marginalized are more likely than not to have undrinkable water. They are the ones driven off their lands and homes for the sake of "development." As a community of faith, what will be our response to the ethical challenge these situations raise?

Members of faith communities are certainly not the only ones challenging their traditions to respond to this crisis. In 1990 a group of international scientists headed by Carl Sagan called upon religious leaders and churches to react to the crisis as "the only social agents with the ethical power to respond to 'crimes against creation.'"[45] The ecological crisis challenges us to examine our way of thinking and behaving in general, and more specifically our attitudes about nature and development. "Ecologists enable us to see our anthropocentric sinfulness in relation to other living beings. They call us to a new pattern of relations with all beings in the cosmos based on mutuality, interdependence and life-giving values."[46]

La tierra theology joins the voices of ecologists to reclaim and reinterpret symbols, and imagine new and hopeful ways to affirm life. The contribution *la tierra* theology offers is that it honors the subject, respects the language and affectivity of the heart; realizes the importance of teaching our future generations how to humanize their will; and increases the ability to understand and draw from an intuitive nature of thinking that is dynamic, fluid, creative, searching, and excludes no one. This theology calls for a radical openness to all, placing as paramount the work of relationships as a consequence of being. As theologians, we must play an active role in this conversation and bring to the table both the life-affirming aspects of our religious and cultural traditions and our skills and commitment to transformation.

The United States Catholic Conference's pastoral statement *Renewing the Earth* (1991) reflects on the interrelationship and interdependence of life, evidenced by the Judeo-Christian scriptures. The pastoral statement argues for an authentic development in moderation, and even calls for austerity in the use of material resources. Authentic development, the document states,

> is a balanced view of human progress consistent with respect for nature . . . It invites development of alternative visions of the good society and the use of economic models with richer standards of well being than material productivity alone. Finally, authentic development requires affluent nations to seek ways to reduce and restructure their over consumption of natural resources.[47]

One of the most controversial issues that arises within the environmental movement is the understanding that the impoverishment of people, and in particular of the most vulnerable of peoples, is closely related to how natural resources, technology, and commerce are distributed, processed, and exploited. It is evident that the level of energy consumption by first-world countries is a key issue. Increasingly, experts are convinced that the way our generation is using energy will not leave enough for future generations.

While I appreciate the development of ecotheology within my own religious tradition, as expressed in *Renewing the Earth*, I also detect the remnants of the emphasis on the dignity of the human person *above* all other beings: the rest of creation is subordinate to the needs of humanity. An alternative Christian view, interestingly enough, was offered by Francis of Assisi. Lynn White tells us that the key to understanding Francis is his belief in humility. Humility is not just an individual virtue but a virtue for humanity as a species. "Francis tried to depose man from his monarchy over creation and set up a democracy of all God's creation."[48]

Indigenous peoples emphasize a more mutually interdependent character, while the church's social teachings challenge us to accept our role as caretakers and stewards for the earth and all of creation. The indigenous traditions teach us that when we separate our existence from the processes of the land, our hearts become fragmented and all that is "other" is objectified.

It seems to me that the contemporary ecological crisis must impress upon our consciousness a new awareness of our dependence on the earth and on each other. We must help our communities understand that we share a common destiny. This common destiny is linked with the earth because we belong to the earth. It calls for re-embracing values laden with the heartfelt meaning of our interconnectedness with creation.

An organic ecological perspective emphasizes interconnectedness and mutual interdependence. This interdependence could provide a resource for a new ethics. Returning to the insights of the indigenous women quoted earlier in this chapter we hear:

> We believe that it is our responsibility to take care of the earth, as if she were our mother. As daughters of the indigenous peoples we witness the destruction of the land. Our Sacred Mother is being violated by the devastation of the forests and excavation for minerals; she is being poisoned through radioactive and chemical waste, and we her daughters and sons are being destroyed in this heartless quest to take over natural resources, and its precious gifts, in order to maintain limitless consumption. We feel the pain and suffering of our Mother Earth as if it were our own. She is being destroyed and, like her, we too are being destroyed so massively that healing and renewal seem impossible.[49]

The most difficult challenge will be to move away from an interest in individual lifestyles and ethnocentrism to a more adequate structural and systemic concern; or, as our tradition has called for, we need a commitment to the common good.

First and foremost, it is imperative to understand that the key issue is survival itself—especially the survival of the most marginalized. K. C. Abraham, director of the South Asian Theological Research Institute, argues that political and social justice are linked to ecological health. He cites connections between economic exploitation and environmental degradation. Global atmospheric changes result from the destruction of forests and indigenous peoples are driven out of their habitat for the sake of "development." The uneven distribution, control, and use of natural resources are just a few of the serious justice issues. It has come to this: the natural resources needed to maintain the lifestyle of one person in the United States equal those required for two hundred to three hundred people in Asia.[50] The rapid depletion of nonrenewable natural resources further raises the question of our responsibility for future generations. We must create and build structures that foster lifestyles that nurture such values. We must make possible the aspirations articulated by film maker Luis Valdez:

> We must re-identify
> with the center and proceed
> outward with love and strength,
> AMOR Y FUERZA, and
> undying dedication to justice.[51]

This dedication to justice begins with the recognition of the myriad voices that must remain in conversation with one another, including those bold enough to defend *la tierra*.

I have presented in this essay some initial reflections implicit in what I have called *la tierra* theology. I have drawn from my own religio-cultural sources, from sources of the wider Latino/a culture, as well as my own Roman Catholic tradition. I have tried to reach back through time and space to the legacy of our ancestors, in their philosophy of *flor y canto*, as well as integrated some contemporary voices, in order to create and generate a contribution to *la tierra* theology.

Finally, I want to emphasize that *la tierra* may be an authentic category for Latino/a theological reflection on ecological concerns for two reasons. First, *la tierra* is more reflective of our experience as expressed in our songs, poems, and literature. As a category, *la tierra* may also help bridge the variety of issues that emerge in ecological reflection: the term in Spanish (*la tierra*) can indicate either the earth, land, or one's country; therefore it refers to the whole. Second, the Latino/a relationship to the earth is necessarily like the Latinos/as themselves; that is, there is a process of *mestizaje* involving both European and Native and/or African influences. Therefore, as with anything *mestizo/a*, ecological reflection is neither totally this or that but rather a bit of this *and* of that, which is its identity and its strength.

Notes

[1] María Pilar Aquino, *Our Cry for Life: Feminist Theology from Latin America* (Maryknoll, N.Y.: Orbis Books, 1993), 109.

[2] Ibid., 31.

[3] Miguel León-Portilla, *Aztec Thought and Culture: A Study of the Ancient Nahuatl Mind* (Norman, Okla.: University of Oklahoma Press, 1963), 182.

[4] Clodomiro Siller Acuña, "El método de la evangelización en el *Nican Mopohua*," *Servir* 17 (1981), 12.

[5] León-Portilla, *Aztec Thought and Culture*, 76.

[6] Ibid., 77.

[7] Ibid., 79.

[8] Ibid., 114.

[9] Ibid., 115.

[10] Jay McDaniel, "Six Characteristics of a Post-Patriarchal Christianity," in *Readings in Ecology and Feminist Theology*, ed. Mary Heather MacKinnon and Moni McIntyre (Kansas City, Mo.: Sheed & Ward, 1995), 302.

[11] Ibid., 309.

[12] Ibid., 310.

[13] Ibid., 312.

[14] Aquino, *Our Cry for Life*, 110-11.

[15] Luis Valdez, *Early Works: Actos, Bernabé, and Pensamiento Serpentino* (Houston, Tex.: University of Houston/Arte Público Press, 1990), 176.

[16] Ibid.

[17] International Organization of Indigenous Women, "Madre Tierra, Madre Creadora," *Con-spirando: Revista Latinoamericana de ecofeminismo, espiritualidad y teología* 2 (1992), 16-17. Note that the word "Creator"—*Creadora*—is in the feminine form throughout.

[18] Leonardo Boff, *Ecology and Liberation* (Maryknoll, N.Y.: Orbis Books, 1995), 11.

[19] Larry L. Rasmussen, *Earth Community, Earth Ethics* (Maryknoll, N.Y.: Orbis Books, 1996), 96.

[20] Ibid.

[21] Teilhard de Chardin, cited in Lorna Green, *Earth Age: A New Vision of God, This Human and the Earth* (Mahwah, N.J.: Paulist Press, 1994), 125-26.

[22] Rudolfo Anaya and Francisco A. Lomeli, *Aztlan: Essays on the Chicano Homeland* (Albuquerque, N.Mex.: Academia/El Norte Publications, 1989), 238.

[23] For Chicanos/as Aztlan refers to an ancient Aztec myth that articulates the longing for a homeland somewhere "in the north." "Aztlan meant that Chicanos and Mexicans shared a common historical origin and identity, grounded in a mestizo people proud of their Indian roots" (Richard Griswold del Castillo and Arnoldo de León, *North to Aztlan: A History of Mexican-Americans in the U.S.* [New York: Twayne Publishers, 1996], 131).

[24] Anaya and Lomeli, *Aztlan*, 238.

[25] This affect-laden image and desire for a return to Aztlan may have eschatological implications. Traditionally eschatology referred to the "last things" and dealt with the themes of death and judgment, heaven and hell. Besides the systematic reflection on the content of our Christian hope, Monika Hellwig suggests that eschatology is also focused on the "realization of the promised reign of God in all human experience and in all creation." I resonate with Hellwig's interpretation of eschatology for two reasons: (1) the incorporation of God's reign and the promise of that reign for all human experience and all of creation; and (2) her understanding of the often undervalued notion of hope. For Chicano/a theology there is an additional nuance to Christian hope: the return to the homeland, Aztlan (see Monika K. Hellwig, "Eschatology," in *Systematic Theology: Roman Catholic Perspectives*, ed. Francis Schüssler-Fiorenza and John P. Galvin (Minneapolis, Minn.: Fortress Press, 1991), 2:349-50.

[26] Anaya and Lomeli, *Aztlan*, 238.

[27] Ibid., 239.

[28] Ibid., 240.

[29] *Cantemos en comunidad* (Cuernavaca, Mexico: Comisión Diocesana de Música y Liturgia, 1982), 42.

[30] Guillermo Bonfil Batalla, *Mexico Profundo: Reclaiming a Civilization* (Austin, Tex.: University of Texas Press, 1996), 33.

[31] Rudolfo A. Anaya, *Bless Me, Ultima* (Berkeley, Calif.: Quinto Sol Publications, 1972), 7.

[32] David Carrasco, "A Perspective for a Study of Religious Dimensions in Chicano Experience: *Bless me, Ultima* as a Religious Text," in *Aztlan*, 13:1-2 (1982), 195-221, 208.

[33] Ibid., 209.

[34] Ibid.

[35] Ibid., 196.

[36] One finds hints of their awareness in early Christian theologians such as Augustine, known as "the theologian of the heart," and later in Pascal. Pascal bridged the important transition from feeling to intellect, from soul to mind, and from knowledge to will. It is the feeling heart that first apprehends truth and, according to Pascal, informs the intellect"(see Stephen Strasser, *Phenomenology of Feeling* [Pittsburgh: Duquesne University Press, 1977], 14).

[37] Buffalo Woman, in Peter Nabakov, ed., *Native American Testimony* (New York: Torchbooks, 1992), 230-231. I am indebted to cultural anthropologist Dr. Ted Fortier, of Seattle University, for his insights and recommendations.

[38] Boff, *Ecology and Liberation*, 38.

[39] National Conference of Catholic Bishops, *Renewing the Earth: An Invitation to Reflection and Action on the Environment in Light of Catholic Social Teaching* (November 14, 1991), no. 6.

[40] Anaya and Lomeli, *Aztlan*, 241.

[41] Chung Hyun Kyung, "Ecology, Feminism, and African and Asian Spirituality," in *Ecotheology: Voices from South and North*, ed. David Hallman (Maryknoll, N.Y.: Orbis Books, 1994), 177.

[42] *Pachamama*, in Quechua, is the generous Earth Mother of Andean cultures.

[43] Kwok Pui-Lan, "Ecology and the Recycling of Christianity," in Hallman, *Ecotheology*, 108.

[44] Rasmussen, *Earth Community, Earth Ethics*, 77. See also Benjamin A. Goldman and Laura Fitton, *Toxic Waste and Race Revisited: An Update of the 1987 Racial and*

Socio-Economic Characteristics of Communities with Hazardous Waste Sites (Washington, D.C.: Center for Policy Alternatives, 1994).

[45] *National Catholic Reporter*, June 6, 1997, 4.

[46] Chung Hyun Kyung, "Ecology, Feminism and African and Asian Spirituality," 177.

[47] National Conference of Catholic Bishops, *Renewing the Earth*, no. 9.

[48] Lynn White, "The Historical Roots of Our Ecologic Crisis," in MacKinnon and McIntyre, *Readings in Ecology and Feminist Theology*, 15.

[49] "Madre Tierra, Madre Creadora," 16—my translation.

[50] K. C. Abraham, "A Theological Response to the Ecological Crisis," in Hallman, *Ecotheology*, 69-70.

[51] Valdez, *Early Works*, 177.

10

Theological Education as *Convivencia*

❦

GARY RIEBE-ESTRELLA, S.V.D.

Catholic Theological Union

INTRODUCTION

This essay might be called a reflection.[1] That is so for two reasons. First of all, it attempts to pull its ideas on theological education out of the other essays in this volume, reflecting their ideas and methodological assumptions. In that sense, it begins not with theory but with the doing of theology by Latino systematicians who themselves use their reflections on their own and our peoples' experience as the starting point for the elaboration of Latino theology.[2] For how to do theological education is a derivative concept; that is, it should flow out of or reflect the way theology itself is done. The emphasis on content in most theological education in the West reflects the dissociation of much North Atlantic theology[3] from the experiential basis out of which it originally arose (with the attendant result that it identifies itself simply as "theology," not as the specific "North Atlantic theology" it actually is). As this theology pays little conscious attention to the praxis out of which it springs, the educational process used to disseminate it in turn pays scant attention to the role of praxis in theological method and pedagogy. In contrast, the ideas about theological education proposed in this essay reflect the way Latinos do theology, that is, intentionally recognizing the praxical starting point of all theology as reflection on experience.[4]

The second way in which this essay is a reflection is that, while more than tentative, its conclusions are directional rather than dogmatic. The conversation around the implications of doing theology *latinamente* for theological education is not a new one. However, a broad and sustained dialogue over the nature of theological education from a Latino perspective is a task yet to be undertaken.[5] As a result, the ideas proffered in this essay are less pronouncements than they are reflections, hoping to lift up the assumptions about theological education embedded in the work of Latino theologians even though these assumptions must yet be culled and refined in a more systematic and intentional way.

Though this dialogue has yet to become a sustained conversation, it is a significant one. As I have argued before, Latino theologians are also Latino theological educators, since the objective of our professional work is not simply the production of a body of content called Latino theology, but rather the mentoring of new Latino theologians.[6] We don't "train" or "form" them, we mentor them. That is, ours is the responsibility to share with them how our minds work as we do theology, passing on to others what we have discovered about method—about the "how" of Latino theology and its centrality. This attention to the question and passing on of method is, I believe, our major contribution as Latino theologians and theological educators. For it is not the cultural specificity itself of the theology we produce that is particularly helpful to non-Latinos in the church, but rather the clear exposition of the contextual nature of all theology, a fundamentally methodological question.[7]

VIVENCIA

The word *vivencia* means "personal experience." Derived from the word *vivir*, the connotation is that the experience is that which makes up life (*vida*), at its core, not simply those happenings through which one passes (*experiencia*).

If theological education is derived from the doing of theology, *vivencia* here carries some of the connotation of praxis, which is held up as the starting place for the doing of Latino theology.[8] Precisely because theology has as its starting point experience understood as *vivencia* or praxis, Leonardo and Clodovis Boff can argue that the term *theology* is not univocal. Rather, there are at least three levels at which theology is done: the popular, the pastoral, and the professional. Where they distinguish one from the other is

> in their logic, but more specifically in their language. Theology can be more or less articulate; popular theology will be expressed in everyday speech, with its spontaneity and feeling, whereas professional theology adopts a more scholarly language, with the structure and restraint proper to it.[9]

The content and the root of these levels are the same, however: "what the base communities do when they read the Bible and compare it with the oppression and longing for liberation in their own lives."[10] This starting point of theology done *latinamente* is open to any person; therefore, any person can be the subject of Latino theological education. The question of academic degrees is one that pertains to the question of levels but not to the truthfulness of the theology done; that is, it may touch the question of how systematically the reflection is done, but the systematization of the reflection is a second if not a third moment of which the first is the *vivencia*—the living of the faith in a concrete situation or context.

In his chapter in the present volume, as well as in previous articles he has published on the subject of popular religion, Orlando Espín speaks of Latino popular religion as arising out of the *sensus fidelium* of Latinos.

It is this "faith-full" intuition that makes real Christian people *sense* that something is true or not vis-à-vis the gospel, or that someone is acting in accordance with the Christian gospel or not, or that something important for Christianity is not being heard. This intuition in turn allows for and encourages a belief and a style of life and prayer that express and witness to the fundamental Christian message: God as revealed in Jesus Christ.[11]

It is on this intuitive level that popular theology (as described by the Boffs) occurs, but for all its being popular it is no less theological.

María Pilar Aquino has helped us to broaden our understanding of what composes the *vivencia* which is the *materia prima* of Latino theology. Just as Roberto Goizueta critiques the Marxist emphasis in much of Latin American liberation theology's understanding of praxis as conceding the modern project and its anthropology of the human person as *homo faber*,[12] Aquino reminds us that the *vivencia* which acts as the basis for theological reflection is daily life, not the dramatic or the history-making. Espín, following Aquino's lead, asserts that it is in *lo cotidiano*, daily life, that Latinos as a whole really live. "It is everyday reality—with its routines and its surprises, its mysterious depths and its pedestrian quality."[13] In fact, it is daily life that is the starting point for all and any theology, for that is where most Christians in fact live their lives.

CONVIVENCIA

The *vida* found in *lo cotidiano*, which forms the basis for *vivencia*, is not an individualistic kind of experience. Rather, *vida* for Latinos is understood within our sociocentric cultural world as a shared reality[14] or, perhaps better put, as what happens in our coming together. As such, *vida* is not simply *vivencia*, but *convivencia*. In fact, the word *convivencia* means "cohabitation" or "living together," and also "get-together" (*"reunión de compañeros"*).[15] As such, *convivencia* speaks of the intimacy out of which *la vida* comes, whether one thinks of the phenomenon biologically or socially.[16]

Miguel Díaz, in chapter 7 herein, notes that, for Latinos, relationships are constitutive of persons, and that the specific persons with whom we relate are mediators of our self-understanding. That is, we Latinos understand ourselves communally, and our identity is founded on relationships. However, as Díaz argues, these are not relationships in the abstract but rather particular, concrete relationships. *Convivencia* is not simply the result of biology or happenstance; it is a togetherness that is conscious and intentional, experienced by *compañeros*, by those who walk with each other. Thus, the experiential basis of Latino theology and of Latino theological education is the communal experience of those who understand themselves as intrinsically related to specific others and who embrace those relationships.

This radical rootedness in concrete and specific relationships also implies that the subjects or themes addressed in Latino theologizing will mirror the specificity of *la vida cotidiana* of the people. When Jeanette Rodríguez wonders why there are no Latino voices in ecotheology, she realizes that the point of identification of Latinos with ecological concerns springs not out of a global concern for the earth, but out of the concrete experiences of the place and function of *la tierra* in personal and family histories.[17] Alejandro García-Rivera works at a retrieval of the role of the particular in the face of the attempts at totalization perpetrated by modern thought. For him, the concrete custom of the *Nacimiento* becomes the "textbook" for reading a Latino cosmology.[18]

In the conversations surrounding the planning of the present volume, what began as an attempt to look at the traditional themes of Catholic systematic theology through Latino eyes soon became the naming of themes that spring out of the concrete ordinariness of the lives of our peoples. As a result, this book's explorations in systematic theology contain some themes that are usually covered by non-Latino systematicians and quite a number that would be new to the systematic canon.

The history of U.S. Latinos, however, keeps us from identifying the *"con"* of *convivencia* too narrowly. Though it certainly refers to the specific relationships *within* the Latino community that constitute the identity of a given Latino/a, our community's experience has been, as well, one of relationship with *other* communities. The marvelous work of Virgilio Elizondo on the *segundo mestizaje* reveals how the relationship of Latino peoples with the dominant culture of the United States is also constitutive of the U.S. Latino community and mediates our self-understanding, even if that relationship has most often been marked by oppression and marginalization.[19] Therefore, such issues as the border, acculturation, immigration, and economic marginalization become truly theological questions for Latinos.[20]

The *"con"* of *convivencia* also embraces the religious dimension of the first *mestizaje* as constitutive of who we are as Latinos. Latino popular religion, which many Latino theologians such as Orlando Espín hold to be "one of the most distinctive and pervasive elements in all of the country's Latino cultures,"[21] is the result of the coming together of indigenous pre-Columbian religiosity and sixteenth-century medieval Spanish Catholicism. It marks our relationship with the Christian tradition as one of the constitutive elements of our identity. Theologically this means that the tradition can and should exercise a kind of critical function vis-à-vis the particularity of any local community. As a result, both our relationship with North American society and our relationship to the universal church keep U.S. Latinos from becoming solipsistic in our self-understanding, and invite us into a dialogue with other sources not originally ours. The result is not a diminution of our particularity but rather a faithful recognition of the dynamic relationship of our particularity to other particularities.

IMPLICATIONS FOR THEOLOGICAL EDUCATION

If, in broad strokes, the above is an outline of the facets of *convivencia* that are relevant for an understanding of theological education under this rubric, what are the concrete implications?

1. *The themes on which theological education focuses should be ones that come from the daily life of a concrete community.* The educational task must decide on its location and from that site map out the areas for reflection. Theological education, therefore, will look different in different communities.

2. *The pedagogy should allow a primacy to the accessing of experience.* At the same time, steps must be taken to ensure that the experience is not simply personal or individual, but that sufficient interaction among the members of the community *in the reflection* preserves the original communal nature of the experience itself. Ana María Pineda's work on the orality of Latino cultures holds promise for thinking about ways of accessing the experience that are themselves Latino.[22]

3. *There should be a "gradualist" approach to theological education that is pegged to the accumulation of experience.* Because current models of theological education are born out of North Atlantic theology, they use a theory-practice approach. The experiential base of the student is generally not determinative in assessing the student's readiness for theological educa-

tion, but rather, the candidate's educational background is fundamental. The fact that programs of study often mandate pastoral experiences as components of the program, and then call for "theological reflection" moments to integrate them with the theology being studied, reveals the operative assumption that education, not experience, is the foundation for theological education in most seminaries today.

4. *The locus for teaching is the community/parish, not the classroom.* The experience of a community is not possessed by a single individual. Accessing that experience demands engagement with a sufficiently representative number of community members so that the experiential basis of the theological reflection may embody the richness and diversity of the experience. In addition, the experience of a community is not static but ongoing. As a result, the education component should be done in conjunction with the living experience of community.

5. *Integration happens throughout the educational process because of the pedagogy used and because of the site of the teaching/learning.* Many theological education programs have an integrating seminar in the final year of study, which is a subtle recognition that the kind of integration that should have been happening throughout the course of study has not really taken place. It reveals a sort of "Humpty-Dumpty" principle at work in theological education: educate in pieces and then try to put it all together at the end. The method of doing theology *latinamente* shows that in theological education integration must be a constant dynamic in the process.

6. *The meaning of integration is broadened to include not just integration among theological disciplines within the student, but also the integration of what the student is learning within the community and the church.* The preference of modernity for rationality has made theological education an "up-front" enterprise. The student is loaded with information, which is then to be applied as pastoral situations occur. The community and the church are not invited to be a part of the learning process through the correction they offer to the theology generated. That is, the praxis-theory-praxis spiral must determine the structure of the educational process. Theological education is not the "theory" part of the spiral; the whole spiral is repeatedly engaged as the fundamental method in the ongoing process of theological education.

7. *Theological education should be done with those who embody the sources.* Because educational background determines entry into programs of study, those who embody the sources are most often excluded. Serious thought needs to be given to better ways to make quality theological education available to those who do not possess the educational background currently demanded for degree programs.

8. *The question of degrees needs to be rethought.* In fact, it would seem that the degree question is really reflective of the types or styles of theology about which the Boffs speak. But a degree does not certify that one can

theologize. Rather, it speaks to the style of the language in which the outcome of the reflection (whether good or bad theology) is phrased.

CONCLUSION

Obviously, taking the above implications seriously means that theological education, as we know it today, needs to be thoroughly revamped in method, pedagogy, and structure. Meeting that challenge will take extraordinary energy and considerable time. Nor is it likely to happen as the result of a headlong assault. A more subversive approach is probably the one called for.

Though one may not be able to change the assessment process for entrance into a theological education program, in order to put more weight on experience than on education a professor is free in the classroom to use experience as the starting point for reflection and to attend consciously with the students to the questions of method. Engagement with the larger community is not prohibited in theological programs, but creativity will be called for if the reflection done is not to run the risk of becoming private and individualistic. Though integration seminars may exist well into the future, the use of assignments that send students out into the community can make the issue of integration a more routine one for students.

In short, it is the small ways in which the ground is prepared for major change that will have results. And those ways are within reach of any theological educator who values the contours of theological education arising out of theology done *latinamente*.

Notes

[1] Readers of the present chapter should consult this volume's Glossary. Throughout this article Professor Riebe-Estrella employs a number of terms that are included in the Glossary—ED.

[2] See the lengthy introductory section of Orlando Espín's article in this volume, in which he deals with the cultural boundedness of all theology as it reflects the lived experience of peoples.

[3] By "North Atlantic theology" I mean that theology originating out of Western Europe, the United States, and Canada.

[4] I say "intentionally" since my argument is that, in fact, *all* theology is based on praxis. The question is whether or not theologians consciously acknowledge this connection and the specificity it gives to the resulting reflections, and whether or not this conscious acknowledgment is incorporated with intentionality into discussions of method.

[5] The very stimulating discussion on the subject among the various authors represented in this volume during an organizational meeting in July 1997—many of whose insights are incorporated into this essay—attests to the concern Latino

theologians have about the question, even though most have not yet had the opportunity to attend to it specifically in their writings.

⁶ Gary Riebe-Estrella, "Latinos and Theological Education," *Journal of Hispanic/ Latino Theology* 4:1 (1997), 5-6.

⁷ Riebe-Estrella, "Latinos and Theological Education," 7.

⁸ See Roberto Goizueta's essay on *fiesta*, chapter 4 herein, particularly the section on Latin American liberation theology. Goizueta critiques those understandings of experience that are static or passive and do not see the role of action in the construction of the human person.

⁹ Leonardo Boff and Clodovis Boff, *Introducing Liberation Theology* (Maryknoll, N.Y.: Orbis Books, 1990), 14.

¹⁰ Ibid.

¹¹ Orlando O. Espín, "Tradition and Popular Religion: An Understanding of the *Sensus Fidelium*," in *Frontiers of Hispanic Theology in the United States*, ed. Allan Figueroa Deck (Maryknoll, N.Y.: Orbis Books, 1992), 46.

¹² See chapter 4 herein for Goizueta, and chapter 1 for Aquino.

¹³ See Orlando O. Espín, "An Exploration into the Theology of Grace and Sin," chapter 6 herein, particularly the section "The 'Birthing Place' of a Latino/a Theology of Grace: *Lo cotidiano.*"

¹⁴ See the sections entitled "A Sociocentric Organic Culture," and "A Contrasting Sense of Peoplehood" in "*Pueblo* and Church," chapter 8 herein. For a fuller discussion of the quite distinct cultural worlds of the sociocentric and the egocentric, see Richard Shweder and Edmund Bourne, "Does the Concept of the Person Vary Cross-culturally?" in *Culture Theory: Essays on Mind, Self and Emotion*, ed. Richard Shweder and Edmund Bourne (New York: Cambridge University Press, 1984), 158-99.

¹⁵ Ramón García-Pelayo y Gross, ed., *Larousse Moderno* (Barcelona: Ediciones Larousse, 1986).

¹⁶ Aquino argues that the construction of social gender, which would locate the female in the private sphere and the male in the public sphere, is challenged precisely by the fact of reproduction, which is in both the private and the public spheres (see María Pilar Aquino, *Our Cry for Life* (Maryknoll, N.Y.: Orbis Books, 1993], 35).

¹⁷ See Jeanette Rodríguez, chapter 9 herein.

¹⁸ See Alejandro García-Rivera, chapter 3 herein.

¹⁹ The classic work on this topic is Virgil Elizondo, *Mestizaje: The Dialectic of Cultural Birth and the Gospel* (San Antonio, Tex.: Mexican American Cultural Center, 1978).

²⁰ For a striking example of this, see Virgilio Elizondo, *Galilean Journey: The Mexican-American Promise* (Maryknoll, N.Y.: Orbis Books, 1983).

²¹ Orlando O. Espín, "Popular Catholicism: Alienation or Hope?," *The Faith of the People: Theological Reflections on Popular Catholicism* (Maryknoll, N.Y.: Orbis Books, 1997), 91.

²² See Ana María Pineda, "Evangelization of the 'New World': A New World Perspective," *Missiology* 20:2 (1992), 151-61.

11

Reinventing Dogmatics

A Footnote from a Reinvented Protestant

JUSTO L. GONZÁLEZ

Emory University/Hispanic Theological Initiative

I was invited to form part of the project leading to this volume both as the Protestant and as the professional historian in the group. That in itself is indicative of the transformations that have taken place in theology, and particularly in Hispanic theology, during my lifetime. As I was growing up, we Protestants were convinced that we knew scripture better than any Catholic. We were quite content leaving history and tradition to the Catholics, for after all, what had happened throughout the course of church history was a process of corruption that could only be undone by a return to the Bible. Now, as Roman Catholic Latino and Latina friends embark on an exploration hoping to "reinvent theology," they invite me, not only to bring a Protestant voice, but also to speak as a historian!

Having been invited into this dialogue both as a Protestant and as a historian, I sought at first to separate these two functions, offering some comments and footnotes, first as a historian, and then as a Protestant. However, I have found it impossible to do that, for two main reasons. First, although throughout the process I have been well aware that this is a project to reinvent Roman Catholic dogmatics, I have never felt excluded from the dialogue. Whatever comments I had to make were heard during the process itself, and if they were of any value they have already been incorporated into the various chapters of this book as they now stand.

217

Our group did indeed practice *teología de conjunto*[1]—theology done in communal conversation—and therefore most of my contributions, as everybody else's, lie in the mix of the various chapters in the present volume. Second, I cannot separate my identity as a Protestant from my identity as a historian. I no longer believe in "objective" history—or in any other version of the common oxymoron "objective knowledge." I do history from the only standpoint from which I can do it—my own. Therefore, my own reading of history, even while I try to be fair to other hearings and to other experiences, remains a Protestant reading—just as it is also marked by various other aspects of my own location in history—social, cultural, chronological, geographic, and so on. The very reasons that led my friends and colleagues to seek a Latino/a Catholic dogmatics— namely, that all dogmatics is done from a cultural and social standpoint— compel me to offer my comments from my own standpoint as a Protestant Latino historian.

Thus, what I offer here is not two different sets of reflections, one from a historical and another from a Protestant standpoint. What I offer rather is my one set of reflections on the entire process, and especially on its outcome—all joined by my own standpoint, experience, and religious identity.

Also, while other chapters in this book center on a particular aspect of theology or head of doctrine, I have seen my task as commenting on the whole, rather than on any of its parts. In other words, I do not see the value of having within this volume a particular chapter on a Protestant Hispanic view of the Trinity, or of the sacraments. My task, as I understand it, is to look at what we have done, and then to offer my reflections on the whole.

Finally, as I seek to define my task, it appears to me that this does not consist only in commenting on what the group has produced, but also in taking that production as the basis for a comment on my own tradition— or perhaps on our various traditions taken together. What I mean by this is that I conceive of this chapter not only as a Protestant footnote to the reinvention of Catholic dogmatics, but also as a preliminary reflection on what such reinvention of Catholic dogmatics may mean for the reinvention of Protestant—specifically Protestant Hispanic—dogmatics, and eventually for the invention of an ecumenical Latino/a dogmatics. I am reflecting not only on what has been discussed and written in the process of our sessions, but also on how this may lead us to read the Catholic-Protestant reality differently.

One of the themes that runs through most of the essays in this book is popular religion—or, more specifically, popular Catholicism. As I reflect on this theme from the perspective of a Protestant historian, it seems that it would be valuable to reread the entire history of the Reformation—both

Catholic and Protestant—and of the ensuing centuries of Protestant-Catholic relations through the prism of popular religion and official attitudes toward it.

In a sense, the Protestant Reformation was an attempt to cleanse Christianity from the accretions of popular religion that had become part of it throughout the centuries. It was a time when scholars had become acutely aware that the passing of time changes any historical reality. Valla, Erasmus, and Calvin disagreed on many things, but they all agreed that the manuscripts of antiquity had been corrupted through generations of copying and recopying and had to be depurated in order to rediscover—or at least to approximate—the original text. Significantly, Luther, Zwingli, Calvin, and most of the other early leaders of the Protestant Reformation, were scholars. As such, they were convinced that the manner in which Christianity had evolved, and the manner in which it was practiced in the religion of the masses, was different from the original faith, and therefore a corruption of it. From their perspective, what was needed was a restoration of that original faith, and of the church which practiced it. Each of them defined the limits of such restoration differently, but they all agreed that depuration from popular accretions—or, as they would say, "superstitions"—was necessary. For them these accretions or superstitions were not only the most obvious ones, such as the cult of relics or the excesses in connection with the sale of indulgences. They also included earlier accretions that had by then become part of accepted Christian tradition, including items such as the interpretation of the presence of Christ in the Eucharist.

In a way, one could say that this was the gist of the debate between Luther and Eck at Leipzig. While Eck saw tradition as the guarantor of Christian truth, Luther wished to use the Bible to cleanse tradition. Hence the famous clash over the decisions of the Council of Constance, particularly regarding Huss and his doctrines. For Eck, to reject those decisions was to reject all of tradition, and therefore to be cast adrift in a sea of incertitude. For Luther, if those decisions contradicted the Bible, then they clearly represented a mistake and a departure from Christian truth.

The example of the Council of Constance and the debate at Leipzig, however, also serve to show that the matter is not as simple as a debate over popular religion. Huss was a scholar, and so were d'Ailly and the others who led the council to his condemnation. Huss wished to reform the church and cleanse it from error, and so did d'Ailly. The two would have agreed wholeheartedly that the church was in urgent need of reformation—indeed, that was the purpose for which the council had been convened, as well as the essence of Huss' teachings. The difference was that each of the two parties went back to a different moment which it took to be normative in its understanding of the faith.

The debate at Leipzig was an almost exact parallel to the one at Constance. Although Protestant hagiography has often presented Luther as a scholar and Eck as an obscurantist, the truth is that Eck himself was also a scholar and had been working on his own German translation of the Bible quite apart from Luther and his reforming movement. Indeed, Eck too was a reformer, just as d'Ailly had been a reformer at an earlier date. The difference between Eck and Luther lay not in their reforming zeal or lack thereof, but rather on the point in the past to which each looked in his quest for reformation.

At this point it may be important to remember that the very word *reformation*, which we use as if its meaning were obvious, implies a looking back to a time in which things were better and doctrines purer. To re-form means to go back to the original form. In the case of Luther and most of the Protestant "re-formers," this meant the Bible. In the case of Eck, Ignatius, and other Catholic "re-formers," this meant a generally undefined time in the past, before the church became tainted with what they viewed as its current failings. (And, as is well known, there was disagreement among the Protestant reformers themselves as to how much of the more recent tradition was to be cast aside for the sake of a "purer" and "scriptural" Christianity.)

In short, the Protestant Reformation did not understand itself as an affirmation of anything that today we would call popular religion. On the contrary, it saw itself as an attempt to cleanse the faith from a number of practices and beliefs that today we would classify as popular religion, and most of the reformers would simply have dubbed superstition.

Yet the matter is not so simple. Soon the Protestant Reformation became a popular movement. Symptomatic of this process is what happened to Luther's famous ninety-five theses. Originally written in Latin, and posted in order to invite scholars to an academic debate such as were common and customary in universities—and which normally drew a prolonged yawn from the rest of the world—they were soon translated into German by an unknown hand, printed, and disseminated widely throughout the area. Almost overnight, what Luther had expected to be an academic debate became a popular movement that eventually would shake the very foundations of Europe.

The role of the printing press in this process is instructive. It was the printing press that stimulated scholars to seek to restore ancient texts that had been corrupted through manuscript transition, for now at last it was possible to produce a large number of identical texts, and thus to preserve and multiply the painstaking work of manuscript comparison and the establishment of the most likely original readings. But the printing press, which provided part of the impulse for this sort of scholarly reformation, was also the tool that soon turned matters previously debated only among scholars into issues of concern and even passion for the people at large. Although Luther did not print the first translation of his theses, he soon became aware of the enormous power of the press and has been credited with being one of the first to use the printing press as a tool for popular dissemination of ideas—or, in perhaps less positive language, as a tool for propaganda.

On the other hand, it was not only the Protestant Reformation that could be described as an attempt to cleanse the Christian faith from the accretions of popular religion. The same is true of the Catholic Reformation. The decrees of the Council of Trent show this abundantly, with their emphasis on the education of the clergy, the writing of a common catechism, the insistence on preaching, explaining the sacraments, the move to make monastic life more uniform, and so forth. The Tridentine church was to be as homogeneous as possible, guided by a hierarchical magisterium that knew what people ought to believe and how they ought to express it. It is even possible that its attempt to suppress expressions of popular religion led people away from it and toward Protestantism. Certainly, if after a time the post–Tridentine church began allowing and eventually even promoting some expressions of popular religion, this was seen by some as a practical strategy against the inroads of Protestantism, and by others as a pastoral lapse.

Here again the matter of the printing press is instructive. Having seen the power of this new invention to take ideas out of the control of the hierarchy and the academic elite, the Catholic Reformation issued the famous Index of forbidden books, which for generations sought to mold popular religion after the dictates of those who controlled the Index.

Thus, neither the Catholic Reformation nor the Protestant Reformation was an affirmation of popular Christianity. On the contrary, they both were attempts to "re-form" the church according to a vision of an earlier time when it had not been polluted by practices and superstitions of which it needed now to be cleansed. It is one of the great ironies of history that, just as Luther's Latin scholarly theses, translated into German and disseminated throughout the nation, became the banner for German nationalist sentiments, so did each of the two branches of the Reformation soon become entrenched in the very ethos of the various peoples who embraced it. The result was a "popular" religion that turned into fanaticism and bloodshed.

Perhaps, with a significant dose of oversimplification, one could say that the difference between the two forms of "re-formation" is that the Protestant sought primarily doctrinal reformation on the basis of the Bible, while the Catholic sought institutional reformation on the basis of the hierarchy. Ever since the time of Bellarmine, Catholics have argued that, if each Christian has the right to read and interpret the Bible for herself or himself, the result will be an endless array of interpretations, leading to the fragmentation of the church. In spite of all theological and theoretical arguments to the contrary, Protestant history and present reality prove Catholics right on this point. On the other hand, ever since the time of Luther, Protestants have argued that placing the authority to interpret scripture solely on the church—understood as its hierarchy and magisterium—is making the Word of God captive to human words. On this point much of recent Catholic theology seems to agree with the more traditional Protestant critique, as may be seen in the various contextual theologies that place the hermeneutical task squarely on the shoulders of the People of God, as well as in our group's interest in religion as it is believed and lived in *lo cotidiano*[2]—the daily life—of the people.

Popular religion, however, has a way of defying official religion, even while outwardly acquiescing to the dictates of hierarchies, magisteria, and theologians. Since the Index of forbidden books has been mentioned above, the story of St. Teresa of Avila in connection with the said Index serves to illustrate this point. It was just as she had become aware that several of the books that she most valued were in the Index, and that she would no longer be able to read them, that Teresa had the famous vision in which Jesus appeared to her, telling her not to worry, for "I will be to you like an open book." In other words, the hierarchy could close as many actual, physical books as it wished. Teresa would still have access to her own, independent source of authority. Thus, it is not surprising that in spite of all the Protestant and Tridentine calls for reformation, Latino popular religion has survived.

This is particularly true in Latin America, where, as Orlando Espín has cogently argued, the Tridentine reforms were never fully implemented. The control that the hierarchy claimed, and in many cases attained, in Europe was not generally present in Latin America, where distances were great, communications difficult, and the native (and later African) populations to be Christianized were enormous.

At this point, however, I find it necessary, as a Protestant, to nuance the matter further. When Protestantism first encountered my culture, it came to us with a reforming zeal reminiscent of the early days of the Reformation—or rather, of the seventeenth century, with its religious fanaticism and its religious wars. It came wrapped in the mantle of modernity, which meant that it was highly critical both of official and of popular Catholicism. Official Catholicism was criticized because it was authoritarian, because it did not allow for free inquiry in "these enlightened times," because it placed authority in the hierarchy and therefore was anti-democratic. The Index of forbidden books came to play a more important role in Protestant proclamation in Latin America than it ever played among Roman Catholic Latin Americans. The authority of the Bible was now proclaimed, not only as the authority of the Bible, but also as the authority of the people to read the Bible, against all the official readings they had been taught by ecclesiastical interpreters.

Thus, it is important to realize that Protestantism came to Latin America, not only with an emphasis on the modern ideals of freedom of inquiry and decision, but also with a strong dose of its earlier aversion to popular religion, now reinforced by the Enlightenment's bias in favor of things Northern European. If official Catholicism was accused of being too much under the control of the hierarchy, popular Catholicism was accused of being under no control—of simply allowing any and all sorts of superstition. If one form of Catholicism was attacked on the grounds that it did not allow for freedom of inquiry, the other was attacked because it did not inquire. Thus, Protestantism developed and prospered in a climate of suspicion both of official and of popular Catholicism.

In all of this, Latin American Protestantism, and its conflict with Catholicism, reflected what was taking place in the rest of the world as each of the two main branches of Western Christianity responded to the challenges and the promises of modernity. In general, throughout the nineteenth century—and in many ways until Vatican II—official Roman Catholicism saw modernity as a challenge and a threat. Witness the *Syllabus of Errors*, the condemnation of modernism, and the refusal of the papacy to come to terms with its loss of temporal power. Meanwhile, Protestantism often took the opposite tack, praising the virtues and the progress of modernity, sometimes coming close to confusing it with the reign of God, and claiming that Protestantism itself was the form of Christianity best suited to the modern age—and in fact, even often claiming that modernity itself was the result or the incarnation of Protestantism. Witness the claims by Schleiermacher that Jesus' promise that his followers would do even greater works than he did was being fulfilled by the wonders of modern science. Witness Harnack's *Essence of Christianity*, which was in truth the essence of modernity. And witness all the talk in the United States of a "manifest destiny," and in Britain of a "white man's burden," which were in fact the destiny and the burden of North Atlantic Anglo-Saxon modernity-cum-Protestantism.

If Trent and Vatican I were Roman Catholicism's version of the attempt to "re-form" the church by centralizing authority against the inroads of localized and therefore centrifugal popular religious expressions, the picture is not as clear when we come to Vatican II. Clearly, in matters of liturgy—especially the use of the vernacular and the affirmation of local cultural expressions—Vatican II allowed more room for the popular to come forth. At the same time, the process of depuration to which the council gave impetus, symbolized in the "demotion" of nonexistent saints such as St. Christopher, gave the first movements of reformation coming out of

Vatican II an official character that was still much in line with Trent, as well as with Protestant reformers such as Luther and Calvin. In our group, Arturo Bañuelas expressed the contrast between the vision of Trent and that of Vatican II by saying that, while Trent sought to educate the clergy in order to produce a more spiritual laity, Vatican II sought both to educate and to empower the laity. If so, Vatican II may be seen as the much belated modernization of the Roman Catholic Church—"modernization" in the sense of coming to terms with modernity. Therefore, thanks to the process of *aggiornamento* advocated by John XXIII, Latin American and Latino Catholicisms stole much of the Protestants' thunder about the anti-modern penchant of Roman Catholicism. However, all of this came at a time when modernity itself was being challenged, and therefore it would appear that official Catholicism's sojourn in modernity will be rather brief.

The Latin American Protestantism that emerged from the conditions described above—and which would eventually shape Latino Protestantism in the United States—bears to this day the mark of those origins. Just as Luther's scholarly ninety-five theses, and the ensuing attacks on the traditional religion of his time, soon became popular and gave rise to a different sort of popular religion, so did the Protestant polemics in Latin America against both official and popular Catholicism become part of popular Protestantism, both in Latin America and eventually among Latinos and Latinas in the United States.

It is important to understand this, for only by doing so will those who are not part of this tradition be able to understand the depth of feeling among many Protestant Latinos and Latinas about many of the items in traditional popular Catholicism. The *Virgen de la Caridad del Cobre* may be very important for Cuban identity, and certainly for Cuban popular Catholicism; for Cuban popular Protestantism, however, she is at best a matter of historical and ethnographic interest, and at worst an idol the devil has produced in order to lead the Cuban people astray. It is true that in some rare Protestant Latino churches one may find an image of Our Lady of Guadalupe. But it is also true that still today for most Protestant Latinos—even those of Mexican origin—rejecting Guadalupe is an essential mark of being truly Christian! Indeed, in some Protestant churches I have heard renderings of the stories of Caridad and Guadalupe that can only be interpreted as counter-myths—stories of how the devil invented these and other national "Virgins" for his own satanic purposes.

We may not like this situation. I do not like this situation. It certainly makes the unity of Latinos/as much more difficult. But it is real and must not be denied, lest we misjudge the depth of the conflicts bequeathed to us by our theological and ecclesiastical ancestors. The notion that Cuban Catholics and Protestants will come together around the image of Caridad, or Mexicans around Guadalupe, may be very beautiful, but is made less than credible by our own histories.

This is not easy to say, and even less easy to accept. Certainly, Caridad is central to much of the Cuban tradition, culture, and self-understanding. The very process whereby the story was changed, so that eventually those represented around the image of the Virgin would include the three major races represented and mixed in Cuba, shows that Caridad is a symbol of national identity. Clearly something similar may be said about Altagracia for Dominicans, and Guadalupe for Mexicans—and respectively for Cuban-Americans, Dominican-Americans, and Mexican-Americans. The result is that there is in much of Latino Protestantism a sense of cultural alienation that is very similar to that produced by the much earlier Spanish colonization of the Americas. Just as Spanish Roman Catholicism told our native ancestors that their religion, and therefore much of their culture, was the work of the devil, so has Anglo Protestantism told us that the Catholic religion of our more immediate ancestors, and therefore much of our culture, must be rejected. In this regard, it is instructive to compare the reaction of native populations to the celebration of the fifth centenary of the "evangelization" of the Americas in 1992 to the similar reaction of many Catholic Latinos/as to the "evangelization" of our people by Anglo Protestants. Just as native populations can accuse the earlier Catholic "evangelization" of undermining their culture and destroying their identity, so do some accuse the later Protestant "evangelization" of similar misdeeds. In many ways, just as for many natives in the sixteenth century it was necessary to abandon much of their cultural traditions in the process of becoming Catholic, so are many Latinas and Latinos forced away from their cultural roots as they become Protestant. And in both cases, this cultural alienation is depicted as good news!

Yet many Latino/a Protestants refuse to abandon their culture and its traditions. The result is, first of all, a serious crisis of identity. Indeed, I have been in more than one Protestant Latino meeting—mainline as well as evangelical and pentecostal—where the main issue under discussion, although often under a different guise, was the matter of identity: How are we Latinas/os and Protestant at the same time? What must we reject of our Latino inheritance? What must we reject of our Protestant tradition? What must we keep of each?

However, at a deeper level it may be that for Latinos and Latinas Catholic popular religion and Protestant popular religion are not all that disparate. I would suggest that this may be the area in which we are to search as we seek to reinvent Christian theology in a manner that is genuinely ours—ours not only in the sense of our owning it, but also in the sense of being truly plural, truly belonging to all of us, and not just to Catholics or Protestants.

Certainly, at the level of official religion we will not be able to come together. We will not be able to come together, first of all, because we have very little say or impact in the official religion of our separate traditions. The official statements of my own denomination[3] were mostly drawn over two centuries ago in Great Britain and the United States. More recently, our official statements, while stressing pluralism and inclusivity, still reflect the ethos, culture, and concerns of middle-class, white, Anglo North America. Thus, while they allow for a Latino presence, and while we Latinas/os are comfortable within the denomination, it is highly unlikely that we shall be able to influence its official pronouncements, or even its decision-making processes, to the point where we can use our common *latinidad*[4] to come together with Christians of other traditions.

Second, it will be very difficult for us to come together at the level of official religion, because that religion is generally fixed on issues that may have been very relevant in the sixteenth or the nineteenth century, but are not the burning issues of today. There are many examples that could be adduced in order to show this. One has to do with the sacraments and their interpretation. This certainly was a bone of contention in the sixteenth century. It still is in our official theologies, in spite of the many strides made by the official ecumenical dialogues, and by theological reinterpretations of traditional doctrine on both sides of the divide. Yet in our everyday religious life, both as Catholics and as Protestants, this issue has often receded to the background. We still hold widely differing views, mostly because our official theologies lead us in that direction. But the fact is that for many Protestant and even Catholic Latinos and Latinas the sacraments are no longer the center of their worship or of their religious sustenance. For most Latino Protestants there are other, more central points to their religious life and devotion—praise and preaching, the witnessing usually called *testimonios*, Bible study, and so on. And I would agree with Gary Riebe-Estrella's argument, in a recent article in *Theology Today*, that for Latino popular Catholicism the sacramentals have largely taken the place of the sacraments.[5]

Thus, as important as the ecumenical dialogue among professional theologians is, and as crucial as it is to overcome the divisions and prejudices of the past by revisiting and reinterpreting official theology, it is not primarily along this route that Hispanic Christians will reinvent theology in such a way that it is both a true expression of our religious life and a way to overcome the divisions and prejudices we have inherited from our missionary ancestors—Spanish or Anglo.

For all of these reasons, the importance popular religion plays in this volume as a central *locus theologicus* from which to set out in the invention of a new theology must be seen as a positive development. Here is indeed the opportunity for a new departure that may allow us to reinvent theology, not merely in the sense of footnoting what we were taught in the past, but as a voice that authentically expresses our faith and our religion.

Yet, as I have stated above, this path too is fraught with difficulties. When Catholics speak of popular religion, and of the manner in which this is expressed in the cultural traditions of our elders, Protestants resonate to the idea. But as soon as this becomes talk about specifics—and in particular about the various "Virgins" that are so central to popular Catholicism—Protestants become very suspicious.

What we must realize in order to carry the process further is that, just as there is a popular Catholicism, there is also a popular Protestantism. In many ways the latter has been created and shaped in opposition to the former—particularly in calling Catholics "idol worshipers." Likewise, to some degree as a matter of reaction, there are dimensions in popular Catholicism that carry a strong anti-Protestant bias.

How, then, can the exploration of popular religion be an avenue toward the reinvention of a theology that is catholic, evangelical, and ecumenical in the wider sense of all three terms? If we remain at the level of the obvious symbols, it is difficult to see an avenue toward mutual understanding and reconciliation—Protestants insisting that Catholics must cease in their "worship" of Guadalupe, and Catholics insisting that they do not really "worship" her. To reinvent Latino Catholic dogmatics, if it is done only at this level of discourse, will result in a theology that, while expressing the religious faith and practice of Latino Catholics, will also reinvent or revive much of the discord that a split imported from sixteenth-century Europe has produced in our midst.

I was asked to be part of this process as a historian. As such, one point that is patently clear to me is that who we are and what we are, are not what we shall be or where we will be, but a single moment in our historical development as individuals, as peoples, and as churches. To a large extent, where we are and what we are—at least in religious terms—are the result of questions raised and debates engaged in the sixteenth and seventeenth centuries. This includes the theological controversies of the Reformation as well as the violent encounter between European and American cultures and religions. We are also the result of debates, hopes, and fears during the nineteenth and twentieth centuries regarding the relationship between Christianity and modernity. Unfortunately, those questions, and the answers given to them in the past, have become so ingrained in our self-understanding that it is difficult for us to go beyond them. Yet, if we are really to reinvent dogmatics, and to reinvent it in an ecumenical fashion with a Latino flavor, we must go beyond the tried and tired answers of the Reformation, and beyond the symbols of our popular religion—which have also become symbols and even banners for our divisions—to the deeply ingrained religious outlook and experience that lie behind them.

I have been asked to engage in this process as a Protestant—although, as Virgil Elizondo has called me, a "Catholic Protestant," or, as I dub myself in the title of this essay, a "reinvented Protestant." As a Latino Protestant, I am caught in the questions of identity I have attempted to describe above. Caridad, Guadalupe, and novenas are not part of my more immediate tradition. Yet they are part of my culture. Does that mean that, like my native ancestors five centuries ago when faced by the initial Catholic "evangelization," I must renounce my cultural heritage in order to affirm my Christianity? I do not believe so. Does it mean that I must denounce those who out of my cultural tradition continue practicing popular Catholicism? I would hope not.

Perhaps what we must do is to move more boldly in the direction of reinventing dogmatics by moving away—at least temporarily—from such prescriptive terms as *dogmatics* and *theology*. The first, with its etymological connection with *dogma*, of necessity focuses on the official and authoritative teaching of the church. The second, also out of its etymological meaning, implies that the best way to approach God is through logic, through orderly reasoned thinking. Therefore, to speak of a reinvention of dogmatics or of theology out of the reality of popular religion almost of necessity leads us to the formulation of that religion in terms that are antithetical to its very nature, rarefying it into the more abstract—although supposedly more precise—language of the academy and of official theology. At the level of such language it will be difficult to achieve a breakthrough over the denominational divisions and the cultural alienations that our popular religions have inherited and sometimes even fostered.

For these reasons I suggest that Roberto Goizueta's proposal of a "theopoetics" may be the direction in which we ought to move as we seek to reinvent what has traditionally been called theology or dogmatics from a Latino perspective. If a Latino perspective involves, as several in our conversation have suggested, a popular perspective, a view "from below," from *lo cotidiano*—the daily—from the lived experience of our people, the aesthetic rather than the cognitive may be the best starting point as well as the best mode of expression.

What would a Christian Latino ecumenical theopoetics look like? I do not know. Perhaps it does not even have to have a single look to it, for poetry, unlike prose, can stand side by side without being forced to agree or even to coincide. I do have some idea, however, what a people moved and inspired by such theopoetics will look like. We already have glimpses of it in the manner in which liturgical elements—especially the songs we call *coritos* or *estribillos*—bring us together in praise and thanksgiving. I imagine that ultimately in its variety and vitality such a community would look something like what John the Seer (also called "the Theologian," although in truth he was more of a "Theopoet") says: "After this I looked, and there was a great multitude that no one could count, from every nation, from all tribes and peoples and languages, standing before the throne and before the Lamb, robed in white, with palm branches in their hands."

Notes

[1] See Glossary.
[2] See Glossary.
[3] Professor González is a member of the United Methodist Church—Ed.
[4] See Glossary.
[5] Gary Riebe-Estrella, "Latino Religiosity or Latino Catholicism," *Theology Today* 54 (1998), 512-15.

12

U.S. Latino/a Theology

A View from Outside

❦

RUY G. SUÁREZ RIVERO

Universidad Iberoamericana

INTRODUCTION

What God do you believe in? This is not a rhetorical question, nor can the answer be ethically or politically neutral. The answer involves a commitment in which one's life is at stake. Among the most serious and keen problems that Catholic systematic theology faces today are questions regarding its intelligibility, its interpretation, and its method. Christian faith focuses on a mystery—God's mystery. It proclaims an insanity—the cross. But in this mystery and in this insanity Christian faith expects humanity's life to be decided. How can one make believable the unbelievable?[1]

Here lies the very core of the challenge faced by the present volume's authors. The University of San Diego's Center for the Study of Latino/a Catholicism presented us with an ambitious project, to be developed in one year: reflect upon method, contents, hermeneutic basis, and epistemological premises of Catholic systematic theology from the perspective of U.S. Latino/a faith, given the latter's complex ethnic, religious, cultural, and socioeconomic reality.

We were asked specifically to discuss the nature, assumptions, shape, methods, and disciplinary concentrations for a truly Latino/a systematic theology. Consequently, we dealt with a number of crucial questions, but the most fundamental of all was: What would Catholic systematic theology be like if it were "reinvented" from the Latino/a experience and perspective? This question brought up an exciting adventure—to open the possibility of making Catholic systematics *latinamente*, within the new methodological context of a *teología de conjunto*.[2]

The modern social sciences have shown to what extent we are all children of culture, of society, and of history. History, society, and culture[3] are not abstract conditions, extrinsic to ourselves. They are within, shaping us. We are children of human groups, and our conduct, values, feelings, attitudes, and ideas about God carry the seal of the human community where we have been formed.

"All human thought," María Pilar Aquino has written, "maintains an intrinsic relation to the historical context in which it originates and to which it seeks to respond, whether to transform or legitimize that context. Theology is not exempt from this principle, even when one acknowledges the internal structure of theology as a discipline that reflects upon the experience of faith in the light of revelation."[4]

Back to the initial question: What God do you believe in? "In the God who has been taught to me," would be a typical answer. But who has taught "God" to you? For the majority of believers, the further answer might be: "I believe in the God my parents taught me, in the God the church taught me." These are not innocent questions or neutral answers; our relationship with God depends on our own particular idea of the Divinity. But not only is our relationship with God involved—our relationship with others and with "otherness" is also at stake. In other words, the believer's entire life. If every human thought maintains an intrinsic relation to the historical context in which it originates, then the idea of God that has been taught to us by our parents and the church, and which in turn had been communicated to them by an earlier generation of the church and by others, is at the same time an idea interpreted through the centuries within concrete historical and cultural contexts.

But is the language that speaks of God within those contexts intelligible? Does it truly speak to modern/postmodern men and women at the dawn of the twenty-first century? And more particularly, is this language intelligible and challenging for Latinos/as, living as they are in historical and cultural contexts very different from the ones that gave birth to the "official" or "mainstream" idea of God?

We know how intense were the "mono-culturizing" processes that seem to have characterized the church from the fourth century on, with very few instances of real dialogue with other cultures. These processes could be summarized in the words of Cardinal Joseph Ratzinger, written at another moment in his life, in reference to Pius IX's *Syllabus* and Pius X's anti-Modernist campaign: "The church denied itself the possibility of living Christianity as something present, because it became excessively attached to its past."[5]

But this is only one side of the coin—the side that tells us from within which historical, social, and cultural contexts the idea of God was communicated to us. The other side is the one that points to the contexts within which that idea of God was *received*.

This point is of capital importance. As Orlando Espín has written:

> No experience of the divine occurs in vacuum. The same testimonies that point to the human encounter with "God" signal precisely that it is an *encounter*. One of the two involved is, by definition, contextualized in a concrete culture, in a concrete society, and in a concrete history. From the perspective of the human partner, the experience of the divine is only possible through cultural, social, and historical means . . . The cultural 'idiom' of an individual or group will shape the language, symbols, etc., used [by that individual or group] in the process of interpreting religious experience, thereby shaping the experience itself as "religious" and the image(s) of the divine therein.[6]

Since the idea of God (that is, the idea of what God is to us and what we are to God), along with everything that this assumes and implies, was communicated to many of us in categories foreign to our historical, cultural, and social roots, the idea has become sufficiently unintelligible and has therefore lost much of its power to speak and challenge. Pretending, for example, to explain God's mystery today by means of ancient or medieval categories of relation and procession is to run the risk of making "God" into something innocuous or, at best, a truth reserved for a few initiates, an inaccessible and unintelligible esoteric reality to most mortals.[7]

Theology is not a static discipline. Its duty is to make faith flow toward social life. Theology must be immersed in the dynamism of everyday life, in a continuous search for new ways, new methods, new languages that make the God of Jesus intelligible and therefore accessible in the ever changing existence of men and women in their "here and now."

If this is so, the theology of everyday life experience cannot be separated from the experience of the "here and now" of concrete men and women; more specifically, in the case of the U.S. Latino/a community, daily experience cannot be separated from its changing contexts, or from its historical density as root of a common identity, or from the search for Latinos/as' understanding of truth. The meaning of Latino/a existence cannot be irrelevant to their encounter with God within their daily experience.

Because theology is a discipline that attempts to articulate the language of faith in its diverse expressions, and because it refers more to the experience rooted in everyday life than to the exposition of abstract truths, theology then originates within the experience of everyday life, only reflecting at a second moment on the self-communication of God in history[8]—a self-communication that expresses itself as love, grace, liberating power, and hope among the poor and oppressed of the earth.

The object of U.S. Latino/a theology is God, but a God who reveals Godself in the reality of everyday life and is discovered in U.S. Latino/a communities from within their own perspective, "named from within their experiences of life and death, word and silence, joy and suffering, liberation and oppression."[9] This basic structure determines in a radical way the methodological articulation, the theological contents, and the central themes of this theology. If Jesus had been a Latino, and if he had been born in the United States, how would he have preached about God? No doubt about it—his preaching would have been done *latinamente*!

Either we encounter God in our everyday life, or we will not encounter God at all. The vital need for serious reflection, to critically discern the impulse of the Spirit in and from the Latino/a community, arises from this premise. Therefore, one of the tasks of U.S. Latino/a theologians has been to provide a language for the faith experience of their community, a language that can help deepen the understanding of the experience of faith in dialogue with the community itself. And this language, as Sixto J. García argues, not without certain irony, "does not flow from the computer-heavy comfort of First World air-conditioned offices, often peripheral to a community's language, but rather from the living contact with the community's experience."[10]

A certainty shared by U.S. Latino/a theologians, which has given life and spirit to their theology, is that reality does not show all its possibilities until the decision to explore it is made with imagination, creativity, boldness, and a mind open to extract from it all of its potential.

Congruent with the maturity of Latino/a theology (whose voice has begun to surpass its national and continental borders), the quest to reinvent Catholic systematics *latinamente* has been a fruitful response to real-life questions arising from Latino/a reality. The articles contained in the present volume represent the extraordinary progress made by Latino/a theologians. These chapters are the conceptualized results of a joint effort at giving shape to a hermeneutic and language that would adequately interpret and express the faith experience of their communities, without negating the language and interpretation of the people.

I was born in the city of Mérida (in the Mexican state of Yucatán), but for the past fourteen years I have lived with my wife and three children in Tijuana (in the state of Baja California). I live, therefore, in the southern half of the huge binational metropolitan area we share with San Diego, in the U.S. state of California. I am, strictly speaking, not part of the U.S.

Latino/a community. And yet, our common border geography, my Latin American origin, and my identification with the theological thinking and struggles of my U.S. Latino/a colleagues, have created an intellectual and affectionate bond between us. My Latino/a colleagues have been, for my family and myself, an enriching source of friendship and witnesses to a committed Christian life.

From my particular perspective, "with one foot in and one foot out," I was asked to take part in this project to reinvent Catholic systematics from the perspective of U.S. Latino/a communities. The particularity of my contribution is that it is done from the outside—that is, from the perspective of a Mexican theologian who knows U.S. Latino/a theology very well. In this essay I will try to answer the following questions: How is Latino/a theology seen, understood, and interpreted in Mexico, and in general, in Latin America? What are the most outstanding contributions that U.S. Latino/a theology, and this attempt at reinventing Catholic systematics, have made or can make to Latin American theological reflection?

The international recognition already achieved by U.S. Latino/a theology, the complexity of the issues it deals with, as well as the importance of the articles in this book, make it practically impossible (in the brief space allocated) to answer fully the questions I just posed in the way this project merits. Apart from the space limitation, I must also admit that the task of analyzing the contents of U.S. Latino/a theology, and of articulating an in-depth response to it, should not be done by a single author but by many other specialists in the different fields of theology, sociology, cultural anthropology, and so forth.

In view of all of this I am compelled to center my attention exclusively on those topics I consider more representative, and that from my point of view reflect more the characteristic notes of Latino/a theology as well as the more important contributions this theology (and this reinvention project) make to Latin American theology and beyond.

MAKING BELIEVABLE THE UNBELIEVABLE: ATTEMPTS BY OTHER THEOLOGIES

U.S. Latino/a theology does not emerge *ex nihilo*. Rather, as every human thought, this theology maintains an intrinsic relation with the historical context from which it originates. Therefore this part, as basic background to my "from outside" general evaluation of U.S. Latino/a theology, begins with an extraordinarily quick *mirada de pájaro* (a bird's-eye view) of the most significative attempts made this century to find theological discourses that could put aside abstract ideas on God and enter into dialogue with human culture, in order to address fundamental questions from within Christian faith.

I am very much aware that the following historically contextualizing summary is brief and incomplete. Indeed, I know that it is very synthetic and selective. Furthermore, I will limit my comments to those theologies born from and as responses to specific cultural contexts. The reader will therefore note that although references will be made to feminist thought, I will not reflect on it except as it has expressed itself within U.S. Latino/a theology. The reason is simple—feminist theologies of the First World still belong, culturally and historically, to Europe and to the United States. No suggestion is implied that feminist theological thought is otherwise unimportant or irrelevant.

I will make some very brief remarks (and in the following order) in reference to contemporary European theology, to the documents of the Second Vatican Council, to the plural reality of contemporary theological thought, and finally, to Latin American theology. By seeking contrasts and similarities with these other theologies, we will have contextualized our approach to U.S. Latino/a theology itself within the overall theological universe.[11]

This quick historical contextualization is not pointless. I consider it necessary not only for the reasons mentioned above, but as an aid to later assess the questioning force that characterizes U.S. Latino/a theology, its progress in relation to other theologies that have preceded it, and, by contrast with the latter, its more significant contributions.

Contemporary European Theologies

From the first decades of the twentieth century it became increasingly clear in Europe that traditional theological discourse—inherited from the metaphysical, abstract, and ahistoric languages of the Middle Ages and of early modernity—did not agree with the mentality and needs of people in the cultural spaces of more recent modernity (and postmodernity). It was perceived as a fact that women and men in contemporary Europe no longer possessed a metaphysical, abstract, and static vision of things, but that they conceived reality in historic, scientific, social, dynamic, and political ways.

It was thus advisable to face the difficult task of translating the Christian message to an accessible language. Both World Wars made evident the insufficiency of the then-current philosophical systems: from idealism to voluntarism, from positivism to spiritualism and vitalism, from intuitionism to pragmatism. The two wars left the values exalted by those philosophical systems in a state of crisis.

Stemming from a deeply felt need for social renewal, due in great mea-
sure to the terribly anguishing situation into which the two World Wars
had sunk humanity, theological languages derived from more contemporary philosophical movements began to appear in the European context.
These renewed languages abandoned many of the old metaphysical speculations and universalizing (and somewhat pompous) systematic constructions. Merely as examples of this shift I mention the existentialist language
developed by Bultmann and Rahner; the so-called secular approaches of
Robinson, Schillebeeckx, and Schoonenberg; the eschatological perspective of Moltmann; the political theology of Metz; Barth's dialectic construction; Tillich's ontological categories; and the aesthetical language of
von Balthasar. These European theological languages are among the most
representative attempts at bringing the Christian message into contemporary cultural and historical categories.[12]

The Second Vatican Council

The Second Vatican Council was more an ecclesial than a theological
event, but it played (as it still does) a decisive role in Catholic theology, in
the sense that it brought about a profound ecclesiological renewal.

The council documents addressed renewal movements that had
emerged during the first half of the twentieth century—and the influence
of the schools at Louvain, Innsbruck, Le Saulchoir, Lyon-Fourviere,
Tübingen, and others is acknowledged in the conciliar texts. Vatican II
was characterized by renewal—biblical, liturgical, patristic, and ecumenical, as well as an openness to the collective and historical dimensions of
human existence.

But the council also "consecrated" central European theology. The great
conciliar theologians were central Europeans, and the problems of the central European world were the ones primarily reflected upon during the
council sessions. Some of Vatican II's documents seem abstract indeed for
non-Europeans.

Vatican II intended, above all, to be a pastoral council. But not a few of
the council fathers had a problem realizing that "pastoral" also meant a
"new dogmatic sensitivity," more focused toward history and toward *lo
cotidiano*.[13] As a consequence, this weakened the council's chance to shape
an authentic theology whose source would be life itself within a church,
as it constantly rethinks and reflects upon God's Word. Therefore, further
reinterpretation from within specific cultural and historical situations became necessary, and this task began to be carried out in many places from
the prophetic perspective of the poor.

Even though sometimes the autochthonous sensitivities and identities
of diverse Christian peripheral communities were present at the council,

it was not until later, with Paul VI's *Populorum Progressio* and *Evangelii Nuntiandi*—and with his explicit support—that a promising awakening was made possible for "global church" thought. The search was on for a theology that would overcome the cultural and historical structures of European Christendom.

Diversity and Plurality

Changes in paradigms during the second half of the twentieth century altered the worldwide theological landscape. The search for new languages and new expressions broke out of the old, expected molds. In the 1960s Karl Rahner pointed out that "modern man asks himself if this talk about 'deification,' 'sonship,' or 'inhabitation in God' is not just another ideological poem, or a series of unproved myths."[14] And Edward Schillebeeckx, in his *Interpretación de la fe*, wrote: "One could easily prove that the use of ecclesiastical language is becoming increasingly less understood by those who speak it, that is, by the faithful themselves. The game of ecclesiastical language has become problematic for the faithful themselves."[15]

In this context, to talk today about the plurality of or diversity among theologies does not surprise anyone. The history of Christian thinking results from mixing and crisscrossing many influences—a process I would hesitate to describe as providential, because it has generated the best as well as the worst in Christian thought. It has been shown that theological constructs are inseparable from ethnic, cultural, social, and economic roots and conditions. Is it by chance that the schisms and heresies of the first several centuries of Christian history were inseparable from the cultural and sociopolitical conflicts of the time?

Post–Vatican II Catholic theologies have a common feature: the metaphysical structure of their discourse tends to disappear. These theologies remind us that the Bible ignores philosophical mediation as we have known it in Western theology. They increasingly emphasize that social mediation of meaning is at the heart of life for real people. These new theological discourses are less and less reducible to one; they are constructed and increasingly received (especially but not exclusively in Latin America) by means and criteria other than or parallel to those of the ecclesiastical institution. They are linked to the social diversification processes that characterize contemporary society—and it is here that we discover the polymorphic and modern equivalent of what in ancient times was precisely called theology.

The effort to find and develop a proper language to express the faith experience has shifted from the center to the periphery. New theologies have emerged that have begun to profoundly affect contemporary theological reflection in Latin America, in Asia and Africa, and very evidently in the U.S. Black and Latino/a communities (in other words, where we find the vast majority of Catholics worldwide).

Latin American Theology

The Latin American bishops at the Puebla Conference (1979) met to critically reflect upon their churches and on their own ministry,[16] in light of the earlier Medellín Conference (1968), which had signaled the defini-tive emergence of Latin America's own ecclesial and theological resources, and which had "read" Vatican II from within the Latin American (and not the European) historical and cultural contexts.

The bishops' Medellín reflections had led to what by the Puebla meeting had become an inductive theology, as opposed to a deductive one, although the bishops did not consider praxis the only foundation capable of solidly grounding all faith discourse. A balanced, dialectical articulation between knowledge and action was called for—an articulation between induction and deduction that would recognize in the process itself the vital space of living faith.

The church was becoming *latinoamericana* by becoming the server of the poor and by making room for real people. A new pastoral sensitivity, which would lead to the option for the poor, was being born with a specific local flavor, supported by theological reflection from within the experience and analysis of situations of poverty and oppression. However, progress did not lack adverse pressures, difficulties, and misunderstandings.[17] I recall the Vatican's challenge to the theology of liberation as one of the many manifestations of the tension between the "center" (Rome) and the "periphery" (in this case, Latin America).[18]

Oriented toward the poor and oppressed, liberation theology and the basic ecclesial communities developed into what could be considered the new spirit and the new face of a genuinely Latin American church. This is where the flux of this church toward the other regional churches began, as well as the refluxes and influxes of its theology. Other regional churches showed interest in "liberation" thought. Latin American theology constitutes the rediscovery of the necessary articulation between Word and praxis,[19] not in theory but in concrete sociohistorical situations.

A theology is Christian only when it allows the poor to speak and consents to be challenged by them. This is *not* about talking *in the name of* the poor. It is about conversion to the gospel, to the point where the poor may recover *their right to speak*. The church's language must be Jesus' language. Nevertheless, it is true that language is not ultimately what matters—love is! But language can bind or break the ties that keep God's people bound, hopeful for and awaiting the fullness of salvation. Granted that this salvation will only be fully perfected in eternity, but without the socio-historical, cultural moment and dimension, there will not be true salvation either.

Humans are *not* "disincarnate souls" or "souls trapped in bodies"; and so if salvation was offered to *real* humans (and if the fullness of Christ's humanness experienced resurrection), then Christian salvation must never be understood *exclusively* as "religious" or "spiritual." Salvation must of necessity involve and include the cultural, the social, and the historical dimensions of human reality, because without these there is no *real* human reality (and consequently, the salvation offered would not affect *real* humans). The *intellectus fidei* must yield the primacy to the *intellectus charitatis* (Jon Sobrino). This, in turn, constitutes a complete theological program.

From this hope new theologies are legitimately born in the church (as in earlier centuries Latin theologies grew together with Eastern theologies). But new theologies do not come about as mere extensions of an officially sanctioned, institutional theology. Indeed, new theologies are not "new" just because they might be interesting "translations" or applications of imposed or acquired theological systems. The impact and importance of any theology must not be measured solely by the number or contents of the books its practitioners may publish, but by the Christian witness and lives of the men and women who create that theology—otherwise we would have to admit that theology (as a Christian task) ultimately has little to do with or effect in real Christians' daily living. It is precisely in the everyday experiences of faith, often lived in the monotony of daily life (which is frequently underestimated by the specialists), that every theology (and theologian) discovers its most fundamental vocation—to encourage, strengthen, enlighten, accompany, reflect on, and thematize the faith of the people by theologizing *in* and *from among* real people.

U.S. LATINO/A THEOLOGY: A PERSPECTIVE "FROM OUTSIDE"

The 1960s social justice and civil-rights struggles became a watershed period for U.S. Latino/a communities. It was in those years that Latino/a social-religious activism blossomed. Milagros Peña has written:

> The history of the struggle, by no mere coincidence, was the same period in which we were coming to our own politically within the larger society, evidenced by the many Latina/o-led social movements of the time . . . Events at the time clearly shaped how, where, and

from whom changes in the churches would come, and the circumstances under which many Latinas and Latinos would come to question their status within their churches and the theologies they were
exposed to.[20]

In this context, and a few years after the publication of Gustavo Gutiérrez's
Teología de la liberación, Virgilio Elizondo published (1972) his article
"Educación religiosa para el méxico-americano."[21] This article marked the
birth of what would become the new Latino/a theological language—a
new theology meant to cross borders, in both the Catholic and the Protestant traditions.

A handful of theologians consolidated, over a decade, what today is
known across most of the world as U.S. Latino/a theology. The foundation of the Academy of Catholic Hispanic Theologians of the United States
(ACHTUS), and later the creation of the respected *Journal of Hispanic/
Latino Theology*, came to significantly support and make better known
the work of these Latino/a scholars. A growing number of Latino/a theologians became actively involved in prestigious theological professional
associations in the United States, Latin America, and Europe. They have
been (and are) frequently invited to address colleagues at international
conferences, and their books and papers are translated and read in several languages.[22] As time has passed, it has become obvious that U.S.
Latino/a theology cannot be defined merely by the fact that its authors
are Latinos/as, or by their continuous use of the expressions and symbols employed by their communities. Latino/a theology is best understood and known through the *sources* of its reflection and through its
method.

One of the most obvious characteristics of this theology is the way it is
rooted in the complex ethnic, social, economic, political, cultural, and religious realities of U.S. Latino/a communities. The Catholic church in the
United States is no longer a church of European immigrants and their
descendants. Demographic studies have pointed to the birth of a new U.S.
church of Latin American roots.[23]

This church of Latin American origin finds itself, however, within the
European-American dominant culture. This fact has come to confirm, in
the words of Fernando Segovia, "that no one culture represents the sole
and superior embodiment of the Christian tradition, and to affirm the richness that cultural diversity represents for church and academy alike."[24] In
this sense, and along the same line of thought, it is easy to agree with
Arturo Bañuelas when he depicts U.S. Latino/a theology as "subversive,"
since Bañuelas understands that this theology "challenges the absolutizing
of any culture as normative, providing further evidence that no one culture can exhaustively embody the gospel or Christian way of life."[25]

In my view "from the outside," the evident contrasts between European-American and Latino/a cultures stand out. This point is important, since European-American theologians very rarely acknowledge themselves to come from and think within very specific and limited historical and cultural contexts, although they often seem very quick to point to (dismissively, perhaps) the specificity of Latino/a theology.

European and European-American theologians claim universal validity for their thought when, in fact, as Orlando Espín has shown, "there is no a-cultural Christianity just as there is no a-cultural option for God, love, or salvation."[26] I need to emphasize that it would be a grave mistake to understand reductionistically U.S. Latino/a theology by the fact that it originates from within a specific cultural universe, and thus somehow dismiss it as "ethnic theology." The evident fact is that *all* Christian theologies originate within specific cultural universes and, consequently, would equally qualify as "ethnic"! This point will become more evident in my exposition of the most outstanding elements of Latino/a theology.

In the paragraphs that follow I will focus mainly, but certainly not exclusively, on Latino/a theology as expressed in the various articles in the present volume.

Mestizaje

U.S Latino/a theology is constructed by men and women who carry in their blood the pride and pain of their *mestizo/a* origins.[27] Their way of looking at life, of understanding their own existence and interpreting their faith experience, links them to the faith experience of the Latino/a communities to which they belong. The criteria employed by them in their theological work, the reflection topics they have chosen, the methods used, and the purpose of their theology are all indelibly marked by the historical density of *mestizaje*.

The articulation that Latino/a theologians make of *mestizaje* as *locus theologicus*,[28] and their critical interpretation of the Conquest, along with the socioreligious and cultural convergence of two worlds on the hill of Tepeyac,[29] have become an epistemological horizon that continuously pervades all Latino/a theology.

For Latino/a theologians, *mestizaje* is not limited to the mingling of races. It also (and primarily) includes a cultural and religious synthesis in its various forms and expressions. *Mestizaje* is employed not only as a paradigm of racial diversity, but of all other diversity found in Latino/a communities. Plurality of origins, of races, of cultures, of human mixing, has not been an obstacle for Latinos/as' identifying and preserving that which is common among them. They have been able to do this without disregarding or oppressing their own internal particularities—thereby also opening a paradigm for a potentially enriching ecumenical theological discourse. *Mestizaje*, as criterion, as reality, and as model, has been crucial to the development of Latino/a theological thought.

It is precisely from the richness of this *mestizaje* that there emerges in U.S. Latino/a theology an all-pervasive cross-cultural and ecumenical awareness that does not necessarily follow the expected models or topics of ecumenical conversation. Nevertheless, Latino/a theology is paving the way for a new dialogue by opening up fresh perspectives and categories still neglected in interdenominational discussions. An example of this new and challenging dialogue can be clearly perceived in the works published by Justo González,[30] and in numerous publications by Catholic and Protestant Latino/a theologians.

Latino/a theology implies the vision of a new Christian universalism—indeed, at the core of theological reflection on *mestizaje* there is the rejection of every exclusion and of every barrier, leading to a new creation where all will share at the festive table of fellowship as brothers and sisters. "The *mestizo* . . . is a foretaste of possible new universal humanity without boundaries . . . The *mestizo* presence in both North and Latin America is a call for solidarity at the historical juncture where God is raising up a new historical moment. For many, the unique *mestizo* border reality is a *kairos*, a moment of grace and opportunity experienced as the decisive action of a bridge people between the Americas."[31]

The Guadalupe Event

The Guadalupe symbol, and what happened at Tepeyac, is a foundational paradigmatic event for U.S. Latino/a Catholic theology. Just as the Guadalupe event helped Náhuatl cultural memory rise from the ashes and destruction of the Conquest,[32] Guadalupe helps the cultural memory of U.S. Latinos/as rise from their own suffering—as expression of eschatological hope and as category in the salvation of identity (J. B. Metz).

The importance that the Guadalupe event has for U.S. Latino/a theology can be summarized in the words of Virgilio Elizondo, who is considered the intellectual father of this theology: "The more I try to comprehend the intrinsic force and energy of the apparitions of Our Lady of Guadalupe to Juan Diego at Tepeyac in 1531, at the very beginning of the Americas, the more I dare to say that I do not know of any other event since Pentecost that has had such revolutionary, profound, lasting, far reaching, healing, and liberating impact on Christianity."[33]

However, I consider it necessary to point out that in order to be able to appreciate the true meaning and depth of the Guadalupe event, for most Latino/a communities and for most Latin Americans, it is important to place oneself not only in the historical context of the violent and unequal sixteenth-century encounter or *encontronazo* (as Fernando Segovia ironically defines it[34]) of two completely different worlds; it is also necessary to move beyond the limits of a traditional anthropology and make an attempt to see, to hear, and to understand Guadalupe through a *mestizo/a* anthropology—an anthropology of inclusive and progressive syntheses.[35]

Beyond the Theology of Liberation

U.S. Latino/a theology is not a sub-theology, dependent on some North Atlantic theological paradigm, nor is it a translation of the Latin American theology of liberation.[36] U.S. Latino/a theology has certainly been inspired by, and taken some foundational insights from, the theology of liberation. But it has delved into them with contributions from the U.S. Latino/a life experience, from within a different sociohistorical context, and with anthropological and theological elaborations made possible thanks to a distinctively U.S. Latino/a systematic reflection on popular religion as epistemology. The very core intuition of Latin American liberation theology, consequently, would admit that Latino/a theology is not and cannot be a mere translation or adaptation thereof. It seems clear that U.S. Latino/a theology, as María Pilar Aquino has said,

> does not exist because of the desire to create a bridge between Latin American liberation theology and European-American critical thought. Neither does it exist to correct the shortcomings of Roman Catholic conservative discourse vis-à-vis today's emancipatory movements and social sciences. Rather our task exists because of the vital need for a coherent formulation of our own faith experience, based on our *mestiza* condition and as we face an oppressive reality that we seek to overcome, there where the liberating traditions of Christianity and the vision and strategies of the liberating socio-ecclesial movements of today dynamically converge.[37]

Latino/a theology has recognized the achievements and extraordinary impact of liberation theology. It has admitted its debt to liberation thought, for example and particularly in U.S. Latino/a theology's own option for the poor and the oppressed. However, Latino/a theology has its own characteristics, which in turn have enriched the theological reflection of many in the Third World with new methods, new intuitions, new epistemological premises, and new fields of reflection. As an example, let me suggest that U.S. Latino/a theology, so rooted in and reflective of popular Catholicism, has deepened and developed an understanding of praxis not only from the perspective of social transformation (as developed by the theology of liberation) but as the basis for understanding aesthetic experience as a key category in the interpretation of human action. The usual understanding of praxis changes radically when the interpersonal action of the human being is defined in aesthetic rather than instrumental categories.[38] And, from this, one must infer that the most profound meaning of the ethical-political option for the poor is not sociopolitical transformation alone, but the hopeful transformation of every dimension of everyday (social, familial, individual) human life. Roberto Goizueta emphasizes and notably elaborates this point in the article he wrote for the present volume, as well as in a number of his other publications.

The Crucial Role of Popular Catholicism

The more deeply I study U.S. Latino/a theology, the more convinced I am that it is practically impossible to understand the cultural and religious universe of the Latino/a communities without considering the crucial role that popular Catholicism has played in the past and still plays today.

Popular Catholicism is conceptualized by Latino/a theology not as a socio-cultural-religious phenomenon to be scientifically analyzed through the instruments of the social sciences, but fundamentally as a legitimate source of Christian theology, assuming it as an epistemological and hermeneutical element essential to the theological task.

As Orlando Espín has demonstrated, popular Catholicism

is a major component of Latino cultural reality that has not been profoundly invaded by the European-American dominant culture. It still acts as indispensable bearer of values, traditions, symbols, and world view for and within U.S. Latino communities. The importance of popular Catholicism in the cultural self-definition and self-preservation of U.S. Latinos cannot be exaggerated.[39]

The fact that popular Catholicism is an epistemological and central hermeneutic element for Latino/a theologians has its deepest root in their own involvement with the experience and popular expressions of faith of the communities to which they belong. However, Latino/a theologians have carefully made the distinction between popular Catholicism and popular religion. Popular religion is certainly assumed as important, but not as coextensive with popular Catholicism. The latter, in turn, is *not* viewed as a "popularized" version of "official" Roman Catholicism.[40] Latino/a theologians have refused to see popular Catholicism as a "pastoral problem"—a view still held by many Latin American and European-American theologians and pastoral agents.

Latino/a theology believes that in popular Catholicism truth is found not in the dimension of cold rationality, but in the dimension of relationality; "not in universal, abstract concepts," as Roberto Goizueta says, "but in particular, concrete sacraments, or symbols; not through observation but through participation, by kissing the statue, or walking with Jesus, or kneeling alongside Mary, or singing to her." Recalling the centrality of the Guadalupe event for U.S. Latino/a communities, he adds: "In the Náhuatl world of Juan Diego, beauty *is* truth, and truth *is* beauty: *'flor y canto.'* It is in the singing of the birds, in the aroma of the roses, and, above all, in the encounter with the Lady of Tepeyac that Juan Diego comes to understand the truth of who he is, who she is, and who God is."[41]

In this context, popular Catholicism is considered a privileged *locus* of divine revelation, its dogmatic/revelatory dimension affirmed by Catholic tradition, especially because this tradition gives a privileged place to the *sensus fidelium*[42] as the "faith-full" intuition of the Christian people as (moved by the Spirit) they sense, adhere to, and interpret the Word of God. Popular Catholicism can then be theologically understood as a cultural expression of the *sensus fidelium*, with everything that this comprehension implies for the theology of the Tradition in the Roman Catholic Church. In the words of Vatican II: "The body of the faithful as a whole, anointed as they are by the Holy One, cannot err in matters of belief" (*Lumen Gentium*, no. 12).

U.S. Latino/a theology also understands popular Catholicism as a source of Christian theology with spatial and geographical dimensions. This point has special importance for the way Latino/a theologians see the option for the poor. From the perspective of popular Catholicism, this implies an option for the preferred *loci* of theology—those places where the poor live, either by choice or by force. "The *locus* or 'place' of theology," Goizueta points out, "should not be understood in a purely metaphorical sense. The very notions of 'social location' and 'experience' themselves remain, after all, mere theoretical categories as does 'praxis.' If we take seriously the concrete particularity of human praxis and, therefore, the option for the poor, we must also take seriously the concrete particularity of the place where theology is done." And then he adds: "If we do this, we are left with only one conclusion, a conclusion which modern theologians and scholars, whether liberal or conservative, have largely evaded, namely, that in its fundamental sense, the *locus* of theology is the *physical, spatial, geographical place* of theological reflection. To walk with the poor is to walk *where* Jesus walks and *where* the poor walk."[43]

In my estimation, an extraordinary contribution made by Latino/a theology to theological reflection in the Third World is the reevaluation of interpersonal relationships from the perspective of the home as a privileged place for theology. This perspective arises from the fact that Latino/a cultures, unlike "mainstream" U.S. culture, are sociocentric in nature—all Latino/a relationships use family as their paradigm. "The fundamental unit of society is envisioned as the group, primarily the family," writes Gary Riebe-Estrella in one of his articles in the present volume. Emphasizing that Latino/a cultures are sociocentric, Riebe-Estrella adds:

> The identity of an individual emerges from his or her membership in the group. In this cultural perspective, human persons mature by recognizing their place within the group and by refining to some extent the mutual obligations and rights which that place entails. But who they are is always bounded by the group.[44]

This assessment necessarily implies a new appreciation evidenced by Latino/a theology—an affective, aesthetic dimension in the option for the poor. In other words, love for and solidarity with the poor must imply not only the public dimension of the ethical, political struggle for justice (as in the theology of liberation), but also the dimension of private, interpersonal relationships—that is, the complete extent of *lo cotidiano*. At the same time, this makes evident how Latino/a theology is a reflection articulated on the basis of "person," the latter understood as "being-with others," as Miguel Díaz explains in his article named after a wisdom phrase much used by Latinos/as: *Dime con quién andas y te diré quién eres.*

There is a further and related development surrounding one of the central themes of Latino/a theology—the relationship between the particular and the universal.[45] The particular, inscribed in the dimension of *lo cotidiano*, is addressed by Alejandro García-Rivera by way of new insights from a reconstructed metaphysics as cosmology. In his contribution to the current volume, García-Rivera introduces the concept of the "Whole," not as the generic "Whole" that scholasticism related to the "particular" as genus to species, but as an aesthetic "Whole" that grounds the "particular" even as the "particular" constitutes the "Whole." García-Rivera points to the Latino/a devotions of the *Nacimiento* and *pastorelas* as explanatory examples.

A theological reflection incarnate in reality, as is U.S. Latino/a theology, cannot be exempt from recognizing the relevance of the paradigms, traditions, and categories that sustain the social construction of that reality which resides and operates in everyday life, in the particular—in other words, *lo cotidiano*. It is from everyday life that transformations emerge. Everyday life has to do with the totality of life, and it is from there that a theological reading of *lo cotidiano* emerges. This theological reading attempts to comprehend God's truth precisely in the historical density of human persons in their "here and now."

The theological reflection on *lo cotidiano* has also become one of the most foundational and richest starting points in the construction of a theology of grace from the Latino/a perspective, as Orlando Espín demonstrates in the chapter he contributes to the present volume. There he emphasizes the prominent role that women, particularly older women, have as living hermeneuts of grace and sin, making their role evident as protagonists and interpreters of Latino/a popular Catholicism, and as the ones with whom Latinos/as sustain the most meaningful and deepest of daily relationships. Espín reminds us in his essay that "mature Latina women (our mothers, grandmothers, aunts, and older sisters) are also our families' wise interpreters of the biblical message and of the heart and mind of God, the teachers of ethics, and the leaders of our prayers, our family's living sacrament of God and the sacred."

Latin American theological reflection has also been enriched by the U.S. Latino/a reading of the scriptures, with a "post-critical" approach to exegesis,[46] and by an interpretation of Tradition that is definitely incarnate in the reality of *lo cotidiano* and immersed in the communitarian dimension. Many examples of the "post-critical" approach to the reading of the scriptures are to be found in the works of the U.S. Latino/a theologians. May it suffice to refer the reader to the chapter by Jean-Pierre Ruiz in this book.

The Voice of Women

Without any doubt, one of the most outstanding aspects of the U.S. Latino/a theology, and one that attracts the most attention in Mexico[47] as well as in many other Latin American countries, is the prominent role of Latina theologians in the United States. In 1992 Allan Figueroa Deck reported that approximately 25 percent of the U.S. Latino/a theological writers were women.[48] A percentage that has certainly increased. From its very beginning Latino/a theology incorporated the scholarship, vision, and experience of women, not as a cosmetic addition, but as a true contribution to and change in the epistemological horizon.

Theology by Latina women in the United States balances and articulates scientific rigor with sensitivity for *lo cotidiano*—the experiential and the systematic. Their research overcomes the partiality of traditionally androcentric theologies that reduced life to abstract speculation. "Living reality is the point of departure for a more systematic theological explanation," states María Pilar Aquino. She further argues:

> theological intelligence, as exercised by women, distances itself from abstract and rationalist discourse, detached from what is real in reality—that is, from the cry of the suffering majority of humanity in

their historical present—in order to allow theology to communicate, in the diverse languages of faith, as a response to God's present action in the struggles and resistance of the poor and oppressed. Theology thus includes a conscious option for a way of exercising intelligence that dynamically articulates life and thought.[49]

Latina theological expressions have had as their central starting point the profound experience of *mestizaje* and of Latinas as *mestizas*. This reality is in turn rooted in the complexity of *lo cotidiano*, of the everyday life of the community to which Latinas belong. *Lo cotidiano* is interpreted in the light of revelation and amply analyzed by Latina theologians through instruments provided by the social and human sciences. U.S. Latina theologians have assumed a clear option for the poor and the oppressed as subjects of their theological task, "since [theology's] internal structure is based on the principle of life, primarily manifested in [the poor's] struggles and hopes, audacity and strength, compassion and deep humanism, *fiesta* and celebration, commitment and prayer."[50]

Incarnate in *lo cotidiano* of their communities, Latina theologians have had to study how culture, economic realities, and sociopolitical structures affect and shape Latino/a faith experience. They have examined how the vision the U.S. dominant society has of itself and of the world—a vision endemic with ethnic, racial, and sexist prejudices—intersects with economic oppression.

"From the outside," which is my perspective as I write this article, one can clearly perceive that the reflection of Latina women has contributed notable richness—expressive and interpretive of U.S. Latino/a theology. This contribution has occurred not only in the process of understanding overall reality but also in responding, from the Latina feminist perspective, to some fundamental questions: How does the U.S. Latino/a community receive, interpret, and express the revelation of the God of Jesus Christ? What symbols and language has that community embraced as its own, in its "here and now," in order to understand itself while it searches for a more liberating identity? What should that liberating identity be, given that it must be found in the midst of profound transculturization, shifting semantic fields, and within a church whose hierarchic structures do not seem to understand that the path of Jesus with the poor demands discipleship there where the poor walk in their "here and now"?

The theology done by U. S. Latina women has shown extraordinary depth and an acute critical sense while responding to such questions. It has demonstrated theological maturity in its reflection and systematic analysis on the reality of U.S. Latino/a communities. On the one hand, Latina theologians have had to situate themselves at the root of the complex gamut of changing influences that make up the intricate context within which *lo cotidiano* of the Latino/a faith experience develops. Furthermore, they have had to sort out the difficulties implied in being accurate interpreters of the faith of the communities, without replacing the latter's language or falling into the very real temptation to mold that language into pre-established categories and formats.[51]

The seriousness, depth, scientific rigor, and high quality of the theology done by U.S. Latina women has earned them a growing and merited international recognition. These theologians and their work are a source of motivation for other Latinas and non-Latinas, inside and outside the United States, to pursue the theological vocation.

The feminist voice in theology, and particularly the voice of Latina theologians, is perceived as extraordinary progress, especially vis-à-vis the current neo-liberal and conservative theologies. The feminist voice has given back to theology the poetic, aesthetical, and passional dimensions of human existence. U.S. Latina theologians have found a new form of expressing the realities of life in the light of the faith, after having themselves lived, listened, felt, and suffered them. This theological expression arises from a new way of being that empowers women critically to confront old dogmatic and excluding postures.

THE PROJECT: REINVENTING CATHOLIC SYSTEMATICS

"Mainstream" theology often asserts that revelation is the foundation of all theological research and, therefore, its starting point. How is it, then, that U.S. Latino/a theologians take as the starting point for their theological task the Latino/a communities' experience, as it is evident in the essays in the present volume? Is it by chance valid to consider experience rather than revelation as the starting point for the theological task?

The theological reflection contained in the various essays in this book depict as false the alternative of opposing experience to revelation—for revelation only takes place in and through the human being. Revelation is by its own nature incarnated. Were human experience to be denied or omitted in theology, this would in turn lead to the denial of the very essence of theology.

Theology fulfills its *razón de ser* (reason to be) insofar as it initiates a dialogue with the experience common to every human being, in his or her own "here and now"—and that is precisely what the authors of this book clearly show.

It is a fact that humans live meaningfully not only by concepts and ideas, but also and especially by symbols and images that have been deeply ingrained in them since childhood and youth, within precise cultural, socioeconomic, historical, political, and religious contexts. It is also a fact that faith is not kept alive solely by dogmas, declarations, and theological or philosophical reasons, but by the great images, symbols, and truths that are directed not mainly to the intellect and to critical-rational discourse, but to the imagination and the emotions as well. Faith would be partial if it affected only the human mind and reason and not the whole person, including affects and dreams, struggles and sufferings, yearnings and hopes.

This being so, the present book's authors have fulfilled their goal. The cultural, epistemological, hermeneutic foundations and premises of Catholic systematics from the Latino/a perspective—as formulated throughout the various chapters of the book—have placed their starting point in the multiform and complex experience that make up the everyday existence, *lo cotidiano*, of the Latino/a communities.

A theological reading of the quality of *lo cotidiano* has been accomplished by the authors while considering the narratives, stories, traditions, familial relations, wisdom phrases, customs, feasts, celebrations, and social relations, along with popular faith experiences and symbols of Latinos/as, as sources for reflection. Immersed in the context of the culture, economics, and sociopolitical structures of U. S. society, Latinos/as struggle to find their own identity while still suffering under ethnic, racist, and sexist oppression.

The themes of Catholic systematic theology that have been considered throughout this book have been expressed in a new language that responds to the "here and now" of the Latino/a community. In my perspective "from outside," and in comparison with Mexican and Latin American theologies, one can clearly appreciate the transcendence that the theological reflection expressed herein has for the Latin American communities outside the United States.

CONCLUSIONS: A VIEW "FROM OUTSIDE"

God's self-communication in history, which expresses itself as love, as grace, as liberating power and hope for the poor and oppressed of the earth, insofar as God's loving self is given to and for us as an expression of that which God is,[52] cannot be imprisoned or manipulated to prevent or resist the transforming power of the Spirit. That dimension of divine self-communication which is grace has empowered Latino/a theologians to reflect seriously on and critically to discern the impetus of the Spirit within their communities.

Throughout its relatively short history, Latino/a theological reflection has impressively matured. Some of the more important gains of that theology have been its treatment and analysis of *mestizaje*, the Guadalupe event, the role of popular Catholicism, the theological import of *lo cotidiano* as hermeneutic, innovative rereadings of scripture and of tradition, and a more consciously incarnate reflection on the trinitarian and communitarian dimensions of *lo cotidiano*. All of these themes gained tremendously from the feminist methodological contributions and theological critique.

Within the diverse paths taken by Latino/a theologians for their original, systematic reflections, one can sense the dawn of new contributions, as shown in the article by Jeanette Rodríguez, included in the present volume, on the earth "as our first and oldest home"—a new reflection that may lead to an authentic ecological solidarity.

U.S. Latino/a theology has done a lot during its relatively short history, but the task and challenges it faces are even greater now. The Latino/a community is not a homogeneous community; it is indeed very diverse ethnically, historically, and culturally. It is also internally different in its multiple levels of inculturation and participation within U.S. society. This implies, as Allan Figueroa Deck has pointed out elsewhere, that "any generalized understanding must be complemented by more detailed analyses of the particular group one is dealing with."[53]

One such analysis (still waiting to be done) interests me very much. It would focus on that specific group of communities located alongside the border between the United States and Mexico. Reality on the binational border is somewhat different from the one U.S. Latino/a theology has concentrated on until now. This needed analysis must look into the everyday life of millions of Latinos/as who share the same geography and the same urban (or rural) realities as millions of Mexicans—the groups artificially separated from each other by an imposed, imaginary line. This field of reflection (a "border theology") is now being taken up within Latino/a theology by Arturo Bañuelas.

I conclude this perspective "from outside" with an intuition, sensed by me in the very heart of the U.S. Latino/a communities and in the work of all U.S. Latino/a theologians: The greatness of a human being depends on the size of his or her hope, on the stature of his or her faith, and on the depth of his or her love. The God of Jesus acts and manifests through weakness. It is in weakness (the cross) that God's greatness is perceived. And if this is so, then it is in the weakness and the oppression of Latino/a communities that we will find their strength and that, in a privileged way, the force of the Spirit and the greatness of God are manifested.

Notes

[1] I wish to express sincere thanks to my friend, Mrs. Carmen Alicia de La Parra, for her help in translating this article into English. I also want to advert the reader that all translations of phrases by other authors included in this paper's text and notes were done by me. Furthermore, some German and Dutch books and articles occasionally referred to in this paper were used by me in Spanish

translations, and it is these translations that I have in turn rendered here in English.

² A brief description of *teología de conjunto* is provided in the present volume's Glossary.

³ The concept of culture used throughout this book is derived from the notions proposed by both the Second Vatican Council (*Gaudium et Spes*, no. 53) and by UNESCO ("World Conference on Cultural Policies," Mexico Declaration Final Report, 1982). Culture, in a broad sense, can be considered today as a set of spiritual and material, intellectual and emotional distinctive traits that characterize a society or a social group. These traits include not only the arts and letters, but also ways of life and fundamental human rights, values, traditions, and beliefs. Culture grants us the ability to reflect upon ourselves. It is this ability that makes us specifically human, rational, critical, and ethically committed. Through it we distinguish values and make our choices. Through it we express ourselves, achieve self-awareness, realize ourselves as unfinished projects, question our own achievements, search untiringly for new meanings, and create transcendent actions.

⁴ María Pilar Aquino, "Doing Theology from the Perspective of Latin American Women," in *We Are a People!: Initiatives in Hispanic American Theology*, ed. Roberto S. Goizueta (Minneapolis, Minn.: Fortress Press, 1992), 79.

⁵ Joseph Ratzinger, *El nuevo pueblo de Dios* (Barcelona: Herder, 1972), 305.

⁶ Orlando O. Espín, *The Faith of the People: Theological Reflections on Popular Catholicism* (Maryknoll, N.Y.: Orbis Books, 1997), 93-94.

⁷ Martín Gelabert Ballester, *Experiencia humana y comunicación de la fe: Ensayo de teología fundamental* (Madrid: Ediciones Paulinas, 1983), 34-35.

⁸ See Roberto S. Goizueta, *Caminemos con Jesús: Toward a Hispanic/Latino Theology of Accompaniment* (Maryknoll, N.Y.: Orbis Books, 1995), 191-96.

⁹ See María Pilar Aquino, "Directions and Foundations of Hispanic/Latino Theology: Toward a *Mestiza* Theology of Liberation," in *Mestizo Christianity: Theology from the Latino Perspective*, ed. Arturo J Bañuelas (Maryknoll, N.Y.: Orbis Books, 1995), 193.

¹⁰ Sixto J. García, "A Hispanic Approach to Trinitarian Theology: The Dynamics of Celebration, Reflection and Praxis," in Goizueta, *We Are A People!*, 114.

¹¹ It will be evident to some readers that in this very synthetical presentation of European, of Vatican II, and of Latin American theologies, I assume as my own the basic insights of Prof. Evangelista Vilanova in his *Historia de la teología cristiana*, vol. III (Barcelona: Herder, 1992). Therefore, I refrain from citing him repeatedly and instead refer the reader to this magnificent work for a more thorough discussion of the historical facts and theological evaluations I present in this section.

¹² Battista Mondin, *Cómo hablar de Dios hoy: El lenguaje teológico* (Madrid: Ediciones Paulinas, 1979).

¹³ See Glossary.

¹⁴ Karl Rahner, "Théologie et anthropologie," in *Théologie d'aujourd'hui et demain* (Paris, 1967), 110, quoted in Mondin, *Cómo hablar de Dios hoy*, 9.

¹⁵ Edward Schillebeeckx, *Interpretación de la fe* (Salamanca: Sígueme, 1973), 16.

¹⁶ Third General Conference of Latin American Bishops, *Puebla Document*, nos. 74ff.

¹⁷ Cardinal Ratzinger made serious accusations (in 1984) against Latin American liberation theology. A number of theologians responded to Ratzinger's arguments. One of them was Juan Luis Segundo, who felt deeply offended by the Vatican document. He confessed that his own theology would be false if the

Ratzinger document were true. See J. L. Segundo, *La teología de la liberación: Respuesta al Cardenal Ratzinger* (Madrid: Ed. Cristiandad, 1985).

[18] See Enrique Dussel, "Teologías de la 'periferia' y del 'centro'" ¿Encuentro o confrontación?," *Concilium* 191 (1984), 141-54.

[19] For a thorough exposition of the meaning and implications of *praxis* for theological method in liberation theology, and on the relationship between orthodoxy and orthopraxis, see Goizueta, *Caminemos con Jesús*, 78-88. On the overall role of praxis in theology, see Juan Luis Segundo, *The Liberation of Theology* (Maryknoll, N.Y.: Orbis Books, 1976).

[20] Milagros Peña, "Border Crossings: Sociological Analysis and the Latina and Latino Religious Experience," *Journal of Hispanic/Latino Theology* 4:3 (1997), 18.

[21] Virgilio P. Elizondo, "Educación religiosa para el méxico-americano," *Catequesis Latinoamericana* 4 (1972), 83-86.

[22] It is an extremely significant fact that non-Latino/a theological associations are increasingly recognizing the importance of Latino/a theological reflection. Besides frequent invitations to make presentations at their annual conferences, in 1997, for the first time, both the Catholic Theological Society of America (CTSA) and the College Theology Society (CTS) included workshop presentations in Spanish in their annual conventions. I had the honor of being invited as speaker in the CTS gathering. The CTSA has also included, for over a decade, an ongoing seminar on Latino/a theology in its annual convention programs. In 1997 a Latino was nominated, for the first time, as candidate for the presidency of the CTSA.

[23] See Allan Figueroa Deck, ed., *Frontiers of Hispanic Theology in the United States* (Maryknoll, N.Y.: Orbis Books, 1992), Introduction.

[24] Fernando F. Segovia, "Aliens in the Promised Land: The Manifest Destiny of U.S. Hispanic American Theology," *Hispanic/Latino Theology: Challenge and Promise*, ed. Ada María Isasi-Díaz and Fernando F. Segovia (Minneapolis, Minn.: Fortress Press, 1996), 16.

[25] Arturo J. Bañuelas, "U.S. Hispanic Theology: An Initial Assessment," in Bañuelas, *Mestizo Christianity*, 74.

[26] Orlando O. Espín, "Grace and Humanness," in Goizueta, *We Are a People!*, 133-64.

[27] For a brief explanation of the terms *mestizo/a* and *mestizaje*, see *mestizaje* in the Glossary in this volume.

[28] See Virgilio P. Elizondo, "*Mestizaje* as a Locus of Theological Reflection," in Deck, *Frontiers of Hispanic Theology in the United States*, 104-23.

[29] See Glossary.

[30] Justo L. González, *Mañana: Christian Theology from a Hispanic Perspective* (Nashville, Tenn.: Abingdon Press, 1990).

[31] Bañuelas, *Mestizo Christianity*, 75.

[32] See Jeanette Rodríguez, "*Sangre llama a sangre*: Cultural Memory as a Source of Theological Insight," in Isasi-Díaz and Segovia, *Hispanic/Latino Theology*, 16.

[33] Virgilio P. Elizondo, *Guadalupe: Mother of the New Creation* (Maryknoll, N.Y.: Orbis Books, 1997), ix.

[34] Segovia, "Aliens in the Promised Land," 16.

[35] Elizondo, *Guadalupe*, 132.

[36] See Bañuelas, "U.S. Hispanic Theology."

[37] Aquino, "Directions and Foundations of Hispanic/Latino Theology," 196-97.

[38] A suggestive and interesting study on praxis as aesthetics may be found in Goizueta, *Caminemos con Jesús*, 77-131.

[39] Espín, *The Faith of the People*, 23.

[40] Ibid., 158-69.

[41] Goizueta, *Caminemos con Jesús*, 140-41. For the expression *flor y canto*, see Glossary.

[42] A thorough and systematic theological study of popular Catholicism, its implications, and its importance for a theology of the *sensus fidelium* can be found in Espín, *The Faith of the People*.

[43] Goizueta, *Caminemos con Jesús*, 191.

[44] See the chapter "*Pueblo* and Church," by Gary Riebe-Estrella, herein. In its first part there is a comparative analysis of Latino/a culture and so-called mainstream U.S. culture, pointing out the differences in their understanding of "person" and highlighting how most (if not all) Latino/a relationships are modeled on family relationships.

[45] See the chapters by Alejandro García-Rivera and Miguel Díaz herein.

[46] Sixto J. García, "Sources and Loci of Hispanic Theology," in Bañuelas, *Mestizo Christianity*, 107.

[47] The production of women theologians in Mexico is minimal. I have no knowledge of the existence of Mexican women with doctorates in theology, with the exceptions of María Pilar Aquino (a Catholic), who has resided in the United States for many years, and Elsa Tamez (a Protestant), who lives in Costa Rica. The example of U.S. Latina theologians, however, has had a strong impact in Mexico, and every day there are more Mexican women interested in the academic study of theology. I can offer as example the growing number of women enrolled in various programs at the Universidad Pontificia de México and at the Jesuits' Universidad Iberoamericana's several campuses throughout the country, especially in the Tijuana campus's graduate program on the theological study of popular Catholicism (the only one of its kind in the Americas).

[48] Deck, *Frontiers of Hispanic Theology*, xvii.

[49] Aquino, "Doing Theology from the Perspective of Latin American Women," 88.

[50] Aquino, "Directions and Foundations of Hispanic/Latino Theology," 202.

[51] Ada María Isasi-Díaz, *En la Lucha/In the Struggle: A Hispanic Women's Liberation Theology* (Minneapolis, Minn.: Fortress Press, 1993), 63.

[52] Espín, "Grace and Humanness," 137.

[53] Allan Figueroa Deck, "The Spirituality of United States Hispanics: An Introductory Essay," in Bañuelas, *Mestizo Christianity*, 227.

Latino/a Catholic Theology

A Selective Bibliography

ARTURO J. BAÑUELAS

Tepeyac Institute

Aquino, María Pilar. "Doing Theology from the Perspective of Hispanic Women." In *We Are a People! Initiatives in Hispanic American Theology*, ed. Roberto Goizueta, 79-105. Philadelphia: Fortress Press, 1992.

———. "Perspectives on a Latina Feminist Liberation Theology." In *Frontiers of Hispanic Theology in the United States*, ed. Allan Figueroa Deck, 23-40. Maryknoll, N.Y.: Orbis Books, 1992.

———. "Directions and Foundations of Hispanic/Latino Theology: Toward a *Mestiza* Theology of Liberation." *Journal of Hispanic/Latino Theology* 1:1 (November 1993), 5-21. This article also appears in Bañuelas, *Mestizo Christianity*, 192-208.

———. *Our Cry for Life: Feminist Theology from Latin America*. Translated from the Spanish by Dinah Livingstone. Maryknoll, N.Y.: Orbis Books, 1993.

Bañuelas, Arturo J., ed. *Mestizo Christianity: Theology from the Latino Perspective*. Maryknoll, N.Y.: Orbis Books, 1995.

Dolan, Jay P., and Allan Figueroa Deck, eds. *Hispanic Catholic Culture in the United States: Issues and Concerns*. Notre Dame, Ind.: University of Notre Dame Press, 1994.

Dolan, Jay P., and Gilberto M. Hinojosa, eds. *Mexican Americans and the Catholic Church, 1900-1965*. Notre Dame, Ind.: University of Notre Dame Press, 1994.

Dolan, Jay P., and Jaime R. Vidal, eds. *Puerto Rican and Cuban Catholics in the U.S., 1900-1965*. Notre Dame, Ind.: University of Notre Dame Press, 1994.

Elizondo, Virgil P. *Galilean Journey: The Mexican-American Promise*. Maryknoll, N.Y.: Orbis Books, 1983.

———. *The Future Is Mestizo: Life Where Cultures Meet*. New York: Meyer-Stone, 1988.

———. "Elements for a Mexican American *Mestizo* Christology." *Voices from the Third World: Journal of the Ecumenical Association of Third World Theologians* 15:2 (1989).

———. "*Mestizaje* as a Locus of Theological Reflection." In *Frontiers of Hispanic Theology in the United States*, ed. Allan Figueroa Deck, 104-23. Maryknoll, N.Y.: Orbis Books, 1992. This article also appears in Bañuelas, *Mestizo Christianity*, 7-27.

————. "The New Humanity of the Americas." *Concilium* 1992:6 (in the U.S. also published as *1492-1992: The Voice of the Victims*. Edited by Leonardo Boff and Virgil Elizondo, 141-47. Maryknoll, N.Y.: Orbis Books, 1992).

————. *Guadalupe: Mother of the New Creation*. Maryknoll, N.Y.: Orbis Books, 1997.

Espín, Orlando O. *Carisma y misión*. Madrid: Ediciones Apostolado, 1983.

————. *Evangelización y religiones negras*. Rio de Janeiro: Edições da PUC, 1984.

————. "Religiosidad popular: Un aporte para su definición y hermenéutica." *Estudios Sociales* 58 (1984), 41-56.

————. "The Vanquished, Faithful Solidarity and the Marian Symbol: A Hispanic Perspective on Providence." In *On Keeping Providence*, ed. Barbara Doherty and Joan Coultas, 84-101. Terre Haute, Ind.: St. Mary of the Woods College Press, 1991.

————. "Grace and Humanness." In *We Are a People! Initiatives in Hispanic American Theology*, ed. Roberto Goizueta, 133-64. Minneapolis, Minn.: Fortress Press, 1992.

————. "Tradition and Popular Religion: An Understanding of the *Sensus Fidelium*." In *Frontiers of Hispanic Theology in the United States*, ed. Allan F. Deck, 62-87. Maryknoll, N.Y.: Orbis Books, 1992.

————. "Trinitarian Monotheism and the Birth of Popular Catholicism: The Case of Sixteenth-Century Mexico." *Missiology* 20:2 (1992), 117-204.

————. "Popular Catholicism among Latinos." In *Hispanic Catholic Culture in the U.S.: Issues and Concerns*, ed. Jay Dolan and Allan Figueroa Deck, 308-59. Notre Dame, Ind.: University of Notre Dame Press, 1994.

————. "Popular Religion as an Epistemology (of Suffering)." *Journal of Hispanic/Latino Theology* 2:2 (1994), 55-78.

————. "Pentecostalism and Popular Catholicism: The Poor and *Traditio*." *Journal of Hispanic/Latino Theology* 3:2 (1995), 14-43.

————. "Popular Catholicism: Alienation or Hope?" In *Hispanic/Latino Theology: Challenge and Promise*, ed. Ada María Isasi-Díaz and Fernando Segovia, 307-24. Minneapolis, Minn.: Fortress Press, 1996.

————. *The Faith of the People: Theological Reflections on Popular Catholicism*. Maryknoll, N.Y.: Orbis Books, 1997.

Espín, Orlando O., and Sixto J. García. "Hispanic-American Theology." *Proceedings of the Catholic Theological Society of America* 42 (1987), 114-19.

————. "The Sources of Hispanic Theology." *Proceedings of the Catholic Theological Society of America* 43 (1988), 122-25.

————. "'Lilies of the Field': A Hispanic Theology of Providence and Human Responsibility." *Proceedings of the Catholic Theological Society of America* 44 (1989), 70-90.

García, Sixto J. "A Hispanic Approach to Trinitarian Theology: The Dynamics of Celebration, Reflection, and Praxis." In *We Are a People! Initiatives in Hispanic American Theology*, ed. Roberto Goizueta, 107-32. Minneapolis, Minn.: Fortress Press, 1992.

————. "U.S. Hispanic and Mainstream Trinitarian Theologies." In *Frontiers of Hispanic Theology in the United States*, ed. Allan Figueroa Deck, 88-103. Maryknoll, N.Y.: Orbis Books, 1992.

————. "Sources and Loci of Hispanic Theology." *Journal of Hispanic/Latino Theology* 1:1 (1993), 22-43. This article also appears in Bañuelas, *Mestizo Christianity*, 105-24.

García, Sixto J., and Orlando O. Espín. "Hispanic-American Theology." *Proceedings of the Catholic Theological Society of America* 42 (1987), 114-19.

———. "The Sources of Hispanic Theology." *Proceedings of the Catholic Theological Society of America* 43 (1988), 122-25.

———. "'Lilies of the Field': A Hispanic Theology of Providence and Human Responsibility." *Proceedings of the Catholic Theological Society of America* 44 (1989), 70-90.

García-Rivera, Alex (Alejandro). "A Contribution to the Dialogue between Theology and the Natural Sciences." *Journal of Hispanic/Latino Theology* 2:1 (1994), 51-59.

———. "San Martín de Porres: *Criatura de Dios*." *Journal of Hispanic/Latino Theology* 2:2 (1994), 26-54.

———. *St. Martín de Porres: The "Little Stories" and the Semiotics of Culture*. Maryknoll, N.Y.: Orbis Books, 1995.

———. *The Community of the Beautiful: A Theological Aesthetics*. Collegeville, Minn.: The Liturgical Press, 1999.

Goizueta, Roberto S. "The History of Suffering as *Locus Theologicus*: Implications for U.S. Hispanic Theology." *Voices from the Third World: Journal of the Ecumenical Association of Third World Theologians* 12 (1989), 32-47.

———. "The Church and Hispanics in the United States: From Empowerment to Solidarity." In *That They Might Live: Power, Empowerment and Leadership in the Church*, ed. Michael Downey, 160-75. New York: Crossroad, 1991.

———. "Theology as Intellectually Vital Inquiry: The Challenge of/to U.S. Hispanic Theologians." *Proceedings of the Catholic Theological Society of America* 46 (1991), 58-69.

———. "*Nosotros*: Toward a U.S. Hispanic Anthropology." *Listening: Journal of Religion and Culture* 27 (1992), 55-69.

———. "Rediscovering Praxis: The Significance of U.S. Hispanic Experience for Theological Method." In *We Are a People! Initiatives in Hispanic American Theology*, ed. Roberto Goizueta, 51-77. Minneapolis, Minn.: Fortress Press, 1992.

———. "U.S. Hispanic Theology and the Challenge of Pluralism." In *Frontiers of Hispanic Theology in the United States*, ed. Allan Figueroa Deck, 1-21. Maryknoll, N.Y.: Orbis Books, 1992.

———. "U.S. Hispanic *Mestizaje* and Theological Method." *Concilium* 1993:4 (in the U.S. also published as *Migrants and Refugees*. Edited by Dietmar Mieth and Lisa Sowle Cahill. Maryknoll, N.Y.: Orbis Books, 1993), 22-30.

———. "*La Raza Cósmica*? The Vision of José Vasconcelos." *Journal of Hispanic/Latino Theology* 1:2 (1994), 5-27.

———. "The Preferential Option for the Poor: The CELAM Documents and the NCCB Pastoral Letter on U.S. Hispanics as Sources for U.S. Hispanic Theology." *Journal of Hispanic/Latino Theology* 3:2 (1995), 65-77.

———. *Caminemos con Jesús: Toward a Hispanic/Latino Theology of Accompaniment*. Maryknoll, N.Y.: Orbis Books, 1995.

———. "In Defense of Reason: Dichotomous Epistemology and Anthropology of Modernity and Postmodernity Oppressive to Hispanics." *Journal of Hispanic/Latino Theology* 3:3 (1996), 16-26.

———. "Bartolomé de Las Casas, Modern Critic of Modernity: An Analysis of a Conversion." *Journal of Hispanic/Latino Theology* 3:4 (1996): 6-19.

————. "U.S. Hispanic Popular Catholicism as Theopoetics." In *Hispanic/Latino Theology: Challenge and Promise,* ed. Ada María Isasi-Díaz and Fernando Segovia, 261-88. Minneapolis, Minn.: Fortress Press, 1996.

Goizueta, Roberto S., ed. *We Are a People! Initiatives in Hispanic American Theology.* Minneapolis, Minn.: Fortress Press, 1992.

Isasi-Díaz, Ada María. "Toward an Understanding of *Feminismo Hispano* in the USA." In *Women's Consciousness, Women's Conscience: A Reader in Feminist Ethics,* ed. Barbara Hilkert Andolsen, Christine Gudorf, and Mary D. Pellauer, 51-61. Minneapolis, Minn.: Winston Press, 1985.

————. "'*Apuntes*' for a Hispanic Women's Theology of Liberation." *Apuntes* 6 (1986), 61-71.

————. "A Hispanic Garden in a Foreign Land." In *Inheriting Our Mothers' Gardens: Feminist Theology in Third World Perspective,* ed. Letty M. Russell et al. Philadelphia: Westminster Press, 1988.

————. "*Mujeristas*: A Name of Our Own." In *The Future of Liberation Theology: Essays in Honor of Gustavo Gutiérrez,* ed. Marc H. Ellis and Otto Maduro, 410-19. Maryknoll, N.Y.: Orbis Books, 1989.

————. "*Mujerista* Theology's Method: A Liberative Praxis, a Way of Life." *Listening: Journal of Religion and Culture* 27:1 (1992), 41-54.

————. "*Mujeristas*: Who We Are and What We Are About." *Journal of Feminist Studies in Religion* 8:1 (1992), 105-25.

————. *En La Lucha/In the Struggle: A Hispanic Women's Liberation Theology.* Minneapolis, Minn.: Fortress Press, 1993.

————. "Defining Our *Proyecto Histórico*: *Mujerista* Strategies for Liberation." *Journal of Feminist Studies in Religion* 9:1-2 (1993), 17-28.

————. "Praxis: The Heart of *Mujerista* Theology." *Journal of Hispanic/Latino Theology* 1:1 (1993), 44-55.

————. "The Task of Hispanic Women's Liberation Theology—*Mujeristas*: Who We Are and What We Are About." In *Feminist Theology from the Third World: A Reader,* ed. Ursula King, 88-102. Maryknoll, N.Y.: Orbis Books, 1994.

————. *Mujerista Theology: A Theology for the Twenty-First Century.* Maryknoll, N.Y.: Orbis Books. 1996.

Isasi-Díaz, Ada María, and Yolanda Tarango. *Hispanic Women: Prophetic Voice in the Church.* Minneapolis, Minn.: Fortress Press, 1992.

Isasi-Díaz, Ada María, and Fernando Segovia, eds. *Hispanic/Latino Theology: Challenge and Promise.* Minneapolis, Minn.: Fortress Press, 1996.

Pineda, Ana María. "*Pastoral de Conjunto.*" In *Mestizo Christianity: Theology from the Latino Perspective,* ed. Arturo J. Bañuelas, 125-31. Maryknoll, N.Y.: Orbis Books, 1995.

————. "The Challenge of Hispanic Pluralism for the Unites States Churches." *Missiology* 21 (1993), 437-42.

————. "The Oral Tradition of a People: *Forjadora de rostro y corazón.*" In *Hispanic/Latino Theology: Challenge and Promise,* ed. Ada María Isasi-Díaz and Fernando Segovia. 104-16. Minneapolis, Minn.: Fortress Press, 1996.

————. "The Colloquies and Theological Discourse: Culture as a Locus for Theology." *Journal of Hispanic/Latino Theology* 3:3 (1996), 27-42.

Pineda, Ana María, and Robert Schreiter, eds. *Dialogue Rejoined.* Collegeville, Minn.: The Liturgical Press, 1995.

Rodríguez, Jeanette. "Hispanics and the Sacred." *Chicago Studies* 29:2 (1990), 137-52.

————. "Experience as a Resource for Feminist Thought." *Journal of Hispanic/Latino Theology* 1:1 (1993), 68-76.

————. *Our Lady of Guadalupe: Faith and Empowerment among Mexican-American Women*. Austin, Tex.: University of Texas Press, 1994.

————. "'*Sangre llama a sangre*': Cultural Memory as a Source of Theological Insight." In *Hispanic/Latino Theology: Challenge and Promise*, ed. Ada María Isasi-Díaz and Fernando Segovia, 117-33. Minneapolis, Minn.: Fortress Press, 1996.

————. *Stories We Live: Hispanic Women's Spirituality*. New York: Paulist Press, 1996.

Ruiz, Jean-Pierre. "Beginning to Read the Bible in Spanish: An Initial Assessment." *Journal of Hispanic/Latino Theology* 1:2 (1994), 28-50.

————. "Naming the Other: U.S. Hispanic Catholics, the So-Called 'Sects,' and the 'New Evangelization.'" *Journal of Hispanic/Latino Theology* 4:2 (1996), 34-59.

Segovia, Fernando F. "A New Manifest Destiny: The Emerging Theological Voice of Hispanic Americans." *Religious Studies Review* 17:2 (1991), 101-9.

————. "Two Places and No Place on Which to Stand: Mixture and Otherness in Hispanic American Theology." *Listening: Journal of Religion and Culture* 27:1 (1992), 26-40.

————. "In the World but Not of It: Exile as Locus for a Theology of the Diaspora." In *Hispanic/Latino Theology: Challenge and Promise*, ed. Ada María Isasi-Díaz and Fernando Segovia, 195-217. Minneapolis, Minn.: Fortress Press, 1996.

Segovia, Fernando F., and Ada María Isasi-Díaz, eds. *Hispanic/Latino Theology: Challenge and Promise*. Minneapolis, Minn.: Fortress Press, 1996.

Vidal, Jaime R. "Popular Religion among Hispanics in the General Area of the Archdiocese of Newark." In *Presencia Nueva*, ed. Office of Research and Planning, 235-352. Newark, N.J.: Archdiocese of Newark, 1988.

Vidal, Jaime R., and Jay P. Dolan, eds. *Puerto Rican and Cuban Catholics in the U.S., 1900-1965*. Notre Dame, Ind.: University of Notre Dame Press, 1994.

Glossary

The definitions that follow are general, only intended for quick reference, and should not be substituted for the particular definitions and nuances employed by individual authors in the present volume.

Amerindian. The native peoples of the Western hemisphere. This term is most frequently used by Latin American historians and social scientists, and increasingly by Latino/a scholars in the United States. See **Nahua**.

Chicano/a. A person born or raised in the United States of Mexican or Mexican-American parents or ancestry. The term is not applicable to any of the other Latino/a communities in the country. Some Mexican-Americans prefer not to apply the term to themselves. See **Latino/a** and **Hispanic**.

Criollo/a. A person born in the Western hemisphere of Spanish parents or ancestry. Although the term was used only in this sense during the colonial period, today it may be (inaccurately) used to indicate anything or anyone who is "typical" of Latin America. The colonial and modern *criollos/as* significantly contributed to *mestizaje* and *mulataje*, just as they in turn have become culturally *mestizos/as* or *mulatos/as*. The term *criollo/a* is *not* synonymous with *creole* in contemporary English. See **Mestizaje, Mulataje, Latino/a, Hispanic, Chicano/a, Nahua,** and **Yoruba**.

Curandero/a. A person who engages in healing practices through means that might range from magic to natural medicine. These practices are often justified through popular religious arguments. *Curanderismo* (these healing practices taken as a whole) is not necessary to popular Catholicism, although it often appears in the same communities.

Dios. The Spanish-language word for "God."

Flor y canto. An expression literally meaning "flower and song." It comes from the pre-Conquest Nahua culture of Mexico, and it was used to signify the divine presence, or truth, and the mediations thereof. See **Nahua**.

Hispanic. A person born or raised in the United States of Latin American or Spanish ancestry. The term, although still used by many, increasingly is being rejected for purposes of self-identification by most U.S. Latino/a communities. Its almost exclusive emphasis on Spain's legacy as the defining element of U.S. Latino/a cultures is regarded as historically inaccurate, unjustified, and misleading. Nevertheless, some authors employ the term because of its gender-inclusive character and because it can refer to the Spanish language as the linguistic base of a common Latino/a identity. See **Latino/a**, **Chicano/a**, and **Criollo/a**.

Latinamente. A Spanish-language adverb literally meaning "Latino/a-ly." Used when something is done in a culturally authentic Latino/a way.

Latinidad. The quality of being Latino/a. The term literally means "Latino/a-ness."

Latino/a. A person born or raised in the United States of Latin American ancestry. The term is increasingly favored for self-identification by the U.S. Latino/a communities. Its emphasis on the Latin American roots of the U.S. Latino/a communities is regarded as historically accurate and appropriate. The Spanish, Amerindian, and African components of the Latin American cultural matrix are equally acknowledged as defining contemporary Latino/a reality. Although "Latino/a" is the currently preferred self-identifying term, it is not gender-inclusive without the awkward addition of "/a," as employed here. See **Hispanic**, **Chicano/a**, **Mestizaje**, and **Mulataje**.

Lo cotidiano. A Spanish-language expression that refers to daily life experience, or to reality as it is experienced in daily life. The expression literally means "the daily." See **Popular**.

Mestizaje. The process of cultural (and often racial) mixing of the Spanish and the Amerindian in the Western hemisphere. The "product" of this process is the **mestizo/a**. The term is often used, in Latino/a theology, to refer to a much broader and deeper mixing of cultures, religious traditions, and so on, including the contributions of the European-Americans to contemporary U.S. Latino/a communities. See **Nahua**, **Criollo/a**, **Mulataje**, and **Latino/a**.

Mulataje. The process of cultural (and often racial) mixing of the Spanish and the African in the Western hemisphere. The "product" of this process is the **mulato/a**. Although occasionally used in Latino/a theology, the terms *mulataje* and *mulato/a* are often and inaccurately subsumed into the categories *mestizaje* and *mestizo/a*. See **Yoruba**, **Criollo/a**, and **Latino/a**.

Nahua. The name of an Amerindian people and culture of the central valley of Mexico before the Spanish conquest. Although sometimes (inaccurately) identified exclusively with the Mexica or Aztec, the latter and their city (Tenochtitlan) were in fact part of the broader Nahua world. The Nahua's language was called Nahuatl. They have had a crucial impact on modern Mexican and Mexican-American self-definitions and cultures. See **Amerindian**, **Mestizaje**, **Latino/a**, and **Criollo/a**.

Pastoral de conjunto. A manner of doing ministry. It is a process whereby a group of ministers along with groups and parishes within a diocese gather to establish common goals and methods. Hence, the "product" ultimately belongs to and is the result of the whole community's evangelizing or ministerial effort.

Popular. The term is applied to practices, worldviews, epistemologies, beliefs, political options, and so forth, whose source and author are "the people" (frequently interpreting the latter to be the culturally and/or socially marginalized Latino/a majority). Consequently, that which is widespread is not necessarily popular in this sense. Furthermore, something may be said to be "popular" when it truly reflects *latinidad* as its core and source. See **Lo cotidiano** and **Latinidad**.

Pueblo. Spanish-language word that means both "town" and "people." See **Popular**.

Teología de conjunto. A manner of doing theology, typical of Latino/a theology. *Teología de conjunto* is the process whereby a group of theologians gathers in order to do theology *jointly*. Hence, the "product" ultimately belongs to the community and not to any one individual scholar. Furthermore, *teología de conjunto* must also spring from and reflect the reality and faith of the people among whom the theologians live and work. See **Lo cotidiano** and **Popular**.

Tepeyac. The hill outside of Mexico City where it is said that the Virgin of Guadalupe appeared to the Amerindian convert Juan Diego in 1531. Before the Spanish conquest of Mexico, Tepeyac (in the Nahuatl language called *Tepeyacac*, or "nose-like hill") was the site of a shrine to Tonantzin, the Nahua goddess identified with motherhood and nurture. Today the Catholic basilica to the Virgin of Guadalupe stands on the same site, and it attracts more pilgrims each year than any other religious site in Christendom. The original painting of the Virgin of Guadalupe, claimed to have appeared miraculously on Juan Diego's outer clothing (his *tilma*), hangs at the basilica's main altar and is the object of great veneration.

Yoruba. The African people (from present-day Nigeria) who were forced into slavery by the Spanish and Portuguese, mainly from the eighteenth through the nineteenth centuries. Several million Yorubas were enslaved and brought to the Americas, although many died in slave ships while crossing the Atlantic. The Yorubas became the main African cultural foundation (mixed with Spanish or Portuguese elements) for the *mulato/a* cultures of Cuba, Puerto Rico, the Dominican Republic, and Brazil. See **Mulataje**, **Latino/a**, and **Criollo/a**.

Process Participants

María Pilar Aquino
Associate Professor of Theological
    and Religious Studies
University of San Diego

Arturo J. Bañuelas
Director of The Tepeyac Institute
Diocese of El Paso

Miguel H. Díaz
Assistant Professor of Theology
St. Vincent de Paul Regional Seminary

Virgilio P. Elizondo
Mexican American Cultural Center
Archdiocese of San Antonio

Orlando O. Espín
Professor of Theological
    and Religious Studies
Director of the Center for the Study
    of Latino/a Catholicism
University of San Diego

Alejandro García-Rivera
Associate Professor of Theology
Jesuit School of Theology
    at Berkeley

Roberto S. Goizueta
Professor of Theology
Boston College

Justo L. González
Director of the Hispanic Theological
    Initiative
Candler School of Theology, Emory
    University

Gary Riebe-Estrella
Vice-President for Academic Affairs
    and Dean
Catholic Theological Union

Jeanette Rodríguez-Holguín
Associate Professor and Chair
    of Theology and Religious Studies
Seattle University

Jean-Pierre Ruiz
Associate Professor and Chair
    of Theology and Religious Studies
St. John's University, New York

Ruy G. Suárez Rivero
Professor of Theology
Universidad Iberoamericana, Tijuana
    (Mexico)

Index